LAWS OF MICHIGAN

CONCERNING THE

ORGANIZATION AND GOVERNMENT

OF TOWNSHIPS,

AND THE

POWERS AND DUTIES OF TOWNSHIP OFFICERS AND BOARDS OF SUPERVISORS:

WITH

NUMEROUS PRACTICAL FORMS, AND NOTES REFERRING TO ADJUDICATED CASES.

BY ELIJAH M. HAINES.

DETROIT:
S. D. ELWOOD, No. 49 GRISWOLD STREET.
1860.

DETROIT, 1859.

S. D. ELWOOD, Esq.:

Dear Sir:—I have looked at the Prospectus of your intended compilation of laws regulating the action of our township and other local officers, with forms for their use in performing the various duties assigned to them.

These officers have entrusted to their care the preliminary steps in assessing taxes, opening roads, and many other matters in which a close adherence to law is absolutely essential. This can be secured in no other way than by furnishing them, not only with the laws themselves, but with convenient and accurate forms. I have no doubt a judicious compilation of this kind will not only facilitate the transaction of business, but remove the occasion for a great deal of annoying and expensive litigation. I am very glad the work has been undertaken, for it is much needed.

Respectfully yours,

JAMES V. CAMPBELL.

DETROIT, 1859.

We concur in the view expressed by Judge Campbell.

GEO. MARTIN.
RANDOLPH MANNING.
I. P. CHRISTIANCY.
J. M. HOWARD, Att'y Gen.
SAMUEL T. DOUGLASS.
B. F. H. WITHERELL.
S. M. GREEN.

PREFACE.

The book here presented to the public, is, as indicated by the title, a compilation of all that portion of the general Statutes of Michigan, concerning the organization and government of townships, and the powers and duties of township officers and Boards of Supervisors, with the addition of notes and forms. The object is to furnish a complete guide for Township Officers as well as Boards of Supervisors, and County Clerks, as Clerks of the Board, to aid them in the discharge of their official duties. The work is therefore designed to contain all the Statute Law relating to the powers and duties of these officers, with numerous practical forms, adapted to every service and duty, and copious notes, by way of instruction or advice, supported by references to adjudicated cases. It is believed that the utility of a work of this nature will be acknowledged by every one who has had any experience as a township officer, or in township or county affairs.

The system of township organization was early adopted in the State of Michigan, but no settled or uniform practice in conducting the details of affairs under this system has prevailed, either by legislative encouragement or private suggestion, and the compiler hereof is the first to undertake this task in those States where this system of government has been adopted.

Under this peculiar system, the execution of the law must of necessity, in many instances, be committed to men of limited experience in legal matters; in consequence of which, in the absence of some reliable guide, many errors are committed, to the injury of innocent persons, and particularly in the matter of laying out and establishing, or removing or vacating, highways. In this compilation, therefore, reliable precedents, or forms, will be given in connection with every essential act or transaction concerning highways, as well as all other township business, together with full instructions which are embodied in the notes also appended, which, together, will form a convenient as well as complete and reliable guide for the most inexperienced officer.

The forms given are principally derived from those most approved and in use in the State of New York, where a settled practice has obtained, and from whence the township system of government, as it exists in Michigan, has been borrowed, to all of which, it will be observed, copious notes have been added by way of instruction, referring to judicial decisions of Michigan, and other States where a like system prevails, and particularly to the decisions of the courts of the State of New York.

It has been the aim of the compiler to arrange the work in as concise and complete a form as possible, and that it should contain so much of the law as the subject of the work ought properly to embrace, and nothing more; this will enable the township officer to turn at once to any portion of his duties, without wading through numberless pages of other matter, as would be the case in consulting a large volume of the Statutes. This fact alone gives great value to such a book. In the *arrangement*, it will be discovered that the *Notes* and *Forms* are carried along in connection with the text; they are not added by way of Appendix, as is often the case with such works, but *are presented upon the same page, or in immediate connection.*

The Plan of this work the Compiler claims to be original with himself; the copyright of which he has secured under the laws of the United States. He is also the compiler of a like work for Illinois and Wisconsin; and as evidence of the merits of those compilations, it may be sufficient to mention that they were, in those States, published by State authority—seven thousand copies being furnished to each State by order of the Legislature, and distributed among the several townships; besides this, several thousand copies have been disposed of at private sale. In Illinois, the private sales, in two years, have reached seven thousand copies, which fact alone proves quite conclusively the utility of a work of this nature.

April, 1860.

PLAN OF THIS COMPILATION AND EXPLANATIONS.

For information as to the matter contained in this compilation, reference will be had to the Table of Contents following.

The different subjects embraced have been classed under several distinct heads, entitled Divisions; each Division comprising a chapter of the Compiled Laws of 1857, reference being made to the number of the chapter, in the margin, at the head of each Division.

The marginal references and foot notes, as contained in the Compiled Laws, are here given, the same as therein contained. The foot notes referred to by small *italic* letters, *a, b, c,* &c., are those taken from the Compiled Laws.

All amendments, since the date of the Compiled Laws, are also inserted in their proper order, with marginal references, as in other cases, showing the date of enactment and page of the Session Laws where the amendments will appear.

TABLE OF CONTENTS.

LAWS OF MICHIGAN

CONCERNING

THE ORGANIZATION AND GOVERNMENT

OF

TOWNSHIPS.

DIVISION I.—OF ELECTIONS.

OF ELECTIONS OTHER THAN FOR MILITIA AND TOWNSHIP OFFICERS.

COMP. L. 1857. Chap. VI. p. 101

An Act to provide for holding General and Special Elections.[a]

[*Approved June* 27, 1851. *Took effect Sept.* 27, 1851. *Laws of* 1851, *p.* 281.]

[25.] SECTION 1. *The People of the State of Michigan enact*, That a general election shall be held in the several townships and wards of this State on the Tuesday succeeding the first Monday of November, in the year eighteen hundred and fifty-two, and on the Tuesday succeeding the first Monday of November, every second year thereafter, at which there shall be elected so many of the following officers as are to be chosen in such years respectively, that is to say: a Governor, Lieutenant-Governor, Secretary of State, State Treasurer, Auditor General, Attorney General, Superintendent of Public Instruction, Commissioner of the State Land Office, Members of the State Board of Education, Electors of President and Vice-President of the United States, Representatives in Congress, the Senators and Representatives in the State Legislature, and the following county officers, viz.: Judges of Probate, Sheriffs, Clerks, Treasurers, Registers of Deeds, Prosecuting Attorneys, and such other officers as may by law be required to be elected at such general election: *Provided*, The provisions of this section shall not apply to the election of the Senator and Representatives in the State Legislature, nor to the election of county officers, in that portion of the State denominated the Upper

General election; when held.

Officers to be elected.

Const. Art. 5, Sec. 3; Art. 8, Sec. 1; Art. 13, Sec. 9.

Art. 6, Sec. 13.

---

[a] This Act, it is believed, supersedes the whole of Chapters 3, 4, 5, 6, 7, 8, 9, 10, and 11 of the Revised Statutes of 1846.

Peninsula, as described in section one, article nineteen of the Revised Constitution, and such other territory as may be attached thereto for election purposes. On the first Tuesday of November, eighteen hundred and fifty-one, there shall be elected a Governor and Lieutenant-Governor, whose term of office shall commence on the first Monday of January, eighteen hundred and fifty-two, and who shall hold their respective offices until the first day of January, eighteen hundred and fifty-three, and until their successors are elected and qualified; which election shall be conducted in the manner provided by the Constitution and laws in force on the thirty-first day of December, eighteen hundred and fifty; and the returns and canvass of votes given thereon shall be proceeded and determined in the same manner herein provided for the same officers to be elected at general biennial elections.

Schedule to Const. Sec. 5.

In what cases special elections may be held.

[26.] SEC. 2. Special elections may be held in the following cases, and for the election of the following officers, viz.:

1. When a vacancy shall occur in the office of Senator or Representative in the State Legislature, Representative in Congress, Judge of the Circuit or District Court, Regent of the University, or member of the State Board of Education;

2. When there has been no choice at a general election of Representatives in Congress;

3. When the right of office of a person elected to any of the aforesaid district or county offices shall cease before the commencement of the term of service for which he shall have been elected;

4. When a vacancy shall occur in either of the said county offices after the commencement of the term of service, and more than six months before the next general election;

5. When, in any other case of vacancy not particularly provided for in this section, the Governor shall in his discretion so direct.

When vacancies may be filled at general election.

[27.] SEC. 3. A vacancy in either of the offices named in the first section of this act, which shall not have been supplied before a general election, may be supplied at such election.

When special elections not to be held.

[28.] SEC. 4. No special election shall be held within three months next preceding a general election, except in cases where the Governor shall order a special election.

When to be ordered by Board of Supervisors.

[29.] SEC. 5. Special elections for the choice of the county officers named in section one of this act, shall, except in cases in which a special election is to be ordered by the Governor, be ordered by the Board of Supervisors.

To be held one day only.

[30.] SEC. 6. Special elections shall be held and continued one day only, and shall be conducted, and the result thereof canvassed and certified in all respects, as near as may be, in like manner as general elections, except as otherwise directed.

Persons having greatest number of votes deemed elected.

[31.] SEC. 7. In elections for the choice of all officers named in the first section of this act, the persons having the greatest number of votes shall be deemed to have been duly elected.

[32.] SEC. 8. Whenever the time fixed by the law of Congress for the election of Electors of President and Vice-President of the United States, shall not occur on the day appointed for holding the general election, such election for Electors of President and Vice-President shall be held on the day so fixed by law of Congress therefor. **Election of Electors of President and Vice-President.**

[33.] SEC. 9. All the provisions of law relating to the notifying and holding of the general elections, and the election of Electors of President and Vice-President thereat, shall apply to every such election held pursuant to the provisions of the preceding section; and the votes given for such Electors shall be returned and canvassed, and the result determined in the same manner in all respects, and with the like effect, as in case of the election of such Electors at a general election.

[34.] SEC. 10. When a vacancy shall occur in the office of Judge of the Circuit Court, Regent of the University, or member of the State Board of Education, thirty days or more before a general election, the Secretary of State shall, at least twenty days before such election, cause a written notice to be sent to the sheriff of each of the counties within the election district in which such vacancy may occur; which notice shall state in which office the vacancy occurred, and that such vacancy will be supplied at the next general election. **Notice of supplying vacancies in certain offices.**

[35.] SEC. 11. The Secretary of State shall, between the first day of July and the first day of September preceding a general election, direct and cause to be delivered to the sheriff of each county in this State, a notice in writing that at the next general election there will be chosen as many of the following officers as are to be elected at such general election, viz.: a Governor, Lieutenant-Governor, Secretary of State, State Treasurer, Auditor General, Attorney General, Superintendent of Public Instruction, Commissioner of the State Land Office, members of the State Board of Education, Electors of President and Vice-President of United States, and a Representative in Congress for the district to which each of such counties shall belong. **Of general elections.**

[36.] SEC. 12. He shall also, between the first day of July and the first day of September preceding such election, direct and cause to be delivered to the sheriff of each county a notice in writing, stating the number of Senators and Representatives to be elected in such county, specifying the number of each district, and the limits of such district, when the county alone does not constitute a senatorial or representative district or districts. **Of elections of Senators and Representatives.**

[37.] SEC. 13. Whenever a special election shall be ordered by the Governor to fill any vacancy, the Secretary of State shall immediately notify the sheriff of each of the counties **Of special elections.**

embraced in said election district, of the time of holding such election, the cause of such vacancy, the name of the officer, and the time when his term of office will expire.

Duty of Board of Supervisors in ordering vacancy to be filled.

[38.] SEC. 14. When the board of supervisors of a county shall order a special election to fill a vacancy in any office, such order shall be in writing and signed by the chairman and clerk of the board, and shall specify how the vacancy occurred; the name of the officer in whose office it occurred; the time when his term of office will expire; and the day on which such special election shall be held, not being more than forty nor less than thirty days from the making of such order; and such clerk shall without delay, cause a copy of such order to be delivered to the township clerk of each township, and to one of the inspectors of election in each ward of any city in the county.

Duty of Sheriff on receiving notice.

[39.] SEC. 15. The sheriff, on receiving either of the notices directed in this act to be sent to him, shall forthwith cause a notice in writing to be delivered to the township clerk in each township, and to one of the inspectors of election in each ward in any city of his county, which notice shall contain in substance the notices so received by such sheriff; but if such county shall be divided into two or more senatorial or representative districts, then such notice, so far as it relates to the election of Senators or Representatives, shall be delivered to the proper officer in each township or ward in each respective district.

Ibid.

[40.] SEC. 16. He shall also give at least twenty days' notice in writing, to be delivered to the township clerk of each township, and to one of the inspectors of election in each ward in any city in his county, of the holding of each general election, for the choice of county officers, designating the officers to be chosen at each and every such election.

Duty of Township Clerk on receiving notice

[41.] SEC. 17. The township clerk or inspector of elections receiving either of the notices directed in this act to be delivered to him, shall, by notice in writing, under his hand, give at least ten days' notice to the electors of the township or ward, of the time and place at which such election is to be held, and the officers to be chosen; and if the notice is of a general election, at which a vacancy is to be filled, it shall state the name of the person in whose office the vacancy shall have occurred, and that such vacancy will be supplied at such election; and such township clerk or inspector shall cause such notices to be posted up in at least three of the most public places in the said township or ward.[1]

---

[1] *Form of Notice of Election by Township Clerk.*

ELECTION NOTICE.

Notice is hereby given to the electors of the Township of *Pontiac,* in the County of *Oakland,* and State of Michigan, that the next ensuing general election will be held on Tuesday succeeding the first Monday of November next, being the —— day of said month, at ————, in said township;

[42.] SEC. 18. At the general election, the supervisor, the justice of the peace not holding the office of supervisor or town clerk, whose term of office will first expire, and the township clerk of each township, and the assessor and alderman of each ward in a city, or if in any city there be not an assessor in every ward, then the two aldermen of each ward, shall be the inspectors of election, two of whom shall constitute a quorum. **Inspectors of elections.**

[43.] SEC. 19. In case three of such inspectors shall not attend at the opening of the polls, or shall not remain in attendance during the election, the electors present may choose, *viva voce*, such number of such electors, as, with the inspector or inspectors present, shall constitute a board of three in number; and such electors, so chosen, shall be inspectors of that election during the continuance thereof. **When electors to choose Inspectors.**

[44.] SEC. 20. The township clerk, if present, shall be required by the board to act as a clerk of the election, and before the opening of the polls, the inspectors in each township shall appoint another competent person to be clerk of the election; and if the township clerk shall not be present, the board shall appoint two such clerks, and the inspectors in each ward in a city shall appoint two competent persons to be such clerks; and each of the clerks so appointed, and each of the inspectors so chosen shall take the constitutional oath of office, which oath either of the inspectors may administer.[1] **Clerks of Elections.** **4 Selden, 67, 68.**

[45.] SEC. 21. The polls of the election shall be opened at eight o'clock in the forenoon, or as soon thereafter as may be, on the day of election, and shall be continued open until five o'clock in the afternoon of the same day, and no longer; but **At what time polls to be opened and closed.**

---

at which election the following officers are to be chosen, to wit: (*Here set forth the officers to be chosen; and if a vacancy is to be filled, state the name of the person in whose office the vacancy has occurred, and that such vacancy will be supplied at such election.*)

The polls of said election will be opened at eight o'clock in the forenoon, or as soon thereafter as may be, and will be continued open until five o'clock in the afternoon, unless the Board shall, in their discretion, adjourn the polls at twelve o'clock, noon, for one hour.

Dated at *Pontiac*, this —— day of ————, A. D. 18—.

JOHN JACKSON,
Township Clerk.

Note.—In case of notice by Inspectors of Election, in wards of cities, the foregoing notice can be easily varied to suit the occasion, by substituting the word "Ward," with its number, or other proper designation, for that of "Township."

[1] *Form of Oath of Office of Clerk or Inspector of Election.*

"I do solemnly swear [or affirm], that I will support the Constitution of the United States, and the Constitution of this State, and that I will faithfully discharge the duties of the office of Clerk (*or* Inspector, *as the case may be*) of this election according to the best of my ability."

The neglect of the inspectors or clerks of an election to take the prescribed oath, does not vitiate an election: neither does the irregular administration of the oath.

An oath irregularly administered—*e.g.* upon a book other than the Holy Evangelists—the parties administering it and taking it supposing it a Bible, is a valid oath.

It is also held that the statute requiring the Inspectors of Election to appoint clerks is directory. If no clerks can be procured, the election is not to fail. The Inspectors are to perform the duty which ordinary is devolved upon the clerks.—*People v. Cook*, 4 *Seld.* 67.

4 Selden, 92.
Adjournments.

the board may adjourn the polls at twelve o'clock noon, for one hour, in their discretion; but the inspectors shall cause proclamation to be made of the opening and closing of the polls, and of each adjournment.[1]

Chairman of Board.

[46.] SEC. 22. When the supervisor shall be one of the board, he shall be chairman thereof; but if he be absent, such one of their number as the inspectors shall appoint, shall be chairman of the board.

How electors to vote.
Const. Art. 7, Sec. 2.

[47.] SEC. 23. The electors shall vote by ballot, and each person offering to vote shall deliver his ballot, folded, to one of the inspectors, in presence of the board.

Ballot, what to contain.
1 Doug. Mich. 59; 3 Mich. 233.

[48.] SEC. 24. The ballot shall be a paper ticket, which shall contain, written or printed, or partly written and partly printed, the names of all the persons for whom the elector intends to vote, and shall designate the office to which each person so named is intended to be chosen; but no ballot shall contain a greater number of names of persons, as designated to any office, than there are persons to be chosen at the election to fill such office.[2]

Oath to be tendered to person challenged.

[49.] SEC. 25. If any person offering to vote shall be challenged as unqualified by any inspector, or any elector entitled to vote at that poll, the chairman of the board of inspectors shall declare to the person challenged the constitutional qualifications of an elector;[3] and if such person shall state that he is

---

1 It is likewise held, in New York, that the provision of the statute as to the time of opening and closing the polls is directory; that, for instance, should the Inspectors, being misled by a defective time-piece, close the polls a few minutes before a particular hour directed by the statute, or receive a few votes after that hour, this will not render the election void. — *People v. Cook*, 4 *Seld.* 92.

2 The *name* of the person for whom the elector intends to vote, must be written in full upon his ballot. It is held that a ballot for J. A. Dyer can not be counted for James A. Dyer. It does not contain the name of the person intended to be voted for, but merely the initial letters; and no evidence is admissible to show that such a ballot was intended for James A. Dyer. — *People v. Tisdale*, 1 *Doug. Mich.* 59; *People v. Higgins*, 3 *Mich.* 233.

But where the designation of an individual, on a ballot, is by an abbreviation sanctioned by common usage, and universally understood, the ballot may be counted for the person for whom it was intended. Thus, a vote for Jas. A. Dyer may be counted for James A. Dyer.

A slight error in the spelling of a name on a ballot, it is presumed, would not prevent the ballot from being counted for the person for whom it was evidently intended. — *People v. Tisdale*, 1 *Doug. Mich.* 59; *People v. Higgins*, 3 *Mich.* 233. Ballots cast for Michael *Finegan*, being of the same sound, it was held, should have been counted for Michael *Finnegan*, the person intended. — *Finnegan v. Mayworm*, 5 *Mich.* 146.

Ballots containing a greater number of names for an office than the number to be elected, can not be canvassed, but must be rejected. — *People v Adams*, 9 *Wend.* 333. Also, if a ballot contains the names of two persons for the same office, it is bad as to both; but such ballots can not be rejected as to candidates for other offices regularly named upon the same ballot. — *Carpenter v. Ely*, 4 *Wis.* 420.

3 The following are the Constitutional qualifications of an elector:

In all elections every white male citizen; every white male inhabitant residing in the State on the twenty-fourth day of June, one thousand eight hundred and thirty-five; every white male inhabitant residing in this State on the first day of January, one thousand eight hundred and fifty, who has declared his intention to become a citizen of the United States, pursuant to the laws thereof, six months preceding an election, or who has resided in this State two years and six months, and declared his intention as aforesaid; and every civilized male inhabitant of Indian descent, a native of the United States, and not a member of any tribe, shall be an elector and entitled to vote; but no citizen or inhabitant shall be an elector, or entitled to vote at any election, unless he shall be above the age of twenty-one years, and has resided in this State three months, and in the township or ward in which he offers to vote ten days next preceding such election. — *Constitution, art. vii. sec.* 1.

Whether a person offering to vote at an election has the requisite qualification as to color or descent, must, on challenge for the want of such qualification, be inquired into, and determined by the inspectors of election.

a qualified elector, and the challenge is not withdrawn, one of the inspectors shall tender to him such one of the following oaths as he may claim to contain the grounds of his qualifications to vote: Const. Art. 7; Sec. 1.

X 1. "You do solemnly swear [or affirm] that you are twenty-one years of age, that you are a citizen of the United States, that you have resided in this State three months next preceding this day, and in this township (or ward, as the case may be) ten days next preceding this day, and that you have not voted at this election"; or Form of oath or affirmation.

2. "You do solemnly swear [or affirm] that you are twenty-one years of age, that you resided in this State on the twenty-fourth day of June, eighteen hundred and thirty-five, that you have resided in this State three months next preceding this day, and in this township (or ward, as the case may be) ten days next preceding this day, and that you have not voted at this election"; or, Ibid.

3. "You do solemnly swear [or affirm] that you are twenty-one years of age, that you resided in this State on the first day of January, eighteen hundred and fifty, that you have declared your intention to become a citizen of the United States, pursuant to the laws thereof, six months preceding this election, that you have resided in this State three months next preceding this day, and in this township (or ward, as the case may be) ten days next preceding this day, and that you have not voted at this election"; or, Ibid.

4. "You do solemnly swear [or affirm] that you are twenty-one years of age, that you have resided in this State two years and six months, that you have declared your intention to become a citizen of the United States, pursuant to the laws thereof, six months preceding this election, that you have resided in this State three months next preceding this day, and in this township (or ward, as the case may be) ten days next preceding this day, and that you have not voted at this election"; or, Ibid.

5. "You do solemnly swear [or affirm] that you are twenty-one years of age, that you are a native of the United States, that you are a civilized inhabitant of Indian descent, and not a member of any tribe, that you have resided in this State three months next preceding this day, and in this township (or ward, as the case may be) ten days next preceding this day, and hat you have not voted at this election." Ibid.

And if such person so challenged will take either of the above oaths, his vote shall be received; but if such person shall therein swear falsely, upon conviction thereof, he shall be liable to the pains and penalties of perjury.

[50.] SEC. 26. There shall be provided and kept by the township clerk in each township, at the expense of such township, and in each ward in any city, by the assessor thereof, at the ex- Ballot box to be provided.

In determining this question, the inspectors act *judicially*, not ministerially; and therefore they are not liable in an action on the case for damages for improperly, and without malice, refusing a lawful vote.—*Gordon v. Farrar*, 2 *Doug. Mich.* 411.

Article VIIth of the Constitution further declares:

SEC. 3. Every elector, in all cases, except treason, felony, or breach of the peace, shall be privileged from arrest during his attendance at election, and going to and returning from the same.

SEC. 4. No elector shall be obliged to do military duty on the day of election, except in time of war or public danger; or attend court as a suitor or witness.

SEC. 5. No elector shall be deemed to have gained or lost a residence, by reason of his being employed in the service of the United States, or of this State; nor while engaged in the navigation of the waters of this State, or of the United States, or of the high seas; nor while a student of any seminary of learning; nor while kept at any almshouse, or other asylum, at public expense; nor while confined in any public prison.

SEC. 7. No soldier, seamen, nor marine, in the army or navy of the United States, shall be deemed a resident of this State in consequence of being stationed in any military or naval place within the same.

SEC. 8. Any inhabitant who may hereafter be engaged in a duel, either as principal or accessory before the fact, shall be disqualified from holding any office under the Constitution and laws of this State, and shall not be permitted to vote at any election.

pense of the city, one suitable ballot box, with lock and key, which ballot box shall have an opening through the lid, of the proper size to admit a single closed ballot, through which each ballot received shall be inserted.

Box to be examined, locked, etc.

[51.] SEC. 27. Before opening the poll, the ballot box shall be examined, that nothing may remain in it; and it shall then be locked, and the key thereof delivered to one of the inspectors, to be designated by the board; and the said box shall not be opened during the election, except in the manner and for the purpose hereinafter mentioned.

Ballot, how deposited.

[52.] SEC. 28. When a ballot shall be received, one of the inspectors, without opening the same, or permitting it to be opened, shall deposit such ballot in the box.

Poll list.

[53.] SEC. 29. Each of the clerks shall keep a poll list, which shall contain the names of all the electors voting at such election.

Comparing and correcting lists.

[54.] SEC. 30. At each adjournment of the poll, the clerks shall, in the presence of the inspectors, compare their respective poll lists, compute and set down the number of votes; and correct all mistakes that may be discovered, according to the decision of the board, until such poll lists shall be made in all respects to correspond.

Lists, box and key; how kept, etc.

[55.] SEC. 31. The ballot [box] shall then be opened, and the poll lists placed therein, and the box shall then be locked, and a covering with a seal placed over the opening of the lid of the box, and the key delivered to one of the inspectors and the box to another, to be designated by the board.

Ibid.

[56.] SEC. 32. The inspector having the key shall keep it in his possession, and deliver it again to the board at the next opening of the poll, and the inspector having the box shall carefully keep it without opening or suffering it to be opened, or the seal thereof to be broken or removed, and shall publicly deliver it in that state to the board of inspectors at the next opening of the poll, when the seal shall be broken, and the box opened, the poll lists taken out, and the box again locked.[1]

Duty of Inspectors to challenge

To keep order.

17 Wendell, 522.

[57.] SEC. 33. It shall be the duty of each inspector to challenge every person offering a vote, whom he shall know or suspect not to be duly qualified as an elector; and the board of inspectors shall possess full authority to maintain regularity and order, and to enforce obedience to their lawful commands during an election, and during the canvass and estimate of the votes, after the poll is closed.[2]

---

[1] The statute specifying the mode in which ballots shall be kept after the election, is held to be directory, merely, and a failure of compliance with its provisions can not operate to the prejudice, or to defeat, the rights of candidates. — *People v. Higgins*, 3 *Mich.* 233.

[2] The board of inspectors may make a parol order for the *removal* of any disorderly person who disturbs the election, or business of the election, or during the canvass. An order in writing is not necessary for such purpose; but where the board design to go further than the mere removal of a disorderly person, and commit the person offending to jail, then their order must be in writing. — *Parsons v. Brainard*, 17 *Wend.* 522.

[58.] SEC. 34. If any person shall refuse to obey such lawful commands of the inspectors, or by disorderly conduct in their presence or hearing, shall interrupt or disturb their proceedings, the inspectors may, by an order in writing, commit the person so offending to the common jail of the county, for a period not exceeding twenty days, and may require such order to be executed by any sheriff, deputy sheriff, or constable to whom the same shall be directed; or if neither of said officers shall be present, such order may be executed by any other person deputed in writing by the inspectors to execute the same.[1]

Penalty for disorderly conduct, and how enforced.

R. S. 1846, Ch. 5, Sec. 21.

[59.] SEC. 35. As soon as the poll of the general election shall be finally closed, the inspectors shall immediately proceed to canvass and ascertain the result of the election, unless they shall deem it necessary to adjourn such canvass to some convenient hour of the next day; if the canvass shall be adjourned, the same course shall be observed in relation to the poll lists, box, and key, as is required in sections thirty-one and two of this act, to be observed upon an adjournment of the poll.

Canvass of votes.

[60.] SEC. 36. The canvass shall be public, and shall commence by a comparison of the poll lists, and a correction of any mistakes that may be found therein, until they shall be found or made to agree.

Canvass to be public.

[61.] SEC. 37. The box shall then be opened, and the ballots contained therein taken out and counted by the inspectors, unopened, except so far as to ascertain whether each ballot is single; and if two or more ballots shall be found so folded together as to present the appearance of a single ballot, they shall be destroyed, when the number of ballots shall be found not to agree with the poll lists, as provided in the next section.

Excess of ballots, how disposed of.

[62.] SEC. 38. If the ballots in the box shall be found to exceed in number the whole number of names of electors on the poll lists, they shall be replaced in the box, and one of the inspectors shall publicly draw out and destroy so many ballots therefrom, unopened, as shall be equal to such excess.

Ibid.

---

[1] *Form of Order of Inspectors to Commit a Person to Jail for Interrupting or Disturbing an Election.*

In the name of the People of the State of Michigan: To the Sheriff, or any Deputy Sheriff, of the County of *Hillsdale*, or any Constable of the town of *Hillsdale*, in said County:

We, the undersigned, Inspectors at a *General* Election held in said town of *Hillsdale*, on the —— day of ———, A. D. 18—, do order that you take the body of A. B. and commit him to the common jail of said County of *Hillsdale*, the keeper whereof is hereby required to keep him in safe custody in said jail for the period of ——— days; said A. B. having been guilty of disorderly conduct in the presence of said Inspectors at said election (*or as the case may be*).

Given under our hands, at *Hillsdale*, this —— day of ———, A. D. 18—.

CHRISTOPHER J. DICKINSON,
TIMOTHY E. DIBELL,
JAMES B. BALDY,
Inspectors of Election.

Canvass and statement of votes.

[63.] SEC. 39. The ballots and poll lists agreeing, or being made to agree, the board shall then proceed to canvass and estimate the votes, and they shall draw up a statement of the result, and cause a duplicate thereof to be made, which statement and duplicate shall be certified by the inspectors to be correct, and shall be subscribed with their names.

What statement to contain, and how disposed of.

[64.] SEC. 40. Such statements shall set forth, in words at length, the whole number of votes given for each office, the names of the persons for which such votes for such office were given, and the number of votes so given for each person;[1] and one of said statements shall forthwith be delivered to the township clerk, to be filed and preserved by him in his office, and the other shall be delivered to one of the inspectors who shall be appointed by the board to attend the county canvass.

Ballots, and copy of defective ballots, how kept.

[65.] SEC. 41. The inspectors shall preserve a true copy of all ballots rejected as defective, with the originals attached, and deliver the same to the township clerk, to be filed in his office; and the other ballots they shall seal up and deliver to said clerk, who shall keep the same in his office until the next election, subject only to the inspection of the proper authorities, in case of a contested election.

Poll lists to be filed, etc.

[66.] SEC. 42. One of the poll lists shall be delivered to the township clerk, and the other to the county clerk, which lists shall be filed and preserved by them in their respective offices.[2]

---

[1] *Form of Statement of Board of Inspectors of the Result of Election.*

A Statement, setting forth the whole number of votes given for each office, the names of the persons for which such votes for each office were given, and the number of votes given for each person, at a *general* (*or special*) election held at ———, in the town of *Spaulding*, in the County of *Saginaw*, and State of Michigan, on the —— day of ———, A. D. 18—.

The whole number of votes given for Governor was *two hundred and fifty.*

The whole number of votes given for Lieutenant-Governor was *two hundred and fifty.*

(*Continue by giving the number of votes for each office.*)

Kingsley S. Bingham had *one hundred and fifty* votes given him for Governor.

——— ——— had *one hundred* votes given him for Governor.

(*Continue by giving the names of persons voted for, and number of votes given for each.*)

Dated this —— day of ———, A. D. 18—.

AARON K. PENNY,
PHINEAS SPAULDING,
JESSE H. QUACKENBUSH,
Inspectors.

We, the Inspectors of the Election mentioned in the foregoing Statement, do certify said Statement to be correct.

Witness our hands, this —— day of ———, A. D. 18—.

AARON K. PENNY,
PHINEAS SPAULDING,
JESSE H. QUACKENBUSH,
Inspectors.

[2] A statement of the number of votes given at an election for the respective candidates, required to be made out and filed in the county clerk's office, by the board of county canvassers, is *prima facie* evidence only of the facts stated in it. The county

In a city, the ballots, and one of such poll lists and statements, shall be delivered to the city clerk, and shall be kept and preserved by him.

[67.] SEC. 43. The several inspectors appointed by the inspectors of election in townships and wards, to attend the county canvass, shall constitute the board of county canvassers, and shall meet on Tuesday next following the election, before one o'clock in the afternoon, at the office of the county clerk, who shall be secretary of the board; or in his absence his deputy shall be secretary; but if such county shall be divided into two or more senatorial or representative districts, the inspectors of election, representing the townships or wards embraced in each of such districts, shall, with the county clerk or his deputy, constitute the board of district canvassers for said districts respectively, so far as the canvass relates to the election of Senators and Representatives in the State Legislature, which several canvasses shall be held immediately after the county canvass.

Who to be the County canvassers, and when to meet.

[68.] SEC. 44. If either of the inspectors appointed to attend the county canvass shall be unable to attend such canvass on the day appointed, he shall, on or before that day, cause to be delivered at the office of the county clerk the original statement of all votes given in his township or ward, which statements said clerk shall lay before said canvassers.

Statement to be delivered to County Clerk in certain cases.

[69.] SEC. 45. On the day appointed for such canvass, if a majority of the canvassers shall not attend, or if such statement of votes shall not be produced, or if there shall be any material defect in any of such statements received, the canvassers then present shall adjourn the county canvass to some convenient hour of the next day; but the inspectors from the several senatorial or representative districts, if there shall be more than one of such districts in such county, may proceed with their secretary to canvass the votes of their respective districts, as far as it can be done, before the county canvass.

When canvassers may adjourn

[70.] SEC. 46. If all the original statements of the votes given in the several townships and wards shall not be produced on the day appointed for such canvass, or if there shall be any material defect in any of the statements received, the county clerk shall, by a special messenger or otherwise, obtain such original or corrected statements as are not produced or are defective, or certified or corrected copies thereof, in time to be delivered to the board of canvassers at their said adjourned meeting.

When messengers to be sent for statement of votes.

[71.] SEC. 47. At the time to which such canvass was adjourned, the canvassers shall again meet; and such of them as

Board to meet on adjourned day.

---

canvass may be corrected by the township canvasses, and these by the ballots themselves.

The determination of the board of county canvassers of the persons elected, is *prima facie* evidence only of their election. A party may go behind the canvass to the ballots to show the number of votes cast for him.

The duties of the board of canvassers are wholly ministerial.—*People v. Vancleve*, 1 *Mich.* 362.

shall be present, although less than a majority of the whole number, shall constitute the board of canvassers.

To organize and canvass votes.

[72.] SEC. 48. The canvassers shall choose one of their number chairman; and said board shall then proceed to examine the original statements certified by the several boards of inspectors of election, or certified or corrected copies thereof, and ascertain the number of votes given in the county for the respective State, county, and district officers when such district shall exceed the limits of such county, and make statements thereof, as the nature of the election may require; after which the several senatorial and representative district boards of canvassers shall proceed to canvass their respective districts, if such county shall be divided for representative purposes.[1]

15 Ill. 492.

Separate statement of votes for certain offices.

[73.] SEC. 49. They shall make a separate statement, containing the whole number of votes given in such county for the offices of Governor, Lieutenant-Governor, Secretary of State, State Treasurer, Auditor General, Attorney General, Superintendent of Public Instruction, Commissioner of the State Land Office, and members of the State Board of Education, the names of the persons to whom such votes were given, and the number of votes given to each; another similar statement of the votes given for Electors of President and Vice-President of the United States, each year in which such Electors are to be chosen; another similar statement of the votes given for Representative in Congress; another of votes given for Senator, when the county alone does not constitute a senatorial district; another of the votes given for Representative in the State Legislature, when the county alone does not constitute a representative district; another of the votes given for Senator or Representative, when the county alone constitutes but one senatorial or representative district; and another of the votes given for county officers.

Ibid.

[74.] SEC. 50. The several senatorial and representative district canvassers shall, where a county is divided for such purposes, also make a statement of the whole number of votes given in each respective district for the office of Senator or Representative, or both, as the case may be, which several statements shall set forth the number of each of such districts, the number of votes given to each of the persons voted for in each of such districts, respectively.

What statement to contain.

[75.] SEC. 51. In each of said statements, the whole number of votes given, the names of the candidates, and the number of votes given to each, shall be written out in words at length; and each statement shall be certified as correct, and attested by

---

1 When no contest is entered, the board of canvassers can only declare the result shown by the statement of inspectors. They do not pass upon the qualification of voters, nor decide as to what ballots should be counted. —*People v. Kilduff*, 15 *Ill.* 492.

The legality of an election does not depend upon the fact of the declaration of the board of inspectors. If withheld, or not made, through illegal causes, the office will vest; the authority, rights, and powers of officers are derived from the election, and not from the returns. — *Ibid.*

the signatures of the chairman and secretary of the respective boards, and a copy of each, thus certified and attested, shall be delivered to the county clerk, and recorded by him in a suitable book, to be provided by him for that purpose, at the expense of the county, and kept in his office.

Statement to be recorded, etc.

Determination by board of persons elected.

[76.] SEC. 52. The county and district boards shall then determine the persons who have been, by the greatest number of votes, elected to the county offices, and members of the Legislature, when the county alone constitutes one or more senatorial or representative districts, and such determinations shall be certified and attested by the chairman and secretary of the respective boards, and be annexed to the statement of votes given for such officers respectively, and shall be recorded with such statements by the county clerk in his office: *Provided*,[b] That in elections for members of the Legislature, or county officers, if it shall appear on the legal canvass of the votes polled at such election, that two or more persons have received an equal number of votes for the same office, such persons shall proceed to draw lots for the election to said office in the following manner: the board of canvassers for the county or district in which such election was held, shall appoint a day for the appearance of all such persons before the proper officer hereinafter provided, for the purpose of determining by lot among such persons the right to such office, and shall cause notice thereof to be given to all such persons interested; the officer before whom such drawing is to take place, shall prepare as many slips of paper as there are such persons, and write the word "elected" on as many slips of paper as there are offices to be filled, and the words "not elected" on the remaining slips, and fold the same so as to conceal the writing, and so that they may appear as nearly alike as possible; said slips shall be placed in a box, and at the time and place appointed for the drawing of said lots, each of such persons aforesaid may draw one of said slips from the box; and any such person drawing a slip on which is written the word "elected," shall be deemed legally elected to the office in question; and the officer conducting such drawing shall forthwith give him a certificate of such election; if the drawings under the provisions of this section are for the office of Senator or Representative in the State Legislature, and the district exceeds the limits of a single county, then the drawing shall take place before the county clerk of the county where the district canvass is held: in all other cases, before the county clerk of the county where each case shall arise: *Provided, further*, That in cases where the office of county clerk is in question, the drawing shall take place before the sheriff of the county.

Proceedings when two or more persons have equal number of votes.

[b] This proviso is from the Act of April 2, 1849; which is retained (Sec. 132) for the reason that an important omission occurs here—the words, "and that a failure to elect to any office is caused thereby," being left out from their appropriate place after the word "office," in the fourth line of the proviso.

Duplicate statement of votes for Senator, etc.

[77.] SEC. 53. The said board shall, without delay, make a duplicate statement of the votes given for Senator, when the county alone does not constitute a senatorial district, and deliver the same to the clerk of the county, to be delivered by him to the senatorial district canvassers; said board shall also make a duplicate statement of votes given for Representative in the State Legislature, when the county alone does not constitute a representative district, and deliver the same to the said clerk, to be by him delivered to the representative district canvassers.

County Clerk to transmit copy of statement to Governor, Secretary of State, and State Treasurer.

[78.] SEC. 54. The county clerk shall prepare and certify under his hand and seal of office, three copies of the statement of votes given for the office of Governor, Lieutenant-Governor, Secretary of State, State Treasurer, Auditor General, Attorney General, Superintendent of Public Instruction, Commissioner of the State Land Office, and members of the State Board of Education; also three copies of the statement of votes given for Representative in Congress; also three copies of the statement of votes given for Electors of President and Vice-President of the United States, after he shall have received such statement from the board of county canvassers; each of which statements he shall seal up in an envelope, and direct one of each to the Governor, one of each to the Secretary of State, and one of each to the State Treasurer, and transmit the same by mail, within five days after the county canvass when a general election has been held, and within three days after the county canvass when a special election has been held.

Certificate of determination to be delivered to persons elected.

[79.] SEC. 55. He shall also prepare as many certified copies of each certificate of the determination of the board of county canvassers, as well as of the several district canvassers, if such county shall be divided for representative purposes, as there are persons declared in such certificates to be elected, and shall, without delay, deliver one of such copies to each person so declared to be elected.

Clerk to transmit list of Representatives and County officers to Secretary of State.

[80.] SEC. 56. Such clerk shall, within thirty days of a general election, transmit to the Secretary of State, a list of the members of the Legislature elected in the county, designating both the Senators and Representatives by their respective districts, and also a list of all the county officers elected in such county at such election.

Votes for and against amendment to Constitution; how taken and canvassed.

Const. Art. 20.

[81.] SEC. 57. Whenever any amendment shall have been proposed to the Constitution, and agreed to and submitted to the people, pursuant to the provisions of the Constitution, if the vote thereon shall be required to be taken at a general election, the votes of the electors for and against such amendment shall be taken, canvassed, certified, and recorded, and certified copies of the statement thereof shall be made and transmitted by the several county clerks to the Governor, Secretary of State, and State Treasurer, at the same time and in the same manner as the votes for State officers are by law required to be taken and canvassed, and statements thereof to be certified, recorded, and transmitted.

[82.] SEC. 58. Whenever any banking law for banking purposes, or amendments thereof, shall have been passed by the Legislature, approved by the Governor, and submitted to the people, pursuant to the provisions of the Constitution, if the vote thereon shall be required to be taken at a general election, the votes of the electors for and against such banking law, or amendment thereof, shall be taken, canvassed, certified, and recorded, and certified copies of the statements thereof shall be made and transmitted by the several county clerks to the Governor, Secretary of State, and State Treasurer, at the same time and in the same manner as the votes for State officers are by law required to be taken and canvassed, and statements thereof to be certified, recorded, and transmitted.

Of Banking Law, or amendments thereto.

Const. Art. 15, Sec. 2.

[83.] SEC. 59. In each election district for the election of a Senator or Representative in the State Legislature, the limits of which shall be greater than those of a county, there shall be a board of district canvassers, and the clerks of the several counties within the district, the judge of probate, and the sheriff of the county in which the meetings of the board are to be held, shall constitute such board.

District canvassers.

[84.] SEC. 60. Any three of said canvassers shall be a quorum for the transaction of the business of said board; and in case there shall not be three of the members of such board present at any such meeting, the register of deeds or the county treasurer of the county where any such meeting is appointed to be held, or both of them, may act as members of such board; and, with the other members in attendance, shall constitute a board of not less than three in number.

Quorum of Board.

[85.] SEC. 61. The board shall meet in the district for the election of a Representative in the State Legislature, on the Tuesday next after the day on which the county canvass is appointed to be made, and in districts for the election of Senators, on the third Tuesday after the county canvass, at the office of the clerk of the county in such district having the greatest number of inhabitants, according to the last preceding census, unless otherwise provided by law.

Times and places of meeting.

[86.] SEC. 62. If either of the county clerks shall be unable to attend such canvass on the day appointed therefor, he shall, on or before that day, cause to be delivered at the office of the clerk of the county in which such meeting is to be held, the original statement of votes given in his county for the officer to be elected in such district, which statement shall be laid before said board.

Original statements to be laid before Board.

[87.] SEC. 63. The canvassers shall then proceed to examine the statement of the votes given in the several counties in the district, and ascertain and determine what persons have been elected, and to what offices, and shall draw up a statement thereof in words at length, which statement shall contain the whole number of votes given in the district for each office, and the names of the persons to whom such votes were given; and

Proceeding of canvassers.

such statement shall be certified to be correct, and to be subscribed by the said canvassers, or a majority of them.

Board to determine persons elected, and deliver certificate to County Clerk

[88.] SEC. 64. The canvassers shall then determine the persons elected to the several offices within the district, as shall appear by such statement, and shall certify such determination under their hands, and annex the same to their said statement, and deliver the same to the clerk of the county in which their meeting shall be held, who shall file the same in his office; and said board shall cause a copy of such statement and certificate to be forthwith published in some newspaper printed in the district.

Duty of County Clerk in relation to statement.

[89.] SEC. 65. The county clerk, by whom the said statement and certificate thereto annexed shall be filed, shall, without delay, transmit by mail to the Secretary of State, a copy of such statement and certificate of determination, certified by him under his hand and seal of office, and he shall also, without delay, prepare and certify as many copies of such certificate of determination as there are persons stated therein to have been elected, and cause one of said copies to be delivered to each person so determined to be elected.

State canvassers.

Const. Art. 8, Sec. 4.

[90.] SEC. 66. The Secretary of State, the State Treasurer, and the Commissioner of the State Land Office shall constitute the board of State canvassers, any two of whom shall be a quorum for the transaction of business; and if only one of said officers shall attend on the day appointed for a meeting of the board, the Auditor General, on being notified by the officer so attending, shall, without delay, attend with such officer, and with him shall form the board.

Secretary of State to record statements.

When to call on Governor and State Treasurer for statement.

[91.] SEC. 67. The Secretary of State, on the receipt of the certified copies of the statement of votes given in the several counties, directed by law to be sent to him by the county clerks, shall record the same in a suitable book to be kept by him for that purpose;[c] and if from any county clerk no such statement shall have been received by the Secretary of State, on or before the second Monday of December next after a general election, and on or before the thirtieth day after a special election, he shall call upon the Governor and State Treasurer, and receive from them, or either of them, the statement from such county [clerk], if the Governor or State Treasurer shall have received such statement.

When to call on County Clerk for statement.

[92.] SEC. 68. If, from any county clerk, no such statement shall have been received by the Secretary of State, the Governor, nor the State Treasurer, within the times limited, the Secretary of State shall forthwith send a special messenger to obtain such statements and certificates from such county clerk; and such clerk shall immediately, on demand being made by such messenger at his office, make out and deliver to him the statements and certificates required.

---

[c] See section 131.

[93.] SEC. 69. For the purpose of canvassing and ascertaining the result of elections, other than for Electors of President and Vice-President, the Secretary of State shall appoint a meeting of the State canvassers to be held at his office, on or before the fifteenth day of December next after a general election, and within forty days after a special election, and shall notify the other members of the board of the same. **Secretary to appoint meeting of Board, etc.**

[94.] SEC. 70. The said board of canvassers, when formed as aforesaid, shall examine the statements received by the Secretary of State, of the votes given in the several counties, and make a statement of the whole number of votes given for the offices of Governor, Lieutenant-Governor, Secretary of State, State Treasurer, Auditor General, Attorney General, Superintendent of Public Instruction, Commissioner of the State Land Office, and members of the State Board of Education, which statement shall show the names of the persons to whom such votes shall have been given for either of the said offices, and the whole number of votes given to each of such persons. **Duty of Board of State canvassers.**

[95.] SEC. 71. The said board shall also proceed to examine the statements received by the Secretary of State, of the votes given in the several counties, and make a statement of the whole number of votes given for the office of Representative in Congress in each congressional district; which statement shall show the names of the persons to whom such votes shall have been given for said office, and the whole number of votes given to each person in each respective district. **Ibid.**

[96.] SEC. 72. The said canvassers shall certify each statement made by them to be correct, and subscribe their names thereto; and they shall thereupon determine what persons have been, by the greatest number of votes, duly elected to each respective office, and make and subscribe on each statement a certificate of such determination, and deliver the same to the Secretary of State. **Ibid.**

[97.] SEC. 73. The Secretary of State shall record in his office, in a book to be kept by him for that purpose, each certified statement and determination, so made and delivered to him by the board of State canvassers; and shall, without delay, make out and cause to be delivered to each of the persons thereby declared to be elected, a copy of such determination, certified by him under his seal of office. **Secretary of State to record certificate of determination and deliver copy to persons elected.**

[98.] SEC. 74. For the purpose of canvassing and ascertaining the votes given for electors of President and Vice-President of the United States, the board of State canvassers shall meet on the Wednesday next after the third Monday of November, or on such other day before that time as the Secretary of State shall appoint; and the powers, duties, and proceedings of said board, and of the Secretary of State, in sending for, examining, ascertaining, determining, certifying, and recording the votes and results of the election of such electors, shall be, in all respects, as near as may be, as hereinbefore provided in relation **Votes for electors of President, etc.; when and how canvassed.**

to sending for, examining, ascertaining, determining, certifying, and recording the votes and results of the election of State officers.

Copy of certificate of determination to be delivered to persons elected.

[99.] SEC. 75. The Secretary of State shall, without delay, cause a copy of the certified determination of the board of State canvassers, declaring the persons elected as such electors, to be transmitted and delivered by special message or otherwise, to each of the persons so declared to be elected, which copies shall be certified under his hand and seal of office.

Canvass of votes on amendment to Constitution and Banking Law.

[100.] SEC. 76. For the purpose of canvassing and ascertaining the result of the vote taken at a general election, upon any proposed amendment to the Constitution, or approval of any banking law, or amendment thereof, the Secretary of State shall appoint a meeting of the State board of State canvassers, to be held at his office, on or before the twentieth day of December next after such election; at which meeting the said Secretary shall lay before the board the statements received by him of the votes given in the several counties for and against such amendment to the Constitution, or for and against the approval of such banking law, or amendment thereof, as the case may be.

Board to ascertain and determine the result.

[101.] SEC. 77. The board shall then proceed to examine such statements, and to ascertain and determine the result, and shall make and certify under their hands, a statement of the whole number of votes given for, and the whole number of votes given against, such amendment of the Constitution, or for or against the approval of such banking law, or amendment thereof, as the case may be; and they shall thereupon determine whether such amendment to the Constitution, or such banking law, or amendment thereof, as the case may be, has been approved and ratified by a majority of the electors voting thereon, and shall make and subscribe on such statement a certificate of such determination, and deliver the same to the Secretary of State.

Determination to be recorded by Secretary of State, and published with Laws.

[102.] SEC. 78. The Secretary of State shall record in his office, in a book to be kept by him for that purpose, such certified statement and determination; and if it shall appear that such amendment to the Constitution, or such banking law, or amendment thereof, has been approved and ratified, as aforesaid, he shall also record such determination in the book in which the original act of the Legislature is recorded, and shall cause any amendment to the Constitution to be published with the laws enacted by the Legislature at the next succeeding session thereof.

Publication of determination of State canvassers.

[103.] SEC. 79. The Secretary of State shall cause a copy of such determination and certificate of election to be published for two successive weeks in a newspaper published at the Seat of Government, immediately after receiving the same from the board of State canvassers.

[104.] SEC. 80. The said board of State canvassers shall have power to adjourn from day to day, for a term not exceeding five days. Adjournment of State canvassers.

[105.] SEC. 81. At the general election to be held in the year eighteen hundred and fifty-two, there shall be elected three members of the State Board of Education, — one for two years, one for four years, and one for six years; and at each succeeding general election, there shall be elected one member of said board, who shall hold his office for six years, and until his successor is elected and qualified; and the ballots for the members of the State Board of Education shall designate which of the persons so balloted for, for member of said board, is to hold the office for two years, which for four years, and which for six years; and the person receiving the greatest number of votes for the term so designated, shall be by the state canvassers declared to be elected for such a term. Election of members of Board of Education.

[106.] SEC. 82. A Representative in the Congress of the United States shall be chosen in each of the congressional districts into which the State is or shall be divided, at each general election; and if a Representative in Congress shall resign, he shall forthwith transmit a notice of his resignation to the Secretary of State; and if a vacancy shall occur, by death or otherwise, in the office of Representative in Congress, the clerk of the county in which such Representative shall have resided at the time of his election, shall, without delay, transmit a notice of such vacancy to the Secretary of State. Representative in Congress. Vacancy.

[107.] SEC. 83. At the general election next preceding the choice of President and Vice-President of the United States, there shall be elected by general ticket as many Electors of President and Vice-President as this State may be entitled to elect of Senators and Representatives in Congress. Electors of President and Vice-President.

[108.] SEC. 84. The Electors of President and Vice-President shall convene at the Capitol of the State on the first Wednesday of December; and if there shall be any vacancy in the office of an Elector, occasioned by death, refusal to act, neglect to attend by the hour of twelve o'clock at noon of that day, or on account of any two of such Electors having received an equal and the same number of votes, the Electors present shall proceed to fill such vacancy by ballot and plurality of votes; and when all the Electors shall appear, or vacancies shall be filled, as above provided, they shall proceed to perform the duties of such Electors, as required by the Constitution and Laws of the United States. To convene at Capitol. How vacancy to be filled.

[109.] SEC. 85. The Secretary of State shall prepare three lists of the names of the Electors, procure thereto the signature of the Governor, affix the seal of the State to the same, and deliver such certificates, thus signed and sealed, to one of the Electors, on or before the said first Wednesday of December. Duty of Secretary of State.

When Senator in Congress to be elected.

[110.] SEC. 86. *On the first Tuesday after the second Monday of January next, before the expiration of the time for which any Senator was elected to represent this State in the Congress of the United States, if the Legislature shall be then in session, and if not, then within ten days after a quorum of both houses shall be assembled at the then next meeting of the Legislature, an election shall be held for a Senator in Congress, at the place where the Legislature shall be then sitting; which election may be continued from day to day until such Senator shall be elected.*[d]

Vacancy; how filled.

[111.] SEC. 87. Whenever the seat of any such Senator shall become vacant before the expiration of the term for which he was elected, another Senator shall be elected to fill his place within ten days after the Legislature shall have notice of such vacancy, at the place where it shall be then sitting.

Manner of conducting election

[112.] SEC. 88. Such election shall be made in the following manner: the Senate and House of Representatives shall each openly nominate one person for the office of Senator in Congress; after which they shall immediately meet in joint convention in the Hall of the House of Representatives, and if they shall agree in their nomination, the person so nominated shall be deemed elected; if they shall disagree, the election shall be made by a joint vote of the Senators and members of the House of Representatives, and a majority of the votes given in such joint convention shall be necessary to an election.

Evidence of election.

[113.] SEC. 89. Whenever any Senator shall be chosen as aforesaid, a copy of the resolutions of the Senate and House of Representatives, certifying such choice, signed by the President of the Senate and Speaker of the House of Representatives, shall be delivered to the Secretary of State, and recorded by him; and he shall forthwith make out a certificate, under the seal of the State, and attested by him as Secretary, certifying such choice, and deliver the same to the person so chosen Senator, by mail or otherwise.

Unorganized counties.

[114.] SEC. 90. Unorganized counties, with other parts of the State which may be attached to any organized county for judicial purposes, unless otherwise provided, shall be considered as a part of such organized county for all purposes concerning the election of officers who may be elected at a general or special election.

Oath of Inspectors and Clerks of elections.

[115.] SEC. 91. The oath directed in this act to be taken by persons chosen to be inspectors, or appointed clerks of elections, shall be in the form prescribed in the first section of the eighteenth article of the revised Constitution of this State.

Compensation to certain officers.

[116.] SEC. 92. Each county canvasser, sheriff, and county clerk, shall receive such reasonable compensation for their services while employed in the business of elections for county

[d] See Sec. 129 and 130, by the latter of which a repeal of this section was designed.

officers as shall be allowed by the board of supervisors or county auditors, to be paid by the county.

[117.] SEC. 93. Each district canvasser, county clerk, or other person employed in canvassing and returning the result of the elections required by law to be certified by district canvassers, to the board of state canvassers, shall receive such compensation as the board of state auditors shall deem reasonable, and be paid out of the State Treasury. **Compensation to certain officers.**

[118.] SEC. 94. During the day on which any election shall be held, pursuant to the provisions of law, no civil process shall be served on any elector entitled to vote at such election. **No civil process to be served on electors on day of election.**

[119.] SEC. 95. The person holding any office, at the expiration of the term thereof shall continue to hold the same until his successor shall be elected or appointed and qualified; and when any person shall be elected to fill a vacancy in any elective office, he shall hold the same only during the unexpired portion of the regular term limited to such office, and until his successor shall be elected and qualified. **Term of office. Term, when elected to fill vacancy.**

An Act to Provide for the Election of Circuit Judges and Regents of the University.

[*Approved March* 10, 1851. *Laws of* 1851, *p.* 20.]

[120.] SECTION 1. *The People of the State of Michigan enact*, That an election shall be held on the first Monday in April, one thousand eight hundred and fifty-one, and every sixth year thereafter, in each of the judicial circuits into which, under the revised Constitution and schedule thereto, and laws, the State is divided, by the electors thereof, of one Circuit Judge and one Regent of the University, who shall hold their offices respectively for the term of six years, and until their successors are elected and qualified. **When Circuit Judge and Regent to be elected, and for what term.**

[121.] SEC. 2. The inspectors of elections in the several townships and wards in cities throughout the State, are hereby required to prepare a ballot box to receive all ballots that may be offered at such election for Circuit Judge and Regent of the University, both of which officers shall be voted for on one ballot. **Duties of Inspectors of election.**

[122.] SEC. 3. The Secretary of State shall immediately after the passage of this act, transmit to the sheriff of each county included within the several judicial circuits of this State a notice in writing, containing a brief statement of the contents of this act, and he shall cause a copy of this act to be published in such newspapers within the several judicial circuits as he may deem proper, once in each week, from the date of the notice till the election aforesaid. **Secretary of State to give notice to Sheriffs.**

[123.] SEC. 4. The sheriffs of the several counties, on receiving the notice hereby provided for, shall forthwith, in writing, notify the township clerk of each township, and one of the inspectors of election of each ward in any city, of such election; and it shall be the duty of the township clerks and inspectors of **Sheriffs to notify Township Clerks, etc.**

Township Clerks to give notice.

election receiving said notice to give eight days' notice, except for the election in eighteen hundred and fifty-one, in writing, under their hands respectively, to the electors of the township or ward, of the time and place of holding such election, by posting the same up in at least three public places in the township or ward.

Election, canvass, etc., to be same as general election.

[124.] SEC. 5. The election provided for by this act shall be conducted in the same manner as by existing laws is provided for the holding of a general election; and the inspectors of elections shall make the same canvass, statement, and returns, and they are hereby invested with the same powers and authority as are provided by the election laws of this State for a general election.

County canvass, when held. Statement, where returned.

[125.] SEC. 6. The county canvass for the several Circuit Judges and Regents of the University, shall be on the second Tuesday succeeding the election, and shall be conducted in all respects in the same manner, and returns shall be made in the same manner, and within the same time as is provided by existing laws for the canvass of Representatives to Congress; but the county clerks of the several counties shall transmit one of the certified copies of the statement of votes to the State Treasurer, instead of the Auditor General.

Board of State canvassers. Const. Art. 8, Sec. 4. Their duty. Proviso as to county of Wayne.

[126.] SEC. 7. The Secretary of State, State Treasurer, and Commissioner of the State Land Office, shall constitute the board of state canvassers; and they are hereby authorized and required to proceed in the canvass and determination of the election of the several Circuit Judges and Regents of the University, in the same manner and within similar periods of time, as near as may be, as is provided by law for the canvass of the election of Representatives to Congress, and shall transmit similar notices to the persons declared to be elected to the offices of Circuit Judge and Regent of the University in the several Judicial districts: *Provided*, That the board of state canvassers shall not determine the result of the election for a Regent of the University in the county of Wayne, until after the receipt of the several statements of votes given for a Regent of the University in the Upper Peninsula; provided such statement shall be received before the third Tuesday of November next ensuing, when said board shall proceed to canvass and determine the election of such Regent, as in other cases.

Commencement of term.

[127.] SEC. 8. The officers elected under the provisions of this act, shall enter upon the discharge of their respective duties on the first day of January succeeding their election.

Oath to be tendered to person challenged.

[128.] SEC. 9. If any person offering to vote shall be challenged as unqualified, by any inspector or any elector qualified to vote at that poll, the chairman of the board of inspectors shall declare to the person challenged the constitutional qualifications of an elector, and if such person shall state that he is a qualified elector, and the challenge shall not be withdrawn, one of the inspectors shall tender to him such of the following oaths as he may claim to contain the grounds of his qualifications to vote:

1st. "You do solemnly swear [or affirm] that you are twenty-one years of age, that you are a citizen of the United States, that you have resided in this State three months, and in this township [or ward, as the case may be] ten days next preceding this election, and that you have not voted at this election"; or, **Form of oath or affirmation.**

2d. "You do solemnly swear [or affirm] that you are twenty-one years of age, that you resided in this State on the twenty-fourth day of June, one thousand eight hundred and thirty-five, that you have resided in this state three months, and in this township [or ward, as the case may be] ten days next preceding this election, and that you have not voted at this election"; or, **Ibid.**

3d. "You do solemnly swear [or affirm] that you are twenty-one years of age, that you resided in this State on the first day of January, one thousand eight hundred and fifty, that you have declared your intention to become a citizen of the United States, pursuant to the laws thereof, six months preceding this election, that you have resided in this state three months, and in this township [or ward, as the case may be] ten days next preeeding this election, and that you have not voted at this election"; or, **Ibid.**

4th. "You do solemnly swear [or affirm] that you are twenty-one years of age, that you have resided in this state two years and six months next preceding this election, that you have declared your intention to become a citizen of the United States, pursuant to the laws thereof, six months preceding this election, that you have resided in this township [or ward, as the case may be] ten days next preceding this election, and that you have not voted at this election"; or, **Ibid.**

5th. "You do solemnly swear [or affirm] that you are twenty-one years of age, that you are a native of the United States, that you are of Indian descent and do not belong to any tribe, that you have resided in this State three months, and in this township [or ward, as the case may be] ten days next preceding this election, and that you have not voted at this election." **Ibid.**

If such person so challenged will take either of the above oaths, his vote shall be received; but if such person shall therein swear falsely, upon conviction thereof, he shall be liable to the pains and penalties of perjury. **If oath be taken, vote to be received. Penalty for swearing falsely**

Sec. 10. This act shall take effect immediately.

An Act to Amend the Sixth Section of Chapter Eleven, Title Two, of Revised Statutes of 1846.

[*Approved January* 29, 1853. *Laws of* 1853, *p.* 24.]

Section 1. *The People of the State of Michigan enact*, That section six of chapter eleven, title two of the Revised Statutes of eighteen hundred and forty-six, be amended so as to read as follows, viz.:

[129.] Sec. 5. Within ten days after a quorum of both houses of the Legislature shall be assembled, at their session immediately preceding the expiration of the time for which any Senator was elected to represent this State in Congress, an election shall be held for a Senator in Congress; which election may be continued from day to day until such Senator be elected." **Senator in Congress, when to be elected.**

[130.] Sec. 2. The eighty-sixth section of an act entitled, "An act to provide for holding General and Special Elections," approved June twenty-seven, eighteen hundred and fifty-one, be and the same is hereby repealed. **Sec. repealed, 1851, p. 301. Ante Sec. 110.**

An Act to Amend Section Two of Chapter Nine of the Revised Statutes of 1846.

[*Approved January* 29, 1853, *Took effect May* 16, 1853. *Laws of* 1853, *p*, 15.]

SECTION 1. *The People of the State of Michigan enact*, That section two of chapter nine of the Revised Statutes of eighteen hundred and forty-six, be amended so as to read as follows:

Secretary of State to record statement of votes given in the several counties.

[131.] SEC. 2. The Secretary of State, on the receipt of the certified copies of the statement of votes given in the several counties, directed by law to be sent to him by the county clerks, shall make a record of the aggregate number of votes given for each person in the several counties, in a suitable book to be kept by him for that purpose, and shall place on file and preserve such certified copies in his office.[e]

An Act Relative to Elections.

[*Approved April* 2, 1849. *Laws of* 1849, *p*. 355.]

Proceedings when two or more persons have equal number of votes for members of the Legislature and County officers.

[132.] SECTION 1. *Be it enacted by the Senate and House of Representatives of the State of Michigan*, That whenever in elections of members of the State Legislature, or county officers, it shall appear, on the legal canvass of the votes, that two or more persons have received an equal number of votes, and that a failure to elect to any office is caused thereby, such persons shall draw lots for election to such office in the manner following: the proper board of canvassers in each case shall appoint a day for the appearance of all such persons before the proper officer hereinafter provided, for the purpose of determining by lot among such persons the right to such office, and shall cause notice thereof to be given to all such persons. The officer before whom said drawing is to take place shall prepare as many slips of paper as there are such persons, and write the word "elected" on as many of said slips of paper as there are offices to be filled, and the words "not elected" on the remaining slips, and fold the same so as to conceal the writing, and so that all may appear as nearly alike as possible; said slips shall all be placed in a box, and at the time and place appointed for the drawing of said lots, each of such persons aforesaid may draw one of said slips from the box, and any such person drawing a slip in which is written the word "elected" shall be deemed legally elected to the office in question; and the officer conducting such drawing shall forthwith give him a certificate of such election.

Drawing of lots, who to be before

[133.] SEC. 2. Drawing of lots, under the provisions of the preceding section, shall take place before the following officers: for the office of State Senator, before the county clerk of the county where the senatorial canvass is held; for the office of Representative in the Legislature, and for any county office, before

[e] See Section 91. The section amended by this act is regarded as superseded by the of June 27, 1851, which comprehends the whole subject of General and Special Elections.

the county clerk of the county where each case shall arise: *Provided*, That in cases where the office of county clerk is in question, the drawing shall take place before the sheriff of the county.

SEC. 3. This act shall take effect and be in force from and after its passage.

An Act to Provide for Holding General Elections in the Upper Peninsula.

[*Approved April* 7, 1851. *Took effect July* 8, 1851. *Laws of* 1851, *p.* 156.]

[134.] SECTION 1. *The People of the State of Michigan enact*, That a general election shall be held in the several townships and wards of that portion of the State denominated the Upper Peninsula, as described in section one, article nineteen of the revised Constitution, and such other territory as may be attached thereto for election purposes, on the last Tuesday of September, A. D. 1852, and on the last Tuesday of September every two years thereafter; at which time shall be elected one Senator and three Representatives in the State Legislature, and such county officers as are authorized by law to be elected in the several counties of this State, *except Prosecuting Attorneys*;[f] which election shall be notified, conducted, canvassed, certified, determined, and recorded, in all respects, as near as may be, according to the provisions of law relative to holding general elections, except as to the time above mentioned, and as is hereinafter provided.[g]

General election

Officers to be elected.

[135.] SEC. 2. The county canvass shall be held on the first Tuesday in October next after such election, and the district canvass shall be held on the last Tuesday of said October, at such places as shall be designated by law.

County and district canvass.

An Act to Provide for the Election of a District Judge, District Attorney, and Regent of the University in the Upper Peninsula.[h]

[*Took effect July* 8, 1855. *Laws of* 1851, *pp.* 157, 213.]

[136.] SECTION 1. *The People of the State of Michigan enact*, That an election shall be held in the several townships and wards of that portion of the State denominated the Upper Peninsula, as described in section one, article nineteen of the Revised Constitution, on the last Tuesday of September, in the year eighteen hundred and fifty-one, and on the last Tuesday of September every sixth year thereafter, at which there shall be elected one District Judge for such district, and *one Regent of the University*,[i] in conjunction with the county of Wayne, and one District

When election of District Judge, District Attorney to be held.

---

f See Section 137.

g As amended by "An Act to amend an Act entitled 'An Act to provide for holding General Elections in the Upper Peninsula, approved April 7, 1851.'" *Laws of* 1851. p. 313.

h Being Act 121 of 1851, p. 157, as amended by Act 180 of 1851, p. 312.

i See Section 6, Article 13 of Constitution, and Section 25 of Schedule to the Constitution.

When election of Regent held, and how conducted. Attorney for said district, who shall be elected on the last Tuesday of September, in the year eighteen hundred and fifty-one, and on the last Tuesday of September, every two years thereafter; which elections shall be notified, conducted, canvassed, certified, recorded, and the result thereof transmitted, in all respects, as near as may be, in conformity with the provisions of an act entitled "An Act to provide for the Election of Circuit Judges and Regents of the University," approved March 10th, eighteen hundred and fifty-one.

An Act to abolish the Office of District Attorney for the Upper Peninsula, and provide for the Election of Prosecuting Attorneys of the several Counties therein.

[*Approved Feb.* 3, 1857. *Laws of* 1857, *p.* 42.]

Prosecuting Attorneys to be elected in Upper Peninsula; when elected. [137.] SECTION 1. *The People of the State of Michigan enact*, At the election to be held in said Upper Peninsula on the last Tuesday of September, in the year eighteen hundred and fifty-seven, and every two years thereafter, a Prosecuting Attorney for each organized county of said Upper Peninsula shall be elected by the electors thereof, whose term of office shall commence (Term of office.) on the first day of January next succeeding his election; and said Prosecuting Attorney shall have all the rights, powers, and duties of Prosecuting Attorneys under the general laws of this State. (Powers and duties.)

Manner of conducting elections. [138.] SEC. 2. The election for said Prosecuting Attorney shall be notified, conducted, canvassed, certified, and recorded, and the result thereof notified and transmitted in all respects, as near as may be, in conformity with the provisions of the Statutes of (Canvass, etc.) this State applicable to the election of county officers, except that the county canvass shall be on the second Tuesday next following the election; and any and each of the Prosecuting Attorneys elected as aforesaid, shall be subject to all provisions of law relative to Prosecuting Attorneys in this State. (Prosecuting Attorney to be subject to general laws.)

Office of District Attorney continued. [139.] SEC. 3. The office of District Attorney for the Upper Peninsula shall remain, and nothing contained in this act shall impair the duties of the office.[j]

SESS. L. 1859. No. 177, p. 483.

An Act further to preserve the Purity of Elections, and guard against the Abuses of the Elective Franchise, by a Registration of Electors.

[*Approved February* 14, 1859. *Laws of* 1859, *p.* 483.]

Registration ordered. SECTION 1. *The People of the State of Michigan enact*, That there shall be, in the year one thousand eight hundred and fifty-nine, a registration of the qualified electors of the State. The alderman of every incorporated city, and the supervisor, (Board of registration.) treasurer, and clerk of every township, shall constitute a board of registration for such city or township, and their duties shall be as follows: They shall respectively provide suitable bound books or registers, one for each township, and one for each ward, (Board to provide books or registers.)

[j] A discrepancy will be noticed between this Section and the first clause of the title to the Act.

so made and arranged as to contain an alphabetical list of the respective names, christian or baptismal, and surnames, in full, of all persons declared by the Constitution of the State to be electors and entitled to vote, residing in their townships or wards, and the date of the registration; and, if the elector resides in a city or incorporated village, also his residence by the number of the dwelling and the name of the street, if any, and, if none, a description of the locality of the same.

Registers, how arranged, and what to contain.

* * * * * * * * * * *[1]

REGISTRATION IN TOWNSHIPS.

SEC. 9. It shall be the duty of the board of registration in each township, to wit: the supervisor, treasurer, and clerk thereof, and in case of the absence of any of them, or his inability to serve, the justice of the peace not holding the office of supervisor or town clerk, whose term of office will first expire, to provide at the expense of the township the like book for their township for the purposes of the like registration of the qualified electors thereof, to be arranged in the same manner, save that in cases where the elector does not reside within the limits of an incorporated village, a description of his residence may be omitted; but in case he resides within such limits and in the township, a description of his residence by the street and the number of the dwelling, or other brief but intelligible method; and the names of such resident electors of the village shall be written in said register in a list separate and distinct from those of other electors of the township, so as to exhibit a correct registration for the village; which list shall be called the village election register.

Registration in townships; who to constitute the board.

Books of registration; how arranged.

REGISTRATION IN TOWNSHIPS IN 1859.

SEC. 10. At the annual meeting of each township on the first Monday of April, in the year one thousand eight hundred and fifty-nine, the township treasurer shall, at a place as near as practicable to that of the meeting, and of convenient access to the electors, have said book or register in readiness for the entry of their names, and each qualified elector residing in the township may then write his name at length in the proper place in said register, if able and willing to do so, or the treasurer shall upon request made in his presence by the elector personally, write the name of such elector in its proper place. And in all cases under this act, the board or the members thereof receiving or making the entry of a name, shall note or cause to be noted, the day and year thereof. During such township meeting and during all future sessions of the board, the township poll list of the next preceding general election or township meeting, shall be before him or them for their better information in making the registration, to be returned to the clerk at the close of the

Proceedings at township elections in 1859.

Board to have access to township poll list.

1 Sections 2, 3, 4, 5, 6, 7, and 8, of this act, being applicable only to cities, have been omitted.

Supervisor to register names while making assessment.

meeting or the session. The supervisor or other person or persons charged by law with the assessment of property in the township for the purpose of State taxation, shall, while making such assessment and in connection with the performance of that duty, in the year one thousand eight hundred and fifty-nine, have with him the said register, and shall allow each qualified elector residing in the township whose name has not been entered therein, to write the same, or shall himself, at the like personal request of the elector, write the same therein at the proper place, and shall, after completing his valuation of property, and on or before the first day fixed by law for reviewing his assessment, deposit said register with the township clerk, who shall carefully keep and preserve the same in his office.

Register to be deposited with township clerk.

Registration after 1859, how made.

SEC. 11. After the year one thousand eight hundred and fifty-nine, it shall be the right of any such qualified elector residing in the township, and entitled to vote at the next election therein, and whose name has not been registered, on any day except Sunday, the days of the session of the board of registration, and the days intervening between them and the next approaching election, to apply to the township clerk in person for the registration of his name; and if upon such examination, as is required by the next following section of this act, the clerk shall be satisfied that such applicant is a resident of the township and otherwise qualified and entitled to vote in such township at the then next election to be held therein, the name of such applicant shall be written either by himself or by the clerk, upon a separate paper to be kept by the clerk, his residence described and the date of the entry noted, as required in the two last preceding sections; which paper shall be laid before the board of registration of each township at its next meeting for examination and review; and the names of such persons appearing thereon as the board shall be of opinion are qualified electors at the then next election, and entitled to vote thereat, may, by some member of the board, and under their direction, be entered in the proper register in the manner above set forth. And every applicant to the clerk so causing his name to be entered upon such separate paper, knowing or having good reason to believe himself not to be such resident and qualified to vote in such township at the then next election, shall, upon conviction thereof, be punished by fine and imprisonment, as provided in the thirteenth section of this act.

Penalty for fraudulent registration.

REGISTRATIONS IN TOWNSHIPS AFTER 1859.

Sessions of boards of registration, when held.

SEC. 12. On the Saturday next preceding the general election, and the annual township meeting, and preceding any special election, after the year one thousand eight hundred and fifty-nine, the board of registration of each township shall be in session at the office of the township clerk, from nine o'clock in the forenoon until five o'clock in the afternoon, for the purpose of completing the list of qualified electors; during which session it shall be the right of each and every person who, at the next approaching election or township meeting, may be a qualified elector and entitled to vote thereat, and whose name is not already registered, to have his name duly entered on such register, which shall be done in the manner above set forth. The board shall have the power, and it shall be their duty, and the duty of the clerk, and of the supervisors individually, when acting under this statute, to question every person presenting himself for registration, touching his residence, and his other qualifications as an elector of the township, and it shall be the duty of the applicant to make truthful answers to all such questions. And the board, supervisor, clerk, or treasurer, as the case may be, may, for the more perfect examination of the applicant, swear and employ an interpreter, truly and impartially to interpret such questions and answers. And if any such applicant shall, in his answers, make any material statement which is false, he shall, upon conviction thereof, pay a fine of not more than one hundred dollars, nor less than five dollars, and be imprisoned in the county jail not more than thirty nor less than five days.

Their powers and duties.

Penalty for false statement.

SEC. 13. The name of no person but an actual resident of the township at the date of the registration, and entitled under the Constitution, if remaining such resident, to vote at the then next election, or township meeting, shall be entered in the register. Neither the board, nor any member thereof, shall write or enter therein the name of any person, nor suffer him to write or enter his name therein, whom they know, or have good reason to believe, not to be such resident and so qualified; nor shall any person, knowing or having good reason to believe himself not to be such resident and so qualified, write his name therein; and every person so offending shall, upon conviction, pay for each offense a fine of not more than five hundred nor less than twenty-five dollars, and be imprisoned in the county jail not more than three months nor less than ten days.

Who not entitled to registration.

Penalty for fraudulent registration.

SEC. 14. At such election or township meeting, and as soon at least as the poll is opened, the township clerk shall cause the register to be placed in the hands of the inspectors of the election, to be used by them during the election, and to be returned to the clerk immediately thereafter; and they shall not receive the vote of any person whose name is not written therein. But in case any person shall offer and claim the right to vote whose name is not so registered, his name may then be registered by the clerk, under the direction of the inspectors, upon the terms and conditions following: One of the inspectors shall administer to him an oath in the following form, viz.: You do solemnly swear that you will true answers make to such questions as shall be asked you touching your qualifications as an elector at this poll, so help you God; or an affirmation to the same effect; which oath or affirmation, if he be unable to under-

Township clerk to deliver register to inspectors on day of election.

Names may be registered on election day.

stand the English language, may be interpreted to him by an inspector, or interpreter sworn by an inspector, which interpreter shall also interpret his answers to the inspectors.

Conditions of such registration.

If, in his answers on oath, he shall state positively that he has resided in the township ten days next preceding said election, designating particularly the place of his residence, and that he possesses the other qualifications of an elector under the Constitution, stating such qualifications; and shall, furthermore, swear that owing to the sickness or bodily infirmity of himself or of some near relative residing in the same household (giving the name of said relative), or, owing to his absence from the township, on public or official business, or his own business, and without intent to avoid or delay his registration, during the then last session of the board, he has been prevented from causing his name to be previously registered; and if, furthermore, some qualified elector of the township, and not a candidate for any office at that election, shall take an oath before said inspectors, which oath any one of them may administer, that he is well acquainted with such applicant, that he has in fact resided in the township ten days previous to such election, and that he, the freeholder, [qualified elector] has good reason to believe, and does believe, that all the statements of such applicant are true, the inspectors may, in their discretion, direct the clerk to register his name in the proper place, with the proper date; and if such applicant or such qualified elector shall in said matter willfully make any

Penalty.

false statement, he shall be deemed guilty of perjury, and, on conviction, be subject to the pains and penalties thereof.

Vote may be challenged.

SEC. 15. Any person offering to vote at any such election, in a city, township, or village, whose name is not written in the proper register, may be objected to, and his vote challenged for that cause by any elector present and entitled to vote at that poll; and on such challenge being made, the inspectors shall, if on inspection they find his name not so written in the proper register, refuse the vote. But nothing in this act contained shall be held or construed in any way to affect or impair the right of any inspector or elector to challenge any person offering to vote, nor the effect of such challenge, as now established by law, or as such right and such effect may hereafter be established:

Proviso.

Provided, however, That the vote of no person shall be received whose name is not so registered.

Penalty for illegal voting.

SEC. 16. Any person knowing that his name is not so registered, who shall vote or offer to vote at any such election, either in a city or township, and every inspector, knowing such name not to be so registered, willfully and corruptly consenting to receive such vote, shall, if the vote be received by reason of such consent, be, for every such offense, punished as above provided in section thirteen of this act; and on the trial of the person so voting or offering to vote, the presumption shall be that he knew his name was not so registered.

SEC. 17. The name of no person shall be registered in any township or ward where he does not actually reside at the time of the registration; and every person who shall willfully register, or cause or procure by enticements or other means, the name of any person to be registered contrary of the provisions of this act, shall, upon conviction of any such offense, be also punished as above provided in section thirteen of this act.

Actual residence a condition of registration.

Penalty.

DEATH AND REMOVAL OF ELECTORS.

SEC. 18. At every session of the board of registration of any township or ward after the year one thousand eight hundred and fifty-nine, it shall be their duty to review the list of names in their register, and if it shall have come to their knowledge that any person whose name has been registered has died or has removed therefrom and ceased to reside therein, they shall place the letter "D" against the name of the deceased person, and the letter "R" against the name of the person who has so removed, with the date of the entry and the initials of the name of the member making it, so as to show by whom and when made, and thereafter such name shall be considered and treated as no longer in the list, and shall be omitted in the copies above provided for. But if it shall happen that such entry was erroneously made and such person shall thereafter appear at any election and claim the right to vote thereat, his name may, on his application, be again registered, but upon the following terms: he shall upon his oath or affirmation, which any member of the board of inspectors or the board of registration may administer, declare that he has not removed from, but is still a resident of the township or ward, and is otherwise a qualified elector and entitled to vote. And on making such oath or affirmation, his name may be registered in the manner above described, either by the board of registration or by the board of inspectors. And if such applicant shall swear or affirm falsely, he shall be liable to the pains and penalties of perjury. But in case such entry shall be made falsely, maliciously, and without credible information, the member of the board making it shall be deemed guilty of a misdemeanor, and be punished as such, and the party aggrieved shall be entitled to recover of him, in an action on the case, treble damages for the injury and treble costs of suit in any court having jurisdiction of the cause, and the record of the defendant's conviction of the criminal's offense duly authenticated, shall be prima facie evidence of his liability.

Board to review and correct lists

Provisions for a subsequent registration.

Conditions.

Penalty.

Penalty for false entry.

SEC. 19. It shall be the duty of any city or township clerk, except during the session of the board or on days of election, on the demand of any qualified elector of the ward in such city, or of such township, on payment or tender of his legal fees, to make out, certify, and at his office deliver to such elector a true copy of the contents of the register of election of such ward or township, for which he shall be entitled to receive at the rate of fifty cents for every one hundred names.

Copy of register furnished by township clerk.

Destroyer, &c., of register, guilty of larceny.

SEC. 20. Whoever shall willfully cut, burn, mutilate, or destroy any such register of electors, or copy thereof filed for preservation, or shall unlawfully take and carry away the same, or unlawfully conceal or refuse or neglect to surrender the same, with intent to prevent its being used as authorized by law, shall be deemed guilty of larceny; and whoever shall falsify any such register or copy, by unlawfully erasing or obliterating any name or entry lawfully made therein, or by unlawfully inserting therein any name, note or, memorandum, with intent thereby to influence or affect the result of any election or to defraud any person of an election to office, shall be deemed guilty of forgery; and the person so offending shall, for every such offense, be punished by imprisonment in the State Prison not more than five years, or by fine not exceeding five hundred dollars, and imprisonment in the county jail not more than one year, nor less than ninety days.

Falsifier, &c., of register, guilty of forgery.

Penalty.

Township clerk to file copies of register with county clerk and township treasurer.

SEC. 21. To the end that the contents of such registers may not be lost, it shall be the duty of every township clerk, within twenty days after each general election, to make, certify and transmit to the county clerk of the proper county, and also to the township treasurer, a true copy of such contents, to be by such county clerk and township treasurer filed and preserved in his office; for which, when received, he shall give such township clerk a receipt; and such township clerk shall be entitled to receive therefor, from the township, at the rate of fifty cents for every hundred names; and such copy, or a copy thereof, certified by the county clerk or township treasurer, shall be prima facie evidence of the contents of the original, and in case of the loss or destruction of the original, shall be used in its stead.

Fees.

Certified copy to be evidence.

VILLAGE ELECTIONS.

Village elections. Duty of President and trustees.

SEC. 22. It shall be the duty of the president and trustees of every incorporated village, or the persons who are by law authorized to make by-laws, and charged with the general power to regulate and control the municipal affairs of the village, to procure from the clerk of the township or of the townships, respectively, within which said village may wholly or in part lie, and it is hereby made his duty to furnish to them, at the expense of the village, from the register of electors of the township or townships within which such village is situated, a true copy of the village election register, to be certified by such township clerk, and to be delivered to the inspectors of election in such village, and used for the purpose of the village election, in the same manner and to the same effect as is above provided for the general election and township meetings in townships, as near as may be; and there are hereby given to the inspectors of any such village election, the same power and authority, and to applicants for registration the same rights and privileges, which are given to township inspectors and to applicants at

Powers and rights of Inspectors of village elections.

township elections, respectively, at such elections; and such inspectors and applicants and other persons mentioned in the foregoing provisions regulating elections in townships, are charged with the same duties, and subjected to the same penalties and liabilities, as are provided in like cases at such elections in townships; and the vote of no person shall be received whose name is not written in such register, or in the copy thereof used by the inspectors of the election. Such copy of the village election register shall be furnished at least ten days before the first village election in the year one thousand eight hundred and sixty, and as often as once in two years thereafter, and oftener if the proper municipal authority shall require it; and the township clerk shall be entitled to receive therefor at the rate of fifty cents for every one hundred names.

When copies are to be furnished.

SEC. 23. If any person, falsely personating any qualified elector whose name is registered, shall, at any election, vote or offer to vote in the name of such elector, or if any person shall knowingly encourage or persuade any such person to vote or offer to vote, or if any person, assuming a false or fictitious name, shall vote or offer to vote by that name, or shall enter or cause to be entered upon the register as his own a false name, the person so offending shall, for every such offense, be punished as above provided in section twelve of this act.

Voting under an assumed name.

Penalty.

SEC. 24. The recorder's court in the city of Detroit shall have cognizance and jurisdiction of all offenses under this act, committed within the limits of said city, and the offender may in all cases be there proceeded against by information, as provided by the charter of said city or any other statute applicable thereto. In all other cases the circuit or district court for the proper county shall have cognizance of such offenses committed within the county; and in cases where the punishment is by such fine or such imprisonment, one or both, as the justice's court may impose, the proper justice's court shall have cognizance and jurisdiction thereof.

What Courts to have jurisdiction, &c.

SEC. 25. Any willful violation of duty by any person charged with the execution of this act, or any provision thereof, not herein particularly provided for, shall be deemed a misdemeanor, and the person guilty thereof shall be punished accordingly. And it is hereby made the duty of every circuit and district court, in its charge to the grand jury, to call their especial attention to the necessity of making diligent and careful inquiry touching offenses arising under this act; and also, the duty of every prosecuting attorney, whenever he shall receive credible information that any such offense has been committed, to cause the same to be prosecuted.

Violation of duty a misdemeanor.

Duties of circuit and district courts and prosecuting attorney.

SEC. 26. It shall be the duty of every city clerk and township clerk, annually, in the month of November, to forward by mail to the Secretary of State of this State, at the seat of government, the aggregate number of names not marked with the

City and township clerks to report to Secretary of State.

letter D. or R., appearing in the register for such city or township, omitting the names; and the Secretary of State is hereby required to keep a record thereof in such manner as to show the number of votes in such city and township, arranged in alphabetical order, in a book to be kept for that purpose. And he shall, within twenty days from the approval of this act by the Governor, cause a printed copy of the same to be forwarded by mail to every such city and township clerk in the State.

Duty of Secretary of State.

Ibid.

Compensation.

SEC. 27. Each member of a city board of registration, while acting under this act, shall be entitled to receive two dollars a day for every day he shall actually serve in performing his duties, to be paid by the city; and each member of a township board shall receive the same compensation as now provided for inspectors of elections.

Oath.

SEC. 28. Each member of a board of registration shall, before he enters upon the discharge of his duties under this act, make and subscribe the oath of office contained in the first section of article eight of the Constitution.

Registers, in what form arranged.

SEC. 29. Every register shall be of good paper, well bound, and arranged alphabetically in the following form as near as practicable:

DATE.	NAME.	RESIDENCE.	REMARKS.

SEC. 30. This act shall take effect immediately.

Approved Feb. 14th, 1859.

DIVISION II.—OF COUNTIES.

COMP. L. 1857. Chap. IX. p. 177.

Chapter Thirteen of Revised Statutes of 1846.

[300.] SECTION 1. The boundaries of the several counties in this State shall remain as now established, unless the same shall hereafter be changed by the Legislature. *Boundaries of Counties.*

[301.] SEC. 2. All the rights, powers, duties, privileges and immunities of the several counties shall remain as now established, until the same shall be altered by law. *Rights, Powers, etc. of Counties.*

[302.] SEC. 3. Each organized county shall be a body politic and corporate, for the following purposes, that is to say: to sue and be sued; to purchase and hold real and personal estate for the use of the county; to borrow money for the purpose of erecting and repairing county buildings, and for the building of bridges; to make all necessary contracts, and to do all other necessary acts in relation to the property and concerns of the county. *For what purposes Counties bodies corporate.*

[303.] SEC. 4. All real and personal estate, heretofore conveyed by any form of conveyance to the inhabitants of any county, or to the County Treasurer, or the Governor of the late Territory of Michigan, or to any committee, trustees, or other persons, for the use and benefit of such county, shall be deemed to be the property of such county; and all such conveyances shall have the same force and effect as if they had been made to the inhabitants of such counties by their respective corporate names. *Conveyances for the benefit of Counties, their force and effect.*

[304.] SEC. 5. The Board of Supervisors of each county, or other public officers having the charge and management of the county lands, may, by their order of record, appoint one or more agents to sell any real estate of their county not donated for any special purpose, and all deeds made on behalf of such county, by such agents, under their proper hands and seals, and duly acknowledged by them, shall be sufficient to convey all the right, title, interest and estate which the county may then have in and to the land so conveyed. *How Real Estate of County may be conveyed.*

* * * * * * * * * * *

COUNTY BUILDINGS.

[315.] SEC. 16. Each organized county shall, at its own proper expense, provide a suitable court house, and a suitable and sufficient jail, and fire-proof offices, and all other necessary public buildings, and keep the same in good repair. *Each County to provide suitable buildings.*

[316.] SEC. 17. The prison limits of each county shall extend to all places within the boundaries of the county. *Prison limits.*

[317.] SEC. 18. In case of the escape of any prisoner, by reason of the insufficiency of the jail, whereby the Sheriff, or other officer performing the duties of Sheriff, shall be made *When County shall reimburse Sheriff, etc.*

liable to any party at whose suit such prisoner was committed, the county shall reimburse and pay all sums of money recovered of the Sheriff, or such other officer, by such party, by reason of such escape.

* * * * * * * * * * *

DIVISION OF COUNTIES, ETC.

Lands of Counties on division.

[319.] SEC. 20. When a county seized of lands shall be divided into two or more counties, or shall be altered in its limits, by annexing a part of its territory to any other county or counties, each county shall become seized to its own use, of such part of said lands as shall be included within its limits, as settled by such division or alteration.

Property, how apportioned on division.

[320.] SEC. 21. When a county possessed of, or entitled to money, rights, credits, things in action, or personal property, shall be so divided or altered, or when any unorganized county or district annexed to any county for judicial purposes, shall be organized into a separate county, such money, rights, credits, things in action, or personal property, shall be adjusted and apportioned, and a settlement thereof made between the counties interested therein by the Supervisors thereof, as to them or a majority of them shall appear to be just and equitable.

Supervisors to meet for settlement.

[321.] SEC. 22. The Supervisors aforesaid shall meet for the purpose of such settlement, at such time as shall be prescribed by the law making such division or alteration; or, if no time is prescribed by such law, at such time as the Board of Supervisors of either of the counties interested shall appoint, at the office of the Treasurer of the county retaining the original name of the county so divided or altered.

Debts to be apportioned.

[322.] SEC. 23. Debts owing by a county so divided or altered, shall be apportioned in the manner prescribed in section twenty-one of this chapter, and each county shall thereafter be charged therewith, according to such equitable apportionment.

Commissioners to be appointed if Supervisors can not agree.

[323.] SEC. 24. In case of the division or alteration of a county as aforesaid, if the Supervisors can not agree upon a settlement, as provided in this chapter, the Supervisors of either of the counties interested may apply to the Circuit Court for any adjoining county, for the appointment of five judicious men residing within a county not interested, to be Commissioners for the purpose of settling and determining the matters aforesaid between such counties; and upon such application, such Circuit Court shall appoint such Commissioners for the purpose aforesaid.

Commissioners to meet and make determination.

[324.] SEC. 25. Such Commissioners shall meet at such time as they may appoint, and after being duly sworn faithfully and impartially to perform their duties as such Commissioners, shall proceed to examine into the merits of the matters aforesaid, and shall make such determination in relation thereto as to them, or a majority of them, shall appear to be just and equitable; which determination shall be entered at length by the clerks of the respective counties so interested as aforesaid, upon the journals of the Board of Supervisors thereof, and shall be final and conclusive between such parties.

OF LEGAL PROCEEDINGS IN FAVOR OF AND AGAINST COUNTIES.

[325.] SEC. 26. Whenever any controversy or cause of action shall exist, between any of the counties of this State, or between any county and an individual or individuals, such proceedings shall be had either in law or equity, for the purpose of trying and finally settling such controversy, and the same shall be conducted in like manner, and the judgment or decree therein shall have the like effect, as in other suits or proceedings between individuals and corporations.

Suits between Counties, etc.

[326.] SEC. 27. In all such suits and proceedings, the name in which the county shall sue or be sued, shall be, "*The Board of Supervisors of* the county of ____"; [the name of the county] except in cases where *other* county officers shall be authorized by law to sue in their name of office, for the benefit of the county.[a]

How Counties to sue and be sued.

[327.] SEC. 28. In all legal proceedings[b] against the Board of Supervisors, the process shall be served on the chairman or clerk of the board; and whenever any suit or proceeding shall be commenced, it shall be the duty of such chairman or clerk to notify the Prosecuting Attorney thereof, and to lay before the Board of Supervisors, at their next meeting, all the information he may have in regard to such suit or proceeding.

Process in proceedings against Counties, on whom to be served; Duty of chairman, etc.

[328.] SEC. 29. On the trial of every action in which a county shall be interested, the electors and inhabitants of such county shall be competent witnesses and jurors.

Who competent Witnesses and Jurors.

[329.] SEC. 30. Any action in favor of a county, which, if prosecuted by an individual, could be prosecuted before a Justice of the Peace, may be prosecuted by such county in like manner, before any such Justice.

What actions may be prosecuted before a Justice.

[330.] SEC. 31. In all suits and proceedings prosecuted by or against counties, or by or against county officers in their name of office, costs shall be recoverable as in like cases against individuals.

Costs.

[331.] SEC. 32. When judgment shall be recovered against *the Board of Supervisors*[c] or against any county officer in an action prosecuted by or against him in his name of office, no execution shall be awarded or issued upon such judgment, but the same, unless reversed, shall be levied and collected as other county charges, and when so collected, shall by paid by the County Treasurer to the person to whom the same shall have been adjudged, upon the delivery of a proper voucher therefor.

Proceedings to collect judgment against Board of Supervisors, etc.

* * * * * * * *

[a] See section 1, article 10 of the Constitution, which provides that "All suits and proceedings by or against the county, shall be in the name thereof."
[b] See last note.
[c] See note (*a*).

COMP. L. 1857. Chap. X. p. 184.

DIVISION III.—OF COUNTY OFFICERS.

BOARDS OF SUPERVISORS.

An Act to define the Powers and Duties of Boards of Supervisors of the several Counties, and to confer upon them certain Local, Administrative and Legislative Powers.

[*Approved and took effect April* 8, 1851. *Laws of* 1851, *p.* 231.]

Annual and Special Meetings.

[335.] SECTION 1. *The People of the State of Michigan enact,* That the Supervisors of the several townships and cities in each of the counties in this State, shall meet annually in their respective counties, for the transaction of business as a Board of Supervisors; they may also hold special meetings when necessary, at such times and places as they may find convenient, and shall have power to adjourn from time to time, as they may deem necessary. The annual meetings of the Board of Supervisors shall be held on the second Monday of October in each year, at the court house in their respective counties, if there be one; and if there be none, then at some place at the county seat, if there be one; and if no county seat be established, then at such place in the county as the clerk of such county may appoint, of which such clerk shall give three weeks' public notice by publishing the same in some newspaper printed in said county, if any, and if none, then in the paper nearest thereto.

City Supervisors.

[336.] SEC. 2. The Alderman of each ward of the City of Detroit, having the shortest time to serve, shall act as Supervisor on the Board of Supervisors; the City of Monroe shall be entitled to one Supervisor for each ward, who shall be the assessor thereof respectively, and the City of Grand Rapids shall be entitled to two Supervisors.

Quorum of Board.

[337.] SEC. 3. A majority of the Supervisors of any county shall constitute a quorum for the transaction of the ordinary business of the county; and all questions which shall arise at their meetings shall by determined by the votes of a majority of the Supervisors present, except upon the final passage or adoption of any measure or resolution, in which case a majority of all the members elect shall be necessary. They shall sit with open doors, and all persons may attend their meetings. They shall at their first meeting in each year chose one of their number as chairman, who shall preside at all meetings of the board during the year, if present; but in case of his absence from any meeting, the members present shall choose one of their number as a temporary chairman. Every chairman shall have power to administer an oath to any person concerning any matter submitted to the board, or connected with the discharge of their duties; to issue subpœnas for witnesses, and to compel their attendance in the same manner as courts of law.

Proceedings at Meetings.

[338.] SEC. 4. The County Clerk of each county, or in his absence, his deputy, shall be the Clerk of the Board of Supervisors of such county, and shall be allowed for his services as such clerk a reasonable compensation, to be fixed by the board, and to be paid by the county. It shall be the duty of such clerk: **Clerk; his compensation and duties.**

1. To record all the proceedings of such board in a book provided for that purpose;

2. To make regular entries of all their resolutions and decisions upon all questions;

3. To record the vote of each Supervisor on any question submitted to the board, if required by any member present;

4. To preserve and file all accounts acted upon by the board;

5. To certify, under the seal of the Circuit Court of his county, without charge, copies of any and all resolutions or decisions on any of the proceedings of such board, when required by such board, or any member thereof, or when required by any other person, upon payment of six cents per folio therefor; and such certificate shall be prima facie evidence of the matters therein set forth;

6. To perform such other and further duties as such board may, by resolution, require.

[339.] SEC. 5. The books, records and accounts of the Board of Supervisors shall be deposited with their clerk, and shall be open without any charge to the examination of all persons. It shall be the duty of the clerk to designate upon every account upon which any sum shall be audited and allowed by the board, the amount so audited and allowed, and the charges for which the same was allowed. **Records to be kept by Clerk.**

[340.] SEC. 6. It shall be the duty of every such Board of Supervisors, as often as once in each year, to examine the accounts of the Treasurer of their county, and to ascertain and enter upon their records a full statement of such account. **Board to examine Treasurer's Account.**

[341.] SEC. 7. It shall by the duty of such board, as often as shall be necessary, to cause the court house, jail, and public offices of their county to be duly repaired at the expense of such county; but the sums expended in such repairs shall not exceed five hundred dollars in any one year, unless authorized by a vote of the electors of such county, as hereinafter provided. **Repairs of Public Buildings.**

[342.] SEC. 8. They shall also cause to be prepared within the jails of their respective counties, at the expense of such counties, so many cells for the reception of convicts as they may deem necessary. **Cells for Convicts.**

[343.] SEC. 9. They shall cause to be made out and published yearly, immediately after their annual meeting, in at least one newspaper, if there be one published in the county, if not, in some paper published nearest thereto, a report of the receipts and expenditures, which shall contain a statement of the names **Annual Report.**

of each claimant, the amount claimed, and the amount allowed, of the year next preceding, the accounts allowed, and a full statement of the amounts of the Treasurer's account on the last settlement, as on his balance sheet or account current in making the settlement.

Special Meetings.

[344.] SEC. 10. A special meeting of the Board of Supervisors of any county shall be held only when requested by at least one-third of the Supervisors of such county; which request shall by in writing, addressed to the County Clerk, and specifying the time and place of such meeting;[1] and upon the reception of such request, the clerk shall immediately give notice in writing to each of the Supervisors, by causing the same of the delivered to such Supervisors personally, or by leaving the same at the place of residence of such Supervisor, at least six days before the time of such meeting.[2]

Powers of Boards of Supervisors.

[345.] SEC. 11. The said several Boards of Supervisors shall have power, and they are hereby authorized, at any meeting thereof, lawfully held:[3]

To purchase real estate for poor-house.

1. To purchase for the use of the county, any real estate necessary for the erection of buildings for the support of the poor of such county, and for a farm to be used in connection therewith;

For county buildings.

2. To purchase any real estate necessary for the site of any court-house, jail, clerk's office, or any other county buildings, in such county;

For sites.

3. To fix upon and determine the site of any such buildings, if not previously located;

Sell or lease real estate.

4. To authorize the sale or leasing of any real estate belonging to such county, and to prescribe the mode in which any conveyance thereof be executed;

Change of site.

5. To remove or designate a new site for any county buildings, required to be at the county seats, when such removal shall not exceed the limits of the village or city at which the county seat is situated, as previously located;

---

[1] *Form of Request for Special Meeting of the Board of Supervisors of any County.*

To *James B. Porter*, Esq., County Clerk of the county of *Allegan:*

The undersigned Supervisors, being one-third of the Board of Supervisors of said county, do request that a Special Meeting of the Board of Supervisors of said county be held, to convene on the — day of ———, 18—, at (*State the hour and place of such meeting.*)

Dated this — day or ——, 18—.

[2] *Form of Notice to each Supervisor, of Special Meeting of the Board.*

To *E. B. Bassett*, Esq., one of the Supervisors of the county of *Allegan:*

You are notified, that in accordance with a request in writing addressed to the undersigned County Clerk of said county by one-third of the Supervisors thereof, a Special Meeting of the Board of Supervisors of said county will be held, to convene on the — day of ——, 18—, at [*State the place of such meeting.*]

Dated at ———, this — day of ——, 18—.

JAMES B. PORTER, *County Clerk.*

[3] This Section is as amended by Act No. 244 of 1859. — *Session Laws*, p. 880.

6. To cause to be erected the necessary buildings for poor-houses, jails, clerk's offices, and other county buildings, and to prescribe the time and manner of erecting the same; **Buildings.**

7. To borrow or raise by tax upon such county any sums of money necessary for any of the purposes mentioned in this act: *Provided,* That no greater sum than one thousand dollars shall be borrowed or raised by tax, in any one year, for the purpose of constructing or repairing public buildings, highways or bridges, unless authorized by a majority of the electors of such county voting therefor, as hereinafter provided; **Raise moneys. Proviso.**

8. To provide for the payment of any loan made by them, by tax upon such county, which shall in all cases be within fifteen years from the date of such loan; **Payment loans.**

9. To prescribe and fix the compensation for all services rendered for, and adjust all claims against, their respective counties; and the sums so fixed and defined shall be subject to no appeal;[1] **Compensation and claims.**

10. To direct and provide for the raising of any money which may be necessary to defray the current expenses and charges of said county, and the necessary charges incident to or arising from the execution of their lawful authority, subject to the limitations prescribed in this act; **County expenses.**

11. To abolish or to revive the distinctions between township and county poor; **Poor.**

12. Shall have power to authorize the making out a new tax roll, to extend and determine, by resolution, the time when each collector or township treasurer in their county, shall make his return to the county treasurer; but such time shall in no case exceed two months from the time fixed by the general law; and in all cases interest shall be charged on all taxes so extended from the time of such extension; **Collectors and treasurers.**

13. To make such laws and regulations as they may deem necessary, and provide for enforcing the same, for the destruction of wild beasts, of thistles and other noxious weeds, within the several counties; **Destruction of wild beasts, &c.**

14. To require any county officer, whose salary or compensation is paid by the county, to make a report under oath to **Officers to report.**

---

[1] A county is not liable to an attorney for defending a prisoner at the request of the court, when the prisoner is poor and unable to employ counsel. — *Bacon v. Wayne Co.* 1 *Mich.* 461.

The power granted to Supervisors of a county to examine, settle, and allow all accounts chargeable against a county involves the right to reject, if sufficient reason in the opinion of the Supervisors is not presented for the allowance. — *People v. Supervisors Dutchess Co.* 9 *Wend.* 508.

A Board of Supervisors, by auditing and paying part of a claim presented, is not thereby precluded from contesting the residue even upon a principle which would show the former allowance to have been improper. A mandamus will not lie to a Board of Supervisors to control them in the exercise of their discretion as to the amount at which an account presented shall be audited. — *People v. Supervisors,* 1 *Hill,* 362.

A Board of Supervisors can not allow a claim on any notions of their own as to its equity. — *Chemung Canal Bank v. Supervisors,* 5 *Denio,* 517.

The necessary lights and fuel for keeping of the several county offices in a suitable condition for the transaction of business, are a proper county charge. So held in Wisconsin. — *Jefferson Co. v. Besley,* 5 *Wis.*

them, on any subject or matters connected with the duties of their offices, and to require any such officer to give such bonds, or further or additional bonds, as shall be reasonable or necessary for the faithful performance of their respective duties; and any such officer who shall neglect or refuse to make such report, or to give such bond, within a reasonable time after being so required, may be removed from office by such board by a vote of two-thirds of the members elect, and the office declared vacant; and such board may fill such vacancy for the unexpired portion of the time for which such officer was elected or appointed: *Provided*, That if the spring or fall election shall occur before the expiration of the said unexpired term, if the office be an elective one, the vacancy shall be filled at such election, and it shall be the duty of said board to give reasonable notice of such election to fill the vacancy;

Proviso.

Roads and bridges.

15. To authorize any township or townships in their respective counties, by a vote of the electors of said township or townships, to borrow or raise by tax upon such township, any sum of money not exceeding one thousand dollars, in any township in any one year, to build or repair any roads or bridges in such township or townships, or in the use of which such township or townships may be interested; and to prescribe the time for the payment of any such loan, which shall be within ten years, and for assessing the principal and interest thereof upon such township or townships; and if any road or bridge is situated partly in one township and partly in another, or on the line between townships, or in case any township have any particular local interest in the construction or repair of any bridge, such Board of Supervisors may determine, under such regulations as they may establish, the relative proportion which each township shall contribute in the building and repairing thereof, and the amount so apportioned to the several townships, shall be assessed and collected in the same manner as other township taxes are now assessed and collected by law;

County property.

16. To represent their respective counties and to have the care and management of the property and business of the county in all cases where no other provision shall be made;

Rules and regulations.

17. To establish such rules and regulations in reference to the management of the interest and business concerns of such county, and in reference to the mode of proceedings before such board, as they shall deem necessary and proper in all matters not especially provided for in this act or in some other law of this State.[1]

---

[1] Boards of Supervisors can not bind their counties by an act not within the limits of the express powers conferred upon them by statute. — *Chemung Canal Bank v. Supervisors of Chemung*, 5 *Denio*, 517.

Where a clear legal duty rests upon the Board of Supervisors, being a matter in which they have no discretion, mandamus will lie, and is the proper remedy to compel them to perform that duty. — *Boyce v. Supervisors of Cayuga* 20 *Barb.* 294.

Where the Supervisors of a county, have neglected to perform any duty required of them, at their annual meeting, they may be compelled by mandamus to meet again and perform it. They can not by their neglect nullify a statute imposing duties upon them. — *People v. Supervisors of Chenango*, 4 *Seld.* 317. This was a case where the

[346.] SEC. 12. None of the powers mentioned in the third, fifth, sixth, eleventh, twelfth, thirteenth, fifteenth and sixteenth subdivisions of the last preceding section, shall be exercised without a vote of two-thirds of all the members elected to such board.

When two-thirds vote required.

[347.] SEC. 13. The said respective Boards of Supervisors in each county entitled to more than one Representative in the State Legislature, shall have power, and it shall be their duty, at their annual meeting in the year eighteen hundred and fifty-one, and at their annual meeting next after each subsequent apportionment of such Representatives by the Legislature, to divide their respective counties into representative districts, equal in number to the number of Representatives to which such county is entitled by law, in accordance with section three of article four of the Constitution of this State; and they shall cause to be filed in the office of the Secretary of State, and in the office of the clerk of such county, within thirty days after such division, a description of such representative districts, specifying the number of each district and the population thereof, according to the last preceding enumeration.

Division of County into Representative Districts.

[348.] SEC. 14. The Boards of Supervisors of the several counties of this State shall have power, within their respective counties, and all territory attached thereto, by a majority of all the members elected, to divide or alter in its bounds any township, or erect a new township, upon application to the board as hereinafter provided, of at least twelve freeholders of each of the townships to be affected by the division, and upon being furnished with a map of all the townships to be affected by the division showing the proposed alterations;[1] and if the application shall be granted, a copy of said map, with a certified statement of the action of said board thereunto annexed, shall be filed in the office of the clerk of such county, and a certified statement of the action of said board shall also be filed in the office of the Secretary of State; and it shall be the duty of the Secretary of State to cause the same to be published with the laws of the next Legislature, after the filing thereof, in the same manner as other laws are published: *Provided, however*, That

Board may divide or alter Boundaries of Townships.

Publication of proceedings thereon with Laws.

Proviso.

Board of Supervisors of Chenango County, in the State of New York, at their annual meeting in 1851, neglected to issue warrants for the military commutation, which it was their duty to do, by law at that meeting. The supreme court issued a mandamus requiring them to meet and issue the warrants. *Held*, That the mandamus was properly issued.

[1] *Form of Application of Freeholders for Erection of a new Township.*

To the Board of Supervisors of the county of *Tuscola:*

The undersigned freeholders of said county, and of the territory hereby asked to be erected into a township, respectfully request the Board to erect and provide for the organization of a new township, to be called *Gilford*, and to consist of the territory bounded as follows, viz.: [*Here insert the boundaries &c., and describe with reasonable certainty*]. And your petitioners attach hereto a map and survey of the said territory. And your petitioners will pray, &c.

Dated this — day of ——, 18—.

no part of the territory of one township shall be detached therefrom, and added to another, unless application in writing for that purpose be made to such board by a majority of all the taxable inhabitants residing on the part of the territory to be so detached, whose names appear on the last preceding assessment roll of the Supervisor of the township from which said territory is to be detached as aforesaid.[a 1]

Notice of application, how to be given.

[349.] SEC. 15. Notice in writing of such intended application, subscribed by not less than twelve freeholders of the township or townships to be affected, shall be posted in five of the most public places in each of the townships to be affected thereby, four weeks next previous to such application to the Board of Supervisors;[2] and a copy of such notice shall also be

---

[a] As amended by the Act of Feb. 17, 1857, following. For a prior amendment, repealed by that Act, see Laws of 1855, p. 108.

[1] *Form of Application to Board of Supervisors to have part of a Township detached, and added to another.*

To the Board of Supervisors of the County of *Cass*:

The undersigned, being a majority of all the taxable inhabitants residing in the Township of *Wayne*, in said County of *Cass*, and on the part of the territory of said Township, described as follows, (*here describe the territory desired to be detached*), and whose names appear on the last preceding assessment roll of the Supervisor of said Township, do respectfully ask that the territory hereinbefore described may be detached from said Township of *Wayne*, and added to the Township of *Silver Creek*, in the county aforesaid.

Dated at *Wayne*, this — day of ——, 18—.

[2] *Form of Notice by twelve Freeholders, of Application to have part of Township detached, and added to another.*

The undersigned, twelve freeholders of the township of *Kinderhook*, in the county of *Branch*, do hereby give notice that application will be made to the Board of Supervisors of said county, at the next meeting thereof, to convene at *Branch* on the — day of ——, 18—, asking that the following described territory, to wit: (*describe the territory desired to be detached*) be detached from said township of *Kinderhook*, and added to the Township of *Ovid*, in the county aforesaid.

Dated at *Kinderhook*, this — day of ——, 18—.

Note.—The foregoing notice should be posted in both the townships from which the territory in question is desired to be detached, and the township to which such territory is to be added.

Form of Notice to be given of Intended Application for Erection of a New Township.

NEW TOWNSHIP.

To all whom it may concern:

Notice is hereby given that an application will be presented to the Board Supervisors of the county of *Oceana*, at their meeting to be held at ——— on the — day of ——, 18—, praying them to erect and provide for the organization of a new township to be called the township of *Greenwood*, to consist of the territory described as follows, viz.: (*Here describe particularly the territory to be included by bounds or otherwise*) a map or survey of which territory will be attached to the application.

Dated at *Greenwood*, the — day of ——, 18—.

Note.—This notice, as will be seen, must be signed by not less than twelve freeholders residing in the contemplated new township, and be posted up in five of the most public places therein, four weeks next previous to the presentation of the application to the Board. This should be carefully attended to in every case, and an affidavit of such posting should be endorsed on a true copy of the notice as signed by the twelve freeholders, which affidavit should be in the following form:

published once in each week four successive weeks immediately preceding the meeting of the Board of Supervisors at which

---

Form of Affidavit of Posting, to be endorsed on Foregoing Notice.

County of Oceana, ss.

Amos Wright being duly sworn, deposes and says: That he posted up true copies of the within and foregoing notice in five of the most public places within the territory therein described; that he posted up one of said copies at ———, on the — day of ——, one at ———, on the — day of ——, one at ———, on the — day of ——, one at ———, on the — day of ——, one at ———, on the — day of ——, A. D. 18—. And further he saith not.

AMOS WRIGHT.

Sworn and subscribed, before me, this — day of ——, A. D. 18—.

H. H. FULLER, *Justice of the Peace.*

Note. — This copy thus sworn to, should be filed with the County Clerk, to be by him laid before the Board; and a copy of the same notice as signed, should also be published in each week, in some newspaper published in said county (if there be one), for five successive weeks immediately preceding said meeting of the Board, and a copy of such printed notice, with an affidavit of the printer or his foreman, of such publication, should also be filed with said County Clerk, to be laid before said Board.

If no paper is published in the county, then the mere posting of the notices will be sufficient.

If the Board grant the application, they should cause to be entered in their book of records the following:

Form of the Order Establishing a New Township.

In the matter of the application of A. B. (*and others named*) for the erection and organization of a new township:

It appearing to the Board of Supervisors that application has been made, and that notice thereof has been signed, posted up, and published, as in the manner required by law; and having duly considered the matter of said application, the Board order and enact that the territory described in said application, bounded as follows, to wit: (*here insert the exact boundaries or description*) be, and the same is hereby, erected into a township, to be called and known by the name of the township of ———. The first annual township meeting thereof shall be held at ———, on ———, the — day of ——, at — o'clock in the ——noon; and at said meeting ———, ———, and ———, three electors of said township, shall be the persons whose duty it shall be to preside at such meeting, appoint a clerk, open and keep the polls, and exercise the same powers as the inspectors of election at any township meeting, as the law provides.

Note. — Two copies of this order of the Board should then be made by the clerk, and a copy of the map or survey be attached to each with the following certificate appended to each:

Form of Authenticating Certificate to be attached to the Order of the Board, and the Map thereto attached.

STATE OF MICHIGAN, }
County of *Oceana.* } ss.

I, *Luther L. Alexander*, Clerk of the County aforesaid, and of the Board of Supervisors thereof, do hereby certify that I have carefully compared the foregoing copy of an order of said Board with the record thereof in my office, as Clerk of said Board, and the copy thereto attached of the map or survey of the new township of *Greenwood*, in my office, and furnished to said Board on the application for the erection and organization of said township, and that said copies are true copies. And I further certify that the foregoing order of said Board was passed by them at their meeting held at ———, in said county, on the — day of ——, 18—, as appears by their record.

[L. S.] In testimony whereof, I have hereunto set my hand, affixed the seal of the Circuit Court of said county, this — day of ——, 18—.

LUTHER L. ALEXANDER, *County Clerk.*

Note. — One of the copies thus authenticated should be filed in his office as County Clerk, and the other transmitted by mail to the Secretary of State at Lansing, to be published with the laws.

such application is to be made, in some newspaper printed in the county, if any shall be published therein.[b]

Proceedings on Organization of New Townships.

[350.] SEC. 16. Whenever the Board of Supervisors shall erect a new township in any county, they shall designate the name thereof, the time and place of holding the first annual township meeting therein, and three electors of such township, whose duty it shall be to preside at such meeting, appoint a clerk, open and keep the polls, and exercise the same powers as the inspectors of election at any township meeting. And in case any of the three electors above mentioned shall refuse or neglect to serve, the electors of said township present at such meeting shall have power to substitute some other elector of such township for each one so neglecting or refusing to serve. Notice of the time and place of such meeting, signed by the chairman or clerk of the Board of Supervisors, shall be posted in four of the most public places in such new township, by the persons so designated to preside at such meeting, or by some person appointed by such Board of Supervisors for that purpose, and in each of the townships whose boundaries may have been altered by the erection of such new township, at least fourteen days before holding the same.[1] They shall also fix the place for holding the first township meetings in the town or towns from which such new township shall be taken, which shall also be stated in the notice posted in such last named township; but nothing in this act shall affect the rights, or abridge or enlarge the term of office of any Justice of the Peace or other town officers in any such township; but such Justice of the Peace or other township officer, residing within the limits of such new township, shall continue to be such Justice or other officer in such new township, till the expiration of the time for which he was elected, in the same manner as if originally elected therein; and the terms of office of the Supervisor, Township Clerk, Commissioners of Highways, Township Treasurer, School Inspectors, Constables and Overseers of Highways, elected at such first township meeting, shall expire on the first Monday of April thereafter, or as soon thereafter as their successors are elected and qualified.

---

[b]As amended by the Act of Feb. 17, 1857, following. For a prior amendment, repealed by that Act, see Laws of 1855, p. 108.

[1] *Form of Notice of First Annual Township Meeting, to be held in a new Township erected by Board of Supervisors.*

ANNUAL TOWNSHIP MEETING.

Notice is hereby given that, as designated by the Board of Supervisors of the County of *Oceana*, the First Annual Township Meeting in the new Township of *Greenwood*, lately erected by said Board in the county aforesaid, will be held on the — day of ——, A. D. 18—, at ———, in said township, which meeting will convene at the time, and be conducted according to the statute regulating annual township meetings.

Dated at ———, this — day of ——, 18—

LUTHER L. ALEXANDER, *County Clerk of the County of Oceana.*

Note.—The foregoing form can be varied to suit the occasion of notice of annual township meetings in townships whose boundaries may have been altered by the erection of a new township.

[351.] SEC. 17. Whenever a county seat is proposed to be removed, the Board of Supervisors for such county shall have power by a vote of two-thirds of all the members elect, to designate a place to which such proposed removal is to be made, and after a majority of the electors of such county voting thereon shall have voted in favor of the proposed location, as hereinafter provided, to make and establish such county seat. Removal of County Seat.

[352.] SEC. 18. Whenever such board shall have designated the place of such proposed removal, as provided in the next preceding section, they shall also provide for submitting such proposition at the next township meeting to the vote of the electors of such county; and they shall thereupon cause notices thereof to be posted up in three of the most public places in each township of such county, for at least thirty days previous to the time fixed for such vote, and shall cause the same to be published in one newspaper printed in the county, if any, and if none in the county, then in the paper published nearest thereto, for at least three successive weeks previous to such vote, setting forth that such proposed location has been designated by two-thirds of such board, and stating the day when the proposition will be submitted to the electors of the county in their several townships.[1] Proposition submitted to the People.

[353.] SEC. 19. At the time specified in such notices, a vote of the electors of such county shall be taken in each of the townships in such county, at the place designated for the next township meeting. The inspectors receiving the votes shall be the same as required at the annual township meeting, and the votes shall be canvassed by the same officers, and in the same manner as required at such annual meeting; and the result of such vote shall be certified by them, and transmitted to the County Clerk within ten days after such vote shall be taken; which certified statements shall be delivered by such clerk to the Board of Supervisors at their next meeting. All voting in the several townships, as provided in this section, shall be by ballot, and those voting in favor of such proposed location, shall have written or printed on their ballots, "For the removal of the County Seat"; and those voting against such proposed location, shall have written or printed on their ballots, "Against removal of the County Seat." Manner of voting on proposition.

---

[1] *Form of Notice of Submitting the Question of Removal of County Seat.*

In pursuance of the direction of the Board of Supervisors of the County of ——, notice is hereby given, that the county seat of said County of ——, is proposed to be removed from its present location at ——, and that by a vote of two-thirds of all the members of said Board elect, the proposed location of said county seat has been designated at (*Set forth the place designated as the place of removal*), as the point to which such proposed removal is to be made; and that the proposition of such removal and location will be submitted to the vote of the electors of said county, in their several townships, at their next township meetings, to be held on the — day of ——, A. D. 18—.

Dated at ——, this — day of ——, 18—, and given by order of the Board.

A. B., *County Clerk.*

Mode of submitting Loan or Tax to a vote of the People.

[354.] SEC. 20. Whenever it shall become necessary, under the provisions of this act, to submit to a vote of the electors of any county the question of raising any sum of money by loan or by tax, the said board, after having determined the sum necessary to be raised, whether the same shall be made by loan or by tax, shall proceed to give the notice of such determination, and of the time when the question will be submitted to the electors of such county in the several townships;[1] which notice shall be for the same length of time, and posted in the same manner, as required by the eighteenth section of this act; and the votes shall be taken, canvassed, certified and returned in the same manner as required by the nineteenth section of this act, except that those voting for such tax or loan shall have written or printed on their ballots the words, "For the Tax," or "For the Loan," as the case may be; and those voting against the tax or loan, shall have written or printed on their ballots the words, "Against the Tax," or "Against the Loan," as the case may be.

Powers of Board with respect to Streams.

[355.] SEC. 21. Every such Board of Supervisors shall have power, within their respective counties, to permit or prohibit the construction of any dam or bridge over or across any navigable stream. They shall also have power to provide for the removal of any obstruction arising from the erection of booms, or collecting of logs or rafts in such streams by any individual, and to direct the time in which, and places where, persons having logs, rafts and boats in such streams shall be allowed to remain, and when the same shall be removed; and may impose such penalties as they deem necessary to enforce such regulations, and authorize the Sheriffs, or their deputies, to carry into effect the regulations made under the provisions of this act.[c]

Powers with respect to Dams and Bridges.

[356.] SEC. 22. Whenever any person or persons, or any incorporation, shall wish to construct a dam across any such stream as is mentioned in the preceding section, such person or persons, or corporation, shall present to the Board of Supervisors, or file with their clerk, to be presented to them at their next meeting, a petition praying for leave to construct such

---

[1] *Form of Notice of submitting to the Electors of any County the Question of raising Money by Loan or Tax.*

In pursuance of the direction of the Board of Supervisors of the County of *Saginaw,* notice is hereby given, that at a meeting of said Board, which convened on the — day of ———, 18—, at *Saginaw,* in said county, said Board did determine that the sum of ——————— dollars was necessary to be raised upon such county, and that the same should be raised by loan (*or* by tax, *as the case may be*), and that the question of raising said sum by loan (*or* by tax, *as the case may be*) will be submitted to the vote of the electors of said county, in their several townships, at their next township meetings, to be held on the — day of ——, 18—, and given by order of the Board.

HEMAN B. FERRIS, *County Clerk.*

[c] As amended by "An Act to amend Section Twenty-One of 'An Act to Define the Powers and Duties of the Boards of Supervisors of the several Counties, and to confer upon them certain Local, Administrative and Legislative powers,' approved April 8, 1851." Approved June 21, 1851.—*Laws of* 1851, *p.* 271.

dam, and setting forth the purpose, location, height, and description of such dam, and whether it is proposed to construct a lock, or shute, or apron, and of what description, for the passage of boats, vessels, rafts, or timber; and before the same shall be heard and determined by such board, it shall be made to appear to the board that notice of such application, signed by the petitioners, and stating substantially the contents of such petition, has been posted up in three of the most public places in each township through which such stream runs, at least three weeks previous to the hearing of such application, and published in some newspaper printed in such county, if any published therein. And on such hearing, any person or persons shall be heard in favor of, and in opposition to the prayer of the petition; and such board may adjourn such hearing to any other time or place; and they may grant or refuse the prayer of such petition. And the determination shall be entered at length upon the record of said board. And if such board shall allow the said dam to be constructed, the petitioners shall be at liberty to construct the same by complying fully with the terms and conditions set forth in their petition; and after having obtained such right, and constructed such dam, such petitioners, their heirs, successors, or assigns, may, if such dam be destroyed or decayed, construct a new dam, subject to all the same terms and conditions, on the same site, without again applying to such board: *Provided*, That nothing in this act contained shall be construed as giving to such Board of Supervisors any power to grant the right to any person or persons, or corporation, to flow, or in any manner to take or injure the lands of any person or persons, by, or in consequence of, constructing such dam.

[357.] SEC. 23. Whenever any person or persons, township officers, or corporation, shall wish to construct any bridge across any stream at a point where the same is navigable for boats or vessels of fifteen tons burden or more, they shall apply to the Board of Supervisors, by petition, and shall give notice of the same, in like manner, as near as may be, as provided in section twenty-two of this act; and the powers, and the mode of proceeding of such board, shall be the same, as near as may be, as provided in the last named section. Every such petition shall set forth the kind and description of the bridge proposed to be constructed, and whether the same is to be constructed with a draw, or whether any and what provision is to be made for the passage of vessels or boats; and such board shall have the power to grant or refuse the prayer of such petition, upon such terms as they may deem just and reasonable, and to prescribe what description of bridge may be constructed, or to prohibit the construction of any bridge on the proposed location, as in their judgment the public interest shall require. Powers with respect to Dams and Bridges.

[358.] SEC. 24. Every such Board of Supervisors shall have power to make general rules and regulations as to the kind of bridges, and the mode of constructing the same over any Ibid.

such stream, as mentioned in section twenty-one of this act, when such stream shall not be navigable for boats or vessels of fifteen tons burden, or to grant permission for building the same, without the notice or hearing above provided, in such manner as shall be judged proper with reference to the passage of boats, rafts, and timber.

Powers with respect to Roads.

[359.] SEC. 25. That the Board of Supervisors of the several counties within this State, are hereby authorized and empowered to cause to be laid out, established, altered, discontinued or opened, all State and Territorial roads heretofore or now laid out, or hereafter to be laid through or within their respective counties, whenever they may deem it for the interest of the public.

Ibid.

[360.] SEC. 26. Whenever the Board of Supervisors of any county are petitioned to by at least twelve freeholders of each of the townships through which any such road or roads may pass, they shall, upon such petition, authorize the Commissioners of Highways of such townships to cause the line of said road or roads, within their respective townships, to be surveyed and located therein; and such Commissioners shall report such survey and location to the Board of Supervisors of their county; and upon examination of said survey and report, said board may declare such road or roads duly laid out, established, discontinued, opened, or altered, as the case may be.

Ibid.

[361.] SEC. 27. Whenever said road or roads shall be surveyed, laid out, altered or established under the provisions of this act, it shall be the duty of the Board of Supervisors to whom such petition and report may have been made as aforesaid, to notify and require the Commissioners of Highways of the several townships through which said road or roads may pass, to furnish to the several Township Clerks of such townships the minutes of all surveys within their respective townships, and the same shall be recorded by said clerks in the same manner that township roads are recorded.

Damages on the laying out, etc., of Roads.

[362.] SEC. 28. Any person feeling himself aggrieved by the laying out, altering, discontinuing, or opening of any road or roads, may have his damages appraised, and obtain the same in the same manner, and under the restrictions made and provided relative to township roads.

Record of orders of Board.

[363.] SEC. 29. Every order, resolution, and determination of such Board of Supervisors, made in pursuance of this act, shall be recorded in the records of such board, and signed by the chairman and clerk of such board.

Compensation of members.

[364.] SEC. 30. Each member of such Board of Supervisors shall be allowed a compensation of one dollar and fifty cents per day for his services and expenses in attending the meeting of such board; and six cents for each mile traveled in going to and returning from the place of such meeting, to be audited by the board and paid by the county.

[365.] SEC. 31. If any Supervisor shall neglect or refuse to perform any of the duties which are, or shall be required of him by law, as a member of the Board of Supervisors, without just cause therefor, he shall for each offense forfeit one hundred dollars. Forfeiture for neglect of duties.

[366.] SEC. 32. Nothing in this act contained shall abridge the powers or duties of any Board of Supervisors, which they now or hereafter may possess, under any other law of this State, and which are not provided for in this act. Powers under other Laws not abridged.

[367.] SEC. 33. All that part of chapter fourteen, title three, of the Revised Statutes of eighteen hundred and forty-six, from and including section one, to and including section twenty-six, is hereby repealed: *Provided*, That such repeal shall not affect any act done, or any right accruing or accrued. Chap. 14 of R.S. repealed.

SEC. 34. This act shall take effect immediately.

An Act to Amend Sections Fourteen and Fifteen of an Act entitled, An Act to Define the Powers and Duties of the Board of Supervisors of the several Counties, and to confer upon them certain Local, Administrative and Legislative Powers, approved April eighth, eighteen hundred and fifty-one.

[*Approved Feb.* 17, 1857. *Laws of* 1857, *p.* 463.]

SECTIONS 1, 2.[d]

[368.] SEC. 3. That act number fifty-nine, approved February tenth, eighteen hundred and fifty-five, of the Session Laws of eighteen hundred and fifty-five be, and the same is hereby repealed. Certain Act repealed. 1855, p. 108.

SEC. 4. This act shall take immediate effect.

COUNTY AUDITORS OF WAYNE COUNTY.

From Chapter Fourteen of Revised Statutes of 1846.

[369.] SEC. 27. There shall continue to be a Board of County Auditors for the County of Wayne, composed of three persons, one of whom shall be elected annually, at the general election in said county, if such election be held, and if there be no such election held, then said Auditor shall be elected by the Board of Supervisors of said county, as follows: Said election shall be by ballot, and shall be held at the hour of ten o'clock, A. M., on the second day of the annual meeting of the Board of Supervisors in said county. Before proceeding to ballot, the board shall choose a teller, whose duty shall be to receive the votes, and, with the chairman and clerk, shall be a board to canvass the same; and the person receiving the majority of said votes cast shall be deemed duly elected, and a certificate of said election, signed by the chairman and clerk of said Board of Supervisors, shall be forwarded by the clerk to the person so elected, within ten days after such election; and a duplicate of said certificate of said election, showing the number of votes given, and the persons for whom they were given, Board of County Auditors. Annual Election. Election by Board of Supervisors.

[d]Amend Sections 14 and 15, as above given.

shall be deposited in the office of the clerk of said county of Wayne, within one week after said election. And each person so elected, whether at general election or by the Board of Supervisors, shall hold his office for the term of three years, and until his successor shall be elected and qualified; but no two of such Auditors shall be residents of the same township or city.[e]

Term of office.

Meetings of Board.

[370.] SEC. 28. The annual meeting of the Board of Auditors shall be holden at the office of the county clerk on the first Monday of October in each year, and the auditor having the shortest portion of a regular term to serve, shall be the chairman of the board; and such board shall have the power to adjourn from time to time, when necessary for the transaction of business; and may hold special meetings at such times and places as a majority of them may deem proper, public notice thereof being first given by the clerk of the board, by publishing the same in a newspaper printed in said county, at least ten days before the holding thereof.

Powers and Duties.

[371.] SEC. 29. The said Board of Auditors shall have and exercise all the powers, and perform all the duties conferred or imposed upon the Boards of Supervisors of the several counties in this chapter, or by any other provisions of law, except those mentioned in the next succeeding section; and the Board of Supervisors of the County of Wayne shall not have or exercise any of the powers herein conferred upon said Board of Auditors.

Powers and Duties of Board of Supervisors for County of Wayne.

[372.] SEC. 30. The Supervisors in the County of Wayne shall hold their annual meeting in each year, at the time and place appointed by law; and shall have and exercise all the powers conferred by law upon the Supervisors of the several counties, in relation to the equalizing and correcting of the assessments in said county, apportioning the State and County Taxes to be collected in the several townships, ascertaining and returning the aggregate valuation of real and personal property in the county, and all other matters connected with the assessment and collection of taxes within said county.

Auditors to report amount of Tax necessary to be raised.

[373.] SEC. 31. The said Board of County Auditors shall, on or before the annual meeting of the Board of Supervisors in said county in each year, ascertain, and report to said Board of Supervisors, the amount of tax necessary to be raised therein for county purposes.

Appeal, how taken.

See Const. Art. 10, Sec. 10.

[374.] SEC. 32. Appeals may be taken from the determination of said Board of Auditors in the same cases, in the same manner, and with the like effect, as provided in relation to appeals from the determinations of Boards of Supervisors of the several counties.

Clerk of Board of Auditors; his duties.

[375.] SEC. 33. The County Clerk of the county of Wayne shall be the clerk of said Board of Auditors, and shall perform the same duties, as clerk of such board, as the clerks of the

[e] As amended by "An Act to provide for the Election of County Auditors in the County of Wayne." Approved February 12, 1855.—*Laws of* 1855, *p.* 152.

several counties are required to perform as clerks of the Board of Supervisors therein.

Compensation of Auditors.

[376.] SEC. 34. Each of said Auditors shall be allowed for his services and expenses in attending the meetings of the board, at the rate of one dollar and fifty cents per day, and six cents per mile for traveling from his residence to the place of meeting; to be certified by the clerk, and audited by the Judges of the County Court for the county of Wayne.

COUNTY TREASURER.

County Treasurer elected for two years, to give bond.

[377.] SEC. 35. The County Treasurer shall be elected at the general election for the term of two years, and shall give a bond for the faithful and proper discharge of the duties of his office, as hereinafter directed.

Bond. By whom approved. Conditions.

[378.] SEC. 36. The said bond shall be given to the Board of Supervisors of the county, with three or more sufficient sureties, to be approved of by the Board of Supervisors, and in such sum as they shall direct, conditioned that such person, and his deputy, and all persons employed in his office, shall faithfully and properly execute their respective duties and trusts, and that such Treasurer shall pay, according to law, all moneys which shall come to his hands as Treasurer, and will render a just and true account thereof whenever required by the Board of Supervisors, or by any provision of law; and that he will deliver over to his successor in office, or any other person authorized by law to receive the same, all moneys, books, papers and other things appertaining or belonging to said office;[1] *Provided, however*, That if the Board of Supervisors, in any case, has neglected or refused, or shall neglect or refuse, for the period of twenty days

Proviso.

---

[1] *Form of Bond of County Treasurer.*

Know all men by these presents, that we, A. B., C. D., E. F., and G. H., ——— of the County of *Barry*, in the State of Michigan, are held and firmly bound unto the Board of Supervisors, of the said County of *Barry*, in the sum of ——— dollars, for the payment of which, well and truly to be made, we bind ourselves, our heirs, executors, and administrators, and each of them, firmly, by these presents. Sealed with our seals, and dated this — day of ——, A. D. 18—.

The condition of the above obligation is such, that whereas the above bounden A. B. has been elected County Treasurer of said County of *Barry:* Now, therefore, if the said A. B., and his deputy, and all persons employed in his office, shall faithfully and properly execute their respective duties and trusts, and if such Treasurer shall pay according to law all moneys which shall come to his hands as Treasurer, and render a just and true account thereof whenever required by the Board of Supervisors, or by any provision of law, and shall deliver over to his successor in office, or to any other person authorized by law to receive the same, all moneys, books, papers, and other things appertaining or belonging to said office, then this obligation to be void and of no effect; otherwise to remain in full force.

In presence of L. M.

A. B. [Seal].
C. D. [Seal].
E. F. [Seal].
G. H. [Seal].

after the commencement of the term for which such Treasurer was elected, to approve of the sufficiency of the sureties to such bond, or direct the sum in which the same shall be given, the Circuit Judge may, on application of the Treasurer elect, approve of the sufficiency of the sureties of such bond, on being satisfied of their pecuniary responsibility to meet the exigency of such bond, and may direct the sum for which such bond shall be given, not, however, in a less sum than that directed for his predecessor.[1]

Circuit judge may approve bond in certain cases.

Deputy.

[379.] SEC. 37. The County Treasurer may appoint a deputy, who, in the absence of the Treasurer from his office, or in case of a vacancy in said office, or any disability of the Treasurer to perform the duties of his office, may perform all the duties of the office of Treasurer, until such vacancy be filled, or such disability be removed.

Office, how supplied in case of vacancy, etc.

[380.] SEC. 38. In case the office of County Treasurer shall become vacant, or in case the Treasurer, from any cause, shall be incapable of discharging the duties of his office, the Board of Supervisors may, if in their opinion the interests of the county require it, by writing under their hands, select a suitable person to perform the duties of the Treasurer; and such person so selected, upon giving such bond for the faithful performance of the duties of the office as the said board shall direct, may perform such duties until such vacancy shall be filled, or such disability be removed.

Who not to be Treasurer.

[381.] SEC. 39. No person holding the office of Prosecuting Attorney, Judge of a County Court, County Clerk, Supervisor, or Sheriff, shall hold the office of County Treasurer.

Treasurer to receive and pay moneys. 6 McLean, 446.

[382.] SEC. 40. It shall be the duty of the County Treasurer to receive all moneys belonging to the county, from whatever source they may be derived; and all moneys received by him for the use of the county, shall be paid by him only on the order of the Board of Supervisors, signed by their clerk, and countersigned by their chairman, except when special provision for the payment thereof is, or shall be otherwise, made by law.

To exhibit books, etc., to Supervisors.

[383.] SEC. 41. At the annual meeting of the Board of Supervisors, or at such other time as they shall direct, the County Treasurer shall exhibit to them all his books and accounts, and all vouchers relating to the same, to be audited and allowed.

Moneys, etc., to be delivered to successor.

[384.] SEC. 42. Upon the death, resignation, or removal from office of any County Treasurer, all the books and papers belonging to his office, and all moneys in his hands by virtue of his office, shall be delivered to his successor in office, upon the oath of the preceding County Treasurer, or in case of his death, upon the oath of his executors or administrators.

Compensation.

[385.] SEC. 43. The County Treasurer shall receive for his services such compensation as the Board of Supervisors shall deem reasonable, to be allowed and ordered by them.

---

[1] As amended by Act No. 57 of 1859. *Session Laws, p.* 96.

[386.] SEC. 44. When directed by the Board of Supervisors, the County Treasurer shall cause to be insured any or all the public buildings belonging to the county, as said board shall direct; and the insurance thereon shall be taken in the name of the Treasurer, and his successors in office.

Insurance of Buildings of County.

1840, p. 161.

[387.] SEC. 45. In case of the destruction of, or damage done to the buildings so insured, the Treasurer shall have authority, and it shall be his duty, to demand and receive the moneys which shall be due on account of such insurance; and in case of neglect or refusal to pay the same, he shall sue for and collect such moneys in his name of office whenever directed by the Board of Supervisors, and pay the same into the County Treasury, to be used in repairing or rebuilding such public buildings.

Treasurer to collect moneys in case of damage.

1840, p. 161, § 1.

[388.] SEC. 46. Whenever the condition of the County Treasurer's bond shall be forfeited, to the knowledge of the Board of Supervisors of the county, they shall cause such bond to be put in suit.

Bond, when to be put in suit.

[389.] SEC. 47. All moneys recovered in any such action, shall be applied by the Board of Supervisors to the use of the county, or to such other use or uses as the same ought properly to be applied to.

Moneys recovered on bond, how applied.

[390.] SEC. 48. The County Treasurer shall keep his office at the seat of justice for the county.

To keep office at Seat of Justice.

SEC. 49, 50.[ee]

* * * * * * * * * *

From Chapter Fourteen of Revised Statutes of 1846; Compiled Statutes 1857, p. 204.

COUNTY CLERK.

[402.] SEC. 61. The County Clerk in each organized county shall be elected at the general election, for the term of two years, and shall give a bond to the people of the State, in the penal sum of two thousand dollars, to be approved by the Circuit Judge, for the faithful discharge of the duties of his office.[f]

Election of County Clerk; his bond.

[403.] SEC. 62. The condition of such bond shall be in substance as follows:

Condition of bond.

"Whereas, the above bounden   hath been elected to the office of Clerk of the County of   at the general election held therein [or at a special election held therein], on the   day of   : Now, therefore, the condition of the above obligation is such, that if the said   shall faithfully, truly, and impartially enter and record all orders, decrees, judgments, and proceedings of the courts whereof he shall officiate as Clerk, and faithfully and impartially perform all other duties of his said office, and shall pay over all moneys that may come into his hands as such Clerk, and shall deliver over to his successor in office all the books, records, papers, teals, and other things belonging to his said office, then the above obligation to be void, otherwise to be and remain in full force."

[ee] These Sections related to the County Judge.

[f] As amended by "An Act to Amend Section Sixty-one of Chapter Fourteen of Revised Statutes," approved February 12, 1853.—*Laws of* 1853, *p.* 114.

Deputy County Clerk.

[404.] SEC. 63. Each County Clerk shall appoint a deputy, to be approved by the Circuit Court, *or the County Judge*, and may revoke such appointment at his pleasure; which appointment and revocation shall be in writing, under his hand, and filed in his office; and the deputy may perform the duties of such clerk.[g]

Clerks, etc., responsible for acts of Deputy.

When Deputy to act as Clerk.

[405.] SEC. 64. The County Clerk, and his sureties, shall be responsible for the acts of his deputy; and in case of the death, resignation, or removal of the Clerk, or in case of a vacancy by any other means, in the said office of Clerk, the deputy shall perform all the duties of such Clerk, until such vacancy shall be filled.

Books to be procured.

[406.] SEC. 65. The books necessary to be kept and used in the Clerk's office, shall be procured by the Clerk, under the direction of the Judge of the Circuit Court, at the expense of the county; and the Board of Supervisors of the county shall audit and allow the account for such books, on the certificate of the said Judge.

Clerk, when to transmit list of Justices to Secretary of State.

1840, p. 52, § 6.

[407.] SEC. 66. The Clerk of each county shall transmit to the Secretary of State, annually, within one week after the fourth day of July, a list, certified by him, of all Justices of the Peace of the county, stating the time of their respective election, and their terms of service, and whether elected to fill a vacancy, and if so, what vacancy; and whenever the County Clerk shall receive information of the death, removal, or resignation of any Justice of the Peace of his county, it shall be his duty forthwith to notify the Secretary of State of such vacancy.

To keep office at Seat of Justice.

[408.] SEC. 67. The County Clerk shall keep his office at the seat of justice for the county, and shall receive such fees and compensation for his services as shall be provided by law.

* * * * * * * * * * *

---

[g] As amended by Act 65, of 1850, p. 54. ¶ The office of County Judge is since abolished

DIVISION IV.—Of Resignations, Vacancies, and Removals from Office, and of Supplying Vacancies.

Comp. L. 1857, Chap. XI. p. 218.

Chapter Fifteen of Revised Statutes of 1846.

* * * * * * * * * * *

VACANCIES.

[475.] Sec. 3. Every office shall become vacant, on the happening of either of the following events, before the expiration of the term of such office: What events to create vacancy.

1. The death of the incumbent;
2. His resignation;
3. His removal from office;
4. His ceasing to be an inhabitant of this State; or, if the office be local, of the district, county, township, city or village, for which he shall have been elected or appointed, or within which the duties of his office are required to be discharged;
5. His conviction of any infamous crime, or of any offense involving a violation of his oath of office;
6. The decision of a competent tribunal, declaring void his election or appointment; or,
7. His refusal or neglect to take his oath of office, or to give or renew any official bond, or to deposit such oath or bond in the manner and within the time prescribed by law: *Provided*, That the Supervisor of any township, in which the office of a Township Treasurer or Justice of the Peace may become vacated by operation of this act, shall immediately transmit to the County Clerk of the county in which such Township Treasurer or Justice of the Peace resides, a notice in writing, officially signed by him, informing the County Clerk that the office of such Township Treasurer or Justice of the Peace is vacated.[a] 3 Gilman, 59.

REMOVALS FROM OFFICE.

* * * * * * * * * * *

[478.] Sec. 6. The Governor shall remove all county officers chosen by the electors of any county, or appointed by him, except County Judges, Judges of Probate, and County Clerks, and shall also remove all Justices of the Peace and township officers chosen by the electors of any township, when in his opinion such officer is incompetent to execute properly the duties of his office; or when he is satisfied that such officer has been guilty of official misconduct, or of wilful or habitual neg- When Governor may remove County and Township Officers.

---

[a] As amended by "An Act to amend Sections Three, Fourteen, and Fifteen, of Chapter Fifteen of the Revised Statutes of 1846, in relation to Vacancies in Office." Approved June 27, 1851.—*Laws of* 1851, *p.* 278.

lect of duty, if in his opinion such misconduct or neglect shall be sufficient cause for such removal; but no such officer shall be removed for such misconduct or neglect, unless charges thereof shall have been exhibited to the Governor, and a copy of the same served upon such officer, and an opportunity given him of being heard in his defense.

DIVISION V.—OF THE POWERS AND DUTIES OF TOWNSHIPS, AND ELECTION AND DUTIES OF TOWNSHIP OFFICERS.

COMP. L. 1857. Ch. XII. p. 225.

From Chapter Sixteen of Revised Statutes of 1846.

[493.] SEC. 1. The limits and boundary lines of every organized township shall remain as now established, until otherwise provided by law.

Boundaries of Townships.

POWERS AND DUTIES OF TOWNSHIPS.

[494.] SEC. 2. The inhabitants of each organized township shall be a body corporate, and as such may sue and be sued, and may appoint all necessary agents and attorneys in that behalf; and shall have power to purchase and hold real and personal estate for the public use of the inhabitants, and to convey, alienate, and dispose of the same; and to make all contracts that may be necessary and convenient for the exercise of their corporate powers, and any orders for the disposal of their corporate property which they may judge expedient.[1]

Inhabitants of Townships to be a body corporate, and may hold and dispose of real estate, &c.

[495.] SEC. 3. The inhabitants of each township shall have power, at any legal meeting, by a vote of the qualified electors thereof, to grant and vote sums of money, not exceeding such amounts as are, or may be limited by law, as they shall deem

May raise money, for what purposes.

---

1 Townships may be considered as *quasi* corporations, with limited powers coextensive with the duties imposed on them by statute or usage, but restricted from a general use of the authority which belongs to corporations by common law. — *Rumford v. Wood*, 13 *Mass.* 193; *Norton v. Peck*, 3 *Wis.* 714.

The whole power and capacity of townships as corporations is derived from and conferred by statute, and is specified and confined to certain functions only. Their authority to contract or assume liabilities is restricted to cases where such action is necessary for the exercise of their appropriate functions, as corporations, and their power to sue and be sued must be limited to cases where the assertion of their corporate rights, or the enforcement of their corporate liabilities, requires such proceeding. — 22 *Barb.* 634.

When a contract is made in pursuance of a vote of a township, but before the contract is performed the vote is rescinded, it seems that the person with whom the contract is made is not affected by the rescission unless he has notice thereof; in which case it would be otherwise. — *Allen v. Taunton*, 19 *Pick.* 485.

A township, as such, has no authority to contract with a plank road company or corporation, granting them the use of a highway in the township. As a corporation a township has nothing to do with, and no interest in, the highways within its limits; the title to the soil is in individuals; the right to their use belongs to the inhabitants of the township, not exclusively, but in common with the whole public. The care and superintendence of highways has been committed to certain officers of the township chosen for that purpose, and whose duties are prescribed by law. — 22 *Barb.* 624.

But it is held in New Hampshire, that townships have a *qualified* interest in the roadways and bridges they have erected, and may maintain an action on the case for the destruction or obstruction of the road, or the conversion of the materials. — *Town of Troy v. Cheshire R. R. Co.* 3 *Porter*, 83.

The electors at township meeting can not direct an officer of the township to perform any act which by law he has not authority to perform, nor to act in any other manner in the performance of his duty, than that which is pointed out by law. — *Keen v. Stetson*, 5 *Pick.* 492.

The powers of the electors to bind the township are conferred by statute, and are limited to such acts as are prescribed by law. — *Cornell v. Guilford*, 1 *Denio*, 510.

necessary for defraying all proper charges and expenses arising in the township.[1]

Orders and By-Laws.

[496.] SEC. 4. The inhabitants of each township may, at any legal meeting, by a vote of the qualified electors thereof, make all such orders and by-laws for determining the time and manner in which cattle, horses, swine, sheep, and other animals shall be restrained from going at large in the highways, and for directing and managing the prudential affairs of the township, as they shall judge most conducive to the peace, welfare, and good order thereof.[2]

Penalties.

[497.] SEC. 5. They may annex to such orders and by-laws suitable penalties, not exceeding ten dollars for any one breach thereof, to be recovered by complaint before any Justice of the Peace of the township or county where the offense shall have been committed.

By-Laws to be published.

[498.] SEC. 6. The by-laws of any township shall, before the same shall take effect, be published, by posting up copies thereof, in three of the most public places in the township; and such by-laws, duly made and published, shall be binding upon all persons coming within the limits of the township, as well as upon the inhabitants thereof.

Suits, etc.

Conveyances made for use of Township.

[499.] SEC. 7. All suits, acts, or proceedings, by or against a township, in its corporate capacity, shall be in the name of such township; but every conveyance of lands within the limits of such township, made in any manner, for the use or benefit of its inhabitants, shall have the same effect as if made to the township by name.[3]

TOWNSHIP MEETINGS.

Annual meeting, when held

[500.] SEC. 8. The annual meeting of each township shall be held on the first Monday of April in each year; and at such

[1] It is competent for the inhabitants of a township to take upon themselves the expense of a suit against their agent or servant, in which the interests of the township are directly involved. Where the servants of the township have made mistakes, which have rendered them liable at law, it has been held legal and proper for the township to meet the expense. — *Babbitt et al. v. Savoy*, 3 *Cush.* 530.

A township is authorized to indemnify its officers against a liability which they may incur in the *bona fide* discharge of their duties, although it turn out that they have exceeded their legal rights and authority. — *Bancroft v. Linfield*, 18 *Pick.* 566.

[2] Any by-law of a township, declaring that all hogs or other animals should be kept shut up, only extends to prevent hogs from going at large on the highway; and it seems that a township has no power to prevent the inhabitants from allowing their hogs or other animals to go at large upon their own lands. — *Shepard v. Hees*, 12 *Johns.* 433.

Every man is bound, upon peril of being accounted a trespasser, to keep such animals as are the subject of absolute property, upon his own soil. If swine, or other animals, depasturing in the highway, break into an adjoining close, though the fence be defective, the owner of such animals will be liable; and it matters not whether there is or is not a township regulation restraining such animals from running at large; they will not in the absence of such regulation be considered free commoners. The public have the full right of passing along and over the highways, but have not the right of pasturage therein. — *Harrison v. Brown*, 5 *Wis.* 27.

[3] It is held in New York that where a cause of action exists in behalf of a township, and no officer is by statute authorized to prosecute for such cause of action, it is proper for the electors, when convened at township meeting, to direct such action to be brought; for which purpose they may appoint an agent to institute and prosecute the same; but such suit must be brought in the name of the town. — *Cornell v. Guilford*, 1 *Denio*, 510.

meeting there shall be an election for the following officers: One Supervisor, one Township Clerk, one Treasurer, one School Inspector, two Directors of the Poor, two Assessors, if the qualified electors present at the opening of the meeting shall so determine by vote, one Commissioner of Highways, so many Justices of the Peace as there are by law to be elected in the township, and so many Constables as shall be ordered by the meeting, not exceeding four in number.[1] Officers to be elected.

[501.] SEC. 9. Each of the officers named in the last preceding section, shall be chosen by ballot; *and before proceeding to choose the officers hereinafter directed to be chosen at such meeting.*[a] Officers to be chosen by ballot.

[502.] SEC. 10. There shall also be elected at such meeting, to be chosen *viva voce*, or in such manner as the meeting may direct, one Overseer of Highways for each road district, and as many Pound Masters as the meeting may direct. Officers to be chosen *viva voce.*

[503.] SEC. 11. Justices of the Peace shall severally hold their offices for four years,[b] except when elected to fill a vacancy in office occurring before the expiration of the legal term of four years, and when elected to fill such vacancy, they shall hold during the unexpired portion of such term: *Provided*, That when there shall have been no previous election and classification of Justices of the Peace in any township pursuant to the sixth article of the Constitution of this State, the Justices elected at such meeting shall be classed and divided by lot, respectively, for one, two, three, or four years, and shall severally hold their offices accordingly. Term of office of Justices.

[504.] SEC. 12. Each Commissioner of Highways shall hold his office for three years, and until his successor shall be elected and qualified, except when elected to fill a vacancy, in which case he shall hold during the unexpired portion of the regular term: *Provided*, That when there shall have been no previous election for Highway Commissioners in any township, there shall be three such Highway Commissioners elected, one for one year, one for two years, and one for three years; and, *Provided, also*, That at the annual township election, in each of the Term of office of Commissioners of Highways.

1 The determination of the electors of a township as to the number of constables or assessors to be chosen, must be by a formal vote or resolution.

When there is no limitation of the number of constables by such formal resolution or order, and more than four persons are voted for, the three having the greatest number of votes are entitled to discharge the duties and receive the emoluments of the office.

When at township meeting the electors limit the number of these officers to be chosen, and ballots are found to contain a greater number of names designated for the office than the number to be elected, such ballots can not be canvassed, but must be rejected. — *People v. Adams*, 9 *Wend.* 33.

If a ballot contains the names of two persons for the same office, it is bad as to both, but it can not be rejected as to candidates for other offices regularly named upon the same ballot. — *Carpenter v. Ely*, 4 *Wis.* 420.

Notwithstanding the determination at township meeting, that the number of constables in the township shall be four, the election of a less number in either case will oust all those of the preceding year, although the number then chosen was three; neither of them can hold over on the pretence that no person is chosen in his place. — *People v. Jones*, 17 *Wend.* 81.

a As to the last clause of this section, see section 531.

b See section 17, article 6, of Constitution.

organized townships, to be held in the year one thousand eight hundred and forty-seven, there shall also be elected three such Highway Commissioners, one for one year, one for two years, and one for three years.

Term of office of School Inspectors. [505.] SEC. 13. Each School Inspector elected as aforesaid, shall hold his office for two years, and until his successor shall be elected and qualified, except when elected to fill a vacancy, in which case he shall hold during the unexpired portion of the regular term: *Provided*, That where there shall have been no previous election for School Inspectors in any township, there shall be two such Inspectors elected, one for one year, and one for two years, who shall severally hold their office accordingly.

1843, p. 99, § 24.

What officers to hold one year. [506.] SEC. 14. Each of the officers elected at such meetings, except Justices of the Peace, Commissioners of Highways and School Inspectors, shall hold his office for one year, and until his successor shall be elected and duly qualified.

Officers elected to fill vacancies. [507.] SEC. 15. Each township officer elected at a special meeting to fill a vacancy, shall hold his office during the then unexpired portion of the regular term of the office, and no longer, unless again elected.

Meetings, where to be held. [508.] SEC. 16. The annual and special township meetings shall severally be held at the place in the township where the last annual township meeting was held, or at such other place therein as shall have been ordered at a previous meeting, or when there has been no such previous meeting, at such place as shall be directed in the act or proceedings by which the township was organized, unless it shall, in either case, become inconvenient to do so.

When place of meeting may be changed, and meeting adjourned. [509.] SEC. 17. Whenever it shall become inconvenient to hold a township meeting at the place designated therefor, the Board of Inspectors, or a majority of them, after having assembled at, or as near as practicable to, such place, and opened the meeting, and before receiving any votes, may adjourn said meeting to the nearest convenient place for holding the same, and at such adjourned place forthwith proceed with the meeting.

1839, p. 122, 123.

Proceedings on adjournment. [510.] SEC. 18. Upon adjourning any township meeting, as provided in the last section, the Board of Inspectors shall cause proclamation thereof to be made, and shall leave a constable, or some other proper person, at the place where such meeting was opened, to notify all persons arriving at such place that the meeting has been adjourned, and the place to which it has been adjourned.

1839, p. 123.

For what purposes meeting may adjourn. [511.] SEC. 19. Any annual or special meeting may, by a vote of the meeting, be adjourned to any other day, and from time to time, for the purpose of transacting any proper business of the township, except for the election of officers.

First meeting in Townships, when held. [512.] SEC. 20. The first township meeting after the organization of any township, shall be held on the first Monday in April after its organization, and at such meeting there shall be an election for such officers as are by law to be elected at township meetings. 1839, p. 16, § 1.

[513.] SEC. 21. At the first township meeting in any township, the qualified electors present, between the hours of nine and ten o'clock in the forenoon, shall choose one of their number as Moderator, one of their number as Clerk, and two others of their number as Inspectors, who shall severally take the oath of office prescribed by the twelfth article of the Constitution, and shall conduct the proceedings of such meeting in all respects as other township meetings are required by law to be conducted, as near as may be, and with the same powers.[1]

Proceedings at first meeting in Township.

1839, p. 17, § 2.

Const., Art. 18. § 1.

[514.] SEC. 22. If the inhabitants of any newly organized township shall fail to hold their first township meeting on the day specified by law, any three qualified voters of such township may call a meeting of the electors of such township, for such township election, at any time thereafter, by posting up notices thereof in not less than three public places in such township, at least ten days previous to the holding of such meeting.[2]

In case of failure, Meeting, how called.

1839, p. 17, § 3.

[515.] SEC. 23. At such first township meeting, the Moderator shall administer the oath of office to the other Inspectors, and either of the other Inspectors, after having been so qualified, may administer the like oath to the Moderator.

Who to administer oaths.

1839, p. 17, § 4.

[516.] SEC. 24. Special township meetings may be held for the purpose of choosing officers to fill any vacancy that may occur, if the Township Board shall deem it expedient, and make their order therefor; and in case the said Township Board become disorganized, or reduced below the number of a quorum, as provided by law, by or through the death or removal of the officers composing the same, or from any other cause, then such special township meeting may be called and proceeded in, in all respects, as in the case of newly organized townships.[c]

Special Township Meetings to fill vacancies; how held.

---

1 *Form of Oath of Moderator, Clerk, or Inspectors at Township Meeting.*

I do solemnly swear (or affirm) that I will support the Constitution of the United States, and the Constitution of this State, and that I will faithfully discharge the duties of the office of Moderator (*or* Clerk *or* Inspector, *as the case may be*) at this township meeting, according to the best of my ability.

Where in pursuance of law, the oath of office is administered to an officer in open township meeting in presence of the township clerk, the clerk's record of the fact is competent evidence of the administration of the oath.—*Briggs v. Murdock*, 13 *Pick.* 305.

2 *Form of Notice by Three Voters, calling Township Meeting in Newly Organized Township.*

The inhabitants and electors of the Township of *Lee*, in the County of *Allegan*, having failed to hold their first township meeting on the day specified by law, are requested by the undersigned, *three* qualified voters of such township, to assemble and hold a township meeting on the — day of ——, 18—, at the hour of — o'clock in the forenoon, at (*state where*), in said township.

Dated at ———, this — day of ——, 18—.

[*To be signed by three electors.*]

c As amended by "An Act to amend Section Twenty-Four of Chapter Eighteen of the Revised Statutes of Eighteen Hundred and Forty-Six, entitled, 'Of the Power and Duties of Townships, and Election, and Duties of Township Officers.'" Approved January 29, 1853. Laws of 1853, p. 22.

Special Meetings for other purposes.

[517.] SEC. 25. Special township meetings shall also be held, for the purpose of transacting any other lawful business, when ordered by the Township Board, on a request to them in writing, signed by any twelve electors of the township, specifying therein the purposes for which such meeting is to be held; and the mode of proceeding at all special meetings shall be the same as at the annual meetings.[1]

Orders for Special Meeting, what to specify.

[518.] SEC. 26. Every order for a special township meeting shall specify the purpose for which it is to be held, and the time when, and the place where it shall be held; and if any vacancies in office are to be filled at such meeting, such order shall state in what offices vacancies exist, how they occurred, and who were the last incumbents, and if the vacancy be in the office of Justice of the Peace, such order shall also state at what time the Constitutional term of office will expire.[2]

Within what time after order meeting to be held.

[519.] SEC. 27. The time appointed for holding any special township meeting shall not be more than twenty nor less than fifteen days from the time of making the order therefor; and such order shall be left with the Township Clerk within two days after the making thereof, and shall be recorded in his office.

Clerk to give notice.

[520.] SEC. 28. The said clerk shall, within two days after such order shall be left with him, cause copies thereof to be posted up in three of the most public places in the township; and if there be a newspaper printed in such township, he shall also cause a copy to be published therein, if practicable, at least five days before the day appointed for such special meeting.

No notice of Annual Meeting.

[521.] SEC. 29. No notice of the annual township meetings shall hereafter be necessary.

---

[1] *Form of Request for Special Township Meeting.*

To the Township Board of the Township of *Albion*, in the County of *Calhoun:*

The undersigned, twelve electors of said Township of *Albion*, do request of you that a Special Township Meeting be held in said township for the purposes of (*Here set forth the purposes*).

Dated at ——, this — day of ——, 18—.

[*To be signed by twelve electors.*]

[2] *Form of Order of Township Board for Special Township Meeting.*

Ionia County,
Township of *Ionia.*

It is ordered by the Township Board of said Township of *Ionia*, that a Special Township Meeting be held for the purposes of (*here set forth the purposes*), which meeting will be held on the — day of ——, A. D. 18—, to commence at 10 o'clock in the forenoon, at ——, in said township, a request in writing having been made to said Township Board for such township meeting, for the purposes aforesaid.

Given under our hands, at *Ionia*, this — day of ——, A. D. 18—.

JOHN C. DEXTER,
L. S. JENKS,
WM. KITTS,
ED. STEPHENSON,
Township Board.

MANNER OF CONDUCTING ELECTIONS.

[522.] SEC. 30. At the election of officers required to be chosen by ballot at the annual township meeting, the Inspectors of Election shall be the same as at the general election. **Inspectors of Election.**

[523.] SEC. 31. The Township Clerk shall be the clerk of the township meeting, and shall keep faithful minutes of its proceedings, and a correct list of the persons voting at the election; and he shall enter at length in his minutes every order or direction, and all rules and regulations made by such meeting.[1] **Township Clerk to keep Minutes.**

[524.] SEC. 32. If the Township Clerk be absent, then such person as shall be appointed by the Inspectors for that purpose shall act as clerk of the meeting, first taking an oath, to be administered by one of the Inspectors, that he will faithfully perform the duties of his office according to the best of his ability.[2] **When Clerk of Meeting to be appointed by Inspectors.**

[525.] SEC. 33. The polls of the election shall be opened at nine o'clock in the forenoon, or as soon thereafter as may be, and shall be closed between the hours of three and six o'clock in the afternoon, and the Inspectors shall cause proclamation to be made at least one hour before the closing of the polls, that the polls of the election will be closed at, or within the specified hour, naming it.[3] **Opening and closing of poll.**

[526.] SEC. 34. When the election is by ballot, the Inspectors shall deposit the ballots in a box, to be constructed, kept, **Ballots to be deposited in box.**

---

1 The clerk's record or minutes of the proceedings of a township meeting will be taken as evidence of the facts therein set forth, as transpiring at that meeting.— *Briggs v. Murdock*, 13 *Pick.* 305.

A person who was formerly a township clerk, but is no longer in office, can not amend a township record made by him when township clerk; but if he continue in office he may amend the record of a previous term; the intervening election is held to be substantially a continuance of the clerk in the same office.— *Hartwell v. Littleton* 13 *Pick.* 229.

Form of Clerk's List of Persons voting at Elections at Township Meeting

A correct list kept of persons voting at an election at a township meeting held at ——, in the township of *Rich,* and county of *Lapeer.*, on the — day of ——, A. D. 18—.

No.	NAMES.	No.	NAMES.
1	Simeon Crawford.	3	James Miles.
2	Horace Fox.	4	John Jackson.

Total number of ballots, 4.

Note.—As a matter of convenience, it is well to enter the number of voters in the margin as the list progresses.

2 *Form of Oath to be Administered to Person appointed to act, in absence of Township Clerk, as Clerk of Township Meeting.*

You do solemnly swear (or affirm) that you will faithfully perform the duties of Clerk at this Township Meeting according to the best of your ability, so help you God.

The following is the usual form of proclamations of this kind:

Form of Proclamation before closing the Polls.

Hear ye! Hear ye! Hear ye! The polls of this election will be closed at *five* o'clock this afternoon.

and disposed of, as near as may be, in the manner prescribed in chapter five.

Ballots, what to contain, etc.

[527.] SEC. 35. The ballot shall be a paper ticket, with the names of the persons for whom the elector intends to vote, written or printed, or partly written and partly printed thereon; and shall designate the office to which each person so named is intended by him to be chosen; but no ballot shall contain a greater number of names as designated to any office, than there are persons to be chosen at such election to fill such office, and each ballot shall be so folded as to conceal the contents, and shall be delivered to one of the Inspectors.

Designation of persons to fill vacancy.

[528.] SEC. 36. If at any election there shall be one or more vacancies to be supplied, in the office of Justice of the Peace, School Inspectors, or Commissioners of Highways, and at the same election, any such officer is to be elected for the full term, it shall be necessary to designate on the ballot the person or persons voted for to supply such vacancy or vacancies.

Challenges.

[529.] SEC. 37. If any person offering to vote at such election, or upon any question arising at such township meeting, shall be challenged as unqualified by any Inspector, or any elector entitled to vote at such meeting, the Inspectors shall proceed thereupon in the manner prescribed in chapter five, in case of a challenge at the general election; and no person whose vote shall have been received upon such challenge, shall be again challenged upon any other question, arising at the same township meeting.[1]

Authority to preserve order, etc.

[530.] SEC. 38. The Inspectors, or officer presiding, shall have the same authority to preserve order, to enforce obedience, and to commit for disorderly conduct, as is possessed by the Board of Inspectors at a general election.[2]

Viva voce votes and elections.

[531.] SEC. 39. Between the hours of twelve o'clock at noon and three o'clock in the afternoon, there shall be elected the other officers to be elected at said meetings; and all business of said meetings requiring a *viva voce* vote (except that required by section eight of said [this] chapter), shall be then transacted.[d]

Questions upon motions, how determined.

[532.] SEC. 40. All questions upon motions made at township meetings, shall be determined by a majority of the electors voting; and the officer presiding at such meeting shall ascertain and declare the result of the votes upon each question.

CANVASS OF VOTES.

Canvass of votes and determination of result.

[533.] SEC. 41. The votes given by ballot shall be publicly canvassed by the Inspectors, at the place where the meeting

---

1 See ante, page —.

2 See ante, page —.

d Substituted for original Section 39, by "An Act to repeal Section Thirty-Nine of Chapter Sixteen, of the Revised Statutes of 1846, and to substitute a new Section therefor, to stand as Section Thirty-Nine of said Chapter." Approved February 10, 1855. Laws of 1855, p. 137.

was held, and the result shall be read by the clerk to the persons there assembled; and such reading shall be sufficient notice to all persons elected at that election to any office, whose names are on the poll list as voters.

[534.] SEC. 42. Before the ballots are opened, they shall be counted and compared with the poll list, and the like proceedings shall be had as to ballots folded together and as to differences in number, as are prescribed in chapter five. **Ballots to be counted and compared with poll list.**

[535.] SEC. 43. The canvass being completed, and the result ascertained, the Inspectors shall draw up a statement in writing, setting forth, in words at full length, the whole number of votes given for each office, the names of the persons for whom such votes for each office were given, and the number of votes so given to each person, which statement shall be certified under the hands of the Inspectors to be correct.[1] **Statement of result, etc.**

[536.] SEC. 44. The Inspectors shall also certify upon such statement, their determination of the persons elected to the respective offices, including as well those elected without ballot, as those elected by ballot; which statement and certificate of determination shall be left with the Township Clerk, and recorded in his office.[2] **Statement of determination to be certified and recorded.**

---

[1] *Form of Statement by Inspectors of Result of Election at Township Meeting.*

The following is a statement setting forth the whole number of votes given for each officer, the names of the persons for whom such votes for each office were given, and the number of votes so given to each person, at an election at a township meeting held at ——, in the township of *Ensley,* in the county of *Newaygo,* and State of Michigan, on the — day of ——, 18—. The whole number of votes given for Supervisor was *two hundred.*

The whole number of votes given for Township Clerk was *two hundred.*

(*Continue by giving the number of votes for each office.*)

Of which *Smith Cook* had *one hundred and twenty* votes given him for Supervisor, and *Otis H. Kellogg* had *eighty* votes given him for Supervisor; *John Kinney* had *one hundred and twenty-five* votes given him for Township Clerk, and *Andrew Flynn* had *seventy-five* votes given him for Township Clerk.

All which statement we certify to be correct.

Given under our hands this — day of ——, A. D. 18—.

OTIS H. KELLOGG,
WILLIAM S. HILLMAN,
HIRAM LUTES,
Inspectors.

[2] *Form of Certificate by Inspectors of Determination of Persons elected to Office at Township Meeting.*

Gratiot County, } ss.
Township of *Bethany,* }

We, the Inspectors of the Election, held at the time and place set forth in the within Statement, drawn up by us, do certify that we have determined that at such election the within named *A. B.* was duly elected Supervisor of said township; that *C. D.* was duly elected Township Clerk of said township (*Continue according to the facts*).

Witness our hands this — day of ——, 18—.

W. J. PARTELOW,
MARTIN CRAYMER,
JAMES GRUETT,
Inspectors.

Note.—This Certificate should properly be endorsed upon the Statement. It will

Who to be deemed elected; when choice to be determined by lot.

[537.] SEC. 45. The persons having received the greatest number of votes given for any office at such election, shall be deemed and declared duly elected; and if two or more persons shall have received an equal number of votes for the same office, the Inspectors of Election shall determine the choice by lot, and shall declare and certify the same accordingly.

TOWNSHIP OFFICERS.

Oath of office.

[538.] SEC. 46. All officers, except Justices of the Peace, required to be elected at township meetings by ballot, shall, before entering upon the duties of their offices, and within ten days after notice of their election, respectively take and subscribe the oath of office prescribed by the twelfth article of the Constitution, before the Township Clerk, or some other officer authorized to administer oaths, and file the same with the Township Clerk, who shall record the same: and such oath shall be administered without reward, and certified by the officer before whom the same was taken, with the date of taking the same.[1]

Clerks, when to notify persons elected.

[539.] SEC. 47. Within two days after the election of any officers at a township meeting, the clerk shall transmit to each person elected to any township office, and whose name shall not have been entered on the poll list at such election as a

---

be observed that the number of votes set forth in the Statement should be written out in words at full length; figures should not be used in place of words.

Where the Inspectors, in case of an equal number of votes, determine the choice by lot, the following may be inse ted in the Certificate, as the form of the clause concerning the determination of such choice:

Form of Clause in Certificate in case of Determination of Choice by Lot.

E. F. and *G. H.* having an equal number of votes for the office of Treasurer, we did determine the choice between said persons for said office by lot, pursuant to the statute in such case made and provided; which resulted in favor of the said *E. F.*

We have therefore determined that the said *E. F.* is duly elected to the office of Treasurer of said township of *Bethany*.

W. J. PARTELOW,
MARTIN CRAYMER,
JAMES GRUETT,
Inspectors.

[1] *Form of Oath of Office of Township Officer.*

I do solemnly swear (or affirm) that I wi'l support the Constitution of the United States, and the Constitution of this State, and that I will faithfully discharge the duties of the office of *Supervisor* of the Township of *Bath*, in the County of *Clinton*, and State of Michigan, according to the best of my ability. So help me God.

T. J. WOODMAN.

Clinton County, }
Township of *Bath*, } ss.

I certify that the foregoing oath was taken and subscribed by the said *T. J Woodman* before me this — day of ——, 18—.

W. M. VAN LENVEN, *Township Clerk.*

voter, a notice of his election,[1] and each Overseer of Highways and Pound Master elected at such meeting, shall, within ten days after notice of his election, file with the said clerk a notice in writing of his acceptance, and in default thereof he shall be deemed to have refused to serve.[2]

[540.] SEC. 48. The persons so elected Justices of the Peace shall enter upon the duties of their offices respectively, as follows: **When Justices to enter upon their duties.**

1. Those elected for the full term of four years, on the fourth day of July next succeeding their election;

2. Those elected to fill vacancies, and those elected at the first township meeting in any new township, immediately upon the filing of their oath of office and security with the County Clerk, as required by law.

[541.] SEC. 49. When a new township shall be organized, if there be one or more Justices of the Peace residing therein, they shall be deemed Justices thereof, and shall hold their offices according to their respective classes; and only so many Justices shall be chosen as shall be necessary to complete the number of four for such township. **Justices residing in new townships.**

[542.] SEC. 50. Within six days after the election of Justices of the Peace in such new township, the Supervisor shall give notice in writing to the Justices elected, and to the Township Clerk, of the time and place when and where he will meet them, to determine by lot the classes of such Justices; which notice shall be served at least six, and not more than twelve days, previous to the time appointed therein for such meeting.[3] **Classification of Justices.** **1836, p. 20, § 6.**

[543.] SEC. 51. At the time and place so appointed, the Supervisor and Township Clerk shall cause to be written on separate pieces of paper, as near alike as may be, the numbers one, two, three, four, or such, and so many of such numbers as **Mode of classifying.**

---

[1] *Form of Notice by Clerk to Person elected to Office at Township Meeting*

To *A. R. Marvin, Esq.:*

Sir,—You are hereby notified that at the *Annual* Township Meeting, held in the Township of *Dewitt,* and county of *Clinton,* on the — day of ——, A. D. 18—, you were elected to the office of Treasurer of said township.

Dated at *Dewitt,* this — day of ——, 18—.

O. F. STRICKLAND, *Township Clerk.*

[2] *Form of Notice of Acceptance of Overseer of Highways or Pound Master.*

To *David B. Dennis,* Township Clerk of the Township of *Coldwater:*

Sir,—Being elected at the late Annual Township Meeting to the office of Overseer of Highways [*or* Pound Master] for Road District No. —, in said township, I hereby notify you that I do accept of that office.

Dated at *Coldwater,* this — day of ——, 18—.

JOHN DOE.

[3] *Form of Notice by Supervisor to Justices for Determination by Lot of Classes.*

To *A., B., C.,* and *D.:*

Sirs,—You, and each of you, having been elected to the office of Justice of the Peace for the Township of *Ovid,* in the County of *Branch,* are hereby notified that I will, on the — day of ——, 18—, at the hour of — o'clock –. M.,

1836, p. 21, § 7. shall correspond with the classes which shall be vacant, and shall cause them to be rolled up as nearly alike as may be, and deposited in a box; and the persons elected Justices shall severally draw one of the said pieces of paper, and shall be classed according to the number written on the paper so drawn by him, and shall hold his office for such number of years, either one, two, three, or four, as shall correspond with such number so drawn.

When Supervisor to draw for absent Justices.

1836, p. 21, § 8.

[544.] SEC. 52. If any person elected a Justice shall neglect to attend such drawing, the Supervisor shall draw for him; but if the Supervisor be absent from his township, or unable to serve, or his office be vacant, the Township Clerk shall give notice, and perform the duties herein enjoined on such Supervisor.

Certificates of classification to be made and recorded.

[545.] SEC. 53. Duplicate certificates of such drawing, and of the result thereof, shall be made and certified by the Supervisor and Township Clerk, or such one of them as shall attend the same, one of which shall be filed with the Township Clerk, and the other with the County Clerk, and shall be recorded by said clerks in the books in which the canvass of votes shall have been recorded, and shall be conclusive evidence of the classes to which the Justices so elected belong.[1]

Classification in case of election to fill vacancies.

[546.] SEC. 54. In case more than one existing vacancy in the office of Justice of the Peace shall be supplied by election

---

at ——, in said township, meet you for the purpose of determining by lot your terms, or classes as such Justices.

Dated at *Ovid*, this — day of ——, 18—.

E. D. CORWIN, *Supervisor.*

Note.—A copy of the foregoing should be delivered to each justice-elect.

Form of Notice to Township Clerk of Meeting of Justices to Determine Classes by Lot.

To *Richard Roe*, Township Clerk of Township of *Ovid:*

Sir:—You are hereby notified that I will, on the — day of ——, 18—, at the hour of — o'clock, –. M., at ——, in said township of *Ovid*, meet you, with *A.*, *B.*, *C.*, *D.*, who have been elected Justices of the Peace in said township, to determine by lot the classes of such Justices.

Dated at *Ovid*, this — day of ——, 18—.

E. D. CORWIN, *Supervisor.*

[1] *Form of Certificate of Drawing for Classes, by Justices.*

Branch County, }
Township of *Ovid.* } ss.

We do hereby certify, that on the — day of ——, at ——, in said Township of *Ovid*, a drawing of lots was had by *A.*, *B.*, *C.*, and *D.*, Justices of the Peace elect for said township, to determine the classes of such Justices. That the said A. drew the term of one year; that the said B. drew the term of two years, &c. (*If any Justice fail to attend, then say*) due notice having been given to all of said Justices, and the said D. neglecting to attend such drawing, the undersigned Supervisor drew for him, and drew the term of *four* years.

In witness whereof, we, the Supervisor and Township Clerk of said township, have hereunto set our hands this — day of ——, 18—.

E. D. CORWIN, *Supervisor.*
RICHARD ROE, *Township Clerk.*

at any township meeting, the classes of the persons elected to fill the same shall be determined by lot, within the time, and in the manner prescribed for classifying Justices elected in new townships.

Penalty on officers for neglect to qualify.

[547.] SEC. 55. If any person elected to any township office, except that of Justice of the Peace, of whom an oath of office is required, who is not excepted by law from holding the office to which he is elected, shall not, within ten days after notice of his election, take and subscribe the oath of office required by law, and cause the same to be filed with the Township Clerk, or if any such officer of whom a bond or security shall be required, shall not file such bond or security within the time above limited for filing his said oath, he shall forfeit and pay the sum of ten dollars; and if any person elected to the office of Overseer of Highways or Pound Master, and not exempted by law from holding such office, shall refuse to serve, he shall forfeit and pay the like sum, unless the person selected shall file with the clerk of his township, within said ten days, a written notice stating that he declines accepting the office.[e] [1]

RESIGNATIONS, VACANCIES, AND SUPPLYING VACANCIES.

How resignations made.

[548.] SEC. 56. Resignations of all officers elected at township meetings shall be in writing, signed by the officer resigning, and addressed to the Township Board, and shall be delivered to and filed by the Township Clerk; and when a Justice of the Peace resigns, such clerk shall immediately transmit a copy of such resignation, certified by him, to the County Clerk.[2]

---

[e] As amended by Act 206 of 1848, p. 313, Section 4.

[1] *Form of Notice by Supervisor of Highways or Pound Master, declining to accept the Office.*

To *E Stephenson*, Township Clerk of the Township of *Ionia:*

Sir:—Being elected at the late *Annual* Township Meeting to the office of Overseer of Highways (*or* Pound Master) for Road District No. —, in said township, I do hereby give notice that I decline accepting said office.

Dated at *Ionia*, this — day of ——, 18—. JOHN P. PLACE.

A person who has been chosen or appointed to a township office, and neglects or refuses to serve, whereby he incurs the penalty imposed by law, can not be again chosen or appointed to such office, or made liable to a second penalty for the second refusal to act. — *Haywood v. Wheeler*, 11 *Johns.* 432.

It is held that an action for the penalty here imposed will not lie except where the township proceed to a new election; that merely neglecting to qualify is not sufficient; the object of the law being to enforce the performance of the duties, and the township proceed to a new election, or appointment, then to exact the penalty. — *Winnegar v. Rae*, 1 *Cowen*, 258.

[2] *Form of Resignation of Officer elected at Township Meeting.*

To the Township Board of the Township of *Bath*, in the County of *Clinton:*

I, *T. J. Woodman*, elected one of the Justices of the Peace in said township, do hereby resign said office, and tender you this my resignation.

Dated at *Bath*, this — day of ——, 18—. T. J. WOODMAN.

Form of Township Clerk's Certificate to copy of foregoing Resignation.

Clinton County,
Township of *Bath.* } ss.

I do hereby certify that the foregoing is a true and correct copy of the original resignation of the said *T. J. Woodman*, now on file in my office.

Witness my hand this — day of ——, 18—.

WM. M. VAN LENVEN, *Township Clerk.*

When office to become vacant.

[549.] SEC. 57. Every township office, including the office of Justice of the Peace, shall become vacant, upon the happening of either of the events specified in chapter fifteen, as creating a vacancy.

Temporary appointments in certain cases to be made by Township Board.

1843, p. 20.

[550.] SEC. 58. Whenever there shall be a vacancy, or when the incumbent shall, from any cause, be unable to perform the duties of his office, in either of the township offices, except that of Justice of the Peace and Township Treasurer, the Township Board may make temporary appointments of suitable persons to discharge the duties of such offices respectively;[1] and such persons, so appointed, shall take the oath of office, or file the notice of acceptance required by law, and shall continue to discharge such duties until the office is filled by election, or until the disability aforesaid be removed.

When Township Treasurer to be appointed by board.

[551.] SEC. 59. In case the Treasurer of any township shall refuse to serve, or shall vacate his office before completing the duties thereof, or be disabled from completing the same, by reason of sickness or any other cause, the Township Board shall forthwith appoint a Treasurer for the remainder of the term, who shall give like security, and be subject to like duties and responsibilities, and have the same powers and compensation as the Treasurer in whose place he was appointed, and the Township Clerk shall immediately give notice thereof to the County Treasurer; but such appointment shall not exonerate the former Treasurer, or his sureties, from any liability incurred by him or them.[2]

---

[1] *Form of Temporary Appointment of Office by Township Board.*

To *John Jackson*, of the Township of *Laketown*, in the County of *Allegan:*

You are hereby appointed a Commissioner of Highways for said Township of *Laketown*, in place of *John Doe*, who has resigned, and on becoming qualified as required by law, you will continue to discharge the duties of said office until the same shall be filled by election.

In witness whereof, the persons composing the Township Board of said township have hereunto set their hands this — day of ——, 18—.

JOHN LUCAS,
GERRIT RUTGERS,
A. J. NEERKEN,
J. R. VOORENCAMP,
Township Board.

[2] *Form of Appointment of Treasurer by Township Board.*

Tuscola County, }
Township of *Wells*, } ss.

Whereas, John Jackson, chosen Treasurer of said Township of *Wells*, has refused to serve (*or* has vacated his office before completing the duties thereof, *or as the case may be*). Now, therefore, we, the Township Board of said township, do hereby appoint *Wm. A. Heartt* to be Treasurer of said township for the remainder of the term of said office.

Dated at *Wells*, this — day of ——, A. D. 18—.

JAMES WRIGHT,
JOSEPH WELLS,
ALANSON R. KING,
B. A. WRIGHTMAN,
Township Board.

After the appointment of any person to a township office to fill a vacancy, the

SUPERVISOR.

[552.] SEC. 60. The Supervisor of each townsip shall prosecute, in the name of the People of this State, or otherwise, as may be necessary, for all penalties and forfeitures incurred within his township, and for which no other officer is specially directed to prosecute. Supervisor to prosecute for penalties.

[553.] SEC. 61. He shall, by virtue of his office, be an Assessor of his township. To be an Assessor. 1843, p. 64, § 12.

[554.] SEC. 62. The Supervisor shall preserve and keep all books, assessment rolls, and other papers belonging to his office, and shall deliver the same on demand to his successor in office; and on application of any person, he shall give certified copies of any such papers, or abstracts from any assessment roll or books in his office; and for making any such copies or abstracts, he shall be entitled to receive from the person applying therefor, six cents for each folio; but no such copy, or abstract and certificate, shall be required for less than twelve and a half cents; and such certified copies or abstracts shall be presumptive evidence of the facts therein continued. Supervisor to preserve books, etc, and give copies. 1843, p. 70.

[555.] SEC. 63. The Supervisor of each township shall attend the annual meeting of the Board of Supervisors of the county, and every adjourned or special meeting of such board of which he shall have notice. To attend Meetings of Board of Supervisors.

[556.] SEC. 64. Each Supervisor shall lay before the Board of Supervisors such copies of entries concerning moneys voted to be raised in his township, as shall be delivered to him by the Township Clerk. To lay before Board entries concerning moneys to be raised.

TOWNSHIP CLERK.

[557.] SEC. 65. The Township Clerk of each township shall have the custody of all the records, books and papers of the township, when no other provision is made by law; and shall duly file and safely keep all certificates of oaths, and other papers required by law to be filed in his office, and record such as are required to be recorded therein. He shall also open and keep an account with the Treasurer of his township, and shall charge such Treasurer with all funds which shall come into his hands by virtue of his office, and shall credit him with all moneys paid out by him on the order of the proper authorities of his township. He shall also open and keep a separate account with each of the several funds belonging to his township, and shall credit each of said funds with such amounts as properly belong to them, and shall charge them severally with all warrants drawn on the Township Treasurer, and payable from said funds respectively.[f] Township Clerk to keep records, etc, of Township.

[558.] SEC. 66. He shall transcribe in the book of records of his township the minutes of the proceedings of every town- Minutes of Township Meeting.

electors can not hold a special township meeting and fill such vacancy by election; the person appointed will hold over untilthe expiration of the time for which his predecessor was elected. — *People v. Van Home*, 18 *Wend.* 515.

[f] As Amended by Act 66, of 1855, p. 55.

ship meeting held therein, and he shall enter in such book every order or direction, and all rules and regulations made by any such township meeting.

To return to County Clerk names of Constables.

[559.] SEC. 67. The Township Clerks, immediately after the qualifying of any constables, chosen or appointed in their respective townships, shall return to the clerks of their respective counties the names of such constables.

To give notice of election of Justices.

[560.] SEC. 68. Each Township Clerk shall, immediately after the election of any Justices of the Peace in his township, transmit a written notice thereof to the County Clerk, stating therein the names of the persons so elected, and the terms for which they were respectively elected; and if one or more of them has been elected to fill a vacancy, he shall state in such notice who was the last incumbent in the office.

To appoint a deputy; duties of deputy.

[561.] SEC. 69. Each Township Clerk shall immediately on entering upon the duties of the office, appoint a deputy, who shall take an oath of office, and file the same with the clerk; and in case of the absence, sickness, death, or other disability of the clerk, such deputy shall perform the duties of such clerk, and receive the same compensation as the clerk would have been entitled to receive therefor.[1]

TOWNSHIP BOARD.

Who shall constitute Township Board.

[562.] SEC. 70. The Supervisor, the two Justices of the Peace, whose term of office will soonest expire, and Township Clerk, shall constitute the Township Board, any three of whom shall constitute a quorum for the transaction of business.[2]

When quorum not present, one of remaining Justices to act.

[563.] SEC. 71. When, from any cause, there shall not be three of the officers constituting such board, competent or able to act, one of the remaining Justices, on being notified by any member of said board, shall meet with any members of the board, and shall have the same authority as the other members of the board.

Annual Meeting of Township Board for auditing accounts, etc.

[564.] SEC. 72. The Township Board shall meet annually on the Tuesday next preceding the annual township meeting to be held in such township, for the purpose of auditing and settling all claims against the township; and they shall state on each account the amount allowed by them; and the amounts allowed by them shall be paid by the Treasurer, on the order of the

---

1 *Form of Appointment of Deputy Township Clerk.*

To *A. R Marvin,* of the Township of *Dewitt,* in the county of *Clinton:*

I do hereby appoint you as Deputy Township Clerk of said Township of *Dewitt,* and in case of my absence, sickness, death, or other disability, you will perform the duties of Township Clerk, and receive the same compensation as the clerk would have been entitled to receive therefor.

Witness my hand this — day of ——, 18—.

O. F. STRICKLAND, *Township Clerk.*

2 Where all the officers constituting the board of township auditors have met, a majority of them may decide upon questions coming before them, and their certificate will be valid, although the supervisor has refused to sign it. — *Onderdonk v. Supervisors,* 1 *Hill,* 195.

board, signed by their clerk, and countersigned by the chairman of the board.

[565.] SEC. 73. The said board shall, at their annual meeting in each year, examine and audit the accounts of the Township Treasurer, for all moneys received and disbursed by him as such Treasurer; and they shall also audit and settle the accounts of all township officers, who are authorized by law to receive or disburse any public moneys by virtue of their offices. **Settlement with Treasurer and other officers.**

[566.] SEC. 74. The Township Clerk shall be the clerk of such board, and shall keep a true record of all their proceedings in his office. **Clerk of Board.**

[567.] SEC. 75. All the accounts audited by such board shall be filed and preserved by such clerk, for the inspection of any of the inhabitants of the township, and shall be produced at the next annual township meeting, and there read by him, if the same shall be required by the meeting. **All accounts to be filed, and produced at Annual Meeting.**

TREASURER.

[568.] SEC. 76. The Township Treasurer shall receive and take charge of all moneys belonging to the township, or which are by law required to be paid into the township treasury, including all moneys that may accrue to his township on account of non-resident highway taxes, and shall pay over and account for the same, according to the order of such township, or the officers thereof duly authorized in that behalf; and shall perform all such other duties as shall be required of him by law. **Duties of Treasurer.** **1841, p. 159, § 4.**

[569.] SEC. 77. Each Township Treasurer, within the time limited for filing his oath of office, and before he shall enter upon the duties of his office, shall give bond to the township in such sum, and with such sureties, as the Supervisor shall require and approve, conditioned for the faithful discharge of the duties of his office, and that he will faithfully and truly account for, and pay over according to law, all moneys which shall come into his hands, as such Treasurer; and the Supervisor shall endorse his approval thereon, and file the same in his office.[1] **Bond of Treasurer.**

[570.] SEC. 78. Each Township Treasurer shall keep a just and true account of the receipts and expenditures of all moneys which shall come into his hands by virtue of his office, in a book to be provided for that purpose at the expense of the township, and to be delivered to his successor in office. **Treasurer to keep account of receipts and expenditures.**

---

[1] *Form of Township Treasurer's Bond.*

Know all men by these presents, that we, *O. F. Strickland, John Jones,* and *Wm. Jackson,* of the Township of *Dewitt,* in the County of *Clinton,* and State of Michigan, are held and firmly bound unto said Township of *Dewitt,* in the sum of ———— dollars, for the payment of which sum, well and truly to be made, we bind ourselves, our heirs, executors and administrators, and each of them firmly, by these presents, sealed with our seals, and dated this — day of ——, A. D. 18—.

The condition of this obligation is such that if the above bounden *O. F. Strickland* shall faithfully discharge the duties of the office of Township

To settle with Township Board.

[571.] SEC. 79. On the Tuesday next preceding the annual township meeting, he shall account with the Township Board of the township for all moneys received or disbursed by him.

CONSTABLES.

Constable to give security.

[572.] SEC. 80. Every person elected or appointed to the office of Constable, before he enters upon the duties of his office, and within the time prescribed by law for filing his official oath, shall execute, with sufficient sureties, to be approved by the Supervisor or Clerk of his township, an instrument in writing, by which said Constable and his sureties shall jointly and severally agree to pay, to each and every person who may be entitled thereto, all such sums of money as the said Constable may become liable to pay, on account of any neglect or default of said Constable, in the service or return of any process that may be delivered to him for service or collection.[g] [1]

Approval and filing security.

[573.] SEC. 81. Such Supervisor or Township Clerk shall endorse on such instrument his approbation of the sureties therein named, and shall then cause the same to be filed in the office of the Township Clerk, and a copy of such instrument, certified

---

Treasurer of said Township of *Dewitt*, and shall faithfully and truly account for, and pay over, according to law, all moneys which shall come into his hands as such Treasurer, then this obligation to be void; otherwise to remain in full force and effect.

In presence of
JOHN DOE. O. F. STRICKLAND, [L. S.]
JOHN JONES, [L. S.]
WM JACKSON, [L. S.]

Form of Supervisor's Approval of Township Treasurer's Bond.

I do approve of the within bond, and the sureties therein named.
Dated this — day of ——, 18—.

A. B., *Supervisor.*

g As amended by "An Act to Amend Section Eighty, of Chapter Sixteen, in Title Four of the Revised Statutes of eighteen hundred and forty-six. Approved February 10, 1855.—*Laws of* 1855, *p.* 84.

[1] *Form of Instrument by Constable and Sureties.*

William Wilson, chosen (or appointed) a constable in the Township of *Bingham,* and County of *Sanilac,* and State of Michigan, and *Lewis Bonell* and *James R. Frank,* as his sureties, do hereby jointly and severally agree to pay to each and every person who may be entitled thereto all such sums of money as the said constable may become liable to pay on account of any neglect or default of said constable, in the service or return of any process that may be delivered to him for service or collection.

In witness whereof, the said constable and sureties have hereunto set their hands and seals this — day of ——, 18—.

In presence of
WM. JACKSON. WILLIAM WILSON, [L. S.]
LEWIS BONELL, [L. S.]
JAMES R. FRANK. [L. S.]

No particular form for a constable's bond seems to be necessary; it will be sufficient if it contains the substance of the statute. It may be in the form of an agreement or in that of a bond, and unnecessary recitals will not vitiate it, but will be mere surplusage. Neither the constable nor his sureties can object that it is not under seal, nor that the sureties had not been approved by the township clerk or supervisor.—*Skellinger v. Yandes,* 12 *Wend,* 306.

by the Township Clerk, shall be presumptive evidence of the contents and execution thereof, and all actions against a Constable or his sureties, upon any such instrument, shall be prosecuted within two years after the expiration of the year for which the Constable named therein shall have been elected.[1]

[574.] SEC. 82. Constables shall serve all warrants, notices, and processes lawfully directed to them by the Township Board, or the Township Clerk, or any other officer, and shall perform such other duties as are required of them by law. **To serve warrants, notices, etc.**

[575.] SEC. 83. Any Constable may serve any writ, process, or order lawfully directed to him, in any township in his county. **Constable may serve process in any Township in his County.**

[576.] SEC. 84. Constables shall be ministerial officers of Justices of the Peace, and shall attend upon the sessions of the Circuit Courts for their respective counties, when notified for that purpose by the Sheriff. **Constables ministerial officers, and to attend Courts.**

COMMISSIONERS AND OVERSEERS OF HIGHWAYS.

[577.] SEC. 85. Every Commissioner of Highways, and every Overseer of Highways, having accepted his office, shall, for every neglect of the duties of his office, forfeit the sum of ten dollars. **Penalty of Commissioners and Overseers of Highways for neglect of duty.**

[578.] SEC. 86. Any of the said Commissioners or Overseers of Highways may be prosecuted by indictment, for any deficiency in the highways within his limits, occasioned or continued by his fault or neglect; and on conviction thereof, may be fined in any sum not exceeding fifty dollars. **May be indicted for deficiency in Highways.**

[579.] SEC. 87. Each of the said Commisioners and Overseers of Highways, before entering upon the duties of his office, and within the time limited by law for filing his official oath, shall give bond to the township in the penal sum of five hundred dollars in the former, and two hundred and fifty dollars in the latter case, with one or more sufficient sureties, to be approved by the Supervisor, or by the Township Clerk, conditioned for the faithful performance of the duties of his office, and the faithful disbursement of all moneys that may come into his hands by virtue of his office: *Provided*, In the case of the Overseer of Highways, the Township Board shall so signify in writing, given under their hands on the day of the election of said Overseer.[h] [2] **Commissioners and Overseers of Highways to give bond.** **Proviso.**

---

[1] *Form of Supervisor's or Township Clerk's Approbation of Constable's Sureties.*

I do approve of the sureties named in the within instrument in writing, this — day of ——, 18—.

A. B., *Supervisor.*

[h] As amended by "An Act to Amend Chapter Sixteen, Title Four, Section Eighty-Seven, of the Revised Statutes of eighteen hundred and forty-six." Approved February 16, 1857.—*Laws of* 1857, *p.* 384.

[2] *Form of Bond of Commissioner or Overseer of Highways.*

Know all men by these presents, that we, *John D. Hayes, James C. Luce,* and *S. M. French,* of the Township of *Gilford,* County of *Tuscola,* and State

Approving and filing bond.

[580.] SEC. 88. The Supervisor or Township Clerk shall endorse his approval on such bond, and shall cause the same to be filed with the Township Clerk, who shall keep the same in his office.[1]

Clerk of Commissioners, his duties.

[581.] SEC. 89. The Township Clerk of each township shall be the Clerk of the Board of Commissioners of Highways, and shall, under their direction, record their proceedings in a suitable book, to be provided for him for that purpose, at the expense of his township, and shall keep an accurate account of all orders drawn by them on the Township Treasurer, stating the amount of each, and in whose favor the same was drawn; and all books and papers relating to the business of said Commissioners, shall be preserved and kept by him in his office.

1841, p. 159, § 2 and 3.

JUSTICES OF THE PEACE.

Oath of Justices of the Peace.

[582.] SEC. 90. Each Justice of the Peace elected to fill a vacancy, and each Justice elected for a term less than four years, within ten days after notice of his election, and each Justice of the Peace elected for the full term of four years, on or before the fourth day of July next after his election, shall take and subscribe his oath of office before some officer authorized to administer oaths, and file the same with the County Clerk.[2]

---

of Michigan, are held and firmly bound to said township of *Gilford*, in the penal sum of —— dollars, for the payment of which, well and truly to be made, we bind ourselves, our heirs, executors, and administrators, and each of them, firmly by these presents. Sealed with our seals, and dated this — day of ——, A. D. 18—.

The condition of the above obligation is such, that if the above bounden *John D. Hayes* shall faithfully perform the duties of the office of Commissioner of Highways, for said Township of *Gilford* (or Overseer of Highways for Dist. No. — in said Township of *Gilford*), and shall faithfully disburse all moneys that may come into his hands, by virtue of his office of Commissioner of Highways (or Overseer) as aforesaid, then this obligation to be void, otherwise to remain in full force and effect.

In presence of
JOHN A. HAYES.

JOHN D. HAYES, [L. S.]
JAMES C. LUCE, [L. S.]
S. M. FRENCH. [L. S.]

Form of Signification of Township Board requiring Bond of Overseer of Highways.

To *John D. Hayes*, Overseer elect for Road District No. —, in the Township of *Gilford:*

This is to signify to you that your bond with sureties, in pursuance of the statute, is required of you as Overseer of Highways of said District No —.

Dated at *Gilford*, this — day of ——, A. D. 18—.

E. B. HAYS,
HAMILTON HOBART,
E. BATTELLE,
JOSEPH SPENCER,
Township Board.

[1] *Form of Supervisor or Township Clerk's Approval of foregoing Bond.*

I do approve of the within bond, and the sureties upon the same, this — day of —— 18—.

A. B., *Supervisor.*

[2] The form of oath of office of justice of the peace will be the same as that of township officer. See ante, page —, being the same as that prescribed by the Constitution, which is uniform for all officers.

Justices to give security.

[583.] SEC. 91. Each Justice of the Peace, before he enters upon the duties of his office, and within the time limited by law for filing his official oath, shall execute, in the presence of the Supervisor of his township, or of the County Clerk, with one or more sufficient sureties, to be approved of by such Supervisor or County Clerk, an instrument in writing, by which such Justice and his sureties shall jointly and severally agree to pay to each and every person entitled thereto, all such sums of money as such Justices shall become liable to pay, for, or on account of any money which may come into his hands as a Justice of the Peace, upon demand thereof made by such person, his agent or attorney.[1]

Approval of sureties and filing of instrument.

[584.] SEC. 92. Such Supervisor or County Clerk shall endorse on such instrument his approval of the sureties therein named, and such Justice shall then cause the same to be filed in the office of the County Clerk, and a copy of such instrument, certified by such clerk, under his hand and seal, shall be presumptive evidence of the contents and execution thereof.[2]

When and how Justice and sureties may be sued, etc.

[585.] SEC. 93. If any Justice of the Peace shall fail to comply with such agreement, it shall be competent for any person to whom such Justice shall have become liable by reason of such failure, to sue such Justice and his sureties, or any of them, in assumpsit, and to declare against them generally, for money had and received to the use of the plaintiff, and if the plaintiff on the trial of such suit, shall establish his right to recover, he shall have judgment for principal, interest, and costs.

Penalty for entering upon his office without filing oath, etc.

[586.] SEC. 94. If any Justice of the Peace shall enter upon the execution of his office before having filed his official oath, or such agreement as aforesaid, as required by law, he shall forfeit the sum of one hundred dollars.

COMPENSATION TO TOWNSHIP OFFICERS.

Compensation of certain Township officers, for certain services.

[587.] SEC. 95. The following township officers shall be entitled to compensation, at the following rates, for each day

---

[1] *Form of Instrument by Justices and Sureties.*

E. Stephenson, being elected a Justice of the Peace in the Township of *Ionia,* and State of Michigan, and *William Kitts* and *L. S. Jenks,* as his sureties, do hereby jointly and severally agree to pay to each and every person entitled thereto all such sums of money as such justice shall become liable to pay for, or on account of any money which may come into his hands as a justice of the peace, upon demand thereof, made by such person, his agent, or attorney.

In witness whereof, said justice and sureties have hereunto set their hands and seals this — day of ———, A. D. 18—.

Executed in presence of
JOHN P. PLACE.

E. STEPHENSON, [L. S].
WILLIAM KITTS, [L. S.]
L. S. JENKS. [L. S]

[1] *Form of Supervisor or County Clerk's Approval of Justices' Sureties.*

I do approve of the sureties named in the within instrument, this — day of ———, 18—.

JOHN C. DEXTER, *Supervisor.*

actually and necessarily devoted by them to the service of the township, in the duties of their respective offices, to be verified by affidavit in all cases:

1. The officers composing the Township Board, Assessors, Inspectors of Election, Clerks of the Poll, Commissioners of Highways, School Inspectors, and Directors of the Poor, one dollar a day, and at the same rates for parts of a day;

1861 p. 27, § 3.
1843, p. 70, § 29.

2. The Township Clerk, as Clerk of the Board of Commissioners of Highways, of the Township Board, and of the Board of School Inspectors, one dollar a day, and at the same rates for parts of a day; but no township officer shall be entitled to pay for acting in more than one capacity at the same time.

Compensation for other services.

[588.] SEC. 96. For services not otherwise provided for by law, rendered to townships by township officers in the duties of their respective offices, the Township Board shall audit and allow such compensation as they shall deem reasonable.

TOWNSHIP BUSINESS, OTHER THAN ELECTIONS.

Moderator of Township Meeting.

[589.] SEC. 97. In the transaction of any business other than the election of officers in any township meeting, the Supervisor, if present, shall be the Moderator of the meeting; and if he shall not be present, any other of the Inspectors of Election, except the clerk, who shall be designated by the Inspectors present, shall be the Moderator; or the meeting, under the direction of the Inspectors present, may elect, *viva voce*, a Moderator of the meeting.

Powers and duties of Moderator.

[590.] SEC. 98 The Moderator shall preside in, and regulate the proceedings of the meeting; he shall decide all questions of order, and make public declaration of all votes passed; and when any vote so declared by him shall immediately upon such declaration be questioned by seven or more of the voters, he shall make the vote certain by polling the voters, or dividing the meeting, unless the township shall, by a previous vote, or by their by-laws, have otherwise provided.

Ibid.

[591.] SEC. 99. No person shall address the meeting before permission obtained of the Moderator, nor while any other person is speaking by his permission; and all persons at such meeting shall be silent at the request of the Moderator.

Disorderly conduct at Township Meetings.

[592.] SEC. 100. If at any township meeting any person shall conduct himself in a disorderly manner, and, after notice from the Moderator, shall persist therein, the Moderator may order him to withdraw from the meeting; and on his refusal, may order the constables, or any other persons, to take him into custody until the meeting be adjourned.

Penalty for disregarding order of Moderator.

[593.] SEC. 101. Any person who shall refuse to withdraw from such meeting, on being ordered by the Moderator to do so, as provided in the preceding section, shall, for every such offence, forfeit a sum not exceeding twenty dollars.

QUALIFICATIONS OF VOTERS AND OFFICERS.

[594.] SEC. 102. Each inhabitant of any township, having the qualifications of an elector, as specified in the Constitution of this State, and no other person, shall have a right to vote on all maters and questions before any township meeting, and when any person claiming the right to vote shall be challenged by a voter, the Moderator shall proceed in the same manner as on challenges at the election of township officers.[1] Who may vote; challenges.

[595.] SEC. 103. No person, except an elector as aforesaid, shall be eligible to any elective office contemplated in this chapter. Eligibility to office.

An Act to Amend Chapter Sixteen of the Revised Statutes of Eighteen Hundred and Forty-Six.

[*Approved April* 3, 1848. *Laws of* 1848, *p.* 253.]

[596.] SECTION 1. *Be it enacted by the Senate and House of Representatives of the State of Michigan*, That the Supervisor of each township shall be the agent for his township, for the transaction of all legal business, by whom suits may be brought and defended, and upon whom all processes against the township shall be served. Supervisor; to be agent for his Township.

SEC. 2. This act shall take effect and be in force from and after its passage.

An Act to Authorize Township Boards to raise Money in certain cases, to defray Township Expenses.

[*Approved March* 31, 1849. *Laws of* 1849, *page* 244.]

[597.] SECTION 1. *Be it enacted by the Senate and House of Representatives of the State of Michigan*, That whenever the qualified electors of any township, at the annual township meeting, shall neglect or refuse to vote such sum or sums of money as may be necessary to defray the ordinary township expenses, the Township Board of any such township is hereby authorized, at any regular meeting, to vote such sum or sums as may be necessary for that purpose, not exceeding such amounts as are, or may be limited by law. Township Boards to raise money for town purposes when Township Meeting have neglected to do so.

SEC. 2. This act shall take effect and be in force from and after its passage.

1 See ante. page 14, title "ELECTIONS"; where will be found the qualifications of an Elector as prescribed by the Constitution.

Comp. L. 1857. Chap. XIII. p. 246.

DIVISION VI.—Of the Division of Townships.

Chapter Seventeen of Revised Statutes of 1846.

Disposition of lands on division of Township, and apportionment of proceeds.

[598.] Section 1. When a township seized of lands shall be divided into two or more townships, the Township Boards of the several townships constituted by such division, shall meet as soon as may be after the first township meetings subsequently held in such townships, and when so met, shall have power to make such agreement concerning the disposition to be made of such township lands, and the apportionment of the proceeds in case of a sale thereof, as they shall think equitable, and to take all measures, and execute all conveyances which may be necessary to carry said agreement into effect.

Proceedings on alteration on Township.

[599.] Sec. 2. When a township shall be altered in its limits, by annexing a part of its territory to another township, or townships, the Township Board of the township from which such territory shall be taken, and of the township, or townships to which the same shall be annexed, shall, as soon as may be after such alteration, meet for the purpose, and possess the powers provided in the preceding section.

If no agreement is made, lands to be sold.

[600.] Sec. 3. If no agreement for the disposition of such lands shall be made by the Township Boards within six months after such alteration or division, then the Township Board of each township in which any portion of such lands shall lie, shall proceed, as soon as may be thereafter, to sell and convey such part of said lands as shall be included within the limits of such township; and the proceeds arising from such sale shall be apportioned between the several townships interested therein, by the Township Boards of all such townships, according to the amount of taxable property in the township divided or altered, as it existed immediately before such division or alteration, to be ascertained by the last assessment roll of such township.

Moneys, etc.; how apportioned in case of division, etc.

[601.] Sec. 4. When a township possessed of, or entitled to, money, rights and credits, or other personal estate, shall be so divided or altered, such moneys, rights, credits and personal estate, including moneys belonging to the township, in the hands of township officers, shall be apportioned between the townships interested therein, by the Township Boards of such townships, according to the rule of apportionment above prescribed; and they shall meet for that purpose as soon as may be after the first township meetings subsequently held in such townships.

Meeting of Township Boards, how called.

[602.] Sec. 5. Whenever a meeting of the Township Boards of two or more townships shall be required, in order to carry into effect the provisions of this chapter, such meeting may be called by either of the Supervisors; but the Supervisor calling the same shall give at least six days' notice in writing to all the other officers, of the time and place at which such meeting is to be held.[1]

[603.] SEC. 6. The preceding sections of this chapter shall not apply to any cemetery or burying grounds belonging to a township; but the same shall belong to the township within which it may be situated, after a division shall have been made. **Qualification of preceding sections.**

[604.] SEC. 7. Debts owing by a township so divided or altered, shall be apportioned in the same manner as the personal property of such township; and each township shall thereafter be charged with, and pay its share of the debts, according to such apportionment. **Debts, how apportioned.**

---

[1]*Form of Notice of Request by Supervisor of Meeting of Township Board for Disposition of Property.*

To A. B., Esq., one of the Township Board of the Township of M———:

You are hereby notified that I have requested a meeting of the Township Boards of the townships of L——— and M———, for the purpose of making an agreement concerning the disposition and apportionment of the property of the former township of L———, pursuant to the statute in such case made and provided, said township having been divided, and the township of M———, created thereby; which meeting will be held on the — day of ——, 18—, at 9 o'clock in the forenoon, at ———, in said township of L———,

Dated at L———, this — of ——, 18—.

C. D———,
Supervisor of the Township of L———.

Comp. L. 1857. Chap. XIV. p. 248.

DIVISION VII.—Of Fences and Fence Viewers; Of Pounds and the Impounding of Cattle.

Chapter Eighteen of Revised Statutes of 1846.

FENCES AND FENCE VIEWERS.

What constitutes lawful fence.

[605.] Section 1. All fences four and a half feet high, and in good repair, consisting of rails, timber, boards, or stone walls, or any combination thereof, and all brooks, rivers, ponds, creeks, ditches and hedges, or other things which shall be considered equivalent thereto, in the judgment of the Fence Viewers within whose jurisdiction the same may be, shall be deemed legal and sufficient fences.

Partition fences, how maintained.

[606.] Sec. 2. The respective occupants of lands enclosed with fences, shall keep up and maintain partition fences between their own and the next adjoining enclosures, in equal shares, so long as both parties continue to improve the same.[1]

Proceedings in case of neglect to repair or rebuild.

[607.] Sec. 3. In case any party shall neglect to repair or rebuild any partition fence, which of right be ought to maintain, the aggrieved party may complain to two or more Fence Viewers of the township, who, after due notice to each party, shall proceed to examine the same; and if they shall determine that the fence is insufficient, they shall signify the same in writing to the delinquent occupant of the land, and direct him to repair or rebuild the same within such time as they shall judge reasonable; and if such fence shall not be repaired or rebuilt accordingly, it shall be lawful for the complainant to repair or rebuild the same.[2]

---

[1] It is held, that any person occupying land, and interested in the making and maintaining a division fence, be his estate or interest in the premises what it may, is entitled to avail himself of the provisions of the Statute in reference to division or partition fences; the remedy is not limited to the owner of the fee. *Bronk v. Becker*, 17 *Ward* 320.

It is held, in Wisconsin, where the law in relation to partition fences is the same as in Michigan, that the provisions of the Statute in relation to fences and fence viewers, does not apply to ornamented partition fences between town, village, or city lots; nor does it prohibit parties from contracting for building such fences.

The fences contemplated by the chapter of the Statute, in relation to fences and fence viewers, are the ordinary fences of the country, built upon, or inclosing agricultural lands. *Brooks v. Allen*, 1 *Wis.*, *R.* 127.

[2] *Form of Determination of Fence-Viewers Directing Delinquent Occupant to Repair Fence.*

To A. B., of the Township of *Carmel* and County of *Eaton:*

The undersigned, two of the fence-viewers of said township of *Carmel*, upon complaint made to us by C. D., of said township, after due notice to each party, have examined the partition fences on the line of lands occupied by you the said A. B., and the said C. D., in said township, being upon the line which divides sections *one and two* (*describe the line with reasonable certainty*) and have determined that the portion thereof which of right you the

[608.] SEC. 4. When any deficient fence, built up or repaired by any complainant as provided in the preceding section, shall be adjudged sufficient by two or more of the Fence Viewers, and the value of such repairing or building up, together with their fees, shall be ascertained by a certificate under their hands, the complainant shall have a right to demand, either of the occupant or owner of the land where the fence was deficient, double the sum so ascertained; and in case of neglect or refusal to pay the sum so due, for one month after demand thereof made, the complainant may recover the same, with interest, at one per cent. a month, in an action for money paid, laid out and expended.[1]

Remedy of Complainant for repairs, etc.

[609.] SEC. 5. When any controversy shall arise about the rights of the respective occupants, in partition fences, or their obligation to maintain the same, either party may apply to two or more Fence Viewers of the township where the lands

In case of controversy, Fence Viewers to assign.

---

said A. B. ought to maintain, being the *South half* (*describe the portion*) of the same is insufficient. You are therefore directed to repair your said portion of such fence within — days from this date.

Dated this — day of ——, A. D. 18—.

E. F.
G. H.
Fence-Viewers.

NOTE.—The complaint to the fence-viewers, and notice to parties, is not required to be in writing; the notice can be given verbally by some disinterested person by whom the fact can be afterwards proved, should it be called in question.

[1] *Form of Certificate of Fence-Viewers, of the Value of Repairing or Building Partition Fence.*

Lenawee County, }
Township of *Dover.* } ss.

Complaint having been made to us, the undersigned, two of the fence-viewers of the said township of *Dover*, by A. B., that C. D. had neglected to repair (*or* rebuild) that portion of the partition fence on the line of lands occupied by them, in said township, which the said C. D. of right ought to maintain. We did proceed to examine said fence, and did thereupon determine that the portion thereof which of right ought to be maintained by the said C. D., being (*describe the portion of fence in question*) was insufficient, and did, upon such determination, direct him, the said C. D., to repair (*or* rebuild) said portion of such fence, within — days from the date of such, our determination being on the — day of ——, 18—; and it appearing to us that the said C. D. has not repaired (*or* rebuilt) his proportion of said fence, as directed by us; but that after the time limited for repairing (*or* re-building) the same by the said C. D., the said A. B. did repair [or rebuild] that portion of said fence which the said C. D. ought to maintain.

Now, therefore, on the application of the said A. B., and on due notice to both parties, we the undersigned, two of the fence-viewers of the said township of *Dover*, having met and examined said fence, have determined and adjudged, that the proportion of said fence, so directed to be repaired [or rebuilt] by the said C. D., has, on his default, been repaired [or rebuilt] by the said A. B., and that the same is now sufficient, and we certify that the value of such repairing [or building up] is — dollars, and that our fees are — dollars.

Given under our hands, at ——, this — day of ——, 18—.

E. F.
G. H.
Fence-Viewers.

lie, who, after due notice to each party, may in writing assign to each his share thereof, and direct the time within which each party shall erect or repair his share of the fence in the manner before provided; which assignment, being recorded in the Township Clerk's office, shall be binding upon the parties, and upon all the succeeding occupants of the lands; and they shall be obliged always thereafter to maintain their respective portions of said fence.[1]

In case of neglect, etc., party erecting and maintaining fence entitled to double the value.

[610.] SEC. 6. In case any party shall refuse or neglect to erect and maintain the part of any fence assigned to him by the fence Viewers, the same may be erected and maintained by the aggrieved party, in the manner before provided; and he shall be entitled to double the value thereof, ascertained in the manner aforesaid, and to be recovered in like manner.

When occupant to pay for portion of fence assigned to him.

[611.] SEC. 7. When, in any controversy that may arise between occupants of adjoining lands as to their respective rights in any partition fence, it shall appear to the Fence Viewers that either of the occupants had, before any complaint made to them, voluntarily erected the whole fence, or more than his just share of the same, or otherwise become proprietor thereof, the other occupant shall pay for so much as may be assigned to him to repair or maintain, the value of which shall be ascertained and recorded in the manner provided in this chapter.

Partition Fences to be kept repaired through the year.

[612.] SEC. 8. All partition fences shall be kept in good repair throughout the year, unless the occupants of the lands on both sides shall otherwise mutually agree.

---

[1] *Form of writing Assigning to each Occupant his share of Partition Fence.*

Branch County, }
Township of *Girard*, } ss.

Whereas, A controversy having arisen between A. B. and C. D., adjoining occupants of lands in said township, in relation to their obligation to maintain (*or* build) the partition fence between their said lands; now, therefore, upon the application of the said A. B. to us, the undersigned, two of the fence-viewers of said township of *Girard,* and after due notice to each party, we have, and do assign to each party, the repairing [or erecting] of said partition fence as follows: [*here describe the fence assigned to each occupant particularly*] and we do direct that each party shall repair (*or* erect) his share of said fence, as above assigned to him, within — days from the date hereof.

Given under our hands, at *Girard,* this — day of ——, 18—.

E. F.,
G. H.,
Fence-Viewers.

Where either party has voluntarily erected more than his own proportion of a partition fence, the fence-viewers may assign the portion to be thereafter repaired or maintained by each, and may ascertain the value of that portion of the fence which has been voluntarily erected by the party, beyond his just proportion thereof. But here the power of those officers in that behalf ceases.

But the fact of payment or non-payment of the value so ascertained, the fence-viewers cannot try or determine.

On suit brought to recover the value of the fence so ascertained by the fence-viewers, the defendant may prove payment made either before or after the award of the fence-viewers.—*Butler v. Barlow*, 2 *Wis. R.*

[613.] SEC. 9. When lands of different persons, which are required to be fenced, are bounded upon, or divided by, any river, brook, pond or creek, which of itself, in the judgment of the Fence Viewers, is not a sufficient fence, and it is, in their opinion, impracticable, without unreasonable expense, for the partition fence to be made in such waters, in the place where the true boundary line is, if in such case the occupant of the land on the one side shall refuse or neglect to join with the occupant of the land on the other side in making a partition fence on the one side or the other, or if such persons shall disagree respecting the same, then two or more Fence Viewers of the township wherein such lands lie, on application to them made, shall forthwith proceed to view such river, brook, pond or creek.

When lands bounded or divided by river, etc., and parties disagree Viewers may be had.

[614.] SEC. 10. If such Fence Viewers shall determine such river, brook, pond or creek in the preceding section mentioned, not to answer the purpose of a sufficient fence, and that it is impracticable, without unreasonable expense, to build a fence on the true boundary line, they shall, after giving notice to the parties, determine how, or on which side thereof the fence shall be set up and maintained, or whether partly on one side and partly on the other side, as to them shall appear just, and shall reduce such determination to writing, and sign the same; and if either party shall refuse or neglect to make and maintain his part of the fence, according to the determination of the Fence Viewers, the same may be made and maintained by the other party as before provided in this chapter, and the delinquent party shall be subject to the same charges and costs, to be recovered in like manner.[1]

Proceedings of Fence Viewers

---

[1] *Form of Determination of Fence-Viewers Where Lands are Divided by River, Brook, Pond, or Creek.*

Monroe County, }
Township of *Raisinville.* } ss.

Application having been made to us, two of the fence-viewers for said township of *Raisinville*, on the -- day of ——, 18---, by A. B., of said township, to view the boundary between the land of the said A. B. and C. D., lying in said township, described as follows: (*describe the lands of each person in question with reasonable certainty*). The River *Raisin* being the boundary between said lands, and it being represented to us that the said A. B. and C. D. disagreed respecting a division fence upon the boundary line aforesaid, (*or as the case may be*), we did on the — day of ——, 18—, proceed to view said river, and, in our judgment, said river is not of itself a sufficient fence, and it is, in our opinion, impracticable, without unreasonable expense, for the partition fence between the lands aforesaid to be made in such waters, in the place where the true boundary line is, and it appearing to us that said A. B. and C. D. could not agree respecting a division fence upon said boundary, and after giving notice to said parties, we do determine that said partition fence shall be set up and maintained upon the *north* side of said *river*, (*or as the determination may be*).

Witness our hands this — day of ——, A. D. 18—

— ——
— ——
Fence-Viewers.

When lands owned in severalty have been occupied in common, any occupant may have lines divided.

[615.] SEC. 11. When any lands, belonging to different persons in severalty, shall have been occupied in common, without a partition fence between them, and one of the occupants shall be desirous to occupy his part in severalty, and the other occupant shall refuse or neglect, on demand, to divide with him the line where the fence ought to be built, or to build a sufficient fence on his part of the line when divided, the party desiring it may have the same divided and assigned by two or more Fence Viewers of the same township, in the manner provided in this chapter.

When Viewers may assign time for making fence; consequence of neglect.

[616.] SEC. 12. Upon the division and assignment as provided in the preceding section, the Fence Viewers may, in writing, under their hands, assign a reasonable time for making the fence, having regard to the season of the year, and if either party shall not make his part of the fence within the time so assigned, the other party may, after having completed his own part of the fence, make the part of the other, and recover therefor double the ascertained expenses thereof, together with the fees of the Fence Viewers, in the manner provided in this chapter.[1]

When partition fence not to be removed.

[617.] SEC. 13. When one party shall cease to improve his land, or shall open his enclosure, he shall not take away any part of the partition fence belonging to him and adjoining the next enclosure, if the owner or occupant of such adjoining enclosure will, within two months after the same shall be ascertained, pay therefor such sum as two or more Fence Viewers shall, in writing under their hands, determine to be the value of such partition fence belonging to such party.[2]

---

[1] *Form of Assignment by Fence-Viewers of a time for making Partition Fence.*

Hillsdale County, }
Township of *Adams.* } ss.

The undersigned, two of the fence-viewers of said township of *Adams*, having divided the line between the lands belonging to A. B. and C. D., in in said township, described as follows: (*describe the lands of each person with reasonable certainty*), said lands having been heretofore occupied by said persons in common; and having in writing dated the — day of ——, 18—, assigned to said A. B. and C. D., each their share of fence to erect on said line, as follows: (*here set the assignment*). We, the said fence-viewers, do now assign to said A. B and C. D., until the — day of ——, 18—, within which each is to make his respective share of said partition fence.

Given under our hands this — day of ——, 18—.

E. F.,
G. H,
Fence-Viewers.

[2] *Form of Determination of Fence-Viewers of Value of Partition Fence.*

Ingham County, }
Township of *Bunker Hill.* } ss.

We, the undersigned, two of the fence-viewers of said township of *Bunker Hill*, do estimate and determine the value of that portion of the partition fence, on the line between the land of A. B. and C. D., in said township, de-

[618.] SEC. 14. When any uninclosed land shall be afterwards enclosed, the occupant or owner thereof shall pay for one half of each partition fence standing upon the line between his land and the enclosure of any other occupant or owner, and the value thereof shall be ascertained by two or more Fence Viewers of the township, in writing, under their hands, in case the parties do not agree; and if such occupant or owner shall neglect or refuse, for thirty days after the value has been so ascertained and demand made, to pay for one half of such partition fence, the proprietor of such fence may maintain an action in the form aforsaid, for such value, and the costs of ascertaining the same.[1]

When occupant owner to pay one half of partition fence, etc.

[619.] SEC. 15. In all cases where the line, upon which a partition fence is to be made, or to be divided, is the boundary line between townships, or partly in one township and partly in another, a Fence Viewer shall be taken from each township.

When a Fence Viewer to be taken from each Township.

[620.] SEC. 16. Where a partition fence running into the water is necessary to be made, the same shall be done in equal shares, unless otherwise agreed by the parties, and in case either party shall refuse or neglect to make or maintain the share belonging to him, similar proceedings shall be had, as in case of other fences, and with the like effect.

Fences running into water.

[621.] SEC. 17 In all cases where the line, upon which a partition fence is to be built between unimproved lands, has been divided by the Fence Viewers, or by agreement in writing between the owners of such lands, recorded in the office of the clerk of the township, or of one of the townships

When line of unimproved lands divided, who to erect fences, etc.

---

scribed as follows: (*describe the fence*), belonging to said C. D., to be ——— dollars.

Given under our hands this — day of ——, A. D. 18—.

E. F.,
G. H.,
Fence-Viewers.

Where a party removes a partition fence without having previously given the required notice, the party injured thereby is not limited to a suit for the recovery of actual damages sustained in consequence of such removal, but may make the fence anew and recover the expense thereof by action.

If actual damages are sustained, as the loss of a crop for instance, caused by the removal of the fence, an action for the recovery of such damages, as well as a suit to recover the expense of making the fence, may be sustained.—*Richardson v. McDougall*, 11 *Wend.* 46.

[1] *Form of Writing by Fence Viewers, ascertaining Value of Partition Fence, where uninclosed Lands become inclosed.*

Cass County,
Township of *Calvin.* } *ss.*

We, the undersigned, two of the fence viewers of said township of *Calvin*, have ascertained and do estimate the value of one half of the partition fence, on the line between the land of A. B. and C. D., in said township, described as follows (*describe the fence or land, as most convenient*), to be ——— dollars.

Given under our hands, this — day of ——, A. D. 18—.

E. F.
G. H.
Fence Viewers.

where such lands lie, the several owners thereof, and their heirs and assigns forever, shall erect and support said fences, agreeably to such division.[1]

Notice on determination not to improve lands.

[622.] SEC. 18. If any person shall determine not to improve any part of his lands adjoining any partition fence that may have been divided according to the provisions of this chapter, and shall give six months' notice of such determination to all the adjoining occupants of lands, he shall not be required to keep up or support any part of such fence during the time his lands shall lie open and unimproved.[2]

Who to be Fence Viewers.

[623.] SEC. 19. The Overseers of Highways of the several townships in this State, shall be Fence Viewers in their respective townships.

Penalty for neglect.

[624.] SEC. 20. Any Fence Viewer, who shall, when requested, unreasonably neglect to view any fence, or to perform any other duty required of him in this chapter, shall forfeit the sum of five dollars, and shall also be liable to the party injured for all damages consequent upon such neglect.

---

[1] *Form of Agreement to divide and Maintain a Partition Fence between Owners of adjoining Lands.*

This agreement, made this — day of ——, A. D. 18—, between A. B., of the township of *Brown*, in the county of *Branch*, and State of Michigan, of the one part, and C. D. of the same township, of the other part, witnesseth, that whereas the said A. B. has heretofore erected a fence on the division line between his lands and the lands of said C. D. in said township, which said fence commences at [*describe the line of fence*] and whereas, after the erection of said fence, the said C. D. enclosed a fence on the *east* side of said division line, so that *sixty* rods of said fence, commencing at, &c. (*describe the portion of fence*) has become and now is a partition fence between the respective fields of the said A. B. and C. D.; and whereas the said C. D. has paid to said A. B. ——— dollars, being in full for one half of the value of said *sixty* rods of fence,—it is therefore agreed, in consideration of the premises between the said parties, that the *thirty* rods of fence on the *north* part of said *sixty* rods, being the *north* half thereof, shall be well and sufficiently maintained and kept in repair by the said A. B. and the remainder of said *sixty* rods shall be kept in like repair by the said C. D.

In witness whereof, the said parties have hereunto set their hands and seals the day and year first above written.

In presence of — A. B., [L. S.]

E. F. — C. D., [L. S.]

Where a dispute arises as to the proportion of a fence to be maintained by each party, it may be settled by the fence-viewers, even where there has been an agreement on the subject.—*Burger v. Kortnight*, 4 *Johns* 414.

The decision of the fence-viewers as to the proportion of fence of each party, is not necessary where there is no dispute between them.—*Willoughby v. Carlton*, 9 *Johns* 136.

[2] *Form of Notice of Determination not to improve Lands adjoining Partition Fence.*

To Mr. *A B.*

Sir: You will take notice that I have determined not to improve any part of my lands adjoining the partition fence, between our adjoining lands in the township of *Barry*, and county of *Barry*, said partition fence being the same fence divided by E. F. and G. H., two of the Fence Viewers of said township (or by agreement), in writing, bearing date the — day of ——, A. D. 18—.

C.D.

[625.] SEC. 21. Each Fence Viewer shall be paid by the person employing him, at the rate of one dollar a day for the time he shall be so employed; and if such person shall neglect to pay the same within thirty days after the service shall have been performed, each Fence Viewer having performed any such service may recover, in an action of assumpsit, double the amount of such fees. Compensation of Fence Viewers.

POUNDS, AND IMPOUNDING CATTLE.

[626.] SEC. 22. Each township may, at its own expense, and in such places therein as the electors shall direct, provide and maintain one or more sufficient Pounds, in which swine, sheep, horses, asses, mules, goats, and neat cattle may be restrained, and kept from going at large contrary to law, or to any by-law of such township. Township to provide and maintain Pounds.

[627.] SEC. 23. If any person shall wilfully injure any Pound maintained by any township, he shall be deemed guilty of a misdemeanor, and on conviction thereof, shall be punished by a fine not exceeding fifty dollars, or by imprisonment in the county jail not exceeding ninety days, at the discretion of the Court. Punishment for injury to Pounds.

An Act to Provide Against the Recovery of Damages done by Beasts on Lands which are not Enclosed by a Lawful Fence.

[*Approved March* 17, 1847. *Laws of* 1847, *p.* 181.]

[628.] SECTION 1. *Be it enacted by the Senate and House of Representatives of the State of Michigan*, That no person shall be entitled to recover any sum of money in any action at law for damages done upon lands by any beast or beasts, unless in cases where, by the by-laws of the proper township, such beasts are prohibited from running at large, except in cases where such lands are enclosed by a fence of the same height and description as is required by the provisions of section one, chapter eighteen of the Revised Statutes of eighteen hundred and forty-six. Damages not to be recovered for trespass on lands not enclosed by lawful Fence. 2 Mich. Rep. 290. 3 do. 163. 5 Gilman, 139.

SEC. 2.[a]

SEC. 3. This act shall take effect and be in force from and after its passage.

[a] Repealed by Act 184 of 1849, p. 228. The Section was, "No Person shall Recover in any action at Law for Trespass on Lands any more costs than the amount of judgment rendered in such case."

Comp. L. 1857. Chap. XV. p. 254.

DIVISION VIII.—OF TAKING THE CENSUS AND STATISTICS OF THE STATE.

An Act to Provide for Taking the Census and Statistic of this State.

[*Approved Feb.* 9, 1853. *Laws of* 1853, *p.* 60.]

Duty of Supervisors to take Census and Statistics.

[629.] SECTION 1. *The People of the State of Michigan enact*. That it shall be the duty of the Supervisor of each township and ward, and Assessor of each assessment district, at the time of taking a list of the taxable property, or between the first Monday of April and third Monday of May, in the year one thousand eight hundred and fifty-four, and every ten years thereafter, to go to every dwelling house in their respective township, ward or assessment district, and by personally inquiring of the head of every family, or some competent person, to ascertain and take an enumeration of all the inhabitants therein (except uncivilized Indians belonging to some tribe), in the following order, to wit: The names of all males of the age of twenty-one years and under forty-five (designating the married from the unmarried); the names of those of forty-five and under seventy-five; the names of those of seventy-five and under ninety; the names of those of ninety and under one hundred; and the names of those over one hundred; the number of females of the age of eighteen years and under forty (designating the married from the unmarried); the number of the age of forty and under seventy-five; the number of the age of seventy-five and over; the number of children under the age of five years; the number of the age of five and under ten (designating the males from the females); the number of males of the age of ten and under twenty-one; and the number of females of the age of ten and under eighteen; the number of colored persons; the number of blind; the number of deaf and dumb; and the number of insane persons and idiots; the number of marriages, and the number of deaths the preceding year, as near as can be ascertained; and the occupation or profession of all males over twenty-one years of age.

Duty of Supervisors and Assessors to take Census and Statistics.

[630.] SEC. 2. And it shall also be the duty of the Supervisor and Assessors of each city and township, at the time mentioned in the preceding section for taking the Census of his township or ward, to ascertain and set down in a table prepared for that purpose, the whole number of acres of taxable land; the whole number of acres of land owned by individuals or companies; the number of acres improved; the number of acres sowed with wheat then on the ground; the number of acres and the number of bushels of corn harvested the preceding

ear; the number of acres harvested and the number of bushels f wheat raised the preceding year; the number of bushels of ll other kinds of grain; the number of bushels of potatoes; id the number of tons of hay the preceding year; the numer of sheep, and the number of pounds of wool sheared the receding year, and the number of sheep; the number of vine over six months old; and the number of pounds of pork arketed; the number of neat cattle (other than oxen and ows), one year old and over; the number of horses one year d and over; the number of mules; the number of work xen, and the number of milch cows; the number of pounds butter and cheese made the preceding year; the number of ounds of sugar manufactured the present year; the number pounds of peppermint oil manufactured the preceding year; e number of flouring mills, the number of runs of stone in ch; the number of barrels of flour made by each the preceding ear; and the number of oil mills, and the number of gallons oil made the preceding year; the number of breweries, the umber of barrels of beer made the preceding year; the numer of distilleries, the number of gallons of liquor made the eceding year; the number of gallons of wine made the eceding year; and the number of barrels of cider made the eceding year; and the number of barrels of fish caught e preceding year, and the amount of capital invested; the mber of saw mills, the number of feet of lumber sawed each the preceding year, and the amount of capital invested; e number and kind of manufactories; the number of persons nployed; the amount of capital invested; and the value of e products for the past year; designating the number of id mills and factories operated by steam, and the number water power; the number of mines worked; the amount capital invested, and the number of men employed, specing the kind of mineral, the aggregate quantity in pounds, d its valuation at the place of mining, the amount of capital vested, and the number of men employed; and the value of the marchandize imported the preceding year for the rpose of sale.

[631.] SEC. 3. The Secretary of State shall prepare proper anks for taking the Census and Statistics, and shall transmit the several County Clerks of all the organized counties of e State a sufficient number for each township, ward, or sessment district in each county, on or before the first y of January, A. D. 1854, and every tenth year thereafter; d it shall be the duty of the County Clerk to receive and tain the same in his office, and on or before the second onday in April next thereafter, cause to be delivered to the pervisor of each township and ward, and Assessor of each sessment district in the county, a sufficient number of said anks for the Supervisor or Assessor to take the Census of his wnship, or ward, or assessment district (as the case may

Duty of Secretary of State.

be), and to make a condensed statement thereof, as prescribed in the next succeeding section.

Census and Statistics to be condensed by Supervisor and Assessor.

[632.] SEC. 4. It shall be the duty of each Supervisor and Assessor to condense the Census and Statistics of his township, ward, or assessment district, so as to show the aggregate number of each class, to write out distinctly the names of all males over the age of twenty-one years; and when so arranged, he shall make duplicate copies, and personnally deliver or forward the same to the County Clerk of their respective counties, on or before the first day of July next thereafter; and it shall be duty of the County Clerk to forthwith seal up one copy and send it by mail to the Secretary of State, and the other he shall file and carefully preserve in his office.

Duty of County Clerk.

When person to be appointed to do the duty of Supervisor or Assessor.

[633.] Sec. 5. If any Supervisor or Assessor shall be sick, or otherwise unable to perform, or omit to perform the duties required by this act, the Township or City Board shall immediately appoint a suitable person to do the duties of such Supervisor or Assessor, who shall take and subscribe the Constitutional oath before entering upon the duties of his office.

Penalty for neglect of duty.

[634.] SEC. 6. Any Supervisor or Assessor neglecting or refusing, without good cause shown, to perform all the duties prescribed in this act, shall forfeit the sum of one hundred dollars, to be recovered by an action of debt, in the name of the People of the State of Michigan, for the use of the county where such failure occurred.

Prosecuting Attorney to sue for forfeitures.

[635.] SEC. 7. It shall be the duty of the County, Township, or City Clerk (as the case may be), to notify the Prosecuting Attorney of the county of any forfeiture under this act, who shall immediately commence a suit for the recovery thereof, and prosecute the same to a final termination.

Compensation of Supervisor and Assessor.

[636.] SEC. 8. The Supervisor of each township and ward, and the Assessor of each assessment district, shall be allowed, in addition to the sum allowed by law for taking the assessment of his township, ward, or assessment district, one dollar for every one hundred persons by him returned, if the number shall exceed one thousand and five hundred, and one dollar and fifty cents per hundred for any number less, and ten cents per mile for conveying the returns to the County Clerk's office, which shall be in full for all services performed under the provisions of this act; and the sum due each Supervisor and Assessor for services, shall be calculated at the rate aforesaid by the County Clerk, to which the proper returns are made, and his certificate of the amount due shall be paid by the Treasurer of said county: *Provided*, That before a Supervisor or Assessor shall be entitled to receive any compensation, he shall attach a certificate to each copy of said returns, signed by him, in the following form, to wit:

Proviso.

Certificate to Returns.

"I do hereby certify that the Census and Statistics set forth in the schedule hereunto annexed, has been consolidated and arranged from enumeration and statistical lists, made by actual inquiry at the dwelling, or personal inquiry at the head of every family, or of a competent person acquainted with the facts, by myself, in the township of or ward number in the city of or assessment district in the city of (as the case may be), and that the said schedule has been made in every respect in conformity with the act for taking the Census and Statistics for the year eighteen hundred and fifty-four, and every tenth year thereafter, and is correct and true, according to the best of my knowledge and belief."

[637.] SEC. 9. The Secretary of State shall condense, in tabular form, the Census and Statistical returns made to him, and as soon as may be, cause three thousand copies to be published in pamphlet form, and transmit four copies to each organized township in the State, one for the use of the Supervisor, one for the use of the Township Clerk, and two to be deposited in the township library; and twenty-five copies to the Mayor of the City of Detroit, and ten copies to the Mayor of any other city in the State, for the use of the several city libraries, and one copy to each of the members of the present Legislature and its officers: *Provided*, That in counties having less than five thousand inhabitants, the Supervisor in each town shall be entitled to three dollars for taking the Census and Statistics in his town extra.

Duty of Secretary of State relative to returns.

Proviso.

Compensation.

[638.] SEC. 10. In the City of Detroit, the Common Council shall appoint a person in each ward to discharge the duties required by this act, to be performed by the Supervisor of each township or ward: *Provided*, There is no Assessor elected in said wards.

Common Council of Detroit to appoint.

[639.] SEC. 11. It shall be the duty of the persons required in this act to take said Census, to have the several columns of figures footed, and the aggregate amount put down.

Columns to be footed.

[640.] SEC. 12. That the Governor appoint marshalls to take the Census in the unorganized territory not otherwise provided in this act, who shall receive such compensation as the Board of Supervisors of the organized county to which such unorganized territory is attached for judicial purposes shall allow.

Governor to appoint Marshals certain cases.

This act shall take effect immediately.

Comp. L. 1857. Chap. XVII. p. 284.

DIVISION IX.—Of the Assessment and Collection of Taxes.

An Act to Provide for Assessing Property at its true Value, and for Levying and Collecting Taxes thereon.[a]

[*Approved and took effect February* 14, 1853. *Laws of* 1853, *p.* 128.]

All property not exempted, liable to taxation. R. S. 1846, Chap. 20, § 1.

[782.] Section 1. *The People of the State of Michigan enact,* That all property, real and personal, within this State, not expressly exempted therefrom, shall be subject to taxation in the manner provided by law.

Real Estate, what to include. R. S., § 2.

[783.] Sec. 2. Real estate shall, for the purpose of taxation, be construed to include all lands within the State, and all buildings and fixtures thereon, except in cases otherwise expressly provided by law.

Personal estate, what to include. R. S., § 2. 1848, p. 313.

[784.] Sec. 3. Personal estate shall, for the purposes of taxation, be construed to include all goods, chattels, moneys, credits, and effects, wheresoever they may be; all ships, boats and vessels belonging to the inhabitants of this State, whether at home or abroad, and all capital invested therein; all moneys at interest, either within or without this State, due the person to be taxed more than he pays interest for, and all other debts due such persons more than their indebtedness; all public stock and securities, all stock in turnpikes, railroads, canals, and other corporations out of the State, owned by inhabitants of this State; all personal estate of moneyed corporations, whether the owner thereof reside in or out of the State, and the income of any annuity, unless the capital of such annuity be taxed within this State.

Corporate property. R. S., § 4.

[785.] Sec. 4. All property of private corporations, except in the cases where some other provision is made by law, shall be assessed in the name of the corporation, in the township or ward where the same shall be situated; and in collecting the same, all the personal property of such corporation shall be liable to be seized wherever the same may be found in the county, and sold in the same manner as the property of individuals may be sold for taxes.

Property exempt from taxation. R. S., 1849, p. 96.

[786.] Sec. 5. The following property shall be exempt from taxation, viz:

1. Household furniture, including stoves put up and kept for use in any dwelling house, not exceeding in value two hundred dollars;

---

[a] For prior laws relative to the Assessment and Collection of Taxes, and the sale of Lands therefor, see Code of 1820, p. 271; Revision of 1827, p. 370, Revision of 1833, p. 88, 98; Laws of 1834, p. 5; 1835-'6, p. 52, 1837, p. 7, 126, 167, 317; 1838, p. 137; R. S., of 1838, Title V, Laws of 1839, p. 159, 168, 1840, p. 6, 80, 254; 1842, p. 68, 85, 108; 1843, p. 34, 55, 60: 1844. p. 3, 22, 159; 1845, p. 79, 85; 1846, p. 13, 87, 102; R. S., of 1846, Title V; Laws of 1847, p. 120, 1848, p. 2, 75, 147, 254, 313; 1849, p. 96, 116, 334; 1850, 40, 161, 218, 395.

2. All spinning wheels and weaving looms, and apparatus, not exceeding in value fifty dollars;

3. All arms and accoutrements, required by law to be kept by any person; all wearing apparel of any person or family;

4. The library and school books of every individual and family not exceeding in value one hundred and fifty dollars, and all family pictures;

5. To each householder, ten sheep, with their fleeces, and the yarn and cloth manufactured from the same; two cows; five swine; and provisions and fuel for the comfortable subsistence of such householder and family for six months;

6. All the property of the United States, and of this State, except lands bid off for the State at tax sales, except as hereinafter provided;

7. All public or corporate property of the several counties, cities, villages, townships, and school districts in this State, used, or intended for corporate purposes.

8. The personal property of all library, benevolent, charitable, and scientific institutions, incorporated within this State, and such real estate belonging to such institutions as shall actually be occupied by them, for the purposes for which they were incorporated; 1857, p. 166. 2 Mich. Rep. 586.

9. All houses of public worship, with the pews, or slips, and furniture therein, and rights of burial, and tombs, while in use as repositories of the dead;[b 1]

10. The estates of Indians, except lands held by them by purchase, and the personal estates of persons who, by reason of infirmity, age, and poverty, may, in the opinion of the Supervisor, be unable to contribute towards the public charges.

[787.] SEC. 6. When a tenant paying rent for real estate shall be taxed therefor, he may retain out of his rent the taxes paid by him for the same, unless there be an agreement to the contrary. When tenant paying taxes, may retain the same from rent. R. S. § 6.

[788.] SEC. 7. All personal estate within this State, except in the cases where other provision is made by the third and eighth sections of this chapter, shall be assessed to the owner in the township where he shall be an inhabitant, on the second Monday of April, and all resident real estate, to the person occupying it on that day, unless the same shall be given in by some other person for assessment to him. Personal estate, when assessed. R. S. Sec. 7.

[789.] SEC. 8. The excepted cases referred to in the preceding section, and not included in said section three, are the following: Cases excepted. 1858, Act 32, p. 176.

---

[b] See the act of February 7, 1857, next following.

[2] It seems the provisions of statutes exempting from taxation "All houses of public worship" were not intended to exempt the *lot or ground* upon which houses of public worship stand.—*Lefevre v. Mayor &c. of Detroit*, 2 *Mich.* 586.

The exemption of houses of public worship from taxation applies only to taxes imposed under the general system of taxation adopted for the State, counties, townships, or other municipal corporation, and does not extend to assessments for the expenses of paving streets, imposed upon the owners or occupants of lots.—*Ibid.*

1st. All goods, wares and merchandise, or stock in trade, including stock employed in the business of the mechanic arts, in any township other than where the owners reside, shall be, if the owner hire or occupy a store, shop, or warehouse therein, shall not be taxable where the owner resides.

2. All horses, mules, neat cattle, sheep and swine, kept throughout the year in any township other than where the owner resides, shall be assessed to such owner in the township where they are kept.

3. All personal property belonging to minors under guardianship, shall be assessed to the guardian in the township where he is an inhabitant, and the personal property of every other person under guardianship, shall be assessed to the guardian in the township of which the ward is an inhabitant.

4. All personal property held in trust by any executor, administrator or trustee, the income of which is to be paid to any married woman or other person, shall be assessed to the person having possession or charge of such property, in the township of which he is an inhabitant, whether such married woman or other person reside within or without this State.

5. Personal property placed in the hands of any corporation as an accumulating fund, for the future benefit of heirs, or other persons, shall be assessed to the persons for whose benefit the same is accumulating, if within this State; otherwise to the person so placing it, or his executors or administrators, until a trustee shall be appointed to take charge of such property, or of the income thereof.

6. The personal estate of persons deceased, which shall be in the hands of executors or administrators, shall be assessed to the executors or administrators in the township where the deceased last dwelt, until they shall give notice to the supervisor that the estate has been distributed and paid over to the parties interested.

7. All property held by any religious society as a ministerial fund, shall be assessed to the treasurer of such society; and if such property consists of real estate, it shall be taxed in the township where such property lies; if it consists of personal property, it shall be taxed in the township where such society usually holds its meetings.

Personal property mortgaged to be deemed property of person having possession. R. S. Sec. 9.

[790.] SEC. 9. When personal property is mortgaged or pledged, it shall, for the purpose of taxation, be deemed the property of the person who has possession thereof.

Undivided Real Estate of deceased persons, how assessed. R. S. Sec. 10.

[791.] SEC. 10. The undivided real estate of any deceased person, may be assessed to the heirs or devisees of such person, unless occupied by some other person to whom it may be assessed, without designating them by name, until they shall have given notice to the Supervisor of the division of such estate, and the names of the several heirs and devisees; and each heir and devisee shall be liable for the whole of such tax, and shall have a right to recover of the other heirs and devisees their respective portions thereof, when paid by him.

[792.] SEC. 11. Any person holding a part-paid certificate of purchase of university, primary school, state building, swamp or salt spring lands, or occupying the same, shall be liable to be assessed therefor, as if he were the actual owner thereof: *Provided however*, That the same shall be assessed as personal property and not as real estate, and the tax thereon shall be collected in the manner hereinafter prescribed.

University, primary school, State building, swamp and salt spring lands.

[793.] SEC. 12. Partners in mercantile or other business, whether residing in the same or different townships, may be jointly taxed under the partnership name, in the township where their business is carried on, for all the personal property employed in such business; and if they have places of business in two or more townships, they shall be taxed in those townships for the proportion of property employed in such townships respectively; and in case of being so jointly taxed, each partner shall be liable for the whole tax.

Partners, how taxed.

R. S., Sec. 12.

[794.] SEC. 13. The term "money," or "moneys," whenever used in this act, shall be held to mean gold and silver coin, and bank notes, and every deposit, which any person owning the same, or holding in trust, and residing in this State, is entitled to withdraw in money on demand. The term "credits," whenever used in this act, shall be held to mean and include every claim and demand for money, or other valuable thing, and every annuity, or sum of money receivable at stated periods, due, or to become due, and all claims and demands secured by deed or mortgage, due, or to become due. The terms "parcel of real property," and "parcel of land," whenever used in this act, shall each be held to mean any contiguous quantity of land in the possession of, owned by, or recorded as the property of the same claimant, person, or company. Every word importing the singular number only, may extend to, and embrace the plural number; and every word importing the plural number, may be applied and limited to the singular number; and every word importing the masculine gender only, may be extended and applied to females as well as males. Whenever the word "oath," is used in this act, it may be held to mean "affirmation," and the word "swear," in this act, may be held to mean "affirm." The term "cash value," whenever used in this act, shall be held to mean the usual selling price at the place where the property to which the term is applied shall be at the time of assessment; and if there be no usual selling price known to the person whose duty it shall be to fix the value thereon, it shall be held to mean the price at which such property shall be appraised in payment of a just debt due from a solvent debtor, or such price as the property assessed may, in the preceding year, have been sold for.

Meaning of certain terms used in this Act.

[795.] SEC. 14. Every person of full age and sound mind, and every firm, body politic or corporate, shall, when called upon, as hereinafter provided, forthwith make a full and true statement in writing, to the Supervisor of the township in which

Statement to be made to Supervisor.

Contents of statement.

he or she resides, in which shall be distinctly and truly set forth a correct description of all the real estate and personal property not by this act exempt from taxation, and not by the laws of this State subject to a specific tax, of which he or she is the owner, or the holder as guardian, parent, husband, or trustee, executor, administrator, receiver, accounting officer, partner, agent, or factor; and also all moneys and credits owned or held, as aforesaid.[c] [1]

Particulars of statement required.

[796.] SEC. 15. Every person required by this act to make or deliver such statement, shall set forth an account of the property held or owned by him or them, as follows:

1. An accurate description of each parcel of land, with the number of acres, and the number of acres improved, and the number and kinds of buildings thereon;
2. The number of neat cattle six months old;
3. The number of horses over six months old;
4. The number of sheep over six months old;
5. The number of hogs over six months old;
6. Every waggon and carriage;
7. Every gold or silver watch;
8. The number of bushels of grain, and the quantity of all other farm produce in the possession of the producer;
9. All merchandize not included in the eighth subdivision of this section;
10. Every musical instrument, of the value of twenty-five dollars and upwards;
11. All moneys and all credits;
12. All other personal property held or owned by him;
13. The amount of money upon which he pays interest, providing he desires to have the same deducted from his moneys and credits;
14. The amount of all other *bona fide* indebtedness: *Provided*, He desires to have the same deducted from his moneys and credits.[d]

---

[c] As amended by "An Act to Amend certain Sections of An Act entitled, 'An Act to Provide for Assessing Property at its true value, and for Levying and Collecting Taxes thereon,' Approved February 14, 1853." Approved February 12, 1855. Laws of 1855, p. 227. This Act amends Sections 14, 15, 16, 18, 19, 20, 22, and 89, as here given,

[1] The city charter of Detroit, and the acts amendatory thereto, empower the Common Council to provide for the expenses of paving streets, &c., either by assessment on the owners or occupants of lots on the street to be paved, or otherwise, as they may direct. The city ordinances adopted in pursuance of such authority, direct such expenses to be raised by assessments upon the owners and occupants of lots, and that the Common Council shall cause an assessment to be made by the city surveyor on the *owners* or *occupants* of lots fronting on the street, &c., to be paved; and the surveyor is also required to state the names of the owners and occupants so to be assessed, in a written report or assessment roll. Under these provisions of the city charter and ordinances: *Held*, that an assessment upon "St. Peter's and St. Paul's Cathedral," the roll neither describing the lots, nor naming the owners or occupants, was void.—*Lefevre v. Mayor, &c., of Detroit*, 2 *Mich.* 586.

An assessment imposed upon a city lot for paving expenses, held not vitiated, on the objection that the paving was contracted for before the assessment was made.—*Ibid.*

[d] See note to Section 795.

[797.] SEC. 16. Such statement the Supervisor may, in his discretion, require to be subscribed by the person making the same; and it shall further mention who is the owner of the property so described, and whether the same is held by him, the maker of such statement, individually, or in his own right, or whether held for any other person, and if held for any other person, then state for whom, in what capacity, or on what account so held, giving the name of the person for whom he holds.[e]

Persons may be required to subscribe statement

To state who is the owner, etc.

[798.] SEC. 17. No person shall be required to include in such statement any share or portion of the capital stock of any company or corporation, which company or corporation is by law exempt from taxation, or by law required to pay a specific tax in lieu of all other taxes on such share or portion of capital stock, or whose corporate property is subject to assessment under the provisions of section four of this act.

Property paying Specific Taxes need not be included in list.

[799.] SEC. 18. It shall be the duty of each Supervisor, on or before the second Monday in May, to call upon each taxable person in his township, at their residence, boarding place, or usual place of business, at which time he shall furnish each taxable person a blank form for the statements required by the fifteenth section of this act; and thereupon said taxable person shall forthwith make and deliver to said Supervisor a full and true statement of the taxable property in his possession, according to the provisions of this act; and immediately thereafter, the said Supervisor shall proceed to examine said property, and estimate and set down the true value thereof, deducting from the moneys at interest and other credits of such person, the amount of money upon which he or she pays interest, together with his other bona fide indebtedness, as set forth in said statement.[f]

Supervisor to furnish blank forms.

1858, Act 32, p. 176.

Taxable person to make and deliver statement to Supervisor.

Supervisor to ascertain and set down true value thereof.

[800.] SEC. 19. In every case where any person shall neglect or refuse to make out and deliver a statement of his real and personal property, moneys and credits, or to exhibit the same to the Supervisor, as required by this act, it shall be the duty of said Supervisor, and he is hereby authorized to examine on oath the person so refusing, and any other person or persons who he may have good reason to believe, and does believe, has knowledge of the amount or value of any property, money, or credits owned or held by such person so refusing; and said Supervisor shall assess any property, money, or credits, owned or held by such person so refusing, at its true cash value; *Provided*, That if any person shall neglect or refuse to make such statement, or in case of any person owning any taxable property in this State, or any money loaned in this State, shall be absent from the township, or can not be found therein by the Supervisor of such township, during the time of the assessment roll is required by law to be made, leaving no agent known to such Su-

Duty of Supervisor in case any person refuses to make statement.

When Supervisors may fix the amount.

[e f] See note to Section 795.

pervisor to make the required statement, such Supervisor is hereby authorized to set down and assess to such person any amount of personal property he may deem just and proper, subject to the reduction on review, upon oath of the party in interest, his agent or attorney.[g]

When assessment to be received and completed. 1858, Act 32, p. 176.

[801.] SEC. 20. On the third Monday of May, it shall be the duty of the Supervisors of the several townships to be present at their respective offices, from eight o'clock in the forenoon until twelve, noon, and from one o'clock in the afternoon till five o'clock in the afternoon, for the purpose of reviewing their assessments, and so on the two next following days, in case they shall have any matter before them for their action under this section; and on the request of any person, his agent or attorney, considering himself aggrieved, on sufficient cause being shown to the satisfaction of the Supervisor, he shall alter the assessment as to the valuation thereof, and he shall also, upon sufficient cause being shown by any creditable person on behalf of any other person whose property is assessed, alter the assessment in such manner as shall to him appear just and equal; and to this end he may in either case examine on oath the person making the application, or any other person present, touching the matter, which oath the Supervisor is hereby authorized to administer.[h]

May alter assessment as to valuation.

Supervisor may administer oath.

Contents of assessment Roll. R. S., Sec. 16.

[802.] SEC. 21. The assessment roll shall contain the names of the resident persons liable to be taxed; a full description of the real estate of such persons; the number of acres in each tract or parcel, as near as the same can be ascertained; the estimated value of each tract or parcel, and the aggregate valuation of the personal estate of each person liable to be taxed, as appears from the statements in the possession of the Supervisor.

Auditor General to transmit blanks to Treasurer. Treasurer to supply Supervisors. R. S., Sec. 17.

[803.] SEC. 22. For the purposes mentioned in the preceding sections of this act, the Auditor General shall, before the first Monday in March in each year, prepare and transmit suitable blanks to the several County Treasurers, who shall, before the first Monday in April, supply all the Supervisors in their several counties with the same. The Auditor General is authorized and instructed to furnish, at the expense of the State, to each Supervisor and Assessor in the several townships and cities in this State, a copy of this law, at the earliest day practicable.[i]

Real Estate, how described. 1858, Act 42, p. 176.

[804.] SEC. 23. The description of real estate may be as follows:

1. If the lands to be assessed be an entire section, it may be described by the number of the section, township and range;

2. If the tract be a sub-division of a section authorized by the United States for the sale of the public lands, it may be described by a designation of such sub-division, with the number of the section, township and range;

---

g h i See note to Section 795.

3. If the tract be less or other than such sub-division, it may be described by a designation of the number of the lot or other lands by which it is bounded, or in some way by which it may be known;

4. In case of lands surveyed or laid out as a town, city or village, and a plat thereof recorded in the register's office of the county, if the tract to be assessed be a whole lot or block, it shall be described by a designation of the number thereof; if it be a part of a lot or block, it may be described by its boundaries, or some other way by which it may be known, and it shall not be necessary to insert the quantity of such land in the assessment roll. When any lands have been, or hereafter shall be laid out as a town, city or village, or as an addition of any town, city or village, and the same has not been duly recorded in the register's office of the county, and any one or more of the lots have been or may be sold by the numbers thereof, according to the plat of said town, city or village, or addition thereto, such land, laid out as aforesaid, may, in the discretion of the Supervisor, be assessed in whole or in part, according to the sub-division as represented on the plat of said town, city or village, or in some other way by which it may be known; and if such sub-division or parcel be a whole lot or block, it shall be described by a designation of the number thereof; if it be a part of a lot or block, such part shall be defined, or it shall be described by its boundaries, or in some other way by which it may be known; and it shall not be necessary to insert the quantity or contents of such land in the assessment roll; **Description of city or village property.**

5. If the land to be assessed be a tract of which the sub-division is not known to the Supervisor, it shall be entered upon the roll by the boundaries thereof, or in some other way by which it may be known;

6. Undivided shares or interests in lands shall be assessed to the owners thereof, if such ownership is known to the Supervisor, and no tract in the same section known to the Supervisor to have been originally entered as one parcel, shall be sub-divided in assessing, unless the fact of a sub-division having been made known to the Supervisor; **Undivided shares.**

7. It shall be sufficient to describe lands to be assessed or sold for taxes in the manner heretofore in use by initials, letters, abbreviations and figures.[1]

[805.] SEC. 24. All lands unoccupied and not claimed to be owned by any resident of the township where they are situated and not exempt from taxation, may be assessed as non-resident **Non-resident lands.**

---

1 Real Estate, for the purposes of assessment, should be "described by its boundaries, or in some other way by which it may be known:" therefore, where premises were described in an assessment and tax roll as follows:

"YOUNG MEN'S SOCIETY—Gov. and J. P., Jeff. av., N. 45 feet— W. pt. lot 11, sec. 1, and E. pt. lot 10, sec. 1. } B 2."

Held, That the assessment was illegal, and the tax levied on the premises invalid.—*Detroit Young Men's Society v. Mayor, &c.*, 3 *Mich.* 172.

The description of lands assessed or sold for taxes, by the use of initial letters, abbreviations, and figures, is a valid description.—*Sibley v. Smith*, 2 *Mich.* 486.

1858, Act 32, p. 176. lands or to the person supposed by the Supervisor to be the owner thereof, and it shall be the duty of the Supervisor to enter the same on a part of the roll separate from that upon which the estates of residents are entered, and when real estate is occupied it may be assessed to the occupant or supposed owner or person exercising control over the same. When a person is assessed as a trustee, guardian, executor, or administrator, a designation of his representative character may be added to his name, and such assessment shall be entered on a separate line from his individual assessment.

Property held in trust, &c.

Certificate to be attached to roll.

[806.] SEC. 25. When the Supervisor has reviewed and completed the assessment roll, it shall be his duty to attach thereto, signed by him, a certificate which may be in the following form:

I do hereby certify that I have set down in the above assessment roll, all the real estate in the township of ——, liable to be taxed, according to my best information, and that I have estimated the same at what I believe to be the true cash value thereof; that the said assessment roll contains a true statement of the aggregate valuation of the taxable personal estate of each and every person named in said roll, and that I have estimated the same at its true cash value, according to my best information and belief.[1]

R. S., Sec. 21.

Lacy v. Davis, 4 Mich. Rep.

1858, Act 32, p. 176.

Clerk of township to deliver statement of amount of money to be raised for township purposes.

[807.] SEC. 26. It shall be the duty of the township clerk of each township, on or before the second Monday of October, of each year, to deliver to the Supervisor of his township a statement of the money to be raised therein for township purposes, and the amount voted for the maintainance and support of common schools, and the township library, stating the amount of each as well as the aggregate amount.[2] The Board of Supervisors in each county shall, at their session in October in each year, examine the assessment roll of the several townships, and ascertain whether the relative valuation of the real estate in the respective townships has been equally and uniformly estimated.[3]

Board of Supervisors to examine assessment roll.

---

1 It seems the provision of the statute requiring the assessor to annex his certificate to the assessment is directory merely, and a non-compliance with that provision will not affect the validity of the roll. — *Sibley v. Smith*, 2 *Mich.* 487.

2 *Statement by Township Clerk, of money to be raised for township and other purposes.*

A statement of money to be raised in the township of *Portland* for township purposes, and the amount voted for the maintainance and support of common schools and the township library.

Money to be raised for township purposes	$500.00
Amount voted for the maintainance and support of common schools ..	500.00
Amount voted for the township library	.00
Aggregate amount	$1100.00

Dated this —— day of —— 18—

A. B., *Township Clerk.*

3 Objection was made to the record of the proceeeings of Supervisors, that it did not show who constituted the board, nor that a quorum was present, and that there was no signature or authentication by the clerk or presiding officer of the board. *Held*, that the presence of the supervisors, or at least a quorum would be presumed.

When the Supervisor, without any action of the electors, or the Township Board, added a certain amount to the tax roll, for township purposeses, that portion of the tax being illegal and void, and from the nature of the case, not distinguishable from the valid part, the sale of premises under and by virtue of the tax so levied, in an action of ejectment for their recovery, was held void.—*Lacy v. Davis*, 4 *Mich.* 140.

The Supervisor and Assessors shall be allowed for their services in assessing property and copying the tax rolls, and for extending the taxes thereon, at the rate of one dollar and fifty cents for each day actually and necessarily spent in perfecting the same, which shall be verified, audited and paid in the townships in the same manner provided by law for the payment of other township officers, and they shall receive payment from no other source.

Supervisors allowed $1.50 per day for services, &c.

[808.] SEC. 27. If, on such examination, they shall deem such valuation to be relatively unequal, they shall equalize the same, by adding to or deducting from the valuation of the taxable property in the township or townships, such an amount as in their judgment will produce relatively an equal and uniform valuation of the real estate in the county, and the amount added to or deducted from the valuation in each township shall be entered upon the records.[1]

How assessment equalized.

[809.] SEC. 28. The Board of Supervisors shall also make such alterations in the description of any lands upon such rolls, as may be necessary to render such description conformable to the requirements of this act.

1858, Act 35, p. 176, Alterations of descriptions. R. S., Sec. 25.

[810.] SEC. 29. After the assessment shall have been equalized, and the descriptions corrected, as provided in the two last preceding sections, it shall be the duty of the chairman of the board to make and sign a certificate upon, or appended to the roll of each township, which certificate may be in the following form, to wit:

Corrected roll to be certified and delivered to Supervisor. 1858, Act 32, p. 176.

I do hereby certify that the Board of Supervisors have equalized and corrected the within roll, by adding to or deducting from the valuation of the real estate made by the Supervisor thereon, or without adding to or deducting from the valution of the real estate made by the Supervisor, as the case may be, and have determined the aggregate value of the taxable property in the township of ———— to be ——— dollars and ——— cents, for the year eighteen hundred ———;

Which assessment roll, certified as aforesaid, shall be delivered to the Supervisor of the proper township, whose duty it shall be to file and keep the same in his office.[2]

[811.] SEC. 30. The Board of Supervisors, at the time of equalizing the assessments, shall cause to be entered upon their records the aggregate valuation of the taxable real and personal property of each township in their county, as determined by them; from which record the Clerk of the Board shall within ten days after their annual meeting, in each year when the State Board of Equalization shall meet, make and transmit to the

Aggregate valuation to be recorded; when transmitted to Auditor General.

---

[1] The fact that the assessment of a township was placed at two different sums first, in the roll as made by the assessor, at one sum, and subsequently in the tabular staiement of the Supervisors at another, is not material; and, therefore, the roll is not void for that reason.

It is competent for the Board of Supervisors to reduce the aggregate of the assessments below that of the assessors.—*Tweed v. Metcalf*, 4 *Mich.* 579.

[2] The certificates of the Assessors and the Chairman of the Board of Supervisors do not, in legal contemplation, form a part of the assessment roll, therefore, proceedings under a roll not having such certificate, are not void for that reason.—*Tweed v. Metcalf.* 4 *Mich.* 579.

R. S., Sec. 27. Auditor General, by mail, or otherwise, a statement of the aggregate valuation of the taxable real and personal property of the county, including the aggregate valuation of property in each township.

MANNER OF ASSESSING TAXES.

Auditor General to apportion State tax.

R. S., Sec. 28.

[812.] SEC. 31. The Auditor General shall apportion the State tax among the several counties, in proportion to the valuation of taxable property therein, and shall, before the October session of the Boards of Supervisors, make out and transmit to to the clerks of the several boards, the amount of such tax so apportioned by him to the county, and shall charge the several amounts of such apportionments to the counties respectively.

Apportionment of Tax by Board of Supervisors.

R. S. Sec. 29.

[813.] SEC. 32. The Board of Supervisors shall, at their annual session in October in each year, ascertain and determine the amount of money to be raised by tax for county purposes, and apportion such amount, and also the amount of State tax required to be raised, among the several townships in the county, in proportion to the valuation of the taxable property therein for the year, as equalized by the board, which determination and apportionment shall be entered at large on their records.

Certificate of apportionment to be made by clerk, etc.

R. S., Sec. 30.

[814.] SEC. 32. The Clerk of the Board of Supervisors shall, immediately after such apportionment, make out two certificates of the amount apportioned to be assessed upon the property of each township, for State and county purposes, one of which he shall deliver to the County Treasurer, and the other to the Supervisor of the township, and the County Treasurer shall charge the amount specified in each certificate to the proper township.[1]

How taxes assessed by Supervisor. 1858, Act 32. p. 176.

Collecting expense not to be more than four nor less than two per cent.

[815.] SEC. 33. The Supervisor of each township shall proceed to assess taxes for the amount specified in such certificate, together with a tax for the amount of money to be raised by his township, adding thereto, and to all other taxes required by law to be assessed by him, not more than four nor less than two per cent., as shall be determined by the electors at their annual meeting, at the same time and in the same manner that overseers of highways are elected, for collecting expenses, upon the taxable property in the township, according and in proportion to the individual and particular estimate and valuation specified

---

[1] *Form of Certificate of Clerk of Board of Supervisors of the amount Apportioned to be Assessed for State and County purposes.*

State of Michigan, } ss.
Lapeer County. }

I do hereby certify that the amount apportioned to be assessed upon the property of each township in said county of *Lapeer*, for State and County purposes, by the Board of Supervisors at their Annual Session in October, A.D., 18—, is (*set forth the amount.*)

In witness whereof, I have hereunto set my hand this ——— day of ——— A. D., 18—.

A. B.,
Clerk of Board of Supervisors.

in the assessment roll of the township for the year, and for the purpose of avoiding fractions in excess in said tax, may add to the several amounts to be raised, on a sum not exceeding one hundred dollars, five per cent. or under, on a sum over one hundred dollars and not exceeding four hundred dollars, three and a half per cent. or under, on a sum not exceeding one thousand dollars and over four hundred dollars, two per cent. or under, and on any sum exceeding one thousand dollars, not over one per cent.; said excess, more or less, to be paid into and to belong to the contingent fund of the township or ward where assessed. May add to the amount to be raised to avoid fractions in excess.

[816.] SEC. 34. The Supervisor of each township, on or before the twenty-fifth day of October in each year, shall notify the Township Treasurer of the amount of State and county tax apportioned to his township; and such Treasurer, on or before the fifth day of November, shall give to the County Treasurer, and his successors in office, a bond in double the amount of such State and county taxes, with good and sufficient sureties, to be approved by the Supervisor of the township, or the County Treasurer, conditioned that he shall duly and faithfully perform the duties of his office, and shall deliver the same to the County Treasurer.[1] Supervisor to notify Treasurer of amount of taxes; Treasurer to give bond. R. S., Sec. 32.

[817.] SEC. 36. The County Treasurer shall file and safely keep such bond in his office; and on the receipt thereof, he shall give to the Township Treasurer a receipt, stating that he has received the bond required by the preceding section, which receipt the Township Treasurer shall deliver to the Supervisor on or before the tenth day of November.[2] County Treasurer to file bond and give receipt. R. S., Sec. 33.

---

[1] *Form of Township Treasurer's Bond to County Treasurer.*

Know all men by these presents, that we *John Doe, Henry Wise,* and *John Lapeer,* of the Township of *Ada,* County of *Kent,* and State of Michigan, are held and firmly bound unto A. B., County Treasurer of said County, and his successors in office, in the sum of (*double the amount of State and County taxes*) for the payment of which sum well and truly to be made, we bind ourselves, our heirs, executors and administrators, and each of them firmly by these presents, sealed with our seals and dated this —— day of—— A. D. 18—.

The condition of the above obligation is such, that if the above bounden *John Doe,* shall duly and faithfully perform the duties of Township Treasurer of said Township of *Ada,* then this obligation to be void, otherwise to remain in full force and effect.

In presence of
JOHN JACKSON.

JOHN DOE, [L. S.]
HENRY WISE, [L. S.]
JOHN LAPEER. [L. S.]

[2] *Form of County Treasurer's Receipt for Bond of Township Treasurer.*

Received of *John Doe,* Township Treasurer of the township of *Ada,* in the County of *Lapeer,* his bond, required as Township Treasurer, by section 816 of the Compiled Statutes of Michigan, said bond being executed by himself, and C. B. and E. F., as sureties, and bearing date the —— day of—— A. D. 8——.

Dated at ———, this —— day of ——— A. D. 18—.

A. B.,
County Treasurer.

When Supervisor to deliver Assessment roll to Treasurer.

R. S., Sec. 34.

1850, p. 161.

[818.] SEC. 36. The Supervisor, after the delivery of such receipt, and on or before the fifteenth day of November, shall deliver to the Township Treasurer, a copy of the corrected assessment roll of his township, with the taxes for the year annexed to each valuation, and carried out in the last column thereof; the school, library, and school house taxes in one column, the highway taxes in another, and the township, county, and State taxes in another column; and if other taxes are at any time required by law, they shall be placed in another column, and the warrant for their collection shall specify particularly the several amounts and purposes for which said taxes are to be paid into the Township and County Treasuries respectively. Before the Supervisor shall deliver such assessment roll and tax list to the Township Treasurer, he shall carefully foot up the several taxes therein levied, and shall give to the Township Clerk of his township a statement thereof; and such Township Clerk shall immediately charge the amount of such taxes to the Township Treasurer.

Warrant to be attached to roll.

R. S., Sec. 35.

Tweed v. Metcalf; 4 Mich. Rep.

[819.) SEC. 37. To such assessment roll and tax list a warrant under the hand of the Supervisor shall be annexed, commanding such Treasurer to collect from the several persons named in said roll the several sums mentioned in the last column of such roll, opposite their respective names, and to retain in his hands the amount receivable by law into the Township Treasury for the purposes therein specied, and to account for, and to pay over to the County Treasurer the amounts therein specified for State and county purposes, on or before the first day of February then next; and the said warrant shall authorize the Treasurer, in case any person named in the assessment roll shall neglect or refuse to pay his tax, to levy the same by distress and sale of the goods and chattels of such persons.[1]

---

[1] *Form of Treasurer's Warrant for Collection of Taxes.*

In the name of the People of the State of Michigan: To *Thomas Jones*, Township Treasarer of the Township of *Burlington*, in the county of *Lapeer*:

You are hereby commanded to collect from the several persons named in the annexed assessment roll, the several sums mentioned in the last column of such roll, opposite their respective names, and to retain in your hands the amount receivable by law into the Township Treasury, for the purposes in said oll specified, and to account for, and to pay over to the County Treasurer the amounts therein specified for State and county purposes, on or before the first day of February next, said several amounts and purposes being as follows: (*Here specify particularly the several amounts and purposes for which said taxes are to be paid into the Township and County Treasuries respectively*); and in case any person named in said assessment roll shall neglect or refuse to pay his tax, to levy the same by distress and sale of the goods and chattels of such persons.

Given under my hands, this ——, this — day of ——, 18—.

A. B.

Supervisor of the Township of Burlington.

The warrant of the Supervisor to the Township Treasurer, authorizing him to collect taxes, is not void by reason of not being "In the name of the People of the State of Michigan." The provision of the Constitution in respect to process, applies only to process issued by courts, or some judicial officer.—*Tweed v. Metcalf*, 4 *Mich.* 579.

[820.] SEC. 38. The taxes assessed upon real estate of any resident or non-resident, and all legal charges made thereon, shall be a charge against the person owning the same on the second Monday of April, and shall be a lien on said real estate from the fifteenth day of November of the year in which such real estate was assessed.

Taxes to be a charge against the owner of real estate on 2d Monday of April. 1858, Act 32, p. 176. When taxes to be a lien on real estate.

OF THE COLLECTION AND RETURN OF TAXES.

[821.] SEC. 39. Every Township Treasurer, upon receiving the tax list and warrant, shall proceed to collect the taxes therein mentioned, and for that purpose shall call at least once upon the person taxed, if a resident, or at the place of his usual residence in the township, and shall demand payment of the taxes charged to him on such list.

Township Treasurer to collect taxes. R. S., Sec. 37.

[822.] SEC. 40. In case any person shall refuse or neglect to pay the tax imposed on personal or real estate belonging to him, the Treasurer shall levy the same by distress and sale of the goods and chattels of said person, whenever the same may be found within his township.

Proceedings in case of refusal to pay. 1858, Act 32, p. 176.

[823.] SEC. 41. The Treasurer shall give public notice of the time and place of sale, and of the property to be sold, at least ten days previous to the sale, by advertisement, to be posted up in three public places in the township where such sale shall be made; and the sale shall be by public auction.[1]

Notice of Sale. R. S., Sec. 39.

[824.] SEC. 42. If the property so distrained can not be sold, for want of bidders, the Treasurer shall return a statement of the fact, and if the tax be assessed on real estate, such real estate shall be returned in the same manner as if the same were non-resident lands.

Proceedings if property not sold. R. S., Sec. 40.

[825.] SEC. 43. If the property distrained shall be sold for more than the amount of the tax and collection fees, the surplus shall be returned to the person in whose possession said property was when the distress was made.

Surplus, how disposed of. 1858, Act 32, p. 176.

[826.] SEC. 44. In case any person, upon whom any tax may be assessed in any township for personal estate, shall have removed out of such township after the assessment, and before such tax ought by law to be collected, it shall be lawful for the Treasurer of such township to levy and collect such tax of the goods and chattels of the person so assessed, in any township

In case of removal of person assessed, tax may be collected in any part of County.

Form of Notice of Sale of Goods and Chattels by Township Treasurer for non-payment of Taxes.

Public notice is hereby given, that, by virtue of the authority vested in me as Township Treasurer of the Township of *Blissfield*, in the county of *Lenawee*, and by reason of the default of *A. B.*, of said town, to pay the taxes imposed on him for the year 18—, I have levied by distress upon the following goods and chattels of the said *A. B.* to wit: (*Here describe the property to be sold,*) which I shall offer for sale at public auction, on the —— day of —— A. D. 18—, at the hour of — o'clock — M., at ——, in said Township *Blissfield*, to make the amount of such taxes.

Dated this —— day of —— A. D. 18—.

C. D., *Township Treasurer.*

R. S., Sec. 42. within the county to which such person shall have removed, or in which he shall reside.

When tax on personal property cannot be collected, Treasurer's warrant may be renewed.

[827.] SEC. 45. Whenever any Township Treasurer shall not be able to collect any tax on personal property, on account of the absence of the person so taxed, or for any other cause, the County Treasurer, if required, shall issue a new warrant to the Treasurer of the township for such tax, and it shall be the duty of the Township Treasurer to renew his office bond; and thereupon the said warrant shall be and remain in force for the purposes of such collection until the next annual meeting of the Board of Supervisors, unless the tax is sooner collected; and the said Township Treasurer shall charge ten per cent. interest on all such taxes from the first day of February until the day of collection: *Provided*, said bond shall not be renewed unless the tax uncollected shall exceed five dollars. 1847, p. 123.

Treasurer may bring suit for tax. On personal property.

[828.] SEC. 46. Whenever any tax which shall have been, or which may hereafter be, assessed on personal property in this State, shall be returned by any Township Treasurer for non-payment, under the provisions of this act, it shall be lawful for the Treasurer of the township from which any such tax is so returned, in the name of such township, to sue the person or persons against whom such tax was assessed, before any Court of competent jurisdiction, and to have, use, and take all lawful ways and means provided by law for the collection of debts, to enforce the payment of any such tax. 1850, p. 193, Sec. 1.

Execution on judgments rendered therefor.

[829.] SEC. 47. Executions issued upon judgments rendered for any such tax, may be rendered upon any property liable to be seized and sold under warrants issued for the collection of taxes by Township Supervisors, and the proceedings of an officer with any execution shall be the same in all other respects as are now directed by law. 1850, p, 193, Sec. 2.

Evidence in suits for such tax.

[830.] SEC. 48. The production of any assessment roll, on the trial of any action brought for the recovery of a tax therein assessed, may, upon proof that it is the original assessment roll, or the assessment roll with the warrant annexed, of the township named as the plaintiff in such action, be read, or used in evidence; and if, it shall appear from said assessment roll that there is a tax therein assessed against defendant in such suit, it shall be *prima facie* evidence of the legality and regularity of the assessment of the same; and the Court before whom the cause may be pending shall proceed to render judgment against the defendant, unless he shall make it appear that he has paid such tax; and no stay of execution shall be allowed on any such judment. 1850, p. 193, Sec. 3.

Treasurer may receive tax on part of lot, or undivided share etc.

[831.] SEC. 49. Such Township Treasurer shall receive the tax, cr any one of the several taxes, on a part of any lot or parcel of land, or on any undivided share or other interest therein, which the tax payer will clearly define; and if the tax on the remainder of such lot or parcel of land shall remain unpaid, the Township Treasurer shall enter a specification thereof in his return to the County Treasurer; but if the part on which the tax is so paid shall be an undivided share, the person paying the same shall state to the Treasurer the name of the owner of such share, that it may be excepted in case of the sale for the tax on the remainder, for which purpose the Treasurer shall enter the name of such owner in his account of arrears of taxes. R. S., Sec. 43.

[832.] SEC. 50. The Township Treasurer shall retain in his hands the amount specified in his warrant to be paid into the Township Treasury, for the purposes therein specified, and shall, within one week after the time specified in his warrant for paying the money directed to be paid to the County Treasurer, pay to such County Treasurer the sum required in his warrant, either in delinquent taxes, or in funds then receivable by law. Moneys collected, how disposed of by Town Treasurer. R. S., Sec. 44.

[833.] SEC. 51. If any of the taxes mentioned in the tax list annexed to his warrant shall remain unpaid, and the Township Treasurer shall be unable to collect the same from the owner or occupant of the premises assessed, he shall make out a statement of the taxes so remaining unpaid and due, with a full and perfect description of such premises from his tax roll, and submit the same to the County Treasurer. Return of taxes not collected. R. S., Sec. 45.

[834. SEC. 52. The County Treasurer shall immediately compare such statement with the tax roll in the hands of such Township Treasurer, and if he finds it to be a true transcript from the same, he shall add to it a certificate, showing that he has examined and compared such statement with the tax roll in the hands of such Township Treasurer, and found it correct; and shall file such statement so certified in his office. Return to be compared with tax roll, etc. R. S., Sec. 46.

[835.] SEC. 53. Upon making an affidavit to be annexed to such statement before the County Treasurer, or his deputy, duly appointed, or before any officer authorized to administer oaths, that the sums mentioned in such statement remain unpaid, and that he has not, upon diligent inquiry, been able to discover any goods or chattels belonging to the person charged with or liable to pay such sums, whereupon he could levy the same, the Township Treasurer shall be credited by the County Treasurer with the amount thereof, and for making the return aforesaid, he shall be entitled to recover [receive] one dollar and fifty cents, and six cents per mile, travelling fee one way, to be allowed and paid to him by the County Treasurer, together with two per cent. on all taxes returned as delinquent; but no such Treasurer shall be allowed more than ten dollars, including said two per cent., for making his return.[1] Affidavit of town treasurer at time of making return. 1858, Act 32, p. 176. Compensation for making return.

Form of Affidavit of Township Treasurer to Statement on Return of Tax List.

STATE of MICHIGAN, } ss.
Ionia County. }

A. B., Township Treasurer of the Township of *Sebewa*, in the county aforesaid, being duly sworn, doth depose and say, that the sums mentioned in the annexed statement remain unpaid, and that he has not, upon diligent inquiry,

Receipt to be given, Township credited, etc.

1850, p. 161.

[836.] SEC. 54. The County Treasurer shall give to the Township Treasurer a receipt, stating the amount of taxes returned by such Township Treasurer unpaid, and for which the township shall receive a credit on the books of the County Treasurer; and shall also give such Township Treasurer a statement of all taxes rejected by such County Treasurer out of such list; which receipt and statement shall be the vouchers of such Township Treasurer for the amounts therein specified.

Endorsement of satisfaction on bond; tax roll and warrant to be deposited with County Treasurer.

R. S., Sec. 48.

[837.] SEC. 55. Upon the settlement of the amount of taxes directed to be collected by the Township Treasurer and paid to the County Treasurer, such County Treasurer shall endorse the bond of the Township Treasurer as paid up; which endorsement shall operate as a full discharge of the Treasurer and his sureties from the obligation thereof, unless it shall afterwards appear that the return of such Treasurer is false; in which case such bond shall continue in force, and such Treasurer and his sureties shall be liable thereon for all damages occasioned by such false return; and the Township Treasurer shall immediately deposit his tax roll and warrant with the County Treasurer, who shall file and preserve the same in his office.

When Township Board shall appoint Treasurer, and proceedings thereupon.

R. S.. Sec. 49.

[838.] SEC. 56. In case the Treasurer of any township shall refuse to serve, or shall die, resign, or remove out of the township before he shall have entered upon, or completed the duties of his office, or be disabled from completing the same from any cause, the Township Board shall forthwith appoint a Treasurer for the remainder of the year, who shall give like security, and be subject to like duties and penalties, and have the same powers and compensation as the Treasurer in whose place he was appointed; and the Township Clerk shall immediately give notice of such appointment to the County Treasurer; but such appointment shall not exonerate the former Treasurer or his sureties from any liability incurred by him or them.

Moneys retained by Township Treasurer, in what order to be paid.

R. S., Sec. 50.

[839.] SEC. 57. In case the Township Treasurer shall not collect the full amount of taxes required by his warrant to be paid into the Township Treasury, such portion thereof as he shall collect shall be retained by him, and paid out for the following purposes, and in the following order, viz.:

1. The amount raised for the general township purposes, to be paid on the order of the Township Board;

2. The amount raised for school and library taxes, to be paid on the order of the School Inspectors, or school district officers, as the case may be;

3. The amount of the highway taxes, to be paid on the order of the Commissioner of Highways.

---

been able to discover any goods or chattels, belonging to the persons charged with or liable to pay such sums, whereupon he could levy the same.

A. B,

Subscribed and sworn to before me this —— day of —— A. D. 18—.

C. D., *County Treasurer.*

[840.] SEC. 58. At the time of paying over the moneys collected to the County Treasurer, pursuant to the provisions of this chapter, the Township Treasurer shall make out, under oath, a statement of all moneys collected by him on account of taxes, and deliver such statement to the County Treasurer, who shall file and preserve the same in his office.[1]

Township Treasurer to make oath to statement of taxes collected. R. S., Sec. 51. Tweed v. Metcalf; 4 Mich. Rep.

[841.] SEC. 59. The Township Treasurer shall receive, not to exceed four nor less than two per cent. on the amount collected, which he shall retain out of the moneys collected by him; and in case of a distress and sale of goods or chattels for the payment of any tax, the Treasurer may also collect, on such sale, one dollar and twenty-five cents over and above the tax, as his fees for making such sale; which per centage and fees shall be in full for his services in collecting such taxes; and said Treasurer shall account to the Township Board for the per cent. added for collection expenses on all non-resident lands returned to the County Treasurer.

Compensation of Treasurer for collecting taxes.

R. S., Sec. 52. 1849, p. 116.

[842.] SEC. 60. In case the Township Treasurer shall neglect or refuse to file his bond with the County Treasurer in the manner and within the time prescribed by law, and the Township Board shall fail to appoint a Treasurer who shall give such bond, and deliver a receipt for the same to the Supervisor by the tenth day of November, the Supervisor shall deliver the tax roll and warrant to the Sheriff of the county, to be executed by himself, or his deputy, who shall execute to the County Treasurer a like bond as is required of the Township Treasurers, and make like collection and returns, and shall be entitled to the same compensation allowed to the Township Treasurers, on all taxes so handed over to him for collection; and, for the purposes of collecting the same, shall be vested with all the powers conferred upon the Township Treasurer.

When Supervisor to deliver tax roll and warrant to Sheriff, and powers and duties of Sheriff thereon.

R. S., Sec. 52.

[843.] SEC. 61. The Township Treasurer, or other collecting officer, on receipt of any tax, shall give a receipt for the same, and shall note on his tax roll the payment thereof; and if any such treasurer or other collecting officer shall wilfully return to the County Treasurer as unpaid any taxes which have been paid to him, except when the same have been duly assessed, he shall be deemed guilty of a misdemeanor, and shall, on conviction thereof, be punished by imprisonment in the county jail not exceeding one year, or by fine not exceeding five hundred dollars, or both, in the discretion of the court, and be liable, together with the surety in his bond, to any person injured by such false return to the full amount of any loss sustained thereby.

Collecting officer to give receipt on payment of taxes

1858, Act 32, p. 176.

[844.] SEC. 62. If any Township Treasurer, ward collector, or other collecting officer in the city shall neglect or refuse to pay to the County Treasurer the sums required by his warrant,

Duty of County Treasurer.

[1] The failure of the Collector to make a statement, under oath, of all moneys received by him as Collector, under Section 41, page 71, Act 1843, does not render the proceedings to sell void; such oath is required to secure an accurate accounting of all the moneys in the Collector's hands, and has no reference to the return of lands for delinqent taxes.—*Tweed v. Metcalf*, 4 *Mich.* 579.

R. S., Sec. 55.

or to account for the same as unpaid, as required by law, the County Treasurer shall, within ten days after the time when such payment ought to have been made, issue a warrant under his hand, directed to the Sheriff of the county, commanding him to levy such sum as shall remain unpaid and unaccounted for, together with his fees for collecting the same, of the goods and chattels, lands and tenements of such Township Treasurer, ward collector, or other collecting officer, and their sureties, and to pay the said sums to such County Treasurer, and return such warrant, within forty days from the date thereof.

Warrant to be delivered to and executed by the Sheriff of the county. R. S., Sec. 56.

[845.] SEC. 63. The County Treasurer shall forthwith deliver such warrant to the sheriff of his county, who shall immediately cause the same to be executed, and shall make return thereof to the County Treasurer within the time specified for the return thereof, and pay to such Treasurer the amount required by such warrant; and such sheriff shall be entitled to collect and receive the same fees as are allowed by law to the sheriffs on executions.

Proceedings against Sheriff for neglect or false returns. R. S., Sec. 57.

[846.] SEC. 64. If any sheriff shall neglect to return any such warrant, or to pay the money collected thereon, within the time limited for the return of such warrant, or shall make a false return thereto, the County Treasurer shall proceed by attachment in the Supreme Court, or any other court of competent jurisdiction, against such sheriff, to collect the whole sum directed to be levied by such warrant, in the same manner and with like effect as for neglecting to return an execution in a civil suit, and the proceedings thereon shall be the same in all respects.

When County Treasurer to prosecute Sheriff and his sureties. R. S., Sec. 58.

[847.] SEC. 65. In case the County Treasurer shall fail to collect such moneys by attachment, he shall forthwith cause a prosecution to be had against the sheriff and his sureties for the sum due on such warrant; which sum, when collected, shall be paid to the County Treasurer.

County Treasurer to enter return of lands delinquent for taxes, and make transcript, etc. R. S., Sec. 59.

[848.] SEC. 66. When any County Treasurer shall receive from a Township Treasurer a statement of unpaid taxes on the lands of residents or non-residents, verified according to law, such County Treasurer shall enter the same at length on the books in his office provided for the purpose, and he shall make a correct transcript thereof, which shall be compared by the County Clerk with the statement of the Township Treasurer; and if he finds it to be a true transcript thereof, he shall add to it a certificate that he examined and compared the same with the certified statement of the Township Treasurer, and found it correct.

Transcript to be forwarded to the Auditor General by the first of March following. R. S., Sec. 60.

[849.] SEC. 67. Such transcript, so made out, compared and certified, shall be forwarded by the County Treasurer to the Auditor General, by the first day of March next after the return of such statement; but such transcript shall be receivable at any time during said month of March.

[850.] SEC. 68. If the taxes on any real estate, assessed to a resident or owner thereof, shall be returned unpaid, the same proceedings shall be had thereon in all respects as in cases of lands assessed as non-resident, and with like effect.

Real estate assessed to residents; proceedings on return of.
1858, Act 32, p. 176.

[851.] SEC. 69. Any person may pay the taxes on any parcel of lands returned as aforesaid, or any undivided share thereof, with interest calculated thereon, from the first day of February next after the same were assessed, at the rate of fifteen per cent. per annum, and the office charges, to the Treasurer of the county in which the lands are situated, at any time before they are sold for taxes, or to the State Treasurer, on the certificate of the Auditor General, at any time before the first day of September next preceding the time appointed for such sale.

Payment of taxes after return.
R. S., Sec. 62.

[852.] SEC. 70. The County Treasurer and Auditor General shall add, for office charges upon each certificate containing one description, twenty-five cents, and for each additional description, in the same certificate, six cents; and the amount received by the County Treasurers for charges, shall go into the County Treasuries, of which they shall keep an accurate account, and the amount received at the State Treasurer's office shall go into the State Treasury, to the credit of the general fund.

Office charges.
R. S., Sec. 63.

[853.] SEC. 71. The County Treasurers shall issue duplicate receipts for all taxes received by them, which shall not operate as a discharge of the taxes until countersigned by the County Clerk, and one of said duplicates shall be left with such clerk; but no additional charge shall be made for issuing duplicate receipts.

Duplicate receipts.
R. S., Sec. 64.

[854.] SEC. 72. The duplicates of such receipts shall be filed by the County Clerk, who shall make an entry of the amount for which every such receipt was given, with the name of the person paying such tax, in a book to be provided by him for that purpose, at the expense of the county; and shall, on the first Monday of each month, forward all receipts on file in his office to the Auditor General, in such manner as he may direct.

County Clerk to enter receipt, transmit duplicate, etc.
R. S., Sec. 65.

[855.] SEC. 73. Every County Treasuer, who shall have received into the Treasury of his county sufficient to make up the amount of taxes assessed for township and county purposes, shall make returns at least once in three months, to the State Treasurer, at such times, and in such manner as he shall direct, of the amount received by him for delinquent taxes, payable to such State Treasurer.

When County Treasurer to make return of moneys to State Treasurer.
R. S., Sec. 66.

[856.] SEC. 74. Until the several counties, which shall have remaining unpaid more delinquent taxes than the amount of the state tax for the year in which the same were assessed, shall have received the amount raised for township and county purposes, they shall be entitled to receive from the State Treasurer, at the close of each month, in specie, or its equivalent, the amount there received for delinquent county or township taxes returned from the several counties, until they shall have received the amounts assessed in such counties for other than State tax.

When County Treasurer to receive taxes paid to State Treasurer.
R. S., Sec. 67.

When County Treasurer to pay excess into State Treasury. [857.] SEC. 75. Immediately after the returns of the several Township Treasurers to the County Treasurers, in all cases where the amount collected shall exceed the amount raised for county and township purposes, the County Treasurer shall forthwith pay into the State Treasury the excess collected as aforesaid, R. S., Sec. 68. for which amount the said counties shall be credited on account of the State tax for the proper year.

OF THE SALE OF LANDS FOR TAXES, AND THE CONVEYANCE AND REDEMPTION THEREOF.

What lands to be subject to redemption and sale, and when to be sold. [858.] SEC. 76. All lands returned to the Auditor General, as provided by law, upon which the taxes, interest and charges shall not he paid, or be charged back to the proper county, shall be subject to sale and redemption, as hereinafter provided, and shall be sold in the same county from which they were returned, R. S., Sec. 69. or in which the lands were situtated at the time such taxes were assessed.

Statement to be made by Auditor General. [859.] SEC. 77. The Auditor General shall make out a separate statement of all such lands as the taxes shall remain due upon, in each of the respective counties; specifying the amount of taxes due upon each parcel, the interest thereon to the first Monday of October thereafter, together with the costs of advertising, postages, expense of sale, and returns thereof, and conveyances, calculated upon each description, by dividing such charges by the whole number of descriptions. And accompany- 1848, p. 257. ing, or preceding such statements, the Auditor General shall cause to be published in the respective counties, a list of all lands not sold by the several County Treasurers at the time prescribed by law, on account of error in advertising, or other cause not affecting the legality of the assessment, or requiring a rejection of the taxes thereon, and on which the taxes, interest and charges still remain unpaid, or not otherwise discharged, for the taxes of any year prior to that for which the statements above mentioned are made up; and deeds given by the Auditor General to purchasers at such sales, or their assigns, shall take effect according to the year's tax for which the deed may be given; the deed for the latest year's tax taking precedence; and the interest on such re-advertised lists shall be computed at the tame rate as in other cases, up to the time of the ensuing annual sax sales.

Auditor General to cause statement to be published. [860.] SEC. 78. The Auditor General shall cause each of such statements to be published in the conntу in which the lands therein described are situate, for eight weeks successively, next previous to the first Monday of October in each year (which shall be construed to mean eight publications, once a R. S. Sec. 72. week), in one newspaper, printed and published in such county, if there be one which shall have been established therein two months prior to the first day of July; and in case there is no such newspaper printed and published in the county, such statement shall be printed and published in an adjoining county, if there be such newspaper established therein for the period aforesaid; but if there is no such newspaper printed, or published in the same, or any adjoining county, such statement shall be printed and published in some other newspaper, to be designated by the Auditor General.[j]

When to be published in adjoining County.

[861.] SEC. 79. The newspapers in which such statements are to be published, shall be designated by the Auditor General, on or before the first day of July in each and every year, and not afterwards, unless the proprietor of any paper so designated shall neglect, or refuse to print and publish such statement, or unless from some other cause it shall become impracticable; in which case the Auditor General shall designate some other paper for that purpose, before the time limited for commencing the publication.[k]

Auditor General to designate paper, etc.

R. S., Sec. 72.

[862.] SEC. 80. The cost of printing and publishing such statement shall not exceed forty (40) cents for each description of land so advertised, and no printer shall be paid for publishing any such statement, who shall not forward to the Auditor General within twenty (20) days after the last publication thereof an affidavit made by some person to whom the facts are known, stating such publications, and also that he has transmitted to each County Treasurer, by mail, copies of the two first numbers of his paper containing such statement, immediately after their publication: *Provided, however*, That such statement shall he published in a newspaper in the county in which the sale takes place, if there be one; and if no newspaper be printed in such county, then such statement shall be published in an adjoining county, or in a newspaper published in the next nearest county to the county in which such sale takes place.

Cost of printing 1858, Act 32, p. 176.

Where statement to be published.

[863.] SEC. 81. The Auditor General shall annex to, and cause to be published with each of said statements, a notice that so much of each tract or parcel of land described in said statement as will be necessary for that purpose, will be sold by the County Treasurer on the first Monday of October next thereafter, at such public and convenient place at the seat of justice of the county, as the County Treasurer may select, for the payment of taxes, interest and charges thereon.[1]

Notice to be published with statement.

R. S., Sec, 74. Niles v. Walker 4 Mich. Rep.

[864.] SEC. 82. As soon after the first Monday of September as shall be practicable, the Auditor General shall prepare and transmit to the several County Treasurers, lists of all lands described in the respective statements, on which the taxes, interest and charges shall have been paid; which lands, together with all the lands whereon the taxes, interest and charges shall

Lists of lands to be withheld to be transmitted by Auditor General to County Treasurer, etc.

---

[j] As amended by "An Act to amend an Act, entitled, 'An Act to provide for Assessing Property at its true value, and for Levying and Collecting Taxes thereon,' approved February 14, 1853." Approved Februry, 12, 1855. Laws of 1855, p. 278.

[k] As amended by the Act of February 12, 1855. See last note.

1 A written notice by the County Treasurer of the place of sale of lands delinquent for taxes, posted in three public places in the town where the sale is to be, about ten days before the time of sale, is insufficient, and renders the sale void.—*Miles v. Walker*, 4 *Mich.* 631.

R. S., Sec. 75. have been paid to the County Treasurer before the sale, shall be struck from the statement of lands advertised to be sold by the respective County Treasurers, and shall be withheld from sale.

Sale how made. [865.] SEC. 83. On the day designated in the notice of sale, the several County Treasurers, under the direction of the Auditor General, shall commence the sale of those lands on which R. S., Sec. 76. 2 Mich. Rep. 192. the taxes shall not have been paid as aforesaid, and shall continue the same from day to day (Sundays excepted), until so much of each parcel thereof shall be sold as shall be sufficient to pay the taxes, interest and charges thereon: *Provided*, That every description of land embraced in said notice, which has been bid off to the State at a previous sale, and which remains unredeemed, or otherwise disposed of, shall be bid off to the State by said County Treasurers.[1]

Where land taken when part of lot only is sold. [866.] SEC. 84. In case less than the whole of any parcel, described in the statements aforesaid, shall be sold for the taxes, interest and charges thereon, the portion thereof sold shall be taken from the north side, or north end of such parcel, and shall R. S., Sec. 77. be bounded on the south by a line running parallel with northerly line thereof, unless the same be an irregular fraction; in which case the portion thereof so sold, shall be bounded on the south by a line running due east and west.

Payment of bids, when to be made, etc. R. S., Sec. 78. [867.] SEC. 85. The County Treasurers may, in their discretion, require immediate payment of any person to whom any parcel of such land shall be struck off; and in all cases where payment is not made in twenty-four hours, he may declare the bid canceled, and, at his discretion, sell the lands again; and any person so neglecting, or refusing to pay any bid made by him, shall not be entitled, after such neglect, to have any bid made by him received by the Treasurer during such sale.

Funds receivable at sales. [868.] SEC. 86. The several County Treasurers shall receive, on such sales, such funds only as shall, at the time, be receivable R. S., Sec. 79. by law at the State Treasury on account of the general and delinquent tax funds; and so much as may be necessary to pay for printing, and charges of sales, shall be paid in specie, or its equivalent.

Notice of am'nt to be paid in specie; State Treasurer to direct remittances, etc. R. S., Sec. 80. [869.] SEC. 87. The State Treasurer shall notify the County Treasurers what amount must be paid in specie, or its equivalent; and the remittance of all moneys received at tax sales shall be made as directed by the State Treasurer; and the expenses of advertising and sale shall be paid therefrom on the Auditor General's warrant, and the remainder shall be placed to the credit of the general fund, as received.

Certificate of sale, etc. [870. SEC. 88. At the sale aforesaid the respective County Treasurers shall give to the purchasers, on the payment of their

1 A County Treasurer having charge of the sale of lands for delinquent taxes, became the purchaser of certain premises at said sale; the purchase by him was declared void. It was held also that his purchase being a nullity, he could not be allowed for improvements made by him on the property.—*Clute et al. v. Barron*, 2 *Mich.* 192.

bids, a certificate in writing, describing the lands purchased, and the amount paid therefor, and such certificate shall be regularly numbered and a copy of each forwarded by the County Treasurers to the Auditor General in such manner as he shall direct. 1858, Act 32, p. 176.

Deed to purchaser.

[871.] SEC. 89. On presentation of such certificate of sale to the Auditor General after the expiration of the time provided by law for the redemption of land sold as aforesaid, he shall execute to the purchaser, his heirs, or assigns, a deed of the land therein described, unless he shall have discovered that the taxes for which said lands were sold had been paid according to law, which deed shall be *prima facie* evidence of the regularity of all the proceedings from the valuation of the lands by the assessors to the date of the deed inclusive, and of title (in fee) in the purchaser, and every such deed when witnessed and acknowledged in the manner prescribed by law for witnessing and acknowledging deeds in other cases, and after it shall have been on record two years in the office of the register of deeds of the county in which the lands therein described are situated shall except:

First. When the same shall be annulled according to law;

Second. When the land sold was not subject to taxation at the date of the assessment of the taxes for which it was sold;

---

1 The Auditor General cannot assume the power to convey lands sold for taxes on forfeiture, unless it is expressly conferred upon him by statute. But section 76 of the act relating to taxes (*Session Laws*, 1843, *page* 683), providing that lands returned for the taxes of 1841 shall be sold at the same time and in the same manner as provided in said act for the taxes of 1843, "And in all respects with *like effect.*" Taken in connection with sections 64 and 65 of said act, expressly confer upon the Auditor the power to execute deeds to purchasers, at tax sales of and for delinquent taxes of 1841.—*Sibley v. Smith*, 2 *Mich.* 487.

The last clause of Section sixty-five of the act of 1843, page 80, which declares that the "Deed shall be *prima facie* evidence of the regularity of all proceedings to the date of the deed," relieves the purchaser having the deed from proving as facts, the proceedings required by statute before the sale, and abrogates the common law rule of strict-construction, otherwise applicable to such cases.—*Ibid.*

The Auditor's deed need not recite the proceedings prior to the sale. The recitals need show no more than the capacity in which the Auditor acts. Under the laws of 1842 and 1843 there is no limitation of the quantity to be sold, for the taxes of a given parcel.—*Ibid.*

To obviate the effect of the law, making the tax deed *prima facie* evidence of the regularity of all proceedings up to its date, such evidence must be produced by the party objecting as will exclude any reasonable presumption of regularity. There must be must be such evidence of irregularity as to require explanation. The evidence must be of matters presumptory and not directory. Some specific defect, the insufficiency of some particular act, or the non-performance of some requisite duty must be shown.—*Lacy v. Davis*, 4 *Mich.* 140.

By the act of 1843 (*Sess. Laws* 1843, *p.* 79) sales for taxes were to commence on the first Monday of October, and continue from day to day (Sundays excepted), until, &c. The Auditor's deed recited the sale of a parcel of land to have been made on the 11th of October; but this was held no evidence to invalidate the sale, and that it was incumbent on the party objecting to the deed to show a non-compliance with the statute. One in possession of land claiming title can acquire no additional interest by suffering the land to be sold for taxes, and becoming the purchaser, if such taxes were a lien upon the land at the time of his taking possession; and it is immaterial whether the land was assessed to the occupant or to one having title, or claim of title, or as non-resident.—*Lacy v. Davis*, 4 *Mich.* 140.

Although it is not competent for one to acquire a cumulative title to lands by allowing them to be sold for delinquent taxes after he has taken possession of them, by virtue of a tax deed, he may bid upon the same lands at a tax sale before the time of redemption unless his former purchase has expired, and to have the benefit of such bid.—*Tweed v. Metcalf*, 4 *Mich.* 579.

To entitle a tax deed given in 1838, to be received as evidence of title, the regularity of the proceedings prior to the tax sale must be shown.—*Ives v. Kimball*, 1 *Mich.* 308.

Third. When the taxes have been paid to the proper officer within the time limited by law for the payment or redemption there; or

Fourth. When a certificate that no taxes were charged against the land has been given by the proper officer within the time limited by law for the payment or redemption thereof;

Be positive evidence that the lands therein described were by such deed conveyed in fee simple to the grantee therein named, and his heirs and assigns, and no suit of ejectment shall be commenced to recover said lands, or title thereto, sustained thereafter by any person claiming or holding possession or title through any other source.

Loss of Certificate.

1847, p. 121, Sec.

[872.] SEC. 90. In case of the loss of such certificate of sale, the purchaser, or his legal representative, as assignee, may file his affidavit of such loss, and that he was, at the time of such loss, the *bona fide* and legal owner thereof; and the Auditor General shall thereupon execute, as aforesaid, a deed for the lands described in such certificate, in the same manner as though it had been presented and surrendered. Any person who shall make an affidavit as above required, or concerning any other matter which may be filed in the office of the Auditor General, shall be liable to the penalties of perjury for any false statement made in such affidavit, with intent to defraud, upon conviction thereof, before a Court having jurisdiction of the offence.

How lands may be redeemed from sale.

1858, Act 32, p. 176.

[873.] SEC. 91. Any person owning any of the lands, sold as aforesaid, or any interest therein, may, at any time within one year next succeeding such sale, redeem any parcel of said lands, or any part or interest in said lands, by showing to the satisfaction of the Auditor General or County Treasurer that he owns only that part or interest in the same which he proposes to redeem, and by paying at his option, into the State Treasury, or to the Treasurer of the county where such land is situated, the amount for which such parcel was sold, or such portion thereof as the part or interest redeemed shall amount to, with interest thereon at the rate of twenty-five per cent. per annum; of which interest twenty per cent. shall be paid by the State Treasurer to the purchaser, and five per cent. shall belong to the State and be passed to the credit of the general fund.

Interest how computed.

R. S., Sec. 84.

[874.] Sec. 92. When any land shall be redeemed as provided in the preceding section, the interest shall, in all cases, be computed from the day of sale up to the end of the current quarter of the year limited for such redemption.

Duplicate certificates of Redemption to be issued, etc.

1847, p. 121.

[875.] SEC. 93. Upon the payment of the redemption money and interest to the County Treasurer, as aforesaid, he shall issue duplicate certificates of redemption, in the usual form, both of which certificates shall be countersigned by the County Clerk, who shall make an entry of the number of each certificate, the amount for which it was given, and the name of the person paying the same; one of which certificates shall be delivered to the person making the payment, and the other shall be transmitted by the County Clerk to the Auditor General, on the first Monday in each month, in the same manner as is now required for the transmission of duplicate receipts.

[876.] SEC. 94. The total amount of such redemption certificate shall be charged by the Auditor General to the county returning the same, if the amount shall be found by the books of his office to be due such county; and if not thus due, then the said amount shall be deposited in the State Treasury by the County Treasurer, at such times as the Auditor General shall require; and if the said County Treasurer shall refnse or neglect for thirty days after such requirement to pay over, or deposit the amount as aforesaid, he shall be subject to a prosecution by the Auditor General, under the provisions of the thirty-sixth section, chapter one hundred and fifty-four of the Revised Statutes of one thousand eight hundred and forty-six; and upon conviction, shall be punished as therein mentioned.

Auditor General to charge County with amount of Certificate, etc.

1847, p. 122.

[877.] SEC. 95. Every County Treasurer shall, on or before the first day of June next succeeding his election, execute to the Auditor General a bond in such sum as the said Auditor shall direct, with three or more sureties, to be approved of by the Prosecuting Attorney, *County Judge*, or Circuit Court Commissioners, of the proper county, and the said Auditor, conditioned that such Treasurer, his deputy, and all persons employed in his office, shall render a just and true account of all moneys received by him, or them, for sales of lands at the annual tax sales, and for redemption thereof, and all other money which may otherwise come into his or their hands, belonging to the State, and that he or they shall faithfully and promptly pay to the State Treasurer all such moneys received as aforesaid, whenever required so to do by the Auditor General; which bond shall be filed in the office of said Auditor.

County Treasurer to execute Bond to Auditor General.

1847, p, 122.

[878.] SEC. 96. In case the said County Treasurer shall refuse, or neglect to execute and file such bond at the time, and in the manner aforesaid, the Auditor General shall employ, in behalf of the State, some other person to conduct the annual sales of lands delinquent for taxes, and to receive payment therefor under his direction, any law to the contrary notwithstanding; upon such person executing and filing with the said Auditor a similar bond, with sureties as above mentioned, to be by him approved, conditioned for the faithful and prompt payment to the State Treasurer of all moneys which may come into his hands, as the proceeds of such sale or otherwise, belonging to the State, whenever required so to do by the Auditor General as aforesaid; and a reasonable compensation for the services of such person shall be allowed, and paid out of said proceeds.

In case County Treasurer neglects to file bond Auditor General may employ some other person to conduct sales.

1847, p. 122.

[879.] SEC. 97. If any parcel of land can not be sold to any person for the taxes, interest and charges, such parcel shall be passed over for the time being, and shall, on the succeeding day, or before the close of the sale, be re-offered; and if, on such second offer, or during such sales, the same can not be sold for

When lands to be re-offered for sale, and when bid in for the State.

R. S., Sec. 85. the amount aforesaid, the County Treasuer shall bid off the same for the State.

Lands bid off to the State liable to taxation. R. S., Sec. 86. [880.] SEC. 98. All lands bid off for the State, as provided in the last preceding section, shall continue liable to be taxed, in the same manner as if they were not the property of the State, and such taxes shall be a charge upon such lands.

Proceedings in case of irregularity. 1858, Act 32, p. 176. [881.] SEC. 99. If the Auditor General shall discover before the sale, or before the conveyance of any lands, as aforesaid, that the same were not subject to taxation at the date of the assessment of the taxes, or that the taxes have been paid, he shall forbear to cause the same to be sold, or withhold a conveyance after sale, as the case may be; and in such case, if a sale has been made, he shall, on demand, cause the money paid therefor to be refunded, with seven per cent. interest thereon.

When amount refunded to be charged against County. R. S., Sec. 88. [882.] SEC. 100. If such errors originated with the county or township officers, the amount so refunded shall be charged against the county from which the tax was returned, and the Supervisors of such county shall cause the same to be refunded to the State Treasury.

Ibid. Persons interested may take proofs before a circuit court commissioner. [883.] SEC. 101. Any person having an interest in any lands sold as aforesaid by the Auditor General, other than such as hold or claim to hold under a tax title, whether in his own right, or in trust, or as executor, administrator, guardian or trustee, may at any time within two years from the date of the deed, and in cases of sales at any time heretofore made, within two years from the time this act shall take effect, and not after that period, present a petition to a circuit court commissioner of the county in which the land or a part thereof is situated, setting forth that the taxes have been paid, or that he had [has] good ground to believe, and does believe, that there are irregularities in the assessment or other proceedings, affecting the rights of such party in interest, and especially setting forth each and all the objections and alleged errors on which he relies, and the names and residences of all persons having any interest in the lands under the tax sale and deed, which petition shall be verified by the affidavit of the person presenting the same, or by his agent or attorney, to be attached to such petition: *Provided*, That he may present such petition at any time:

1st. When the land sold was not subject to taxation at the date of the assessment of the taxes for which it was sold;

2d. When the taxes have been paid to the proper officer within the time limited by law for the payment or redemption thereof;

3d. When a certificate that no taxes were charged against the land has been given by the proper officer, within the time limited by law for the payment or redemption thereof.

On the presentation of such petition, such commissioner shall make and endorse thereon an order for receiving evidence, and for taking examination of witnesses on the part of the parties to said petition, before him, in the matter of said petition; and shall in said order fix the time, not less than twenty days from the presentation of the petition, and the place in his county when and where he will proceed to take such evidence or examination of witnesses. A copy of such petition, affidavit and order, shall be served upon the person or persons holding such tax title, or claiming any interest therein in law or equity, if residing in in the county and in the same manner prescribed for the service of a summons from the circuit court, at least twenty days before the commissioner shall take such evidence or examination. If such person or persons reside in any other county in this State, the commissioner shall allow such further reasonable time for making such service, and the appearance of such parties, as shall be just; and after the first time fixed for the hearing, the commissioner shall, upon the application of any party to the petition, and upon good cause shown, continue the hearing from time to time for the purpose of taking the evidence. In case any party entitled to such service is not a resident of this State, and can not be served as aforesaid, on filing an affidavit of that fact with the commissioner, the petitioner shall be entitled to an order of the commissioner for the appearance of such party, such as is or may be authorized by law for the appearance of such parties in suits in chancery in the circuit courts, which order shall be published as required by law in such suits; or in case of failure of appearance in accordance with such order, the commissioner may proceed *ex parte* to take the evidence and examination, and the same shall be binding on the parties failing to appear. All statutes and rules of the circuit court sitting in chancery, in force during the pending of such petition before the commissioner touching infants and persons under guardianship, as parties to a suit, shall, so far as may be, apply to the proceedings before the commissioner, and he shall apply the same. The commissioner shall have power to administer oaths to all such witnesses, who may be examined and cross-examined, and who shall subscribe to their respective depositions; and the commissioner may take all affidavits requisite in the matter, and may issue subpœnas, which may be served on witnesses in any part of the State. And when the evidence and the examination of witnesses shall be completed, the commissioner shall certify them; [and,] thereupon, and within four days thereafter, render his decision thereon, and within ten days after the rendition of said decision or judgment, either party, or any person interested in such proceeding, may appeal therefrom to the circuit court for the county in which such proceedings may be had, by giving notice in writing of his intention to appeal, and such commissioner shall within ten days after receiving notice of such appeal, file the petition, certified copies of all his orders, the originals of all proof of service and depositions taken by him, together with his decision, in the office of the clerk of the circuit court of his county, and shall in his return set forth, briefly, all objections taken before him, to any portion of the evidence, to the competency thereof,

Petition and mode of proceeding thereon.

Commissioner shall enter his decision.

Party aggrieved may appeal to circuit court.

or to any order made by him. And upon such filing, the circuit court shall have jurisdiction of the matter, and full power and authority to determine all questions of law or fact therein, and to render judgment annulling or affirming the title in controversy, which judgment shall be rendered and recorded like other judgments in said court, subject to be reviewed on writ of *certiorari*, by the supreme court, at any time within two years: *Provided, however*, That on the application of any party to said petition, to the circuit court, he or they shall be entitled to have any issue of fact arising in the matter, tried by a jury, in which case the court shall, by order, cause the issue to be made up and tried, as in other cases of trial of issues of fact.

Clerk of the circuit court to deliver certified copy of judgment. 1858. Act 32, p. 176.

[884.] SEC. 102. Whenever any judge of the circuit court shall have annulled, for any of the reasons enumerated in the preceding section, the title to any description of land conveyed in any deed executed by the Auditor General, as aforesaid, or any part thereof, the clerk of the circuit court of the county in which the land is situated, shall, on application of either party, and payment of fifty cents, make and deliver to such party, a certified copy of such judgment. And whenever such copy of judgment shall be presented to the register of deeds of said county, where said deed shall have been recorded, the register shall record the same, and make a short written memorandum on the margin or face of the deed of the description of the land, and that the title has been annulled or affirmed, as the case may be, and the date of the judgment, and of the recording thereof.

Register to record, etc.

Auditor General to certify to County Treasurer. 1858, Act 32, p. 176.

[885.] SEC. 103. In all cases where lands sold for taxes have been conveyed by deed, and the title has been annulled pursuant to law, the Auditor General shall, on presentation of a copy of the judgment annulling the same, refund to the holder of said title the purchase money and interest thereon, as the law requires, and certify the fact to the proper County Treasurer.

Money to be refunded to State. State not liable for costs. R. S., Sec. 90.

[886.] SEC. 104. Such money, when paid by the State Treasurer, shall be refunded to the State Treasury by the proper county; and in any action of ejectment brought by the owner to recover such lands, the State shall not be liable to costs.

Accounts of County Treasurers to be stated by Auditor General. R. S., Sec. 91.

[887.] SEC. 105. The Auditor General shall state the account of the several County Treasurers, on the first day of July in each year, allowing to the several counties ten per cent. interest on such portions of the taxes unpaid on the first day of February in the same year as shall belong to them for township and county purposes, and shall transmit a copy thereof by mail, or otherwise, to the County Clerk, who shall lay the same before the Board of Supervisors at their first meeting after the receipt of the same.

OF REJECTION AND ASSESSMENT.

When tax rejected, etc., Supervisor to reassess the same.

[888.] SEC. 106. Whenever the County Treasurer shall be notified by the Auditor General, or shall otherwise become satisfied that any tax has been paid to the Township Treasurer, or that there was a double assessment upon any lands, or that any parcel is so erroneously or defectively described that it can not be sold, he shall deliver to the Board of Supervisors an accurate statement thereof; and the said board shall cause the same to be re-assessed upon the same land in the next year's tax, or raise the amount upon the proper township, or otherwise correct such errors, as they shall consider just.[1]

R. S., Sec. 92.

How rejected taxes, etc., to be charged back. R. S., Sec. 92.

[889.] SEC. 107. The Auditor General is authorized and required, in all cases where taxes upon lands returned delinquent to his office shall be rejected for any cause, or having been credited, shall be charged back on the books of his office, to charge the same over to the county from which such taxes were returned, unless the lands upon which the same same were assessed, shall have been set off to some other county, or attached to some other county for judicial purposes; and in case such lands shall have been so set off or attached, they shall be charged to the county to which they may belong at the time of such rejection.

Supervisors to furnish list of land detached from County on which Taxes are charged back. R. S., Sec. 94.

[890.] SEC. 108. It shall be the duty of the Board of Supervisors to furnish to the Auditor General a list of all taxes which shall have been rejected or charged back to their county by him, upon lands which shall have been detached from such county subsequent to the time when such taxes were assessed, and the Auditor General shall thereupon credit to such county the amount which he may have so charged back, and charge the same to the county in which such lands may be then situated, provided such taxes shall not have been previously paid or re-assessed.

Auditor General to forward to County Treasurer a description of lands, etc. R. S., Sec. 95.

[891.] SEC. 109. The Auditor General, immediately after ascertaining the amount of taxes, interest and charges, due upon any lands which may have been, or may hereafter be rejected or charged back as hereinbefore provided, shall forward to the Treasurer of the county in which such lands shall then be situated, or to which they may be attached, a description of such lands, together with a statement of the amount of taxes, interest and charges thereon, and specifying for what year or years such taxes were originally assessed.

County Treasurer to lay statement before Board of Supervisors. 1858, Act 32, p. 176.

[892.] SEC. 110. The County Trersurer receiving such certificate of Auditor General, shall lay the same before the Board of Supervisors at their next session thereafter, and if such taxes shall have been rejected or charged back by the Auditor General for any error or informality, excepting an insufficient description of the land, or for the reason that it was not subject to taxation, the Board of Supervisors shall cause the same to be re-assessed upon the same land, and collected with the taxes of the then current year, and in the same manner.

---

[1] Where an amount was re-assessed upon a township on error on account of the assessment of the previous year, the board having authority to re-assess, under the assessment law of 1845, such re-assessments will be good in legal presumption until some error is shown.—*Tweed v. Metcalf*, 4 *Mich.* 579.

Proceedings when tax cannot be properly re-assessed on same lands. R. S., Sec. 97.

[893.] SEC. 111. If such taxes can not be properly re-assessed upon the same lands, the Board of Supervisors shall cause the same, or any part thereof to be re-assessed upon the taxable property of the proper township, as may appear equitable.

Proceedings when tax exceeds limits fixed by law. R. S., Sec. 98.

[894.] SEC. 112. Whenever the Auditor General shall have rejected any State, county, or township tax, for the reason that the amount assessed for any such purpose exceeds the limitation established by law, the County Treasurer of the county in which the lands so assessed shall be situated shall make out and present to the Board of Supervisor thereof, at their next session, a list of the lands, with the taxes assessed, and the interest accrued thereon.

Ibid. R. S., Sec. 99.

[895.] SEC. 113. The Board of Supervisors shall cause so much of said taxes as shall remain unpaid, and as shall not exceed the limit fixed by law, for the year in which they were originally assessed, to be re-assessed upon the same lands, if they can legally do so, and collected with, and in the same manner as the taxes for the year in which the same shall be re-assessed as aforesaid.

Ibid. R. S., Sec. 100.

[896.] SEC. 114. If any such taxes cannot be properly re-assessed upon the same lands, the Board of supervisors shall cause the same, or any part thereof, under the limitations aforesaid, to be assessed upon the taxable property of the proper township, as may appear equitable.

Taxes assessed on Village property, rejected for informality to be re-assessed. 1848, p. 75.

[897.] SEC. 115. All taxes assessed on any lot or block, or any part thereof, in a town or village, or addition thereto, which have been rejected subsequent to the first day of January, eighteen hundred and forty-seven, or which may hereafter be rejected on account of any informality or defect in the execution, filing, acknowledgment, or recording of the plat of said town or village, or any addition thereto, the Board of Supervisors of the respective counties may cause the same to be re-assessed by the same lots or blocks, or parts thereof, which are respectively chargeable with said taxes, as provided by law in other cases of re-assessments, excepting such lots, or parts of lots, as have been sold since the rejection of said taxes; and all the provisions of law concerning the assessment, collection, and return of taxes, and of the sale of the lands chargeable therewith, shall be applicable to the re-assessments made as aforesaid, and to the sales of the lands delinquent in the payment thereof.

Liability of Collector, who has received tax returned unpaid.

[898.] SEC. 116. If at any time it shall be discovered that the Treasurer of any township has received the tax assessed upon property which he has returned delinquent, the Supervisor shall have power, and he is hereby required to collect the same, in the name of his township, from such Treasurer, or his sureties, together with interest and charges.

OF LANDS BID OFF TO THE STATE FOR TAXES; THEIR REDEMPTION AND SALE.

[899.] SEC. 117. All lands heretofore bid off, or that may hereafter be bid off to the State, for taxes, which have not been redeemed, or otherwise discharged, shall be offered for sale at the annual tax sales in October in each year.

Lands bid off to the State to be offered at October sales.

[900.] SEC. 118. The Auditor General shall furnish to each of the County Treasurers, in the month of August in each and every year, a full and accurate statement of all the lands in his county that may have been bid in for the State, remaining unredeemed, or not otherwise discharged.

Auditor General to furnish statements to County Treasurers. 1847, p. 124.

[901.] SEC. 119. Such statement shall exhibit the aggregate amount of all sums due to the State on each description of land, including interest thereon at the rate of twenty-five per cent. per annum, from the time the lands were bid in by the State, to the first Monday in October in the year in which they shall be first offered as State tax lands, as contemplated in the preceding section: *Provided*, That on all State tax lands, which have, or should have been once previously offered at public sales, and which, remaining unsold, are again to be offered as above, there shall be charged upon the amount for which each description thereof has, or should have been so offered, interest at the rate of ten per cent. per annum, from the time when they were so, or should have been so first offered, to the said first Monday of October.

Contents of statements; interest, etc. 1847, p. 124.

[902.] SEC. 120. The Auditor General shall cause to be published for eight weeks successively (which shall be construed to mean eight publications, once a week), next previous to the first Monday of October in each year, a notice that the lands described in such statement will be sold at public auction by the Treasurer of the county in which such lands are situated, at the time and place designated for the ordinary tax sales, under the direction of the Auditor General.

Notice of sale. 1847, p. 124.

[903.] SEC. 121. At the time designated in the notice, and immediately previous to the sale of other lands advertised to be sold for taxes at the same time, such County Treasurer shall commence the sale at the place designated, and continue the same from day to day, if necessary (Sunday's excepted), until he has offered all the lands embraced in his list which have not been redeemed, or otherwise discharged; and he may re-offer and sell any parcel, when a bidder shall refuse to pay his bid for twenty-four hours after the lists have been gone through, or he may, in his discretion, demand immediate payment; and if not paid, cancel the bid and re-offer the lands.

Time and manner of sale. Lacy v. Davis, 4 Mich. Rep.

[904.] SEC. 122. In all cases when a description of land is offered as State tax land, and the same description, or any part thereof, shall be offered in the regular list of land delinquent for taxes, as provided in section eighty-three of this act, it shall be the duty of the County Treasurer to inform the person bid-

Purchaser must buy for subsequent year, etc.

ding for the description offered as State tax lands of the fact, and such person shall be required to purchase the description so offered in the regular list, at the same time the description offered as State tax land is bid off by him; and in case of his neglect or refusal so to do, the Treasurer shall withhold said description of State tax land from sale; but may re-offer the same as provided in the next preceding section.

County Treasurer to issue certificate of sale.

[905.] SEC. 123. The County Treasurer shall, on payment of the purchase money at such sale, issue certificates of sale to the purchasers, in such form, and make such returns to the Auditor General, as shall be prescribed by him, and shall also transmit the moneys received on such sale to the State Treasurer, in such manner as he shall have directed.

Auditor General to execute deed for State tax land.

1858, Act 32, p. 176.

[906.] SEC. 124. The Auditor General shall, on the presentation and surrender of the State tax land certificate of sale at his office, or as soon thereafter as may be, (except in cases where the land has been previously sold at the Auditor General's office, or redeemed, when the purchase money only shall be refunded) execute a deed of the land to the purchaser or his assigns, which shall convey all the right acquired by the State under the original sale or sales. And such deed shall be *prima facie* evidence of the legality of all the proceedings to the date of the deed, and of the title in the fee, in the grantee therein named; and when duly acknowledged, may be recorded and admitted as evidence in the same manner as other deeds of conveyance; and every such deed, when witnessed and acknowledged in the manner prescribed by law for witnessing and acknowledging deeds in other cases, and after it shall have been recorded for two years in the office of the register of deeds, in the county in which the land therein described is situated, shall, except:

First. When the same has been annulled according to law.

Second. When the land sold was not subject to taxation at the date of the assessment of the taxes for which it was sold;

Third. When the taxes have been paid to the proper officer within the time limited by law for the payment or redemption thereof; or

Fourth. When a certificate that no taxes were to be charged against the land has been given by the proper officer within the time limited by law for the payment or redemption thereof.

Be conclusive evidence that the land therein described was by such deed conveyed in fee simple to the grantee therein named, and his heirs and assigns; and no suit of ejectment or other suit for the recovery of possession shall be thereafter commenced to recover said lands, nor the title thereto [sustained] by any person claiming or holding possession or title through any other source.

Redemption of lands bid off to the State.

[907.] SEC. 125. Any person may redeem any lands, or any part or interest which shall be clearly defined in any lands heretofore bid in, or that may hereafter be bid in for the State, at any time within one year next succeeding the sale at which the same was bid in, by paying into the State Treasury, on the certificate of the Auditor General, the amount for which the same was so bid in, with interest thereon at the rate of twenty-five per cent. per annum, as is contemplated and provided in sections ninety-one and ninety-two of this act. 1847, p. 123.

Purchaser of State bids at Auditor General's office, etc.

[908.] SEC. 126. All such lands remaining unredeemed, except such description as the State may have a title to for another year or years, shall be subject to sale at any time at the office of the Auditor General, and upon the payment therefor, on his certificate to the State Treasurer of the amount for which such lands were bid off to the State, with interest at twenty-five per cent. per annum, to be computed from the first Monday in October, when such lands were bid off to the State to the time of such application, the Auditor General shall issue to the purchaser a certificate of purchase.

Amount to be refunded. in case of redemption, etc,

[909.] SEC. 127. If such lands shall be redeemed, the purchaser shall be entitled to the amount of the bid, together with twenty per cent. interest, as contemplated and provided in section ninety-one of this act; if otherwise discharged, then to the amount paid by him, with interest at seven per cent. per annum, to be computed from the date of the purchase to date of such discharge. But if such lands are not redeemed or otherwise discharged according to law, the Auditor General shall, on the surrender of such certificate of purchase, execute to the purchaser a deed for the lands therein described.

If not redeemed, etc., Deed to be executed by Auditor General.

Purchase of unsold State tax lands at Auditor General's office.

[910.] SEC. 128. Any person may purchase any unsold State tax land, upon application therefor at the office of the Auditor General, and upon paying to the State Treasurer, on the certificate of the Auditor General, the amount for which the same was, or should have been first offered in the county as State tax land, with interest upon said amount at ten per cent. per annum, to be computed from the first Monday in October, in the year in which the lands was, or should have been so first offered in the county, to the day of making such application and payment.

Deed to be executed by Auditor General.

[911.] SEC. 129. Upon application and payment being made as above mentioned, the Auditor General shall execute to such purchaser a deed, conveying all the right, title and interest of the State in and to said State tax lands, acquired by virtue of the original sale or sales to the State.

What provisions applicable to State tax land deeds.

[912.] SEC. 130. All the provisions of this act relative to deeds executed by the Auditor General, on the surrender of certificates of sale of State tax lands, issued by the several County Treasurers, shall be applicable to deeds executed by him for lands purchased at his office pursuant to the provisions of this act. 1858. Act 32, p. 176.

Office charges.

[913.] SEC. 131. The purchaser of any lands bid in for the State at the annual tax sales, and sold pursuant to the provisions of this act, on application to the Auditor General for a deed, shall pay an office charge of twenty-five cents for the first, and six cents for each subsequent description contained in such deed, R. S., Sec. 114.

which shall be paid into the State Treasury, to the credit of the general fund.

Expense of sale; Postage, etc. 1847, p. 125.

[914.] SEC. 132. All expenses of sale, postage and other charges, incident to the sale of lands, bid in for the State as aforesaid, shall be audited by the Auditor General, and paid out of the general fund on his warrant.

Who to be made defendant in case of prosecution of ejectment. 1858, Act 32, p. 176.

[915.] SEC. 133. In case it shall become necessary in the prosecution of an action of ejectment by any person holding an adverse claim to any land bid in for the State, as provided in this chapter, the Auditor General may be defendant, and in all cases in the prosecution or defence of an action of ejectment or trespass, by any person holding or claiming land, under any deed or deeds or other conveyance of land bid off or purchased for delinquent or unpaid taxes, the party so claiming, under and by virtue of such purchase for unpaid taxes as aforesaid, may show his title to said land and premises, whether the same was derived under one or more purchases or sales for taxes or otherwise, and may give in evidence any and all deeds of conveyance or other evidence of such purchase as aforesaid, which he may at any one or more different times have received on sales for taxes, and may claim title under any or all of them.

Right of the State to enforce collection of taxes for subsequent years, not to be prejudiced etc. 1848, p. 225.

[916.] SEC. 134. Neither the sale of any State tax lands, nor the sale of any of the bids of the State for which the time of redemption has not expired, shall in any wise prejudice the right of the State to enforce the collection of any tax subsequent to the year or years for which the same have been sold as aforesaid, and for the taxes and charges remaining unpaid for such subsequent year or years, the Auditor General shall cause such lands to be offered in regular succession, at the next ensuing annual sales for taxes, in the proper county, giving the notice required by law, unless previously redeemed or otherwise discharged.

When State acquires absolute title to tax lands 1858, Act 32, p. 167.

[917.] SEC. 135. Any description of land bid off to the State at the annual sales, which shall have remained undisposed of for five years from the date when it was so bid off, shall vest in the State an absolute title in fee simple, and no suit of ejectment shall be commenced to recover said lands or title thereto, [or be] sustained thereafter by any person claiming or holding possession or title through any other source; but such lands shall be subject to sale at any time by payment in like manner as other State tax lands, the amount of taxes due thereon and interest at the rate of ten per cent.; and after the expiration of five years, as aforesaid, said lands shall be stricken from the assessment roll, but shall be restored thereto after the same shall have been sold.

When lands to be struck from assessment roll.

Auditor General to transmit lists of lands to be struck from assessment rolls to county clerks and county Treasurers.

[918.] SEC. 136. The Auditor General shall, in the month of March in each year, transmit to the several County Clerks and County Treasurers, lists of all lands to be so struck from the assessment rolls, in their respective counties, and lists of such as have been previously struck from the rolls, but are to be restored and again assessed; and the said clerks respectively, on or before the first Monday of April thereafter, shall transmit a list to the several Supervisors, designating such lands in their respective townships as are to be left out of the assessment roll, and such as have been previously left out, but are to be restored.

[919.] SEC. 137. When any single description of State tax land shall be sold for the taxes of two or more years, and it shall be made to appear to the Auditor General, within the time prescribed by law, that the taxes for any year for which the same was originally bid off to the State were paid before sale, or were illegally assessed, or would be void for any other cause, he shall, on application, cause to be refunded to the purchaser the amount due and paid on account of said year's tax, with interest at the rate of seven per cent. from the day of sale until said purchaser was notified that said amount would be refunded; but the deed shall remain a valid conveyance to the purchaser of all the rights acquired by the State under the sale or sales for taxes of other years, not thus proved to have been illegal or void.°

When description sold for taxes of two or more years, and sale void for one year, conveyance to remain good for balance.

1848, p. 256.

[920.] SEC. 140. All sales of State tax lands, or the bids in behalf of the State, at the Auditor General's office, under the provisions of the act to provide for the sale of certain unsold State tax lands, and for other purposes, approved February seventeenth, eighteen hundred and forty-six, and act number seventy-two, amendatory thereof, approved April twenty-third, eighteen hundred and forty-six, which were made after the said acts were repealed, and also the sales at the said office, of the bids in behalf of the State on lands sold for the taxes of eighteen hundred and forty-one, eighteen hundred and forty-two, and eighteen hundred and forty-three, and which were previously held by the State as State tax lands, for the taxes of eighteen hundred and forty, and previous years, and the deeds or certificates of purchase issued, or to be issued on account of such sales, shall be as valid as if said acts had not been repealed.

Certain sales to remain valid.

1848, p. 257.

1846, p. 18.

1846, p. 87.

MISCELLANEOUS PROVISIONS.

[921.] SEC. 141. Any person who has a lien upon any lands returned for non-payment of taxes, may pay the taxes, interest, and charges thereon, and the receipt of the County Treasurer, or State Treasurer therefor, duly countersigned, shall constitute an additional lien on such land to the amount therein specified; and the amount so specified shall be collectable with interest thereon, in the same manner as the original lien.

Person having Lien may pay taxes, and acquire additional Lien.

R. S., Sec. 117.

[922.] SEC. 142. If any Township Clerk or Supervisor shall wilfully neglect or refuse to perform any of the duties required of him by the provisions of this chapter, he shall forfeit and pay a sum not exceeding five hundred dollars to any person injured

1858, Act 82, p. 176.

Penalty for neglect of duty by certain town officers.

°There are no Sections numbered 138 and 139 in this Act.

by each [case of] such neglect, but such sum shall not exceed the injury sustained.

Duty of Board of Supervisors as to forfeitures, etc. R. S., Sec. 119.

[923.] SEC. 143. The Board of Supervisors of each county shall, at their annual session in each year, transmit to the Prosecuting Attorney, the names and places of abode of all Township Clerks and Supervisors within their county, who shall have incurred any forfeiture under the provisions of this chapter, and such Prosecuting Attorney shall immediately prosecute for such forfeiture.

Losses sustained by default of county or township Treasurer, chargeable to county or town, etc. R. S., Sec. 120.

[924. SEC. 144. All losses that may be sustained by the default of the Treasurer of any township, shall be chargeable on such township; and all losses that may be sustained by the default of any County Treasurer in the discharge of the duties imposed by this chapter, shall be chargeable on such county, and the Board of Supervisors of such county shall add such losses to the next year's taxes of such township or county.

Auditor General to furnish blanks. R. S., Sec. 121.

[925.] SEC. 145. The Auditor General shall, from time to time, furnish suitable blanks, in addition to those required by the preceding provisions of this chapter, for returns of unpaid taxes, receipts and certificates of sale, which shall be sent to the several County Treasurers.

Detroit; who to perform duties of Township Treasurer therein. R. S., Sec. 122.

[926.] SEC. 146. The Assessors of the several wards in the City of Detroit shall have, and exercise the powers and duties of Supervisors, and the Collectors of the several wards of said city shall have, and exercise the powers and duties of Township Treasurers, under the provisions of this chapter.

Auditor General to cause this Act to be printed, etc. R. S., Sec. 123.

[927.] SEC. 147. The Auditor General shall, from time to time, whenever he shall find it necessary, cause to be printed at the expense of the State, a sufficient number of copies of this chapter, with such forms of proceeding under the same as may be necessary and proper, to furnish one copy to each Supervisor, Township Treasurer, Township Clerk, and County Clerk, and three copies to each County Treasurer; and shall transmit to each County Treasurer, at the expense of the county, a sufficient number for such county; and every County Treasurer receiving such copies shall immediately transmit to the Township Clerk of each township five copies, to be distributed by him to the officers entitled thereto.

Officer refusing to perform duties, etc.; guilty of misdemeanor. R. S., Sec. 124.

Any officer who shall wilfully neglect, or refuse to perform any of the duties imposed upon him by this chapter, shall be deemed guilty of a misdemeanor, and, on conviction thereof, shall be punished by imprisonment in the county jail not exceeding one year, or by fine not exceeding five hundred dollars, in the discretion of the Court.

Property distrained for taxes, proceedings in case of surplus in certain cases. R. S., Sec. 125.

[928.] SEC. 148. Whenever a surplus arising from the sale of any property distrained for taxes, shall be claimed by any other than the person for whose tax such property was sold, and such claim shall be contested by such person, such claimant may prosecute an action against such person; or the person for whose tax such property was sold may prosecute such action against such claimant, as for money had and received; in which action the right of the respective parties to such surplus shall be tried and determined.

Property distrained for taxes; proceedings in case of surplus in certain cases.

[929.] SEC. 149. For the purpose of such action, the defendant shall be deemed to be in possession of the surplus in the hands of the Township Treasurer, and upon the presentation to such Treasurer of a certified copy of the final judgment rendered in such action, the said Treasurer shall pay over the same to the party recovering such judgment; and no Township Treasurer shall be liable to any claimant of such surplus, the right to which is contested, as provided in this chapter, until he shall have refused to pay over such surplus upon the production of a certified copy of a judgment as aforesaid.

R. S., Sec. 126.

Ibid.

[930.] SEC. 150. In any action brought pursuant to the two last preceding sections, no other cause of action shall be joined, nor shall any set off be allowed; and if an execution issue on a judgment so rendered, it shall direct the costs only of such action to be levied by virtue thereof.

R. S., Sec. 127.

Value of property distrained and sold may be recovered in certain cases.

[931.] SEC. 151. When any property shall be legally distrained and sold for the tax of any person, and such property shall be owned by another person, such owner may recover of the person for whose tax the same was sold the value of such property, in an action of assumpsit, as for goods sold and delivered, deducting therefrom the amount of any surplus which may have been claimed or recovered by such owner, as provided in this chapter.

R. S., Sec. 128.

Duty of Prosecuting Attorney to advise Treasurer and Supervisor.

[932.] SEC. 152. It shall be the duty of the Prosecuting Attorney of each county to give his counsel and advice to the County Treasurer, and the Supervisors of the county, whenever they, or any of them, may deem it necessary for the proper discharge of the duties imposed upon them in this chapter, free of charge.

R. S., Sec. 129.

County Treasurer paying money to Town Treasurer to notify clerk.

[933.] SEC. 153. Whenever any County Treasurer shall pay to any Township Treasurer any moneys on account of taxes returned from such township, it shall be the duty of such County Treasurer immediately to notify the clerk of the proper township of the amount so paid to such Township Treasurer.

In case of death of purchaser or assignee.

[934.] SEC. 154. In all cases of sales of land for taxes, if the purchaser or his assigns shall die before a deed shall be executed on such sale, the deed may be executed by the Auditor General to and in the name of such deceased person, if such person being still alive would be entitled to the same; which deed shall vest the tax title in the heirs or devisees of such deceased person in the same manner and liable to like claims of creditors and other persons as if the same had been executed to such deceased person immediately previous to his death; or the deed may issue to the assignee of said deceased person, [his] executors or administrators; and in like cases which have heretofore occurred, the same rules shall apply, and [to] all deeds hereto-

1858, Act 32, p. 176.

fore issued in the name of any deceased person, who, if living at the time of the execution thereof, would have been entitled to said deed as above provided.

University, primary school, State building, normal school, asylum, swamp and salt spring land to be returned, etc.

1858, Act 32, p. 176.

[935.] SEC. 155. The Supervisor of every township in which there shall be assessed the interest of any purchaser of university, primary school, State building, normal school, asylum, swamp or salt spring lands, as personal property, shall, on or before the first day of November, in the year when the same was so assessed, transmit to the Treasurer of his county a list of all such lands, containing a full description thereof, together with the names of the person to whom the same was so assessed.

County Treasurers to return to State Land Office.

1858, Act 32, p. 176.

[936.] SEC. 156. That the several County Treasurers shall at the same time and in the same manner they are now required to return to the office of the Auditor General, lands delinquent for taxes in their respective counties, return to the State land office a statement of all university, primary school, State building, normal school, asylum, swamp and salt spring lands, upon which, from returns made to them by the Township Treasurer, it appears the taxes assessed have not been paid and can not be collected.

Improvements made by purchasers under this act to be paid for.

[937.] SEC. 157. If any person dispossessed of lands purchased in pursuance of the provisions of this act shall have made valuable improvements thereon, he shall be entitled to receive what such improvements are reasonably worth, to be assessed on the trial of said cause, and the same so assessed shall be a lien on said land till paid.

Forfeiture in case of neglect to pay Taxes.

1850, p. 396.

[938.] SEC. 158. The purchaser or purchasers of any parcel of the land so returned, or the person or persons claiming to have any interest in the same as the assignee or legal representative in any other capacity of such purchaser, shall, under pain of forfeiting his or their interest in such lands, and in the certificate of sale thereof, within the time in which the annual interest is required to be paid on the purchase money of such lands, pay to the State Treasurer the mount of taxes assessed upon any description of the lands so returned, with interest thereon from the first day of February following the assessment of the same, at the rate of fifteen per cent. a year, and in addition thereto, on each description, the sum of twenty-five cents, to defray the expenses of the collection of such taxes.

Forfeiture in case of neglect to pay Taxes.

[939.] SEC. 159. Every parcel of land returned under the provisions of this act, upon which the taxes, and the interest and charges aforesaid, shall remain unpaid at the expiration of the time within which such payment thereof is required to be made by the next preceding section, shall be deemed to have been forfeited to the State by the purchaser thereof, his assignee, or other legal representative; and the lands so forfeited shall be subject to sale in the same manner that other forfeited and unsold university and primary school lands are.

Commissioner to furnish statement to Auditor General of Taxes so paid.

[940.] SEC. 160. The said Commissioner shall, on or before the first day of May and November in each year, make out and furnish to the Auditor General a statement containing a description of the lands upon which the taxes have been paid, and the amount of taxes, interest and charges paid on such lands.

Auditor General to credit Counties.

[941.] SEC. 161. The Auditor General shall credit to the proper counties the taxes so paid, with the rate of interest allowed on other delinquent taxes, and place the balance of moneys arising from such interest and charges to the credit of the general fund.

Board of Supervisors of organized County, to which unorganized Territory is attached, may appoint one or more Assessors; their duties, etc

[942.] SEC. 162. The Board of Supervisors of any organized county, to which is attached any unorganized territory for judicial purposes, may appoint one or more Assessors, who shall hold their office until others are appointed, to be duly qualified, whose duty it shall be to assess the property liable to taxation in such unorganized territory, in the same manner as is herein prescribed for the Supervisors of organized towns, who shall take, complete, and deliver the same to the County Clerk of such organized county, on or before the first day of October, which roll shall be equalized, and go to make the aggregate valuation of said county, the same as the other township rolls, and the relative amount of State and county tax, together with the expense of assessment and collection, shall be apportioned to the property of said rolls, the same as that of the several township. It shall be the duty of the County Clerk to affix the taxes so apportioned to a true copy of said roll, to annex his warrant thereto, to deliver the same to the Sheriff, who shall give bond to the County Treasurer that shall be approved by him, to collect and pay over the same, in the time, manner, and under the same restrictions as is herein prescribed for the Town Treasurer to collect and pay to the County Treasurer their several State and county taxes. Said Assessors shall be empowered at any time before the first day of October, to make amd complete an assessment in any organized town that may fail or neglect to make or complete an assessment roll within the time required by this act, and shall deliver the same to the County Clerk, who shall affix the taxes to a true copy thereof, and deliver the same to the Sheriff of said county, who shall give bonds to the County Treasurer, collect and pay over the same in like manner as is required for the unorganized portion of said counties.

Conflicting enactments repealed.

[943.] SEC. 163. That all acts, and parts of acts, contravening the provisions of this act be, and the same are hereby repealed.

SEC. 164. This act shall take effect immediately.

An Act Amending the Fifth Section of the Twentieth Chapter of the Revised Statutes Relative to Exemption from taxation. p

[*Approved February* 7, 1857. *Laws of* 1857, *p.* 166.]

[944.] SECTION 1. *The People of the State of Michigan enact* That the fifth clause of the fifth section of the twentieth

p The Section here amended was re-enacted, and the exemptions increased by section Five of the preceding Act. For that reason it is not re-published here.

chapter of the Revised Statutes be amended by inserting after "therein," the following words: "Also the lands on which such houses of worship may stand, so far as actually occupied by such houses of worship, and for no other purpose," so that the clause shall read as follows:

Houses of Public Worship and lots exempted from Taxation.

"(5.) All houses of public worship, with the pews, or slips and and furniture therein; also the land on which such houses of worship may stand, so far as occupied by such houses of worship, and for no other purpose; also the rights of burial and tombs, while in use as repositories of the dead."

From Chapter Twenty of Revised Statutes of 1846. [q]

Assessors may divide Townships into districts.

[945.] SEC. 14. The assessors may divide their townships into districts, for the purpose of ascertaining the property liable to be taxed, and the persons subject to the payment of taxes thereon, and assign one district to each Assessor; but such property and persons, and the valuation of such property, shall be finally determined by them, or a majority of them, jointly, and if any Assessor shall neglect his duties within his district, the other Assessors shall perform them.[r]

If sale found to be invalid after conveyance, amount to be refunded; interest thereon.

[946.] SEC. 89. If, after the conveyance of any land sold for taxes, the Auditor General shall discover that the sale was invalid, he shall, on demand, cause the money paid therefor to be refunded, with seven per cent. interest; and in all such cases, when the Auditor General, deeming a title invalid, shall have offered to the purchaser his money and interest upon a delivery and cancelment of the deed, and the purchaser shall have refused to receive the money and cancel the deed, such purchaser shall never be entitled to receive any more than the purchase money, and seven per cent. interest thereon, to the day of such offer and refusal.[s]

Purchasers not entitled to interest after notice.

[947.] SEC. 111. No person who shall refuse to receive back his purchase money and interest, and surrender his deed, shall be entitled to any interest after he shall have been notified by the Auditor General that the sale has been canceled.[t]

---

q The whole of Chapter Twenty of R. S. is believed to be either repealed or substantially re-enacted, except the Sections which follow.

r Although the Constitution of 1850 does not provide for the election of Assessors, yet as the provision in the Revised Statutes which permits the Electors of Townships to choose them, is not expressly repealed, this Section is retained.

s The last clause of this Section seems to be wanting in the corresponding Section in the Law of 1853. See Section 903.

t Relates to the Refunding of Moneys on the Cancelment of Deeds given on sales of State Tax Lands. See Section 932, and note thereto.

DIVISION X.—Of Specific State Taxes and Duties.

From Chapter Twenty-one of Revised Statutes of 1846.

TAX UPON BANKS.

[948.] Section 1. Every Bank now incorporated, or hereafter to be incorporated, shall pay a yearly tax of one and one half per cent. on the amount of capital stock paid in; one half thereof on or before the first Monday of April, and the other half on or before the first Monday of October in each year; which tax shall be in lieu of all State, county, township, or other taxes in this State, on the capital stock of said Bank and of all State tax imposed by the charter of any such Bank heretofore incorporated. Tax on Capital Stock of Banks.

[949.] Sec. 2. Any portion of the capital stock of any Bank, which shall, in accordance with the provisions of its charter and the laws of this State, have become vested in real, or personal estate, within this State, subject to taxation, and which shall be actually assessed within this State, for ordinary State, county, and other taxes, upon proof thereof to the satisfaction of the State Treasurer and Attorney General, shall be exempt from said tax of one and one half per cent. for the year succeeding said assessment, to the amount of the valuation of such property on the assessment roll. When certain portion of stock exemptied.

[950.] Sec. 3. If any part of the capital stock of any Bank shall have been paid in within six months next before either of the days specified for the payment of said tax, the tax on such part shall be paid in proportion to the time that shall have elapsed after such part of the capital stock shall have been paid in. When stock paid in within six months.

[951.] Sec. 4. If any Bank shall neglect to make such payment, the State Treasurer shall forthwith notify the Attorney General thereof, who shall thereupon immediately institute proceedings against such delinquent Bank, by bill in Chancery, or by an action at law, for the recovery of such tax, with interest and costs, in the same manner, and with the like effect, as is hereinafter provided in cases of delinquent railroad, canal and turnpike corporations. Proceedings in case of neglect to pay tax.

TAX UPON RAILROAD, CANAL AND TURNPIKE CORPORATIONS.

[952.] Sec. 5. Every company heretofore incorporated, or hereafter to be incorporated within this State, for the purpose of constructing and using any railroad, canal, or turnpike therein, shall pay a yearly tax to the State of three-fourths of one per cent. on the amount of the capital stock of such company paid, or secured to be paid, which tax shall be paid into the Tax on Capital Stock of Railroad and other Corporations.

State Treasury by said corporations respectively, on or before the first Monday of October, in the year one thousand eight hundred and forty-seven, and in each year thereafter.

Such tax to be in lieu of all other taxes.

[953.] SEC. 6. Such tax shall be in lieu of all State, county, township, or other taxes in this State, on the capital stock of said corporations, and on the railroad, canal, or turnpike constructed, or used by any such corporation, and on all the real and personal property in which said capital stock shall be invested, and which shall be used and occupied by any such company, in accordance with the provisions of its charter, and the laws of this State, in the construction or use of such railroad, canal, or turnpike.

Proceedings in case of neglect to pay.

[954.] SEC. 7. If any such incorporated company shall neglect or refuse to pay the tax aforesaid, on or before the said first Monday of October, the State Treasurer shall immediately furnish the name of every such company so neglecting or refusing to pay such tax to the Attorney General, with the amount due from each; and the Attorney General shall thereupon file a bill in the Court of Chancery against every such company, for the discovery and sequestration of its property.

Sequestration, injunction, etc.

[955.] SEC. 8. *The Chancellor*, on the filing of such bill, or on the coming in of the answer thereto, shall order such part of the property of such company to be sequestered, as he shall deem necessary for satisfying the taxes in arrear, with the costs of prosecution; and he may also, at his discretion, enjoin such company, and the officers thereof, from any further proceedings under their act of incorporation, and may order and direct such other proceedings as he may deem necessary to compel the payment of such tax and costs.

Proceedings at Law to recover tax.

[956.] SEC. 9. The Attorney General may also recover such tax, with costs, from such delinquent company, by action in the name of the People of this State, in any Court of competent jurisdiction.

BROKERS AND EXCHANGE DEALERS.

No person to be Broker, etc., without license

[957.] SEC. 10. No person shall be engaged in the business of a Broker, or of buying or selling current or uncurrent money, or bank notes, or in the exchange thereof, or in the exchange of coins, without first paying into the State Treasury the sum hereinafter mentioned, and obtaining a license from the State Treasurer, to carry on the business of a Broker and exchange dealer, in the manner hereinafter provided, except as provided in the next section.

Prohibition not to apply to certain Corporations and persons.

[958.] SEC. 11. The prohibition in the preceding section contained shall not apply to corporations authorized by law to carry on the business of exchange, and the buying and selling of money, nor to persons engaged in commercial or mercantile operations, as forwarders, dealers in products of the country, grocers, merchants, and millers, or others, whose regular business, other than that of Brokers and exchange dealers, renders the purchase and sale of exchanges, or the purchase or sale of current or uncurrent money, a legitimate part of their said business or occupation.

Proceedings to obtain license.

[959.] SEC. 12. Any person desiring to carry on the business of Brokers and exchange dealers as aforesaid, may, before commencing such business, obtain from the Treasurer of this State a license for each office or concern which they propose to establish; for which purpose they shall file with the said Treasurer a certificate, specifying:

1. The name of every person who is to be connected with such business, and constitute a part of the firm;

2. The actual amount of capital to be invested in the business of the concern, and the precise amount that each partner is to put in;

3. The city or village, township and county wherein said business is intended to be carried on; which said certificate shall be duly verified by the oath of the party applying for the license.

Amount to be paid before license granted.

[960.] SEC. 13. The persons applying for such license shall, at the time of filing such certificate, pay to the State Treasurer therefor at the rate of one and one half per cent. on the amount of the capital stock to be used in such business; whereupon the said Treasurer shall grant, under his hand and official seal, to the person or persons applying therefor, a license to carry on the business of Brokers and exchange dealers, with the capital mentioned in the certificate, and at the place therein specified, for a term not exceeding one year from the date thereof; but such license may be renewed annually, from time to time, upon payment therefor at the rate aforesaid; and the proceeds of all such licenses shall be placed to the credit of the general fund.

Violation of prohibition to be deemed a misdemeanor.

[961.] SEC. 14. If any person shall carry on the business of a Broker, or exchange dealer, contrary to the provisions of this chapter, such person shall be deemed guilty of a misdemeanor, and, on conviction thereof, shall be punished by fine not less than one hundred, nor more than two thousand dollars, in the discretion of the court.

Affidavit to be filed.

[962.] SEC. 15. Every person who shall obtain a license to carry on the business of a Broker and exchange dealer, as provided in this chapter, before he commences the business, shall make and file with said State Treasurer an affidavit, stating therein that he has not, and will not have any connection, directly or indirectly, with any bank or banks, and that no bank is, or shall be entitled to any share of the profits of such business.

HAWKERS AND PEDELRS.

No person to be a Hawker and Pedler without license.

[963,] SEC. 16. No person shall be authorized to travel from place to place within this State, for the purpose of carrying to sell, or exposing to sale any goods, wares, or merchandise, unless he shall have obtained a license as a Hawker and Pedler, in the manner hereafter directed.

Applications for licenses as Hawker and Pedler.

[964.] SEC. 17. Every person desirous to obtain a license as a Hawker or Pedler, shall apply to the Treasurer of this State, and shall deliver to him a note in writing, signed by such applicant, stating in what manner he intends to travel and trade, whether on foot, or with one or more horses, or other beasts of burthen, or with any sort of carriage.

Payment of duties.

[965.] SEC. 18. Every such applicant, before he shall be entitled to a license, shall pay into the State Treasury the following duties: if he intend to travel on foot, the sum of ten dollars; if he intend to travel and carry his goods with a single horse, or other beast carrying or drawing a burthen, the sum of twenty-five dollars; and if he intend to travel with any vehicle or carriage drawn by more than one horse, or other animal, the sum of fifty dollars.

When Treasurer to grant license.

[966.] SEC. 19. Upon the presentation of such note in writing and the payment of the proper duties herein required, the State Treasurer shall grant to such applicant a license under his hand and seal of office, and authorizing such applicant to travel and trade as a Hawker or Pedler, in the manner stated in such note, for the term of one year from the date of the license.

Licenses to be issued for any term less than a year, and may be renewed annually.

[967.] SEC. 20. Licenses may be granted by the Treasurer for any term less than one year, upon payment of a rateable proportion of the duties hereinbefore prescribed; and every license granted, or to be granted for the purpose aforesaid, shall be renewed annually by the State Treasurer, if such renewal be applied for, on the same terms and conditions that the original license was granted.[a]

Penalty for Hawking, etc. without license.

[968.] SEC. 21. Every person who shall be found traveling and trading within the limits of this State, contrary to the provisions of this chapter, or contrary to the terms of any license that may have been granted to him as a Hawker or Pedlar, shall, for each offence, forfeit the sum of twenty-five dollars.

Construction of this chapter.

[969.] SEC. 22. Nothing contained in this chapter shall be construed to prevent any mechanic residing in this State from selling his work anywhere in the State.

Penalty for refusing to produce license.

[970.] SEC. 23. Every person who shall be found traveling and trading as aforesaid, and who shall refuse to produce a license as a Hawker or Pedler, to any officer, or citizen who shall demand the same, shall, for each offence, forfeit the sum of ten dollars.

Costs in case of Prosecution.

[971.] SEC. 24. In every case of a prosecution against any person, for the recovery of any penalty given in this chapter, no costs shall be allowed to the defendant, if it shall appear that, before the commencement of the prosecution, such defendant had refused to produce his license, or to disclose his name when lawfully required.

Limitation of Prosecution for Penalty.

[872.] SEC. 25. No prosecution for the recovery of any penalty imposed for any violation of the provisions of this chapter, relating to Hawkers and Pedlers, shall be maintained, unless it

[a] As amended by Act 105 of 1847. Laws of 1847. p. 168, Sec. 5.

shall be brought within sixty days after the commission of the offence charged.

OF AUCTIONEERS, AND OF DUTIES UPON SALES AT AUCTION.

[973.] SEC. 26. Any citizen of this State may become an Auctioneer within the county in which he resides, on executing and delivering to the Treasurer of such county a bond in the penal sum of two thousand five hundred dollars, with two or more sufficient sureties, to be approved by such Treasurer, conditioned for the payment to such Treasurer of all auction duties upon goods or property which may be sold by him, according to law.

How person may become an Auctioneer.

1839, p. 145.

[974.] SEC. 27. Every person who shall have executed and delivered such bond to the County Treasurer, shall, for the term of four years next after the date of such bond, be an Auctioner within such county, and be authorized to carry on and perform the business of an Auctioneer, and shall conform to the provisions hereinafter contained.

For what term.

[975.] SEC. 28. If such Auctioner reside in either of the cities of this State, he shall, on the first Monday of each month, and if he reside in any other place, then on the first Monday of April and October in each and every year, make out a statement in writing, verified by his oath, and deliver the same to the County Treasurer, in which statement he shall designate particularly;

Auctioneer to render statement on oath.

1. The sums for which all the goods, at every auction held by him after delivering such bond, or the date of his last preceding statement, were sold;

2. The days on which sales were so made by him, and the amount of sales on each day;

3. The amount of duties chargeable under the provisions of this chapter.

[976.] SEC. 29. Every such statement verified as aforesaid, shall, within ten days after the date thereof, be delivered by such Auctioneer to the Treasurer of the county in which he resides, and such Auctioneer shall, at the time of delivering such statement, pay over to such County Treasurer the duties chargeable by law upon the sales specified in such statement, and take the Treasurer's receipt therefor, which receipt shall be countersigned by the clerk of the same county, who shall make an entry of the amount thereof, in a proper book to be kept by him for that purpose.

Delivery of statement and payment of duties.

[977.] SEC. 30. Each County Treasurer shall, immediately after receiving such statement, forward the same to the Auditor General, and shall pay over all auction duties received by him to the State Treasurer, in such manner as such Treasurer shall direct.

County Treasurer to forward statement to Auditor General, and pay over duties.

[978.] SEC. 31. The following articles, and no others, shall be subject to the payment of the following duties, if sold at auction:

Articles subject to duties.

1. All ardent spirits, wines and intoxicating liquors, whether foreign or domestic, shall be liable to the payment of a duty of two and a half per cent.;

2. All goods, wares and merchandise of every description, imported from any place without the United States, shall be liable to the payment of a duty of one and a half per cent. at each and every time they are so exposed for sale.

When chattels exempt from Auction duties.

[979.] SEC. 32. Goods and chattels otherwise liable to auction duties, shall be exempt therefrom, if sold under the following circumstances:

1. If they shall belong to the United States, or to this State;

2. If they shall be sold in pursuance of any judgment, order, or decree of any court of law or equity, or under any seizure or distress by any public officer;

3. If they shall belong to an estate of a deceased person, and be sold by his executors or administrators, or by any other person duly authorized by any Judge of Probate;

4. If they shall be the effects of a bankrupt or insolvent, and be sold by his assignee, appointed pursuant to law, or by a general assignment for the benefit of the creditors of such bankrupt or insolvent.

Sales, how made by Auctioneer.

[980.] SEC. 33. All goods, property and effects, liable to the payment of duties, shall, in all cases when sold at auction, be struck off to the highest bidder, and when the Auctioneer, or owner, or any person employed by them or either of them, shall be such bidder, they shall be subject to the same duties as if struck off to any other person; but this section shall not be construed to render valid any sale which would otherwise be deemed fraudulent and void.

Duties how calculated.

[981.] SEC. 34. All duties shall be calculated on the sums for which the goods and property exposed for sale shall be respectively struck off to the purchaser thereof.

Persons acting as Auctioneer without authority, guilty of misdemeanor.

[982.] SEC. 35. If any person shall act as an Auctioneer in the sale of any goods or property liable to the payment of duties under the provisions of this chapter, without first having delivered to the County Treasurer the bond herein required, such person shall be deemed guilty of a misdemeanor, and, on conviction thereof, shall be punished by a fine not exceeding five hundred dollars.

An Act Relative to Specific State Taxes on Plank Road, Mining and other Corporations, not enumerated in the Revised Statutes of Eighteen Hundred and Forty-six.

[*Approved March* 14, 1848. *Laws of* 1848, *p.* 67.]

State to have lien for specific taxes.

[983.] SECTION 1. *Be it enacted by the Senate and House of Representatives of the State of Michigan*, That in all cases, when any incorporated company hereafter to be incorporated, is made subject to the payment of a specific State Tax, this State shall have a lien on all of the property of said company, to secure the payment of said tax, which lien shall take precedence of all other liens or incumbrances whatever.

How taxes may be enforced.

[984.] SEC. 2. The payment of any such tax may and shall be enforced according to the provisions of sections seven, eight and nine of chapter twenty-one, of title five of the Revised Statutes of eighteen hundred and forty-six.

SEC. 3. This act shall take effect and be in force from and after its passage.

An Act to Provide for Filing certain Reports in the Auditor General's Office, and for other purposes.

[*Approved January* 29, 1853. *Took effect May* 16, 1853. *Laws of* 1853, *p.* 21.]

[985.] SECTION 1. *The People of the State of Michigan enact*, That all reports of the amount of capital stock of incorporated bodies paying specific taxes, hereafter received by any State officer, shall be placed on file in the Auditor General's office within one week after their receipt.

Reports of Corporations to be filed in Auditor General's office.

[986.] SEC. 2. The Auditor General is authorized and required, upon the receipt of such copies, to estimate and charge upon the books of his office, the amount of specific tax due from the company making such report; and in case any company shall neglect or refuse to pay the tax required by its charter, within twenty days after the same is due, it shall be the duty of the Auditor General to issue his warrant to the Sheriff of the county in which such company is located commanding him to forthwith levy the same, together with ten per cent. for his fees, by distress and sale of any of the property of said company, wherever the same may be found within his county, and to pay over the same, reserving his fees, to the State Treasury, within ten days after the same is collected.

Auditor General to estimate and charge specific tax.

Proceeding on neglect to pay.

[987.] SEC. 3. The Sheriff shall give public notice of the time and place of sale, and of the property to be sold, at least ten days previous to the sale, by advertisement, to be posted up in three public places in the township, city or village where such sale is made, and the sale shall be by public auction.

How Sheriff to collect.

[988.] SEC. 4. If the property so distrained can not be sold for want of bidders, or if the property of the company is insufficient to pay the tax, the Sheriff shall forthwith return a statement of the same to the Auditor General; and if the company shall still neglect or refuse to pay such tax within thirty days, if the place of business of such company be in the Lower Peninsula, if in the Upper Peninsula, then within sixty days after such return, it shall be deemed a forfeiture of all its chartered privileges.

How Sheriff to collect.

[989.] SEC. 5. In case any corporation fails to make the report contemplated in the first section of this act, it shall be the duty of the Auditor General, and he is hereby required, to ascertain the amount of the specific tax of any such corporation, as appears from their last report, and to issue his warrant as provided in the preceding sections, and for double the amount of such tax.

Proceedings when corporations fail to report.

An Act to Provide for the payment of Specific Taxes to the Counties in the Upper Peninsula.

Approved February 12, 1853. *Took effect May* 16, 1853. *Laws of* 1853, *p.* 76.

Specific tax in Upper Peninsula,

[990.] SECTION 1. *The People of the State of Michigan enact*, That one half of the taxes received, or which may be hereafter received into the Treasury of the State, from mining corporations in the Upper Peninsula, paying an annual tnx of one per cent., shall be paid to the Treasurers of the counties from which they respectively have been, or hereafter may be received, upon the written order of the County Clerk of the county from which such tax has been, or shall be received, to be used for county and township purposes, as the Board of Supervisors in said counties respectively shall direct, as provided in section seven of article nineteen of the Constitution.

An Act to provide for the payment of the expenses of the State government.

[*Approved February* 15, 1859. *Laws of* 1859, *p.* 507.]

Tax authorized.

SECTION 1. *The People of the State of Michigan enact*, That one mill on the dollar of the aggregate of real and personal estate as equalized by the State Board of equalization for the year eighteen hundred and fifty-six, be levied and collected upon the taxable property of the State for each of the years eighteen hundred and fifty-nine and eighteen hundred and sixty, and the same is hereby appropriated for the payment of the expenses of the State government, the interest upon the State debt, not otherwise provided for, and the State debt falling due within said years, not otherwise provided for.

Auditor General to apportion and transmit the amount to county Treasurer.

SEC. 2. The Auditor General shall apportion each year the sums herein directed to be raised among the several counties, in proportion to the taxable property therein, as determined by the State board of equalization; and he shall, on or before the fifteenth day of September, in each year, make out and transmit to the clerks of the several Boards of Supervisors, the amount of such tax, so apportioned by him to the county, and shall charge the several amounts of such apportionment to the counties respectively.

Supervisors to apportion am't among the several Townships.

SEC. 3. The Board of Supervisors shall, at their annual session in each year, ascertain and determine the amount of money to be raised by tax for county purposes in their respective counties, and apportion such amount, and also the amount of State tax apportioned to the respective counties by the Auditor General, among the several townships of the county, in proportion to the valuation of taxable property therein, as equalized by the Board of Supervisors for said year, which determination and apportionment shall be entered at length on the records.

DIVISION XI.—Of the Officers having the Care and Superintendence of Highways and Bridges, and their General Powers and Duties.

Comp. L. 1857. Chap. XIX., p. 389.

Chapter Twenty-Two of the R. S. of 1846.

N.Y. Rev. Stat., Art. 1, Title 1, Chap. 16, Part 1.

Commissioners of Highways, their duties.

[991] Section 1. The Commissioners of Highways in the several townships of this State, shall have the care and superintendence of highways and bridges therein, and it shall be their duty:

1. To give directions for the repairing of roads and bridges within their respective townships;

2. To regulate the roads already laid out, and to alter such of them as they shall deem inconvenient;[1]

3. To cause such of the roads used as highways, as have been laid out, but not sufficiently described, and such as shall have been used for twenty years, but not recorded, to be ascertained, described, and entered of record in the Township Clerk's Office;[2]

---

1 It is held in New York that Commissioners of Highways can not by virtue of their office bring suits to recover damages against individuals or corporations, for illegally entering upon and taking possession of the public highways or bridges of their town. Neither have the electors of a town, at town meeting, power, by resolution or otherwise, to authorize such commissioners to bring an action in their own names, or in their name of office, for such injuries. Such a resolution, if passed at town meeting, would not bind the town.

In the case cited, the electors of a town, at town meeting, directed the commissioners of highways to prosecute a Turnpike Company for entering upon and taking possession of a public highway and bridge in that town, and the commissioners accordingly brought a suit for the cause of action in their names as commissioners, and had judgment against them,—*Held*, that they could not sustain an action against the town, to be re-imbursed, their costs and expenses, or the costs recovered against them in that suit. The electors of a town can not bind the town except in manner prescribed by law.—*Cornell v. Guilford*, 1 *Denio* 510.

2 Under this provision of the law, it becomes the duty of the Commissioners of Highways, without an application, to proceed and re-survey all such roads laid out, and used as highways, but not sufficiently described, as well as such as have been used for twenty years but not recorded, that the same may become a matter of town record, or more definite record; and their precise location be the more easily determined which may avoid disputes between parties that might otherwise arise.—*Bumpus v. Miller*, 4 *Mich.* 161.

Twenty years uninterrupted user of a way is *prima facie* evidence of a prescriptive right.—1 *Saund.* 323 *a*; 10 *East*, 476. Hence all such roads as have been used and traveled by the public for twenty years, without interruption, become public highways by *prescription;* which in law is defined to be the manner of acquiring property, or any particular right, by long, honest, and uninterrupted possession or use during the time required by law.

The public, however, have not the right to use and occupy the soil of an individual, adjoining navigable waters, as a public landing and place of deposit of property in its transit, against the will of the owner, although such user has been continued for more than twenty years. The user can not be urged by the public, either as a foundation of a legal presumption of a grant, and thus justify a claim by prescription, or as evidence of dedication of the premises to public use.—*Pearsoll v. Post*, 20 *Wend.* 111 *S. C. on Error*, 22 *Wend.* 425.

The provision of the Constitution,—That private property shall not be taken for public use without just compensation—therefore, does not affect cases of this kind. It applies to cases where private property is taken for public use without the consent of the owner; and not to cases where the owner actually gives or dedicates his property to the public for their use; or where, from his long acquiescence in the use of it by the public, a donation or dedication is presumed by law.

It seems that, whether the highway is acquired by user only, or under the provisions of the Constitution, it must be of the width prescribed by law; the dedication or donation, when not expressly or impliedly restricted by the owner is not confined to the

3 Barb., S. C. R. 645, 2 Hill, 619. 6 Hill, 463. 4. To cause the highways, and the bridges over the streams intersecting highways, to be kept in repair;[1]

5. To divide their respective townships into so many road districts as they shall judge convenient, by writing, under their hands, to be entered of record in the Township Clerk's office;

mere track which is beaten by carriages, and the feet of animals, in passing along but includes and carries with it the width as provided by statute.--*Bumpus v. Miller*, 4 *Mich.* 164.

But Commissioners of Highways have no authority under this provision, to change the width of the road, or to change its location; and if the Commissioners, in such cases, encroach upon the lands which do not belong to the highway as it had been actually opened and used, the owner thereof can not take his remedy by appeal, as in other cases, but must seek it in some other form. The statute in relation to appeals from the determination of Commissioners of Highways, in *laying out, altering*, or discontinuing or in refusing to *lay out, alter*, or discontinue any road, it is held, does not extend to such cases.--24 *Wend.* 491.

Form of Order of Commissioners of Highways ascertaining a Road used as a Highway, and laid out, but not sufficiently described.

Oakland County, }
Township of *Pontiac.* } ss.

Whereas, it appears that a certain road in said Township of *Pontiac,* leading from (*here insert a description of the road with convenient certainty, giving the place of commencement and termination*) is used as a highway, and has been laid out as such, but is not sufficiently described:

Now, therefore, we, the undersigned Commissioners of Highways for the said Township of *Pontiac,* do order that said road be ascertained, described, and entered of record in the Township Clerk's office in said township, according to a survey thereof, which we have caused to be made as follows: (*Here insert the survey.*) The line of said road being the centre thereof; said road being —— rods in width.

Witness our hands, this —— day of ———— A. D. 18—

A. B.,
C. D.,
E. F.,
Commissioners of Highways.

Form of Order of Commissioners of Highways ascertaining and describing Road used for twenty years, but not recorded.

Monroe County, }
Township of *Monroe.* }

Whereas it appears that a certain road in said Township of *Monroe,* leading from (*here describe the road with convenient certainty, giving the place of commencement and termination*) has been used as a highway for twenty years but not recorded:

Now, therefore, we, the undersigned Commissioners of Highways for the said Township of *Monroe,* do order that said road be ascertained, described and entered of record in the Township Clerk's office of said township, according to survey thereof, which we have caused to be made, as follows: (*Here insert the survey.*) The line of said road being the centre thereof.

Witness our hands, this —— day of ———— A. D. 18—

A. B.,
C. D.,
E. F.,
Commissioners of Highways.

[1] In England the liability to keep highways in repair, is of common right incumbent in general upon the parishes in which they respectively lie; but in some cases, it attaches, by prescription to particular townships or other divisions of parishes, and occasionally to private individuals or corportions, bound *ratione tenrae*, or in right of their estates or franchises to repair some particular highway; but the case of bridges is differently provided for. The expense of maintaining these is incumbent, not on the parishes, but on the counties at large, in which the bridges are situated.

In this country, the construction of roads and bridges is, for the most part, o-but no such division shall be made within five days next preceding the annual township meeting;[1]

6. To assign to each of said districts such of the inhabitants, liable to work on highways, as shall reside in such district, or own lands therein: and,

7. To require the Overseers of Highways, from time to time, and as often as they shall deem it necessary, to have all persons assessed to work on the highways, perform their labor thereon, with such teams, carriages, sleds, or implements as said Commissioners, or any of them, shall direct.

---

complished through our township organization; the counties contributing towards the construction of bridges, in cases where the expenses would be too onerous to be wholly borne by the townships in which they are situated. The statute, in express terms, gives to Commissioners of Highways, when elected, the care and superintendence of the highways and bridges of the town, and confers upon them all powers requisite for the execution of their trust. They are in no way responsible to the town, but are themselves a species of *quasi* corporation, with power to sue and be sued, having legal succession, and deriving their authority, not through the town, but directly from the statute. The towns have no power to give the slightest direction or instruction to these officers, as to the performance of their duties.—*Commissioners of Niles v. Martin*, 4 *Mich.* 557.

If damages are sustained by individuals, in consequence of the non-repair of bridges and highways: towns are not liable to actions therefor either at common law or by statute. Nor can they be subjected to any liability for such non-repair through the means of an action against the Commissioners of Highways.—*Ibid.*

A claim against a town, for damages thus occasioned, being entirely without foundation, will not support a promise by the electors of the town, assembled in town meeting, to pay the same, on the ground of its being made for the purpose of compromising a doubtful claim, and therefore upon a sufficient consideration.—*Morey v. Town of Newfane*, 8 *Barb.* 645.

The existence of funds or other specific means provided by statute, is a condition precedent to the obligation of Commissioners of Highways to repair bridges; and an indictment against such Commissioners, for not repairing a bridge, is defective, unless it aver that they had funds or other means to defray the expenses of the repairs.—*People v. Adlit et al.*, 2 *Hill.* 619.

The Commissioners of Highways are not bound to build or repair either roads or bridges, until the necessary funds or means are provided. Commissioners of Highways have no power to contract a debt against the town, by borrowing money for the repair of roads and bridges. Accordingly, when Commissioners of Highways, borrowed $1000 for this purpose on a note purporting to bind them in their official capacity;—*held*, That the town was not liable thereby, and that an action could not be maintained against their successors to recover the amount.—*Baker v. Loomis*, 6 *Hill.* 463.

At common law the counties and not towns were liable to build and repair the necessary bridges, and the remedy for neglect was by indictment.—17 *Johns.* 452.

Held in New York that where a bridge is built by an individual over a natural stream for his own benefit, if the bridge be a public utility and is used by the public, they are bound to keep it in repair; but not so when the necessity for the bridge is created by the individual.—*Dygert v. Schenck*, 23 *Wend.* 446.

[1] *Form of Order dividing Townships into Road Districts.*

Allegan County,
Township of *Allegan*. } ss.

We, the Commissioners of Highways for said Township of *Alegan*, do hereby order that said Township be divided into *six* road districts, as follows: Road district number one shall embrace all the highways contained within the following territory: (*or boundaries, giving the description by sections, or outward boundaries, as may be thought proper,*) and all the inhabitants liable to work on highways as shall reside in said district, or own lands therein, shall be and are hereby assigned to work on the highways of said district number one.

District number two shall embrace, &c., [*Continuing as aforesaid until the whole township is divided.*]

Witness our hands, this —— day of —— A. D. 18—

A. B.,
C. D.,
E. F.,
Commissioners of Highways.

To lay out and discontinue Roads.

[992] SEC. 2. The Commissioners of Highways shall have power, in the manner and under the restrictions hereinafter provided, to lay out and establish, upon actual survey, such new roads in their respective townships as they may deem necessary; and to discontinue such old roads and highways as shall appear to them to have become unnecessary.[1]

To render account to Township Board.

[993] SEC. 3. The Commissioners of Highways of each township shall render to the Township Board, at the annual meeting of such board in each year, an account in writing: stating,

1. The labor assessed and performed in their township;

2. The sums paid for delinquencies and commutations, and other moneys received by them, and the application thereof;

3. The improvements which have been made on the roads and bridges in their township during the year preceding such report, and the condition of such roads and bridges; and

4. The improvements necessary to be made on the same, and an estimate of the probable expense thereof beyond what the labor to be assessed in that year will accomplish.

Statement to be presented at Township Meeting; Moneys may be voted and collected.

[994] SEC. 4. The Township Board shall cause such statement to be presented at the next annual township meeting, and such meeting may vote for the raising of such sum, not exceeding two hundred and fifty dollars in any one year, for the improvement of the roads and bridges within the township, as a majority of the electors present shall deem necessary; and the sum so voted shall be levied and collected in the same manner as other township expenses.[2]

---

1 A town can not by vote authorize or compel Commissioners of Highways to lay out, alter, or discontinue a particular town way or public road; their duty being expressly pointed out by law, and they can only act in obedience to its provisions.—*Keen v. Stetson*, 5 *Pick*. 492.

2 *Form of Account of Commissioners of Highways to be rendered to Township Board.*

To the Township Board of the Townsnip of *Assyria*, in the County of *Barry*.

The annual account of the Commissioners of Highways of said Township of *Assyria*, for the year ending the —— day of —— A. D. 18— shows as follows, to wit:

1st. The labor assessed in said township during the year ending on the —— day of —— A. D. 18—, is —— days, and the amount of said labor performed is —— days, as appears by the returns made to us by the several Overseers of highways in said township.

2d. There has been paid for delinquencies and commutations, and other moneys have been received by us, and application thereof made, as follows

185—.			
June 4.	Received	from A. B., C. D., and E. F., penalties for refusing to work on highway, $1 each	$3 00
June 6.	"	from G. H., commutation	5 00
Aug. 1.	"	from I. J., Township Treasurer, being money received by him from Overseers	200 00
			$208 00
Sept. 1.	Paid for rebuilding bridge at ——————	. . . . .	208 00

[995] SEC. 5. It shall be the duty of the Overseers of Highways: Duties of Overseers.

1. To repair and keep in order the highways, within the several districts for which they shall have been elected or appointed respectively;

2. To warn all persons assessed to work on the highways in their respective districts to come and work on such highways according to law;

3. To cause the noxious weeds within the limits of the highways in their respective districts to be cut down or destroyed twice in each year, once before the first day of July, and again before the first day of September; and the requisite labor shall be considered highway work; and

4. To collect all sums due for delinquencies and commutation money, and to execute all lawful orders of the Commissioners of Highways.[1]

[996] SEC. 6. It shall be the duty of the Overseers of Highways, once in every month, from the first day of April to the first day of December, to cause all the loose stones lying on the beaten track of every road within their respective districts to be removed. To remove loose stones.

[997.] SEC. 7. Two-thirds of the assessment of highway taxes shall be collected from all the resident inhabitants in each district, before the first day of July, and all the remainder of said assessment in the discretion of the Overseer. When Assessment to be collected.

[998.] SEC. 8. The Commissioners of Highways of each township shall cause guide posts, with proper inscriptions and devices thereon, to be erected and kept in repair at the intersection of all post roads in their township, and at the intersection of such other roads therein as they may deem necessary. Guide posts.

The following improvements have been made on the roads and bridges in said township during the preceding year: (*Here set forth the improvements, and the condition of the roads and bridges.*)

4th. The improvements necessary to be made on the roads and bridges in said township are as follows: (*state what improvements are necessary.*) We estimate the probable expense thereof, beyond what the labor to be assessed in this year will accomplish, at —— dollars.

Given under our hands, this —— day of ————, A.D. 18—.

A. B.
C. D.
E. F.
Commissioners of Highways.

A town has no authority, however, to raise money to aid in the construction of a road which by law is to be made at the expense of the county; and consequently a tax laid by the town for the purpose of collecting the money is illegal and void. So held in Massachusetts.—*Pearson v. Goshen*, 71 *Pick.* 396.

[1] An Overseer of Highways is bound to remove obstructions from the highways within his district, although not specially directed to do so by the Commissioners.—*McFadden v. Kingsbury*, 11 *Wend.* 667.

Labor assessed for highway purposes can only be bestowed upon such roads or highways as are established by law. When lands are dedicated by the owner to public use as streets, they do not become public highways until accepted as such by the public authorities.—*Oswego v. Oswego Canal Co.*, 2 *Seld.* 263.

Townships under the laws of Michigan, and in other Strtes under similar laws, could probably only accept of such dedication, by the action of the Commissioners of Highways, upon proper application, as in other cases of creating roads or highways.

Scrapers and Ploughs.

[999.] SEC. 9. Any Overseer of Highways may procure a good and sufficient iron or steel shod scraper, and a suitable plough, or either of them, for the use of his road district, to be paid for with moneys arising from commutations, delinquencies, or non-resident highway taxes within such district.[a]

Excess of work by Overseer, how paid for.

[1000.] SEC. 10. If any Overseer shall be employed more days in executing the several duties enjoined upon him by this chapter, than he is assessed to work on the highways, he shall be paid for the excess at the rate of seventy-five cents per day, and be allowed to retain the same out of any moneys that may come into the his hands for delinquencies or commutations, under this chapter; but he shall not be allowed to commute for the days he is assessed.

When Commissioners to appoint Overseer, etc.

[1001.] SEC. 11. If any person chosen to the office of Overseer of Highways shall refuse to serve, or if his office shall become vacant, the Commissioners of Highways shall, by warrant under their hands, appoint some other person in his stead; and the Overseers so appointed shall have the same powers, be subject to the same orders, and liable to the same penalties, as Overseers chosen in township meetings.[1]

Warrant to be filed, notice to be given, etc.

[1002.] SEC. 12. The Commissioners of Highways, making such appointment, shall cause such warrant to be filed in the office of the Township Clerk, who shall forthwith give notice thereof to the person appointed, which person shall give written notice of his acceptance to such clerk, within ten days after receiving notice of his appointment.[2]

Penalty for neglect, etc., by Overseer.

[1003.] SEC. 13. Every Overseer of Highways, who shall refuse or neglect to perform any of the duties required of him by law, or which may be lawfully enjoined on him by the Commis-

---

[a] As Amended by Act 51 1848. Laws of 1848, p. 49.

[1] *Form of appointment of Overseer of Highways in case of vacancy.*

Branch County,
Township of *Algansee.* } ss.

Whereas, A. B., who was lately chosen to the office of Overseer of Highways for road district number —— in said Township of *Algansee*, has refused to serve [*or* has removed from said township, by which his said office has become vacant, *or as the case may be.*] Now, therefore, be it known, that we, the Commissioners of Highways of said township, do hereby appoint C. D., to be Overseer of Highways for said road district, number —— and to have the same powers, be subject to the same orders, and liable to the same penalties as if chosen in township meeting.

Given under our hands this —— day of —— A. D. 18—.

E. F.,
G. H.,
I. J.,
Commissioners of Highways.

[2] *Form of Notice of appointment of Overseer of Highway.*

To A. B.,

SIR,—You are hereby notified that the Commissioners of Highways of the Township of *Albion*, have by warrant under their hands bearing date the —— day of —— A. D. 18—, and filed in my office, appointed you Overseer of

sioners of Highways of his township, and for the omission of which a penalty is not hereinafter provided, shall, for any such neglect or refusal, forfeit the sum of ten dollars.[1]

When Commissioners to prosecute for penalty.

[1004.] SEC. 14. It shall be the duty of the Comissioners of Highways of each township, whenever any person resident in their township will make complaint that any Overseer of Highways in such township has refused or neglected to perform any of the duties required of him by law, or shall give, or offer to such Commissioners sufficient security to indemnify them against the costs which may be incurred in prosecuting for the penalty annexed to such refusal or neglect, forthwith to prosecute such Overseer in the name of the People of this State, for the recovery of such penalty.[2] If any Overseer of Highways shall neglect or refuse to warn the residents in his district, liable to do work on the highways, to do such work as the law requires, and his warrant directs, such Overseer shall be liable to pay for all the work not so done or commuted for, at the rate of sixty-

---

Highways for road district No. ——, in said township, instead of C. D., who was chosen to said office and has refused to serve [*or as the case may be.*]

Dated at *Albion*, this —— day of —— 18—.

E. F.,
Township Clerk.

Form of Notice of Acceptance of Office of Overseer of Highways.

To A. B., Township Clerk of the Township of *Calvin*, in the County of *Cass*.

SIR,—You are hereby notified that I accept of the appointment to the office of Overseer of Highways for road district No. —, in said Township of *Calvin*, made by the Commissioners of Highways, by warrant under their hands, bearing date the —— day of ——— A. D. 18—.

Dated this —— day of ——— A. D. 18—.

A. B.

1 An Overseer of Highways is not liable in a *private* action for any error of judgment in the execution of his trust. He is only responsible for any neglect or refusal under the section of the act which subjects him in such case to a penalty.—*Freeman v. Cornwell*, 10 *Johns*. 125.

If, however, he acts maliciously or oppressively, it is otherwise.—5 *Johns*. 135.

2 *Bond of Indemnity to Commissioners of Highways in prosecuting Overseer for Penalty.*

Know all men by these presents, that we, A. B. and C. D., of the Township of *Bath*, in the County of *Clinton*, and State of Michigan, are held and firmly bound unto E. F., G. H. and I. J., Commissioners of Highways, of said township, in the penal sum of ——— dollars, for the payment of which sum, well and truly to be made, we bind ourselves, our heirs, executors and administrators, and each of them firmly by these presents, sealed with our seals and dated this ——— day of —— A. D. 18—.

The condition of the above obligation is such, that whereas the above bounden A. B., has this day made complaint, that L. M., an Overseer of Highways, in said township has refused (*or* neglected) to (*Here state the duty refused or neglected*) duties required of such Overseer by law. Now, if the said A. B., shall promptly pay all costs which may be incurred in prosecuting for the penalty annexed to such refusal [or neglect] by said Overseer, and shall save and keep harmless said Commissioners against all such costs in prosecuting for such penalty, then this obligation to be void, otherwise to remain in full force and effect.

In presence of
O. P.

C. D. [L. S.]
A. B. [L. S.]

When Overseer liable.

two and a half cents per day; and it shall be the duty of the Commissioners of Highways in each township to prosecute any Overseer who may so neglect, or refuse to do his duty, before any Justice of the Peace, or any other Court of competent jurisdiction, and collect of him what he may be liable to pay under the provisions of this act, unless such Overseer shall show satisfactory cause to such Justice of the Peace, or such Court, why he should not pay the same: *Provided*, That in all cases where judgement shall be recovered against any such Overseer, under the provisions of this section, such Overseer shall not be further liable to an action for the penalty incurred by such neglect or refusal.[b]

An Act to Authorize the perfecting of the Records of Public Highways, and for other purposes.

[*Approved March*, 28, 1849. *Laws of* 1859, *p.* 175.]

Defective Highway Records to be transcribed by Township Clerk.

[1005.] SECTION 1. *Be it enacted by the Senate and House of Representatives of the State of Michigan*, That the clerk of any township where the records of highways, filed and recorded prior to the first day of January, eighteen hundred and forty-seven, may be found defective, may and he is hereby authorized to transcribe the legal survey-bill of every such road, having thereon the signature of the Surveyor who made the survey, and the names of the Highway Commissioners of the township for the time being, or a majority of them.

How Clerk to transcribe the same.

[1006.] SEC. 2. The clerk in transcribing, where characters, initials, signs and figures are used in the survey bills herein required to be transcribed, shall write the same in words at full length, but the names of the Highway Commissioners, where there is no order establishing the survey as a public highway, shall be omitted.

When transcribed, Commissioners to meet at office of Township Clerk.

[1007.] SEC. 3. Where clerk of any township shall have transcribed the survey bills of his township, according to the provisions of the preceding sections of this act, it shall be his duty to give notice thereof to the Commissioners of Highways of his township, and it shall be the duty of said Commissioners, or a majority of them, within ten days after the receipt of such notice, to meet at the office of such Township Clerk.[1]

---

[b] As Amended by Act 69 of 1848. Laws of 1848, p. 71.

[1] *Form of Township Clerks' Notice to Commissioners of Highways of Transcribing Survey Bills.*

To the Commissioners of Highways of the Township of *Bellevue*, in the County of *Eaton*.

You are hereby notified, that I have transcribed according to the statute in such case, made and provided, the legal survey bill of every road in said township of *Bellevue* having thereon the signature of the surveyor, who made the survey, and the names of the Highway Commissionars of the township for the time being, or a majority of them; the records of which were filed and recorded prior to the 1st day of January, 1847, and which were found defective.

Dated at *Bellevue*, this —— day of ——— A. D. 18—.

A. B.,
Township Clerk.

[1008.] SEC. 4. When so met, it shall be the duty of said Commissioners, and they are hereby authorized to affix their order and determination, establishing as public highways so many roads as there are survey bills transcribed according to the provisions of this act, or so many thereof as, in their opinion, the public interest may require: *Provided*, That nothing herein shall be construed as authorizing the Commissioners of Highways to establish by their order, or in any manner to affect the record of any road, except such as was surveyed, opened and traveled as late as January first, eighteen hundred and forty-nine.[1]

Commissioners to establish as Highways such of the Roads as the public interest may require.

[1009.] SEC. 5. The said Commissioners, after having made their order on the corrected copies of the survey bills, as prescribed in the last preceding section of this act, shall deliver the same to the Township Clerk, whose duty it shall be to cause the same to be filed and recorded, as provided in chapter twenty-five, section one, of the Revised Statutes of eighteen hundred and forty-six.

Determination of Commissioners to be recorded.

[1010.] SEC. 6. The corrected copy of the survey bill of any township road, filed and recorded in pursuance of the provisions of the last preceding section, shall be denominated the corrected record of highways of said township, and as such, shall be deemed of the same force and effect that they would have had in law had they been made perfect at the time the surveys were taken.

Effect of corrected Record.

SEC. 7. This act shall be in force from and after its passage.

An Act authorizing the Commissioners of Highwags of Townships to establish Water-Courses, and locate ditches in certain cases.

Laws 1859, p. 1064.

SECTION 1. *The People of the State of Michigan enact*, That if the persons interested in any water-course, or in draining their lands by a ditch, shall agree to the establishment of such water-course, or location of such ditch, and the apportionment of the labor, cost and expenses, that each person or tract of land interested in or benefitted by such water-course or ditch shall bear in opening and maintaining the same, they shall make a map thereof, showing the commencement and termination of such water-course or ditch, by courses and distances from the

Agreement of persons as to location of water-courses or ditches.

---

[1]*Form of Order of Commissioners, establishing public highways where survey bills have been transcribed.*

Genesee County,
Township of *Agentine* } ss.

We, the Commissioners of Highways for said Township of *Genesee*, do order and determine, that the road described in the survey bill hereto affixed, be and the same is hereby established as a public highway.

Witness our hands, this —— day of ——— A. D. 18—.

A. B.,
C. D.,
E. F.,
Commissioners of Highways.

NOTE.—A separate order may be affixed to each survey bill, or the whole may be embodied in one, referring particularly to, and describing each survey bill.

Proceedings. nearest section corner, or quarter post, or other permanent monument, and the intermediate courses and distances, the width and depth thereof, and divide the same into as many sections, numbering them, as there shall be persons or tracts of land contributing to the construction and maintenance of the same, in accordance with the apportionment of labor to each person or tract of land, and shall attach thereto a certificate describing such water-course or ditch, its commencement, courses, distances, termination, width, depth, number of sections, and length of each section, giving the name of each person, and description of each tract of land, benefitted by such water-course or ditch, and designating the section, by number, that each person or tract of land shall open and maintain, and shall sign such certificate, and file the same with the clerk of the township or townships in which such water-course or ditch shall be located, and said clerk shall file and keep the same in his office with the town records, in the same manner that records of highways are now required by law to be filed and kept; and said persons shall, before filing said map and certificate, as aforesaid, cause a measurement to be made of each section on the ground, a stake or boundary, numbered as aforesaid, to be placed at the end of each section, for the benefit of each person interested, which ditch or water-course, located and apportioned by agreement, as aforesaid, duly filed as aforesaid, shall have all the force and effect, and be as binding in law as if located and established by the Commissioners of Highways under the provisions of this act.

Agreement binding in law.

Highway Commissioners to apportion labor in case of disagreement.

SEC. 2. If such persons shall agree as to the location and dimensions of such water-course or ditch, but shall be unable to agree upon the apportionment of the labor, costs and expenses of opening and maintaining the same, they may make a map and certificate, as provided in the first section of this act, omitting therein the division into sections, and the apportionment of labor, costs and expenses in opening and maintaining the same, sign the same, and deliver it to the Highway Commissioners of the township or townships in which the water-course or ditch is located, and such Commissioners shall at once proceed to measure said water-course or ditch, and apportion the labor, costs and expenses thereof, among the persons signing said certificate and the land benefitted in its proportion, in the same manner and with like effect as provided in this act in cases of locating and establishing without the agreement of parties, and shall file their certificate of apportionment, together with said maps and certificate of agreement, with the clerk of the township or townships wherein located, who shall file and return the same, as in other cases in this act, which water-course or ditch, when so located, established and apportioned, partly by agreement and partly by Commissioners shall have the same force and effect as if done entirely by agreement or by commissioners, as provided by this act.

Certificate filed.

SEC. 3. That the Commissioners of Highways shall have power, upon application of any party interested, to enter upon any lands in their townships, to view any water-course or proposed ditch, for the purpose of draining such swamps, marshes, and other low lands, and lands owned and held by one or more persons as do, in their judgment, affect injuriously the health of the inhabitants; and in case the parties interested in such lands can not agree where such water-course or ditch shall be located and opened, or as to the apportionment of the labor, costs and expenses that each person interested, or tract of land drained or benefitted by said water-course or ditch shall bear said Commissioners shall cause such water-course or ditch to be located and surveyed, if necessary, and shall set apart to each person, or tract of land drained or benefitted by the same, such portion thereof, to be opened and maintained by such person, or tract of land as the said commissioners shall deem just and right, according to the benefits to be derived by him or advantage to such tract of land drained and benefitted by opening such water-course or ditch.

Power of Commissioners to locate ditches.

Apportion labor, expenses, &c.

SEC. 4. That when any person shall make application to said commissioners, as prescribed in the third section of this act, said commissioners shall at once appoint a time and place for making such examination and hearing, and such persons shall give notice in writing to all persons interested in the proposed ditch or water-course, if known to such person, of such application and the time when, and place where, said commissioners will meet to make such examination, which notice shall be served personally upon said parties, or by copy left at the residence of such party, at least three days before the day appointed by said commissioners as aforesaid; and a copy of such notice, together with the affidavit of service thereof, and the publication of notice as herein provided shall be taken as evidence that the same has been regularly served and published; and if any parties reside without the State, or county or township, it shall be lawful to give such notice by publication thereof for two successive weeks before such time appointed, as aforesaid, in some newspaper of general circulation in the county, and said commissioners shall have power to administer oaths as to verification of services and publication of notice, and in all other cases, necessary in enforcing the provisions of this act.

Proceedings on application for Commissioners to locate, &c.

Notice to parties.

SEC. 5. On such examination, if said commissioners shall determine to locate such ditch or establish such water-course, they shall make a survey of the proposed route, if necessary, and shall make a map or diagram thereof, showing its commencement, courses, distances, termination and dimensions, and divide the same into as many sections, numbered, as there are tracts of land to be drained or benefitted by such water-course or ditch; and shall attach thereto their official certificate showing the commencement and termination of the same, from the nearest section corner or quarter post, or other permanent

Survey maps, &c.

What map to show.

Certificate of Commissioners. boundary, and the intermediate courses and distances and dimensions thereof; and in case the owners of land through which the same is located, shall not release all claim for damages on account of locating and opening the same, the said commissioners shall make a list of twenty-four disinterested free-holders of said county, residing in the vicinity of such property, from which said commissioners shall strike off the names of six, and the persons claiming damage, six; and if no such persons appear, or appearing, refuse or neglect to act, then said commissioners shall strike off other six, and the remaining twelve shall be the jurors elected; and said commissioners shall at once issue a venire, signed by them, directed to the sheriff or any constable of said county, commanding him to summons said jurors, naming them, to be and appear before him forthwith, and at such other time as they shall direct, not more than three days from the date of said venire, to serve as jurors to ascertain the necessity of taking certain property for the purpose of such ditch or water-course, and to appraise the damage thereon; and if all said jurors shall not appear, the said sheriff or constable shall summons talesmen to make a full jury. The said jurors shall be sworn by said commissioners, or one of them, to ascertain the necessity of locating and opening such ditch or water-course described in said certificate, and to appraise the just compensation thereof, and damages thereon, if any. The said jury shall take said map and certificate of said commissioners, and after viewing the premises described therein, they shall make return to said commissioner in writing, signed by them, of their doings, which shall state the necessity of such water-course or ditch, and the amount of compensation or damage appraised, if any, to all persons injuriously affected or damaged by said ditch or water-course, and to whom payable, which venire and return of said jury shall be filed in the office of the clerk of said township or townships, and in case said jury can not agree another may be chosen and sworn in like manner, on the same or some other day, to be appointed by said commissioners, who shall act and make returns as aforesaid, and successive jurors may be chosen, sworn and act as aforesaid, until they shall agree, if the parties interested desire it, or said commissioners may then or in the first instance, apply to the probate court of their county for the appointment of the [three] commissioners to act in place of said jury, who shall take the same oath of said jurors, and shall perform the same duties prescribed above for said jury, and the certificate of their appointment by said probate court with their return shall be filed in the town clerk's office in same manner as return of the jury: *Provided*, That if said jury or commissioners shall certify that said water-course or ditch is not necessary, all further action in that case shall be suspended for six months; at the expiration of which time another jury or set of commissioners may be called or appointed as aforesaid, if the parties interested desire it, and in case such jury or commis-

Margin notes: Provision for jury for estimate of damage. — Oath of jurors. — Return of jury. — What to state. — New jury. — Proviso.

sioners agree and make return as aforesaid, the commissioners of highways shall proceed as aforesaid.

Commissioners to apportion labor, expenses, &c.

SEC. 6. If the said jury or said commissioners of appraisal, so appointed, shall return that said water-course or ditch is necessary, and shall award the compensation or damage as aforesaid, the said Commissioners of Highways shall, as soon thereafter as may be, proceed to apportion the labor, costs and expenses of opening and maintaining said ditch or water-course, among the several persons interested therein, and upon the lands drained and benefitted thereby, in such amount and proportion as they shall deem just and right, and shall cause a measurement to be made of such portion thereof, as they shall award to each person or tract of land, and cause a stake or monument to be placed at each boundary line, and number the same, to correspond with the said numbers on said map and certificate for the benefit of those interested, and shall officially certify the number of each section they so award to each person or tract of land; which certificate, together with said map and certificate of location and dimensions, and other papers in the case, shall be filed in the office of the clerk of the township in which the same is located, to be there preserved as the records of such townships for the benefit of those interested; and such award and apportionment of labor as aforesaid, by said Commissioners of Highways when duly filed as aforesaid, shall thenceforth be an obligation against such owner of lands benefitted and assessed, and a lien upon such tract of land to open and always maintain such portion of such ditch or water-course in accordance with the order of the Commissioners of Highways of such townships.

Boundaries defined.

Filing of certificate.

Apportionment to be a lien.

Notice to owners.

SEC. 7. Said Commissioners of Highways, after having made said apportionment and filed certificate thereof, shall, within a reasonable time, cause a written notice to be served upon the persons owning or interested in the land drained and benefitted as apportioned, if known to said commissioners, setting forth the section or sections of said ditch or water-course he is bound to open and maintain by his agreemant or by said apportionment, and shall order him to open said ditch or water-course of the width and depth described in said map and certificate so filed by agreement or by said commissioners, within such reasonable time as they shall, in said order, specify, and that he may keep open and sustain without obstruction, his said portion thereof, of the width and depth designated in said map or certificate, and in all cases of non-residence of such persons, such order and notice may be posted in three public places nearest to the said land so owned and assessed for draining as aforesaid, and the certificate of the commissioners or affidavit of other persons as to such service and posting, filed in said clerk's office, shall be deemed conclusive evidence of the regular service and posting of said notice and order.

Order to open water-course.

Commissioners to contract for opening ditches in case of refusal by owner.

SEC. 8. If any person interested in said water-course or proposed ditch, and assessed, as aforesaid, for opening the same, shall fail to procure the cutting of said ditch, or opening of said water-course, through that section of the same so apportioned to him, and against his land, as aforesaid, by said commissioners, or by agreement, at the time and manner designated by said commissioners in such order and notice, said commissioners shall cause the same to be done, either by public or private contract, on such reasonable terms as they are able to procure, and give to such person having performed the labor aforesaid a certificate of the amount and value of the labor by him performed, or caused to be performed, with a description of the land against which such labor was apportioned; and the person holding such certificate shall be authorized, after demand and refusal to pay, to file the same with the Supervisors of the township where the land is situated, who shall enter the same upon the tax roll of his township against the land described in said certificate benefitted by the cutting and opening of said ditch or water-course, in a column entitled "delinquent ditch tax," in the same manner that delinquent highway taxes are required by law to be entered, and the amount so entered, together with the legal interest thereon, shall be collected by the Township Treasurer, the same as other taxes, and when collected, shall be paid over to the person or persons entitled to receive the same: *Provided*, That if the person owning any land so benefitted, and assessed and interested in said ditch or water-course, reside out of the State or county, shall fail to pay the Township Treasurer for the use of the person holding such certificate, for thirty days after the labor has been performed, the person holding the same may file it with the Supervisor of the township where said land is situated, who shall levy the same upon the tax roll of his township, in the manner above stated, and the same shall be collected and paid over as provided in other cases in this section: *Provided further*, That no Supervisor shall be obliged to levy the tax as aforesaid, unless said certificate contain a perfect description of the land subject to the amount so claimed.

Expenses how paid.

Proviso.

Unpaid tax.

SEC. 9. If the tax on the land so assessed on the tax roll for delinquent ditch tax shall not be collected by the Treasurer of said Town, the same shall be returned, advertised and sold, the same as lands are returned and sold for other taxes.

Ditches in two or more townships.

SEC. 10. In cases where any proposed ditch or water-course shall be in more than one township, application shall be made to the Highway Commissioners of each of said townships, and in such case a majority of the commissioners of such townships shall be competent to create and establish the ditch or water-course: *Provided, always*, That no commissioner shall serve in any case wherein he is personally interested. Any two commissioners may form a quorum for the transaction of business, and should such township be without a quorum, it shall be law-

Proviso.

ful for the commissioners of any adjoining township to perform like duties with like powers, as residents of any such township.

SEC. 11. All persons to whom damages shall be awarded, as herein provided, for cutting any ditch, or opening water-course, or throwing up any embankment, or changing any water-course, shall be paid therefor by the persons interested, the amount of such award, on demand of said commissioners, within thirty days after damage shall have been ascertained, as in this act provided. **Damages, by whom paid.**

SEC. 12. The person interested in said ditch or water-course shall be responsible for the fees of the officers, juries, and commissioners under this act, and for the amount of damages awarded by the jury or commissioners for the opening of the proposed ditch or water-course, and shall be by them, or some of them, deposited with the said Commissioners of Highways, before said commissioners shall order the same cut and opened; and in case such person, or persons, advance the whole of such sum, or an undue proportion thereof, he shall notify said commissioners of the amount he or they have advanced, and the same shall be credited to him in said apportionment of labor in opening said ditch. **Fees of officers juries, amount of damages, &c., by whom paid.**

SEC. 13. Highway Commissioners and other persons refusing, failing or neglecting to perform any of the duties imposed by this act, shall forfeit and pay a fine of five dollars for every such neglect and refusal, to be recovered before any justice of the peace in his township, for the benefit of common schools in such township, at the suit of any person feeling aggrieved thereby. **Penalty.**

SEC. 14. The Commissioners of Highways shall receive for service under this act, each one dollar per day, and half dollar for each half day for the time actually employed. The judge of probate the sum of fifty cents for making appointment of commissioners and certificate thereof. The sheriff and constable the same as in other cases of serving venire, and juries the same fees as in cases before justices of the peace. **Compensation of commissioners.**

SEC. 15. Whoever shall wilfully obstruct any such ditch or water-course, or injure the same, shall forfeit for every such offense a sum not exceeding twenty-five dollars, to be recovered before a justice of the peace of such township, for the benefit of common schools in such township, at suit of any person making complaint, and shall also remove such obstruction, and in default thereof for three days shall be liable to action therefor, before any justice of the peace of the town, at the suit of the Commissioners of Highways, to be expended by said commissioners in removing such obstructions, and the fees of commissioners in superintending the same, and attending to such suit. **Penalty for obstructing water course.**

SEC. 16. The power herein conferred upon Highway Commissioners, shall also extend to, and include deepening, widening and cleaning out any ditches or drains that have been heretofore made or shall hereafter be construed. **Power extended**

Approved February 15, 1859.

An Act Relative to the Streets of Recorded, but Unincorporated Village Plats.

[*Approved March* 6, 1844. *Laws of* 1844, *p.* 28.]

Streets on plats of unincorporated villages to be under care of Overseers of Highways,

[1011.] SECTION 1. *Be it enacted by the Senate and House of Representatives of the State of Michigan,* That such Streets of Recorded, but unincorporated Village Plats, as the Commissioners of Highways shall deem to be required for public highways, shall be included in the several road districts of the respective townships in which they are situated, and shall be subject to the care and superintendence of the Commissioners and Overseers of Highway relative to repairs, and in like manner as other highways are now by law provided for.

16 Barb. S. C. R. 251.

SEC. 2. This act shall take effect and be in force from and after its passage.

An Act Relative to State Roads.

[*Approved March* 28, 1836. *Laws of* 1836, *p.* 102.]

State Roads to be in charge of Commissioners of Highways.

[1012.] SECTION 1. *Be it enacted by the Senate and House of Representatives of the State of Michigan,* That all State Roads which are now, or hereafter may be laid out in this State, shall be under the care of the Commissioners of Highways of the several townships through which the same shall pass, and subject to be by them opened and kept in repair, in the same manner as Township Roads may be by them opened and kept in repair.

DIVISION XII.—OF PERSONS LIABLE TO WORK ON HIGHWAYS, AND MAKING ASSESSMENTS THEREFOR.

Comp. Laws, 1857, CHAP. XX p. 346.

Chapter Twenty-Three of Revised Statutes of 1846.

N. Y. Rev. Stat. Art. 2, Title 1, Chap. 16, Part 1.

Persons liable to be Assessed.

[1013.] SECTION 1. Every person owning or occupying land in the township in which he resides, and every male inhabitant above the age of twenty-one, and under fifty years, except as hereinafter provided, residing in the township where the assessment is made, shall be assessed to work on the highways in such township; and the lands of non-residents, situated in such township, shall be assessed for highway labor as hereinafter provided.

When Tax to be Assessed.

Laws 1859, p. 473.

1844, p. 69, Sec. 2.

[1014.] SEC. 2. The Commissioners of Highways of the several townships shall meet at the office of the Supervisor, on the third Monday of May in each year, for the purpose of assessing a highway tax, and they shall have free access to the assessment roll until they shall have completed their assessment.[a]

List to be furnished by Overseers.

[1015.] SEC. 3. Each of the Overseers of Highways shall, within sixteen days after his election, or appointment, deliver to the Township Clerk a list subscribed by him, of the names of all the inhabitants in his road district who are liable to work on the highways.[14]

Statement and description of Property.

[1016.] SEC. 4. The Commissioners of Highways in each township shall make out from the assessment roll, a separate list and statement of the valuation of all the taxable personal property, and a description of all lots or parcels of land within each road district in such township, inserting in a separate part of such list descriptions of land owned by non-residents of the township, with the value of each lot or parcel set down opposite to such description, as the same shall appear on the assess-

---

[a] An Act to Amend Chapter Twenty-Three of the Revised Statutes of 1846, relative to Highway Taxes. Aproved April 2, 1850. Laws of 1850, p. 296.

SECTION 1. *Be it enacted by the Senate and House of Representatives of the State of Michigan,* That section Two, of Chapter Twenty-Three of the Revised Statutes of eighteen hundred and forty-six, shall not apply to the counties of Chippewa, Marquette, Houghton, Schoolcraft and Ontonagon.

SEC. 2. That the Commissioners of Highways of each of the counties above named, shall meet at the office of the Supervisor on the third Monday of July in each year, for the purpose of Assessing a Highway Tax, and shall have free access to the Assessment Roll until they shall have completed their Assessment.

[14]*Form of list of names of Inhabitants liable to Work on Highway.*

The following is a list of the names of all the inhabitants in my road district, being district No. —— in the Township of *Adams*, and County of *Hillsdale*, who are liable to work on the highways.

John Jones, *George Church,*
Jeremy Jackson, *John Doe,*

Witness my hand, this —— day of —— A. D. 18—.

A. B.,
Overseer of Highways.

M

ment roll; and if such lot or tract was not separately described in such roll, then in proportion to the valuation which shall have been affixed to the whole tract of which such lot or parcel forms a part.[15]

Assessment, how made.

[1017.] SEC. 5. In making the estimate and assessment of highway labor, the Commissioners shall proceed as follows:

1. Every male inhabitant in each road district, being above the age of twenty-one, and under the age of fifty, except paupers, persons of color not possessing taxable property, idiots and lunatics, shall be assessed one day;

1840, p. 81, Sec. 3.

2. The residue of the highway labor to be assessed, not exceeding one day's work upon one hundred dollars of the valuation, shall be apportioned upon the estate, real and personal, of every inhabitant in each of the road districts in such township, and upon each tract or parcel of land in the respective road districts, of which the owners are non-residents, as the same shall appear by the assessment roll;

3. The Commissioners shall affix to the name of each person named in the lists furnished by the Overseers, and not assessed upon the assessment roll, and also to each valuation of property within the several road districts, the number of days which such person or property shall be assessed for highway labor, adding one day to the assessment of each person liable to a poll tax, and assessed upon the township assessment roll.

Clerk to make duplicates.

[1018.] SEC. 6. The clerk of the Board of Commissioners shall, under their direction, make duplicates of the several lists, which shall be subscribed by the Commissioners, one of which

---

[15] *Form of list and statement of Assessment of Highway Taxes.*

At a meeting of the Commissioners of Highways of the Township of *Delhi*, in the Couuty of *Ingham*, at the office of the Supervisor of said Township, on the —— day of May, A. D. 18—, being the second Monday thereof, for the purpose of assessing a highway tax, said Commissioners did proceed and have made out from the assessment roll, the following separate list and statement of the valuation of all the taxable personal property, and a description of all lots and parcels of land, within each road district in said Township; inserting in a separate part of such list, descriptions of lands owned by non-residents of said township, with the value of each lot or parcel set down opposite to such description, as the same appears on the assessment roll.

NAMES.	VALUE OF PER. PROP.	DESCRIPTION OF LAND.	VALUE OF EACH LOT.	NO. OF DAYS. POLL TAX.	TAX.
A. B.	500.00	E. ½ of the N. E. ¼ Sec. 10.	1000.00	11	
C. D.	500.00	W. ½ of the N. E. ¼ Sec. 10.	800.00	9	
		LANDS OWNED BY NON-RESIDENTS.			
Unk'wn		E. ½ of the N. E. ¼ of Sec. 11.	600.00	7	
"		W. ½ of the N. E. ¼ of sec. 11.	600.00	7	

Dated this —— day of —— A. D. 18—.

A. B.,
C. D.,
E. F.,
Commissioners of Highways.

lists for each road district shall be filed by such clerk in his office, and the other shall be forthwith delivered to the Overseer of Highways of the district in which the highway labor therein specified is assessed.

Names of persons omitted. [1019.] SEC. 7. The names of persons left out of any such list, and who ought to have been included therein, and of new inhabitants who have not in the same year been assessed in some other place for highway labor, shall be, from time to time, added to the several lists, and rated by the Overseers in proportion to their taxable real and personal property, as others are rated on such lists by the Commissioners, to work on the highways, subject to an appeal to the Commissioners.

Credit to persons working Private Roads. [1020.] SEC. 8. It shall be the duty of the Commissioners of Highways of each township to credit such persons as live on private roads and work the same, so much upon their assessment on account of such work, as such Commissioners may deem necessary to improve and keep such private roads in repair; or they may annex any such private road to some highway district.

Certain Assessments to be made separate. [1021.] SEC. 9. Whenever the occupant of any land not owned by him, shall be assessed therefor by the Commissioners, they shall distinguish in their assessment list the amount charged upon such land from the personal tax, if any, of such occupant; but when any such land shall be assessed in the name of the occupant, the owner thereof shall not be assessed, during the same year, to work on the highways on account of such land.

When Assessment may be deducted from Rent. [1022.] SEC. 10. Whenever any tenant of any land for a less term than twenty-five years, shall be assessed to work on the highways on account of such land, pursuant to the last section, and shall actually perform such work, or commute therefor, he shall be entitled to a deduction from the rent due, or to become due from him for such land, equal to the full amount of such assessment, or he may recover the same of his landlord in an action for money paid for his benefit, estimating the same at so much as is, or shall be prescribed by law for commutation per day for highway labor, unless otherwise provided by agreement between such tenant and his landlord.

Comp. Laws, 1857. Chap. XXI p. 349.

DIVISION XIII.—Of the duties of Overseers in regard to the performance of labor on highways; and of the performance of such labor, or the commutation therefor, and application of moneys by the commissioners.

N. Y. R. S., Art. 3, Title 1, Chap. 16, Part 1.

Chapter Twenty-Four of Revised Statutes of 1846.

Notice to persons Assessed.

[1023.] Section 1. It shall be the duty of the Overseers of Highways to give at least twenty-four hours' notice to all persons assessed to work on the highways in their respective districts, and residing in their townships, of the time and place when and where they are to appear for that purpose, and with what implements.[16]

When Agent of non-resident to be notified.

[1024.] Sec. 2. It shall be the duty of the several Overseers of Highways to notify the agent of every non-resident owner of lands within their respective districts, if they shall know that any such agent resides within the township, of the number of days assessed upon the lands of such non-resident, and of the time when, and place where the labor is to be performed; which notice shall be given at least five days previous to the time appointed.

Commutation for work, etc.

[1025.] Sec. 3. Every person liable to work on the highways, shall work the whole number of days for which he shall have been assessed; but every such person, other than an Overseer, whether resident or non-resident, may elect to commute for the same or any part thereof, at the rate of one dollar for each day, in which case such commutation money shall be paid to the Overseer of Highway of the district in which the labor is required to be performed, and shall be applied and expended by such Overseer in the purchase of implements, or construction and repair of the roads and bridges in the same district, except when said taxes are otherwise appropriated, or disposed of by law.[a]

When Commutation to be paid.

[1026.] Sec. 4. Every person intending to commute as aforesaid, shall within twenty-four hours after he shall be notified to appear and work on the highways, pay the commutation money

---

[16] *Form of notice to work on highways.*

To *James Jackson,* residing in the road district No. —— in the Township of *Berlin,* in the County of *Ionia.* You have been assessed to work on the highways in said district —— days, you will therefore appear at (*here state the place where*) on the —— day of —— A. D. 18—, at —— o'clock, A. M., with (*here state with what implements.*)

A. B.,
Overseer.

[a] As Amended by "An Act to Amend Sections Three and Sixteen of Chapter Twenty-Four, Title Six, of the Revised Statutes of 1846, so as to increase the rate of Commutation for Labor assessed on the Highways." Approved February 3, 1857. Laws of 1857, p. 45.

for the work required of him, and the commutation shall not be considered as complete until such money be paid.

[1027.] SEC. 5. Every Overseer of Highways shall have power to require a cart, wagon, plough or scraper, with a yoke of oxen or span of horses, and a man to manage them, to be furnished by any person having the same within his district, who shall have been assessed and shall be liable for three days or more; and the person furnishing a man and team, with a cart, wagon, plough or scraper, upon such requisition, shall be entitled to a credit of three days for each days' service therewith.

Overseer may require cart, etc., to be furnished.

[1028.] SEC. 6. Every person assessed to work on the highways, and warned to work thereon, may appear and work in person, or by a substitute; and the person so appearing shall actually work eight hours in each day.

Work by substitute.

[1029.] SEC. 7. If any person assessed, or his substitute, shall, after appearing, remain idle, or not work faithfully, or hinder others from working, such offender shall, for each offence, pay the sum of one dollar.

Forfeiture for idleness, etc.

[1030.] SEC. 8. Every person so assessed and duly notified, who shall not commute, and who shall refuse or neglect without good cause to appear as above provided, shall, for every day's refusal pay the sum of one dollar; and if he was lawfully required to furnish a team, carriage, man, or implements, and shall refuse or neglect, without good cause, to comply, he shall pay as follows:

Liability for refusal to work, etc.

1. For wholly refusing to comply with such requisition, three dollars and fifty cents for each day;

2. For omitting to furnish a cart, wagon, plough or scraper, one dollar and twenty-five cents for each day;

3. For omitting to furnish a yoke of oxen or span of horses, one dollar and twenty-five cents for each day;

4. For omitting to furnish a man to manage the same, one dollar and twenty-five cents for each day.

[1031.] SEC. 9.[17] It shall be the duty of every Overseer of Highways, within six days after any person shall become liable for the payment of any sum of money under the provisions of either of the last three preceding sections, unless a satisfactory

Overseer, when to make complaint against persons liable for neglect, etc.

---

[17] *Form of complaint of Overseer against persons refusing to work on highways.*

Jackson County, }
Township of *Columbia*. }

The complaint of A. B., Overseer of Highways, in road district No. —— made before C. D., a Justice of the Peace in said township, on the —— day of —— A. D. 18—, The said A. B., being duly sworn doth depose and say that (*here set forth the matter of complaint.*)

A. B.

Subscribed and sworn to before me this —— day of —— A. D. 18—.

C. D.,
Justice of the Peace.

excuse be rendered to him by the person so liable, to make complaint in writing and on oath, to some Justice of the Peace of the township, stating the default, neglect, refusal, or other cause, by reason of which such person became so liable.

Proceedings on complaint,

[1032.] SEC. 10. The Justice to whom such complaint shall be made, shall forthwith issue a summons directed to any constable of the county, requiring him to summon the person against whom the complaint shall have been made, to appear forthwith before such Justice, at some place to be specified in the summons, to show cause why a judgment should not be rendered against him according to law for the cause mentioned in the complaint; which summons shall be served personally.[18]

Judgment and execution.

[1033.] SEC. 11. On the return of such summons, or within such reasonable time thereafter as the Justice shall allow, if no sufficient cause shall be shown to the contrary, the Justice shall render a judgment in favor of the people of this State against such person for the sum which such person shall have become liable to pay on account of the default, neglect, or other delinquency mentioned in the complaint, with the costs of prosecution; and shall forthwith issue an execution under his hand, directed to any constable of the county, commanding him to levy the amount of such judgment, including the costs of the proceedings, of the goods and chattels of such defendant.

Proceedings on execution.

[1034.] SEC. 12. The constable to whom such execution shall be delivered, shall forthwith proceed to collect the moneys therein mentioned, by distress and sale of the goods and chattels of the defendant therein named, giving at least ten days' notice of the time and place of sale; and he shall pay such moneys, when collected, to the Justice who issued the execution, who shall pay the same to the Overseer who entered the complaint, to be by him expended in improving the roads and bridges in his district.

Moneys collected to be set off against Assessment.

[1035.] SEC. 13. Every sum of money collected for a refusal or neglect to appear and work on the highways, shall be set off against the assessment upon which it was founded, estimating every one dollar and twenty-five cents collected, exclusive

---

[18] *Form of Summons against person refusing to work on the highways.*

Kalamazoo County,
Township of *Alamo.*

To any constable of said county, greeting: Whereas, complaint has been made before the undersigned, a Justice of the Peace in and for said township, by A. B., setting forth that [*here set forth the matter of complaint.*]

These are therefore, in the name of the People of the State of Michigan, to command you to summon the said E. F. to appear forthwith before the undersigned Justice of the Peace, at his office in said township, to show cause why a judgment should not be rendered against him according to law for the cause mentioned in said complaint; and hereof make due return as the law directs.

Given under the hand and seal of said Justice, this — day of — A. D. 18—

C. D., [L. S.]
Justice of the Peace.

of the costs of the proceedings, as a satisfaction for one days' work.

[1036.] SEC. 14. The acceptance by an Overseer of an excuse for a refusal or neglect, shall not in any case exempt the person excused from commuting for, or working the whole number of days for which he shall have been assessed during the year.

Excuse, effect of.

[1037.] SEC. 15. Every Overseer of Highways shall, on or before the first Monday of October in each year, make out and deliver to the Supervisor of his township, a list of all the lands of non-residents and of persons unknown, which are taxed on his list, upon which the labor assessed has not been paid, and the amount of labor unpaid; and said Overseer shall make and subscribe an affidavit thereon, before some person competent to administer oaths, or before the Supervisor, that the labor assessed upon the lands so returned has not been performed, and remains unpaid.[19]

List of non-resident Lands, etc., to be delivered to Supervisor.

1844, p. 69, Sec. 4.

[1038.] SEC. 16. The Supervisor of each township shall cause the amount of such arrearages of labor, estimating the same at one dollar for each day, to be levied on the lands so returned, and to be collected in the same manner that the contingent charges of the township are collected; and the same, when collected, shall be paid into the Township Treasury, to be applied by the Commissioners of Highways, in the construction and improvement of roads and bridges in the road district for the benefit of which the labor was originally assessed, except

Supervisor to cause delinquent taxes to be collected, etc.

---

[19]*Form of Overseer's return to Supervisor of unpaid taxes upon lands of unknown persons and non-residents.*

The following is a list of all the lands in road district No. ——, in the Township of *Ada*, of non-residents and of persons unknown, which are taxed on my list for the year 18—, upon which the labor assessed has not been paid, and the amount of labor unpaid.

NAMES OF OWNERS.	DESCRIPTION OF LAND.	AM'T OF LABOR UNPAID.
A. B.	N. W. 1-4 of Sec. 12.	3 days.
C. D.	N. E. 1-4 of Sec. 12.	3 Do.
E. F.	S. E. 1-4 of S. E. 1-4 of Sec. 12.	2 Do.
Unknown.	N. E. 1-4 of S. E. 1-4 of Sec. 12.	2 Do.

Dated this —— day of —— A. D. 18—.

G. H.,
Overseer.

Form of affidavit to be attachad to foregoing statement.

Township of } ss.

G. H., an Overseer of Highways, whose name is subscribed to the foregoing list, being duly sworn, doth depose and say, that the labor assessed upon the land so returned has not been performed and ramains unpaid.

G. H.,

Subscribed and sworn to before me this —— day of —— A. D. 18—.

A. B.,
Supervisor.

when said taxes are otherwise appropriated, or disposed of by law.[b]

Account to be rendered by Overseer.

[1039.] SEC. 17. Every Overseer of Highways shall, on or before the second Saturday next preceding the time of holding the annual township meeting, render to the Commissioners of Highways an account in writing, verified by his oath, to be administered by the Township Clerk, or some other person competent to administer such oath, and containing:

1. The names of all persons assessed to work on the highways in his district;

2. The names of all those who have actually worked on the highways, with the number of days they have so worked;

3. The names of all those against whom judgments have been recovered by virtue of this chapter, and the sums so recovered;

4. The names of all those who have commuted, and the amounts paid by them, and the manner in which the moneys arising from judgments and commutations have been expended by him;

5. A list of all the non-resident lands in his district upon which the labor has been performed or commuted for.[c][20]

---

[b] As Amended by Act of February 3, 1857. See note to Section 1025.

[c] See the Act of March 6, 1849, next following.

[20] *Form of annual account of Overseer of Highways.*

The annual account of A. B., Overseer of Highways for road district number —— in the Township of *Allison* and County of *Lapeer*, render to the Commissioners of Highways of said township;

1st. The names of all persons assessed to work on the highways in said district are as follows: (*here insert the names.*)

2d. The names of all those who have actually worked on the Highways with the number of days they have so worked are as follows:

NAMES.	NO. OF DAYS WORKED.
Oliver Owen,	2
Alfred Gregory,	3

3d. The names of all those against whom judgments have been recovered by virtue of chapter 21 of the Compiled Statutes, and the sums so recovered are as follows:

NAMES.	SUMS RECOVERED.
George Johnson,	$3.00
Andrew Fiddler,	4.00

4th. The names of all those who have commuted, and the amounts paid by them, and the manner in which the moneys arising from judgments and commutations have been expended by me are as follows:

NAMES OF PERSONS COMMUTING.	AMOUNT.
John Winslow,	$2.25.

I have received for amount of judgments and commutations as above set forth the sum of $——, of which amount I have expended the sum of, in

[1040.] SEC. 18. Every such Overseer shall, immediately upon the rendering of such account, pay over to the Township Treasurer all moneys collected by him for judgments and commutations, and remaining unexpended, to be applied by the Commissioners in the construction and improvement of roads and bridges in the road district of the Overseer who paid over the same.

Overseers to pay over Moneys collected in their hands, etc.

[1041.] SEC. 19. If any Overseer shall neglect or refuse to pay over any moneys remaining unexpended in his hands, as required by the preceding section, it shall be the duty of the Township Treasurer forthwith to sue for the same in his name of office, in an action for money had and received to the use of such Treasurer, which moneys, when collected, shall be applied as provided in the preceding section.

When Township Treasurer to sue for Moneys, etc.

[1042.] SEC. 20.[21] No money shall be drawn by the Commissioners of Highways from the Township Treasury, in payment of any labor, contract, or materials furnished, except by an order signed by a majority of them, and accompanied by their certificate that the labor has been actually performed, or the

Highway Moneys how drawn.

1841, p. 159, Sec. 5

(*here state how the money has been expended*) and no moneys remain in my hands unexpended, (*or the sum of $—— remains in my hands unexpended.*)

5th. The following is a list of all the non-resident lands in my district upon which the labor has been performed or commuted for.

NAMES.	DESCRIPTION OF LANDS.
George Sands,	N. E. 1-4 of S. E. 1-4 of Sec. 10.
John Myers,	N. 1-2 of N. W. 1-4 of Sec. 10.

Dated this —— day of —— A. D. 18—.

JOHN JONES,
Overseer.

Subscribed and sworn to before me this —— day of —— A. D. 18—.

A. B.,
Township Clerk.

[21] *Form of Order of Commissioners of Highways on Township Treasurer.*

To the Township Treasurer of the Township of *Blissfield.*

Pay to A. B., or to his order, —— dollars in payment of amount in full (*or in part as the case may be*) for (*here state what for and also out of what fund payable.*)

Given under our hands this —— day of —— A. D. 18—.

C. D.,
E. F.,
G. H.,
Commissioners of Highways.

Form of certificate to accompany foregoing order.

We, the Commissioners of Highways of the township of——, do hereby certify that the labor for which the amount of the accompanying warrant is to apply in payment has been actually performed [*or as the case may be.*]

Given under our hands this —— day of —— A. D. 18—.

C. D.,
E. F.,
G. H.,
Commissioners of Highways.

N

contract fulfilled, or materials furnished, for which the amount of such warrant is to apply in payment.

Letting of contracts for repairs, etc.

[1043.] SEC. 21. Whenever the Commissioners of Highways shall determine to appropriate any portion over ten dollars of the moneys accruing to their township on account of non-resident highway taxes, in the repairing or construction of roads or bridges therein, they shall contract at public auction, with the lowest bidder giving good and sufficient security, for the performance thereof; and not less than ten days' notice shall be given by said Commissioners, of the time and place of letting such contracts, by posting up such notice in at least three of the most public places in their township.[d] [22]

141, p. 159, Sec. 6.

An Act to Amend Chapter Twenty-Four of the Revised Statutes of One Thousand Eight Hundred and Forty-Six.

[*Approved March* 6, 1849. *Laws of* 1849, *p.* 61.]

Commissioners of Highways may administer certain oaths.

[1044.] SECTION 1. *Be it enacted by the Senate and House of Representatives of the State of Michigan*, That any Commissioner of Highways be, and is hereby authorized to administer the oath required by section seventeen of chapter twenty-four of the Revised Statutes of one thousand eight hundred and forty-six.

Where the plaintiff sued the defendant on the following instrument: "The Commissioners of Highways of the township of Rowland will pay the bearer twenty-two dollars when funds in road district number three and four.

ALEXANDER PALMER,
HENRY CORNWELL,
Commissioners of Highways in said Township.

ROWLAND, Feb. 22d, 1841."

Held,—It was not a warrant or order upon the Township Treasurer under the Act Sess. L., 1841, p. 159, Sec. 5; but a draft drawn by Commissioners upon themselves, and that an action could not be sustained upon it against the Township.—*Monroe v. Township of Rowland*, 1 *Mich.* 318.

d As Amended by Act 206 of 1848, p. 313 Section 2.

[22]*Form of Commissioner's notice of letting contract to build bridge.*

Public notice is hereby given that the undersigned Commissioners of Highways of the Township of *Dover*, in the County of *Lenawee*, will on the —— day of —— A. D. 18—, at the hour of— o'clock, — M., at ——, let at public auction, to the lowest bidder giving good and sufficient security for the performance thereof, contracts for the construction of bridges in said township as follows: (*here set forth the place where the bridge or bridges are to be constructed with the proper description thereof.*)

A. B.,
C. D.,
E. F.,
Commissioners of Highways.

DIVISION XIV. — OF LAYING OUT, ALTERING AND DISCONTINUING PUBLIC ROADS.

COMP. L. 1857, Chap. XXII., p. 355.

An Act to Repeal Chapter Twenty-five of the Revised Statutes of 1846; also, Act Eighty-Eight, entitled an Act to Amend Chapter Twenty-Five of the Revised Statutes of 1846, relative to Laying Out, Altering and Discontinuing Highways, Approved March Eighteen, 1848; also, Act No. Seventy-Two, entitled, an Act to amend Chapter Twenty-Five of the Revised Statutes of 1846, Approved March Fifteen, 1848, and to Provide for Altering, Laying Out, and Discontinuing Highways. *a*

1848, p. 99.
1848, p. 74.

[*Approved February* 17, 1857. *Laws of* 1857, *p.* 413.]

[1045.] SECTION 1. *The People of the State of Michigan enact*, That whenever any ten freeholders, or more persons in any township liable to be assessed for highway labor, shall wish to have a highway in such township laid out, altered or discontinued, they may, by writing, under their hands, make application to the Commissioners of Highways of the township for that purpose, who shall proceed to lay out, alter or discontinue such highway as hereinafter directed: *Provided*, That no second application shall be made within twelve months for the same purpose.

Application to have Road laid out, altered or discontinued.
3 Mich. Rep. 121.
Laws of 1848, p. 99.

[1046.] SEC. 2. Whenever the Commissioners of Highways shall be applied to, as mentioned in the preceding section, to alter, lay out, or discontinue any highway, they shall cause an accurate survey to be made of such road, and shall incorporate such survey in an order to be signed by them, and shall cause such order to be filed in the office of the Township Clerk, who shall note upon the order the time of filing the same.

Survey of Road and order.
3 Mich. Rep. 121.

[1047.] SEC. 3. It shall be the duty of the Township Clerk, whenever any order of the Commissioners for altering, laying out, or discontinuing any road, shall be received by him, forthwith to post a copy of such order on the outer door of the house or building where the township meeting is usually held, or if there be no such building, then in three public places in the township.

Copy of Order to be posted.

[1048.] SEC. 4. The Commissioners, or one of them, shall, within five days after recording the survey order, as provided in the preceding section, make application to a Justice of the Peace of the same, or an adjoining township, for the appointment of a jury of twelve freeholders of the county, to ascertain the necessity of altering or laying out such road, and to appraise the damage thereon, which application shall be in writing, and describe the premises through which it is proposed to alter or lay out such highway.

Application to Justice of the Peace for appointment of Jury.

[1049.] SEC. 5. Upon the receipt of such application, the Justice shall appoint a time and place for that purpose, and shall issue a citation or notice stating a time and place of meeting, which shall be

Justice to appoint time for hearing application for Jury.

---

a For prior Statutes on the same subject, see code of 1820, p. 102; Revision of 1827, p. 388; Revision of 1833, p. 102; Laws of 1837, p. 98; Revised Statutes of 1838, p. 120; Laws of 1839, p. 217; Revised Statutes of 1846, p. 133; Laws of 1848, pp. 49, 99; 1850, p. 57.

Note.—It would seem to have been the intention of the Legislature to entirely supersede the above Act by the Act following, approved Feb. 3, 1858; but such does not appear to be the effect of that Act, and so much at least of the above Act as relates to the manner of laying out and establishing township roads, by Commissioners of Highways, within their respective townships, seems to remain in force.

served by the Highway Commissioners, on the owners or occupants of lands through which it is proposed to alter or lay out said road, at least ten days before such time, and in case any such land is unoccupied, the notice may be served by posting up the same in three public places in the township, ten days before the time of meeting.

Manner of appointing Jury.

[1050.] SEC. 6. If the Commissioners, or any one of them, and the owners or occupants of such lands, or such as may be present, cannot agree upon any other mode of appointing such jurors, they shall be appointed in the following manner: The Justice may make a list of twenty-four disinterested freeholders residing in the county, and each party may object to six on the list, and if either party fails to appear, or refuse to act, the Justice and the other party, or the Justice alone, may strike out the names of twelve, and the remaining twelve shall be the jurors elected, and the same Justice shall continue the hearing of the application for not less than fifteen, and not more than twenty days to a time and place certain.

Warrant for summoning Jury.

[1051.] SEC. 7. The Justice shall then annex to the application a warrant under his hand, returnable on said adjourned day, and issue the same, directed to any constable in the county, commanding him to summon the said jurors to be and appear at his office on the said adjourned day, to serve as jurors, to ascertain the necessity of taking certain property for highway purposes, and to appraise the damages thereon, and if all the jurors shall not appear, the Justice may summon talismen to make a full jury.

Jurors to be sworn.

[1052.] SEC. 8. The jurors shall be sworn to ascertain the necessity of altering or laying out the highway described in the application, and to appraise the damage thereon, if any is claimed. They shall then proceed to view the premises described, and shall, within five days thereafter, make return to the said Justice, in writing, to be signed by them, of their doings, which shall state the necessity of altering or laying out such road, the amount of damages appraised, to whom payable, if known, and a statement of the time spent by them for that purpose, which return shall be certified by such Justice, and filed in the office of the Township Clerk.

Duties of Jury.

Compensation of Jurors.

[1053.] SEC. 9. Such jurors shall be entitled to receive one dollar per day, and fifty cents for each half day, and the Justice and constable one dollar each for their fees, and the damages which shall be assessed by the jury as hereinbefore provided, upon altering or laying out any highway, and all the lawful charges against the township for services, fees and expenses consequent upon laying out or altering such highway, shall be levied and collected in the township within which such highway is situated, and shall be paid upon the order of the Township Board, as other township charges, except as hereinafter provided.

Damages, charges, fees and expenses; how collected.

Proceedings in case of disagreement between Commissioners of adjoining Townships.

[1054.] SEC. 10. Whenever the Commissioners of Highways in one township shall disagree with the Commissioners of an adjoining township, whether in the same or another county, in any matter relating to a highway on the line between the two townships, the Commissioners of both townships, or a majority of them, shall meet at the request of the Commissioners of either township, and make their determination upon such subject of disagreement.

[1055.] SEC. 11. Whenever it shall become necessary to have a highway altered or laid out upon the line between two townships, application for that purpose may be made to the Commissioners of either township, who shall proceed to lay out or alter such road in the manner hereinbefore provided; but they shall cause the survey order to be filed in the office of the Township Clerk of each township; and the said Township Clerks are required to post up a copy of the same in their respective townships, as required by section three of this act.

Highways laid on the line between Townships.

[1056.] SEC. 12. Upon altering or laying out a road on the line between two townships, application may be made to a Justice of the Peace of either township for the appointment of jurors, who shall be drawn equally from each township, and shall appraise the amount of damage to be paid by each township, and the return of their doings shall be certified by the Justice, and filed in the office of the Township Clerks of each township.

Application for appointment of Jury upon altering or laying out road on line between two Townships.

Duties of Jury.

[1057.] SEC. 13. The Commissioners of Highways of such adjoining townships, upon altering or laying out a highway upon the line thereof, shall determine what part of such highway shall be made and repaired by each township, and each township shall have all the rights, and be subject to all the liabilities in relation to the part of such highway to be made and repaired by such township, as if the same was located wholly in such township.

Apportionment of Highway to be made or repaired by each Township

[1058.] SEC. 14. Public roads to be laid out according to the provisions of this act, shall not be less than three rods wide, except in cities and villages where the Commissioners or other proper authorities may otherwise determine.

Width of Roads.

[1059.] SEC. 15. Whenever Commissioners of Highways are applied to, as provided in section one of this act, to discontinue a road, they shall give at least ten days' notice, in writing, to the owners or occupants of land through which such road runs, of the time when, and place where they will meet for that purpose; and in case such land, or any part is unoccupied, such notice may be given by posting up the same in three public places in the township. In case the Commissioners shall deem it advisable to discontinue such road, they shall make and sign an order to that effect, and cause the same to be filed in the office of the Township Clerk, from and after the time of filing which, such road shall cease to be a public highway.

Notice of meeting of Commissioners to discontinue road.

[1060.] SEC. 16. Any person or persons wishing to have a private road opened, shall cause an accurate survey to be made thereof, and filed in the office of the Township Clerk; application may then be made to a Justice of the Peace, as in case of public highway, for the appointment of jurors, who shall be appointed in the same manner, and all the subsequent proceedings shall be the same as in laying out public highways, except that the applicant or applicants shall act in the place of Highway Commissioners, and the amount of damages appraised in consequence of the opening thereof, together with the

Private Roads, how laid out.

expenses of all proceedings, shall be paid by the person or persons to be benefitted thereby, before said road shall be opened or used.[b]

Damages and expenses of laying out or altering Highway in cities or villages; how collected.

[1061.] SEC. 17. Whenever a highway is altered or laid out in a city or village, and the damages therefor appraised, and the doings of the jury filed in the office of the Township Clerk, as is required in section eight of this act, it shall be the duty of the Township Clerk to certify a copy of the same to the Supervisor of the township, who shall proceed to assess the amount thereof upon the taxable property of the township, and shall, on his warrant to the Township Treasurer, direct him to pay the amount so appraised to the order of the person or persons to whom the same is made payable in the return of the jury.

Upon altering or laying out Highway; Fences to be removed.

[1062.] SEC. 18. Whenever a public highway shall have been altered or laid out according to the provisions of this act, the Commissioners of Highways shall give the owners or occupants of the land through which said road shall have been laid out or altered, notice thereof, in writing, requiring him or them to remove his or their fence or fences within such time as they shall deem reasonable, not less than sixty days after giving such notice, and in case such owner or occupant shall neglect or refuse to remove his fence or fences within the time specified in such notice, the said Commissioners shall have full power and suthority, and it shall be their duty to enter with such aid and assistance as shall be deemed necessary upon the premises, and remove such fence or fences, and open such highway without delay, after the time specified in such notice shall have expired: *Provided*, no person shall be required to remove his fence or fences between the first day of April and the first day of November.

Duties of Commissioners upon neglect or refusal to remove fences.

How damages estimated when discontinued highway attached to land through which new highway is laid out.

[1063.] SEC. 19. If any discontinued highway shall be attached to a tract of land through which a new highway shall be laid out, the same may be taken into consideration in estimating the damages sustained by the owners; and in estimating the damages which may be sustained by any person owning or interested in said lands, by reason of laying out or altering any highway, the benefit which such person shall receive thereby shall be taken into consideration.

What Highways to be deemed Public Roads.

[1064.] SEC. 20. That all highways heretofore regularly laid out and established, in pursuance of existing laws or statutes heretofore passed by the Legislature, and approved by the Governor, are hereby declared to be legal highways.

Commissioners of Highways may apply to Court of Record for appointment of Commissioners.

[1065.] SEC. 21. The Commissioners of Highways, or one of them, may, instead of making application for the appointment of jurors, as is provided in section four of this act, make application to any Court of Record for the appointment of three Commissioners, whose duty it shall be to ascertain the necessity of altering or laying out said road, and to appraise the damages thereon, if any is claimed; the application shall be in writing, and describe the premises proposed to be taken for such highway purposes, and notice thereof shall be given at least five days previous to making such application to the owners or occupants of the lands described in the application, and such no-

How application made.

b See Chapter 27 and Note a thereto.

tice may be served by the Highway Commissioners in the same manner as provided in section five of this act.

[1066.] SEC. 22. The Commissioners so appointed shall be sworn to ascertain the necessity for altering or laying out the road described in the application, and justly and impartially to appraise the damages thereon, if any is claimed. They shall then proceed to view the premises, and shall, within five days thereafter, make return of their doings, in writing, signed by them, to the Township or Village Clerk, or Recorder, which returns shall state if such road is altered or laid out, the necessity therefor, the amount of the damages appraised thereon, to whom payable, if known; and shall be filed in the office of the Township or Village Clerk, or Recorder. The said Commissioners shall be entitled to the same compensation as jurors are entitled to under the provisions of this act. The damages appraised by said Commissioners, together with all the costs of the proceeding, shall be levied, collected, and paid in the manner prescribed by this act.

Commissioners to be sworn.

Proceedings of Commissioners.

Compensation of Commissioners.

Damages, costs and expenses; how collected.

[1067.] SEC. 23. All acts, or parts of acts, contravening the provisions of this act, are hereby repealed.

Repeal of Contravening Acts.

This act shall take effect immediately.

An Act to amend an act entitled "an act to repeal chapter (25) twenty-five of the Revised Statutes of (1846) eighteen hundred and forty-six; also, act (88) eighty-eight, entitled "an act to amend chapter (25) twenty-five of the Revised Statutes of (1846) eighteen hundred and forty-six, relative to laying out, altering, and discontinuing highways," approved March (18) eighteenth, (1848) eighteen hundred and forty-eight, also, act No. (72) seventy-two, entitled "an act to amend chapter (25) twenty-five of the Revised Statutes of (1846) eighteen hundred and forty-six, approved March (15) fifteenth, (1848) eighteen hundred and forty-eight, and to provide for altering, laying out, and discontinuing highways," approved February, (17) seventeenth, (1857) eighteen hundred and fifty-seven.

Laws 1858, p. 28.

[*Approved February* 3, 1858. *Laws of* 1858, *p.* 28.]

SECTION 1. *The People of the State of Michigan enact*, That an act entitled an act to repeal chapter (25) twenty-five of the revised statutes of (1846) eighteen hundred and forty-six; also, act (88) eighty-eight, entitled an act to amend chapter (25) twenty-five of the revised statutes of (1846) eighteen hundred and forty-six, relative to laying out, altering and discontinuing highways, approved March (18) eighteenth, (1848) eighteen hundred and forty-eight; also, act No. (72) seventy-two, entitled an act to amend chapter (25) twenty-five of the revised statutes of (1846) eighteen hundred and forty-six, approved March (15) fifteenth, (1848) eighteen hundred and forty-eight, and to provide for altering, laying out and discontinuing highways, approved February (17) seventeenth, (1857) eighteen hundred and fifty-seven, be so amended as to read as follows:

"That whenever any (10) ten or more freeholders of any township shall wish to have a highway in any part of such township, not included within the corporate limits of any city or village, altered, laid out or discontinued, they may, by writing under their hands, make application to the Commissioners of Highways of the township for that purpose, who shall proceed to alter, lay out, or may discontinue such highway, as hereinafter directed: *Provided*, That no second application shall be made within (12) twelve months for the same purpose: *Provided*, That whenever the person or persons through whose land

Number of Freeholders necessary to make application.

Application, to whom made.

the proposed highway is to be altered or laid out, shall give his, her or their consent, in writing, according to the provisions of section (17) seventeen of this act, and release any claim for damages, the Commissioners of Highways shall have power to alter or lay out the proposed highway, without the intervention of a jury or Commissioners appointed by a Court of Record, as hereinafter provided, and shall certify their action to the Township Clerk.[23]

Powers of Commissioners.

---

[23]*Form of Application to Commissioners to lay out a Highway.*

To the Commissioners of Highways of the township of *Brighton*, and thecounty of *Livingston.*

The undersigned freeholders of said township of *Brighton*, wishing to have a highway laid out in such township as hereinafter described, not included within the corporate limits of any city or village, do make application to you, said commissioners, for the purpose of having the same laid out, and do therefore respectfully ask that you will proceed to lay out a highway as follows: commencing, at &c., (*here describe the route of the proposed highway; state the point of commencement, the general course, and point of termination.*)

Dated at——this——day of——A. D. 18

(*To be signed by ten freeholders.*)

Note.—The foregoing form can be varied to suit the occasion of an application to alter or discontinue a highway.

The second section of the eighteenth article of the constitution of 1850 provides: That when private property for the use or benefit of the public, the necessity for using such property, and the just compensation to be made therefor, except when to be made by the State, shall be ascertained by a jury of twelve freeholders residing in the vicinity of such property, or by not less than three Commissioners appointed by a Court of Record, as shall be prescribed by law. It seems that no law was passed in relation to township roads after the adoption of the constitution, until February 17th, 1857, and the laws relating to township roads previously adopted being repugnant to the provisions of said section of the constitution, it appears that there was no law from 1851 to 1857 at least, authorizing the laying out of township roads.—*People vs. Kimble*, 4 *Mich.*, 95.

It is requisite to the valid laying out of a highway under the statute, that application therefor should be made, in writing, by ten or more freeholders, and that notice of the proceedings be given to the persons interested in lands through which the road is to pass; a survey of such land should be made and incorporated in an order, to be signed by the Commissioners of Highways and filed in the office of the Township Clerk, who should note the time of filing. Where it was not shown that any of these requirements were complied with, and the road had never been opened or used, or regarded by the Commissioners as a highway, the Court refused a mandamus to the Township Board, to show cause why they should not pay the damages to a party through whose lands a highway was claimed to have been laid.—*People vs. Township Board of Scio*, 3 *Mich.*, 121.

The Commissioners of Highways have no authority to proceed and lay out a highway, except upon the application of the requisite number of freeholders of the township, in writing, and an order made by them, establishing a highway without such application, would be void.—*Harrington vs. People*, 6 *Barb.*, 607.

It is no objection, however, to an application, that more than the requisite number of persons have signed it, and where ten of the number are freeholders and reside in the township, it will be no objection, because others whose names are upon the application, are not freeholders or do not reside in the township.—*See Carmel vs. Judges of Putnam*, 7 *Wend.*, 64.

But in order to give the Commissioners of Highways jurisdiction, it is necessary that the application should be signed by at least ten freeholders of the township, otherwise it would be utterly nugatory. It is not sufficient that in the body of the petition or application it is stated that the "undersigned are freeholders," &c., but in order to render the application competent evidence in a proceeding where it is called in question, it must be affirmatively shown that the application is signed by ten freeholders of the township. The *onus probandi* is on the party who seeks to avail himself of the application and the proceedings under it.—*Williams vs. Homes*, 2 *Wis. R.*, 129.

But it will not be necessary in the first instance to introduce title deeds or documentary evidence of the property qualification of the signers. Peacable possession under claim of title is *prima facie* evidence of seizure in fee, which will be proved by parol, and will be sufficient until the contrary appears.—*Austin vs. Allen*, 6 *Wis. R.*

A highway must be laid out in conformity with the route described in the petition; otherwise, the doings of the Road Commissioners will be without authority and invalid.—*Cole vs. Town of Canaan*, 9 *Porter's R.*, 88.

The applicants for a road designate the general course desired, the commissioners the particular route, and the latter may make such variations as they may think proper, provided the departure is not of such a character as to induce the court to suppose that these officers had wholly disregarded the preliminary proceedings of the application.—*Hallock vs. Woolsey*, 23 *Wend.* 328.

Where Commissioners were appointed by an act of the Legislature, to lay out a road on the most direct and eligible route, commencing at or near a certain village, and the road was laid out, commencing at a distance of sixty rods from the village, in a field where there was no road with which the new road could be connected, and the route, instead of being the most direct and eligible, was, as expressed by the court, strikingly injudicious; yet, notwithstanding these facts, the court awarded a peremptory *mandamus* to the Commissioners of Highways of the town, through which the road was laid, to proceed forthwith to open and work the road, as laid out by the State Commissioners.—*People vs. Collins*, 19 *Wend.*, 56.

SEC. 2. Whenever the Commissioners of Highways shall be applied to as mentioned in the preceding section, to alter or lay out any highway, they, or one of them, shall, within (5) five days thereafter, make application to a Justice of the Peace of the same or adjoining township, for the appointment of a jury of (12) twelve freeholders of the county, to ascertain the necessity of taking the property described in such application, and to appraise the damage thereon, which application shall be in writing, and describe the premises through which it is proposed to alter or lay out such highway.[24] — Provision for a Jury.

SEC. 3. Upon the receipt of such application, the justice shall appoint a time and place for that purpose, and shall issue a citation or notice stating the object, time and place of such meeting, which shall be served by the Highway Commissioners on the owner or occupants of lands through which it is proposed to alter or lay out such road, at least (10) ten days before such time; and in case any such land is unoccupied, the notice may be served by posting up the same in three — Duty of Justice.

It was held in this case that the court would not collaterally review the doings of the Commissioners, and hold as void the final determination made by them, in the exercise of their discretion or judgment. That the proper way of taking advantage of an error of this kind would be by *certiorari*, or writ of error, if no other mode of appeal is given by statute. Hence, we see the necessity of setting forth in the application the points of commencement and termination of the road, with a degree of certainty that may show clearly the wishes of the applicants, and thereby avoid disputes that may thereafter arise.

It has been held in New York that, where an application is made to Commissioners of Highways for laying out a road, they may refuse to act, and should do so, unless, in their opinion, the application presented to them is regular and in accordance with the requirements of the law. If they err in their refusal to act, the remedy by *mandamus* is at hand.—*Warnick vs. Orange Co.*, 13 *Wend.*, 432.

In laying out highways, the Commissioners before whom the matter is brought, exercise a special and limited jurisdiction, and although it may be presumed till the contrary appear, that they have proceeded legally, yet their acts may be impeached, by showing that they exceeded their powers.—3 *Hill*, 458.

The laying out of highways upon inducements or considerations, other than the public good, is illegal.

Thus, where a road was laid out by selectmen, both because they thought the public good required it, and because G. and F. stated to them that, if they would lay the road, the petitioners would make it without any expense to the town; both of which were taken into consideration by the selectmen in deciding to lay the road—*held* by the court, that a laying out upon such inducements would be clearly illegal.—*Gurnsey vs. Edwards*, 6 *Porter R.*, 224.

The laying out of highways partakes of the character of judicial proceedings. It is a judicial act.—*State vs. Richmond*, 6 *Porter*, 232.

The Commissioners of Highways have no jurisdiction in the matter of laying out a highway, which is not to be wholly within their township, unless under some express provision of law.—*Griffin's Petition*, 7 *Foster*, 343.

A public highway may be created by a long use of land by the public for the purposes of a highway. But the way, to become public, must be used in such a manner as to show that the public accommodation requires the way, and that it is the intention of the owner of the land to dedicate it to the public for that purpose, and the travel should be confined to the same place.—*State vs. Nudd*, 3 *Porter*, 327. See *Gardner vs. Tisdale*, 2 *Wis. R.*, 153.

[24]*Form of Application of Commissioners to Justice of the Peace for Jury to appraise Damage on Highway.*

To A. B., Esq., a Justice of the Peace of the Township of *Armada*, in the County of *Macomb*.

The undersigned Commissioners of Highways of said township do hereby make application to you, the said Justice, for the appointment of a Jury of twelve freeholders of said county, to ascertain the necessity of taking the property required in laying out a highway described as follows: *(Here describe the route of the highway.)* The premises through which it is proposed to lay out such highway, are described as follows: *(Here describe the premises with reasonable certainty.)*

Dated at this —— day of —— A. D. 18—.

C. D.,
E. F.,
G. H.,
Commissioners of Highways.

public places in the township, (10) ten days before the time of meeting.[25]

SEC. 4. If the Commissioners, or any one of them, and the owners or occupants of such lands, or such as may be present, cannot agree upon any other mode of appointing such jurors, they shall be appointed in the following manner:

Mode of appointing Jurors.

The Justice may make a list of twenty-four disinterested freeholders residing in the county, and each party may object to six on the list, and if either party fail to appear, or refuse to act, the justice and the other party, or the justice alone, may strike out the names of (12) twelve, and the remaining (12) twelve shall be the jurors selected, and the justice may continue the hearing of the application for not less than six, nor more than (12) twelve days.

SEC. 5. The Justice shall then annex to the application a warrant under his hand, returnable on said adjourned day, and issue the same, directed to any constable of the county, commanding him to summon the said jurors to be and appear at the place appointed on the said adjourned day, to serve as jurors, to ascertain the necessity of taking certain property for highway purposes, and to appraise the damages thereon; and if all the jurors shall not appear, the Justice shall cause a sufficient number of talismen to be summoned to make a full jury. And if said jury shall fail to agree and return a verdict to the parties (Justice) within the time provided by this act, they shall be,

---

[25]*Form of Citation or Notice by Justice of time and place of meeting to selec Jury to appraise damages on highways.*

To the persons whom it may concern.

You are hereby notified, that application has been made to me, the undersigned, Justice of the Peace of the Township of *Ash* in the County of *Monroe*, for the appointment of a jury of twelve freeholders of said county to ascertain the necessity of taking the property required in laying out a highway described as follows: *(Here describe the route of the highway.)* The premises through which it is proposed to lay out such highway being described as follows: *(Here describe the premises as in the application.)* And that a meeting will take place at —— on the —— day of —— A. D. 18—, at —— o'clock —M., for the purpose of appointing such jury, when and where you are requested to attend.

Given under my hand this —— day of —— A. D. 18—.

A. B.,
Justice of the Peace.

In laying out a highway, due and proper notice to parties interested is essential to the validity of the road.—*Pritchard vs. Atkinson*, 3 *N. H. Rep.*, 335.

But want of proper notice to land owners of the laying out of a highway, does not render the proceedings void, but voidable only; but cannot be avoided by those who have in any way waived their rights in the premises. The proceedings cannot be avoided by strangers. So held in New Hampshire.—*State vs. Richmond*, 6 *Porter R.*, 232.

But where the selectmen do not acquire jurisdiction to lay out a road, the proceedings are void, and must fail under all circumstances.—*Gurnsey vs. Edwards*, *id.*, 229.

It would seem, that where notice to occupants or land owners is not given in manner required by law, but such occupants or land owners nevertheless have due notice from any other source of the hearing, &c., or do actually appear, it will be a waiver of the formal notice required by law; and the proceedings will be good as to them.—*Ibid.*, *citing* 6 *Wend.*, 564, 565.

When A., upon the laying out of a highway, was a petitioner for the road, and admitted notice of the hearing, and released the land damages to which he was entitled, and the road was illegally laid out by his inducements, held out by him, and by his approval,—*held*, that B., who subsequently acquired the title of A. to the premises over which the road was laid, could not take advantage of the illegality of the laying out, and maintain trespass for subverting the soil.—*Gurnsey vs. Edwards*, 6 *Porter R.*, 224.

The road was held legal as to A., and those claiming under him.

When parties, entitled to notice of the time and place of meeting of road Commissioners, appear before them, and make no objection at the time to the notices or the service of them, such appearance is a waiver of all right to notice, and consequently, of the right to object to the form or sufficiency of the notices.—*Guilford's Petition*, 5 *Foster R.*, 124.

by such Justice, discharged, and a new jury empanneled within (12) twelve days, upon the same application and in the same manner and form as herein provided for empanneling a jury.[26]

Provision for new Jury.

SEC. 6. The jurors shall be sworn by such Justice, to ascertain the necessity of taking the property described in the application, and justly and impartially to appraise the damage thereon, if any is claimed. They shall then proceed to view the premises described, and shall, within (5) five days thereafter, make return to the said Justice in writing, to be signed by them of their doings, which shall state, if such road be altered or laid out, the necessity of taking the property described in such application, the amount of damages appraised, if any, to whom payable if known, and a statement of the time spent by them for that purpose, which return shall be certified by such Justice, and filed in the office of the Township Clerk.[27]

Duty of Jurors.

---

[26] *Form of Warrant for Jury to appraise damages on laying out highway.*

STATE OF MICHIGAN, } ss.
Montcalm County, }

To any Constable of said county, Greeting.

In the name of the people of the State of Michigan, you are hereby commanded to summon *(here insert the names of the persons appointed as jurors,)* to be and appear at —— on the —— day of —— A. D. 18—, at —— o'clock —M., to serve as jurors to ascertain the necessity of taking certain property for highway purposes, and to appraise the damages thereon; and hereof fail not.

Given under my hand this —— day of —— A. D. 18—.

A. B.,
Justice of the Peace.

[27] *Form of Oath of Jurors to appraise damages on highways.*

You and each of you do solemnly swear, that you will ascertain the necessity of taking the property required in laying out a highway as follows: *(here recite the description of the proposed highway,)* and that you will justly and impartially appraise the damages thereon, if any is claimed.

Form of Jury's Return in relation to appraising damages on highway.

To A. B., Esq., Justice of the Peace.

The undersigned, a jury of twelve freeholders of the county of ——, being appointed to ascertain the necessity of taking the property required in laying out a highway described as follows: *(here describe the route of the highway,)* being first duly sworn, did proceed to view the premises through which such highway was proposed, and said highway being laid out, we do consider the taking the property described in the application for said jury to be necessary, and we have appraised the following amounts of damages, sustained by the following individuals and payable to them, in consequence of the laying of such highway and the taking such property as follows, to wit:

AMOUNT OF DAMAGES.	TO WHOM PAYABLE.	DESCRIPTION OF PREMISES.
$300 00	John Jones,	N. E. ¼ of S. E. ¼ of sec. 12.
300 00	James Jackson,	S. E. ¼ of N. E. ¼ of sec. 12.
150 00	Unknown,	N. E. ¼ of N. E. ¼ of sec. 12.

The time spent by us for the purpose of viewing said premises and making such appraisal is ——— days.

Witness our hands this —— day of —— A. D. 18—.

(To be signed by the Jurors.)

I hereby certify the foregoing return to be the same as returned to me by the said jury.

Witness my hand this —— day of —— A. D. 18—. C. D.,
Justice of the Peace.

Compensation of Jurors, how paid.

SEC. 7. Such jurors shall be entitled to receive ($1) one dollar per day, and (50) fifty cents for each half day, and the Justice and constable each ($1) one dollar for their fees; and the damages which shall be assessed as hereinbefore provided, upon altering or laying out any highway, and all the lawful charges against the township for services, fees and expenses consequent upon altering or laying out such highway, shall be levied and collected in the township within which such highway is situated, and shall be paid upon the order of the Township Board as other township charges, except as hereinafter provided.[27a]

Action in case Commissioners disagree.

SEC. 8. Whenever the Commissioners of Highways of one township shall disagree with the Commissioners of an adjoining township, whether in the same or another county, in any matter relating to a highway on the line between the two townships, the Commissioners of both townships, or a majority of them shall meet at the request of the Commissioners of either township, and make their determination upon such subject of disagreement.

It is held in New Hampshire, that the doings of selectmen in laying out highways cannot be supported, unless it appear that due recompense was allowed to the owners of lands through which such highway was laid out, and that the owners had an opportunity to be heard upon the subject of damages.—*Pritchard vs. Atkins*, 3 *N. H. Rep.*, 335.

Where a highway is laid out along the line of a farm, taking no portion of the land of the owner, but subjecting him to the expense of maintaining the whole of a fence, the expense of the half of which only was formerly borne by him, such owner, under the law, is not entitled to compensation for damages.—*People vs. Sups. Oneida Co.*, 19 *Wen.*, 120.

It is held in Massachusetts, that where damages upon laying out a road have been assessed or awarded to an individual, the town would be liable for the amount thereof, although the road had been discontinued before payment and in fact never entered upon. That the owner had a vested right to such damages and was entitled to a writ of *mandamus* to compel payment.—*Harrington vs. Berkshire*, 22 *Pick.*, 263.

Where a road was opened by order of the proper authority, according to law in every respect, except that no damages were assessed by the jury to the owners of the land—*held*, that none but those owners could impeach the order for that cause.—*Woolard vs. McCullough*, 1 *Iredell R.*

A township is not liable for interest on damages appraised for laying out a highway.—*People vs. Township Board of LaGrange*, 2 *Mich.*, 187.

Form of Order of Commissioners of Highways, laying out a Road.

Oakland County,
Township of *Pontiac.*

Application having been made to us, the undersigned Commissioners of Highways of said Township of *Pontiac* by ten freeholders of said township for a highway as hereinafter described, and a jury having been summoned and sworn according to law, to ascertain the necessity of taking the property required for said highway and to appraise the damages thereon, and said jury having declared the taking thereof necessary and appraised the damages thereon, we did on the —— day of —— A. D. 18— proceed and cause an accurate survey to be made of said highway which is as follows: *(Here incorporate the survey.)* It is therefore ordered and determined, and we do hereby order and determine, that a highway be and the same is hereby laid out and established according to said survey, —— rods in width, and that the line of said survey be the centre of said highway.

In witness whereof, we have hereunto set our hands this —— day of —— A. D. 18—.

A. B.,
C. D.,
E. F.,
Commissioners of Highways.

[27a] Mere irregularities which would not render the proceedings absolutely void, questions involving the merits of the controversy before the Commissioners or Appraisers, and fraud or misconduct in the parties or officers, cannot be inquired into by the Township Board upon an application for an order on the Treasurer for the amount of damages assessed.—*People vs. Township Board of LaGrange*, 2 *Mich.*, 187.

SEC. 9. Whenever it shall become necessary to have a highway altered or laid out upon the line between two townships, application for that purpose may be made to the Commissioners of either township, who shall proceed to lay out or alter such road in the manner provided by this act; but they shall cause the survey, or a copy thereof certified by them, to be filed in the office of the Township Clerk of each township. Upon proceeding to alter or lay out such road, application may be made to a Justice of the Peace of either township for the appointment of jurors who may be drawn equally from the townships on the line between which said road runs. The said jurors shall appraise the amount of damage to be paid by each township, and the return of their doings shall be certified by the Justice and filed in the office of the Township Clerk of each township. **Proceedings as to roads between two townships.**

SEC. 10. The Commissioners of Highways of such adjoining townships, upon altering or laying out a highway upon the line thereof, shall determine what part of such highway shall be made and repaired by each township, and each township shall have all the rights and be subject to all the liabilities in relation to the part of such highways to be made and repaired by such township as if the same was located wholly in such township. **Duties of Commissioners.**

SEC. 11. Public roads to be laid out according to the provisions of this act, shall not be less than (4) four rods wide, except in cities or villages, where the Commissioners or other proper authorities may otherwise determine. **Width of road.**

SEC. 12. Whenever Commissioners of Highways are applied to, as provided in section (1) one of this act, to discontinue a road, they shall give at least (10) ten days notice, in writing, to the owners or occupants of lands through which said road runs, of the time when and place where they will meet for that purpose; and in case such land or any part is unoccupied, such notice may be given by posting up the same in (3) three public places in the township.[28] In case the Commissioners shall deem it advisable to discontinue such road, they shall make and sign an order to that effect, and cause the same to be filed in the office of the Township Clerk, from and after the time of filing which, such road shall cease to be a public highway, unless an appeal **Length of notice.** **Order filed with Township Clerk.**

---

[28]*Form of Notice of Commissioners to owners or occupants of lands, of meeting to discontinue a road.*

To Mr. A. B.

You are hereby notified, that the undersigned Commissioners of Highways of the Township of —— will meet on the —— day of —— A. D. 18—, at —— o'clock —M., at ——, for the purpose of considering and determining upon the question of discontinuing the highway described as follows: *(here describe the road to be discontinued,)* agreeably to an application duly made to said Commissioners for the discontinuance thereof.

Dated at ——, this —— day of —— A. D. 18—.

C. D.,
E. F.,
G. H.,
Commissioners of Highways.

shall be taken from the determination of said Commissioners as hereinafter provided.[29]

Appointment of Commissioners.

SEC. 13. The Commissioners of Highways, or (1) one of them, may, instead of making application for the appointment as (of) jurors, as provided in section (2) two of this act, make application to any court of record, for the appointment of (3) three Commissioners, whose duty it shall be to ascertain the necessity of taking the property described in such application, and to appraise the damage thereon, if any is claimed. The application shall be in writing, and describe the premises proposed to be taken for such highway purposes, and notice thereof shall be given, at least (5) five days previous to making such application, to the owners or occupants of lands described in the application, and such notice may be served by the Highway Commissioners, in the same manner as provided in section (3) three of this act, and such court shall be entitled to receive for his services on each application for the appointment of Commissioners, as provided in this act, the sum of ($1) one dollar.[30]

Notice given to owners.

Compensation of the court.

Commissioners, their duties and compensation.

SEC. 14. The Commissioners so appointed, shall be sworn by one of the Commissioners of Highways, to ascertain the necessity of taking the property described in the application, and justly and impartially to appraise the damage thereon, if any is claimed. They shall then proceed to view the premises, and shall, within (5) five days thereafter, make return of their doings in writing, signed by them, to the Township Clerk, which return shall state if such road is altered or laid out, the necessity of taking the property described in such application, the amount of damage appraised thereon, to whom payable, if known, and shall be filed in the office of the Township Clerk. The said Commissioners shall be entitled to the same compensation as jurors are, under the provisions of this act. The damages appraised by said Commissioners, together with all the costs of the proceeding, shall be levied, collected and paid in the manner prescribed in this act.

---

29 *Form of Order of Commissioners of Highways discontinuing a road.*

Oakland County,
Township of *Addison.*

Application having been duly made to us, Commissioners of Highways of said Township of *Addison*, by twelve freeholders of said township, for the discontinuance of the following highway: *(here describe the highway,)* and we having given ten days' notice to the owners and occupants of lands through which said road runs, of the time and place of our meeting to consider and determine upon the question of the discontinuance of the said road, and we having met accordingly, do order and determine that the said road be and the same is hereby discontinued.

Given under our hands this —— day of —— A. D. 18—.

A. B.,
C. D.,
E. F.,
Commissioners of Highways.

30 The forms which have been given in case of application to a Justice of the Peace by Commissioners of Highways, can be varied to suit the occasion of an application to a Court of Record.

SEC. 15. If any discontinued highway shall be attached to a tract of land through which a new highway shall be laid out, the same may be taken into consideration, in estimating the damages sustained by the owners, and in estimating the damages which may be sustained by any person owning or interested in said lands, by reason of laying out or altering any highway, the benefit which such persons shall receive thereby, shall be taken into consideration. Damages, &c.

SEC. 16. All highways heretofore regularly laid out and established in pursuance of existing laws, or statutes heretofore passed by the Legislature and approved by the Governor, are hereby declared to be legal highways, and it shall be the duty of the Township Clerk to record, in a book to be kept by him for that purpose, all papers filed in his office, relating to the laying out, altering or discontinuing of roads, as provided in this act. Existing highways legalized.

SEC. 17. Whenever the owner or owners of lands shall give the same or any part thereof, to the township for highway purposes, such owner or owners shall make a statement in writing, signed by him or them, to that effect, and cause the same to be filed in the office of the Township Clerk, of the township in which such lands are situated, and if a road shall be opened and worked thereon within the time limited by the (25) twenty-fifth section of this act, for opening and working highways, the person or persons signing such statement, or any one claiming under him or them, shall be precluded from having any action to recover possession of such land, or any compensation therefor, so long as the same shall be used for such highway purposes.[31] Lands given for highway purposes.

SEC. 18. Any person who shall conceive himself aggrieved by any determination of the Commissioners of Highways of any township, in discontinuing or refusing to discontinue any road, may, within Grievances, how redressed.

---

[31]*Form of Release of Damages by owner of lands.*

Know all men by these presents, that I, A. B., of the Township of *Chester* in the County of *Ottawa*, for and in consideration of one dollar to me in hand paid, do hereby give my consent to the laying out of a highway as follows: *(here describe the highway)* over my premises described as follows: *(here describe the premises)* in manner following: *(here state the manner in which the road is to run, if it is desired to restrict the location,)* and in consideration of the sum aforesaid, the receipt whereof is hereby acknowledged, I do hereby release to said township all claim for damages in consequence of the laying out of such road upon such premises.

Witness my hand and seal, this —— day of —— A. D. 18—.

A. B. [SEAL.]

The owner of the soil over which a highway is laid, retains all his rights not incompatible with the public right of way, and may maintain trespass for cutting timber therein.—*Babcock vs. Lamb*, 1 *Cow.*, 238.

The grant or laying out of a highway gives only a right of way to the public; the fee or right of soil remains in the original owner, and an action of trespass will lie for any exclusive appropriation of the soil.—3 *Hill*, 567; 12 *Wen.*, 98; 14 *Johns.*, 483; 2 *Johns.*, 357; 15 *Johns.*, 447.

As a public highway is a mere easement, and the seizin and right to convey still continue in the owner of the land over which it is laid out, it is no breach of the covenant of seizin and power to convey contained in the deed, that part of the land conveyed was a highway and used as such. *Whitbeck vs. Cook*, 15 *Johns.*, 483. Held otherwise in New Hampshire. See *Pritchard vs. Atkinson*, 3 *N. H. Rep.*, 335.

It seems that the title to the land over which a turnpike road passes, is vested in the company solely for the purpose of a road, and that when the road is abandoned, the land reverts to the original owner.—12 *Wen.*, 371.

The right of way, public or private, is but an incorporeal hereditament, an easement which *per se* does not divest the owner of the fee of the land. The soil is nevertheless the owner's, and he is entitled to the same remedies for an injury to his residuary interest, that he would be entitled to if it was entire and absolute.—*Gidney vs. Earl*, 12 *Wen.*, 98.

(10) ten days after such determination, appeal to the Township Board of such township, but an appeal by one person shall not conclude nor affect the rights of any other person, who shall appeal within the time limited; and the said Township Board shall suspend all proceedings upon appeals received by them, from any such determination, until the time limited for such appeals shall have expired, to the end that their decision, when made, may embrace the whole subject.

Appeals, to whom made. SEC. 19. In case of an appeal from a determination of the Commisioners of Highways of adjoining townships in the same county, or in different counties, relating to a road upon the line of such township, such appeal may be made to the Township Boards of the said adjoining townships, who shall act jointly in deciding upon the determinations of the said Commissioners: Proviso. *Provided,* That any Commissioner who may be a member of the Township Board shall not act on such appeal.

How made. SEC. 20. Every appeal from a determination of Commissioners of Highways shall be in writing, addressed to the Township Board or boards, as the case may be, and signed by the party appealing, and shall briefly state the grounds upon which it is made, and whether it is brought to reverse entirely the determination of the Commissioners, or only to reverse a part thereof, and in the latter case it shall specify what part.[32]

Duty of Township Boards. SEC. 21 It shall be the duty of the Township Boards, to whom the appeal is made, as soon as may be after the time limited for taking such appeals shall have expired, to give notice to the appellant, and to one or more of the Commissioners from whose determination such appeal was taken, of the time when they will proceed to view the premises and hear the appeal.[33]

---

[32]*Form of Appeal from determination of Commissioners in discontinuing or refusing to discontinue any road.*

To the Township Board of the Township of *Ridgeport* in the County of *Saginaw.*

The undersigned, feeling himself aggrieved by the determination of the Commissioners of Highways of said township of —— in discontinuing *(or refusing to discontinue, as the case may be,)* the following described road: *(here describe the road,)* does hereby appeal to you from the determination of said Commissioners, and asks that you will proceed to consider the same according to the statute in such cases made and provided. The grounds upon which the appeal is made, are: *(here briefly state the grounds,)* and said appeal is brought to reverse entirely the determination of said Commissioners, *(or as the case may be.)*

Dated this —— day of —— A. D. 18—. A. B.

[33]*Form of Notice to Appellant by Township Board in case of road appeal.*

To Mr. A. B.

SIR:—You are hereby notified, that the undersigned Township Board of the Township of *Berlin* in the county of *St. Clair,* will on the —— day of —— A. D. 18—, at —— o'clock —M., proceed to view the premises and hear the matter of your appeal from the determination of the Commissioners of Highways of said township in discontinuing the following highway: *(here describe the highway.)*

Dated this —— day of —— A. D. 18—.

C. D.,
E. F.,
G. H.,
J. I.,
Township Board.

Sec. 22. Every such notice shall be in writing and served at least (4) four days before the time mentioned therein, by delivering a copy of the same to the appellant and to one of such Commissioners, or by leaving a copy thereof at the dwelling house of such appellant and Commissioner. Ibid.

Sec. 23. The said Township Board or boards shall proceed at the time specified in the notice, to view the premises and to hear the proofs and allegations of the parties, and may adjourn from time to time as may be necessary, and their decision shall be conclusive in the premises, and every such decision shall be reduced to writing, be signed by the Township Board or boards making the same, and filed by them in the office of the clerk of the proper township, who shall file the same, and give notice thereof to the Commissioner of Highways, but nothing herein contained shall be construed to prevent a new application under the provisions of this act.[34] Ibid.

Sec. 24. Whenever a highway shall be altered or laid out and the same does not run upon a section line, the Commissioners of Highways shall, if they shall deem the same necessary, cause an accurate Survey may be made.

Form of Notice by Township Board to Commissioner of Highway in case of road appeal.

To Mr. A. B., Commissioner of Highways of the Township of *Constantine* in the County of *St. Joseph.*

You are hereby notified, that an appeal having been taken by A. B. to the undersigned Township Board of said township, from the determination of the Commissioners of Highways of said township in discontinuing the following highway: *(here describe the highway,)* the said Township Board will on the—— day of —— A. D. 18—, at —— o'clock —M. proceed to view the premises and hear said appeal.

Dated this —— day of —— A. D. 18—.

C. D.,
E. F.,
G. H.,
I. J.,
Township Board.

The attendance of the Commissioners of Highways without notice will be a waiver of notice —20 *Wen.*, 186.

Where Commissioners of Highways have acted upon a petition and treated it as valid, they cannot afterwards, in any proceeding in which they may be concerned, deny its sufficiency.—See *Carmel vs. Judges of Putnam*, 7 *Wen.*, 264.

[34]*Form of Decision by Township Board in case of road appeal.*

Whereas, an appeal having been taken to the undersigned Township Board of the Township of *Antrim* in the County of *Shiawassee*, by A. B. from the determination of the Commissioners of Highways of said township in discontinuing the following highway: *(here describe the highway,)* and said Township Board, having given notice to said appellant and to one of said Commissioners of Highways of the time when they would proceed to view the premises and hear said appeal; and said Board, having at such time met and proceeded according, do consider and decide that the determination of said Commissioners in discontinuing said highway was erroneous, and that the same should continue hereafter to be a highway.

Given under our hands this —— day of —— A. D. 18—.

A. B.,
C. D.,
E. F.,
G. H.,
Township Board.

survey to be made of the line of said road, and shall file the minutes of such survey in the office of the Township Clerk of the township in which such road is situated: *Provided*, That in all cases where the premises taken for a highway are required to be set out or described, the said premises or the said highway shall be construed to be the parcel of land not less than (2) two rods wide on each side of the line of survey, and shall be sufficiently set forth and described for all the purposes of this act by setting forth the line of survey.

Line of survey, how construed.

Commissioners to give sixty days' notice to owner to remove fences.

SEC. 25. Whenever a public highway shall have been laid out and established, or altered through any enclosed or improved land, and the ascertained damages for such highway shall have been paid or tendered to the owner or occupant, or an order on the treasurer of the proper township for the amount of such damages, shall have been executed and delivered, or tendered to such owner or occupant by said commissioners, said Commissioners of Highways shall then give the owner or occupant of the land through which said road shall have been laid out or altered, notice thereof, and require him to remove his fence or fences, within such time as they shall deem reasonable, not less than (60) sixty days after giving such notice, and in case such owner or occupant shall neglect or refuse to remove his fence or fences, within the time specified in such notice, the said commissioners shall have full power and authority, and it shall be their duty to enter with such aid and assistance as shall be necessary upon the premises and remove such fence or fences, and open such highway without delay, after the time specified in such notice shall have expired: *Provided*, No person shall be required to remove his fence or fences, between the (1st) first day of April and the (1st) first day of November.[35]

Duties in case of refusal.

Proviso.

---

[35] *Form of Notice for the Removal of Fences.*

To Mr. A. B.

SIR:—You will take notice that the Commissioners of Highways of the Township of *Antwerp* in the County of *Van Buren*, having laid out and established a public highway through certain lands owned by (*or* occupied by) you described as follows: *(here describe the land with reasonable certainty,)* and the ascertained damages for such highway having been paid, (*or* tendered, *or as the case may be,)* you are, therefore, hereby required to remove your fences from within the bounds of said highway within sixty days after the service of this notice.

Dated this —— day of —— A. D. 18—.

A. B.,
C. D.,
E. F.,
Commissioners of Highways.

Note.—This notice should be served by leaving a copy with the owner or occupant, and should be served by or in the presence of some indifferent person, having no interest in the matter; and a true copy should in all cases be retained by the Commissioners of Highways, as actual notice must be proved, should it ever be questioned, and will not be presumed. The presumption, which is sometimes indulged in favor of public officers, does not extend to such a case.—*Case vs. Thompson*, 6 *Wen.*, 634.

If fences are removed without giving sixty days' notice, all persons concerned therein are trespassers.—*Kelly vs. Horton*, 2 *Cow.*, 424.

Where Commissioners of Highways had laid out a road in pursuance of law, but neglected to file their proceedings, and a mandamus directed to their successors, commanding them to open it, by mistake misdescribed the road; on application for a rule requiring the defendants to furnish the original application, and that the mandamus be amended thereby, it appeared that the paper sought for had remained in the hands of H., a former Commissioner, and was beyond the control of the defendants. Motion, therefore, denied as to the defendants. But a rule was made upon H., that he file a paper with the Clerk of the town, &c., or show just cause why he should not do so.—*People vs. Vail*, 1 *Cow.*, 589.

Limitation.

SEC. 26. Every public highway already laid out, no part of which shall have been opened and worked within (4) four years from the time of its being so laid out, and every such highway hereafter to be laid out, no part of which shall be opened and worked within the like period, shall cease to be a road for any purpose whatever.

Public highways legalized.

SEC. 27. All public highways now in use, heretofore laid out, and allowed by any law of this State, or of the late Territory of Michigan, of which a record shall have been made in the office of the clerk of the county or township, and all roads not recorded, which have been used (10) ten years or more, and all roads which shall be hereafter laid out and not recorded, and which shall be used (10) ten years or more, shall be deemed public highways, but may be altered or discontinued according to the provisions of this act.

Powers of corporations in relation to highways.

SEC. 28. In cities and villages, application may be made by (10) ten freeholders, as provided in section (1) one of this act, to the corporate authorities of such city or village, as (and) the corporate authorities of such city or village shall have power, upon such application, to lay out and establish, open, alter or discontinue such streets, commons, lanes, alleys, sidewalks, highways, water-courses and bridges, as may be necessary for the public convenience.

Ibid.

SEC. 29. In case the corporate authorities of any city or village, should require the lands of any person for such purposes, such corporate authorities may cause notice to be given to the owner or party interested, his, her, or their agent or attorney, either by personal service, or by written or printed notice, posted up in at least (3) three public places in said city or village (3) three weeks next preceding the meeting of the corporate authorities for the purpose aforesaid, and the said corporate authorities of such city or village, are hereby authorized to contract for and purchase such lands for the purposes aforesaid.

Provision for calling a jury.

SEC. 30. In case the owner or owners of such lands, shall refuse to sell the same for the purpose aforesaid, or if the parties fail to agree,

---

Where the Commissioners of Highways refuse to open a road laid out, a mandamus lies to compel them to do so, which writ need not in the first instance be directed to the Commissioners by their individual names. It is only in case of disobedience to the writ, that they are to be proceeded against personally.—*People vs. Champion*, 16 *Johns.*, 61.

A mandamus to Commissioners of Highways to open and work a road will be granted without regard to the near approach of the expiration of their offices; when the term of office expires, their successors must obey the command of the writ.—*People vs. Collins*, 19 *Wen.*, 56.

Where a road is used and traveled by the public as a highway, and is recognized and kept in repair as such, by the authority whose duty it is by law to open and repair public roads, proof of these facts furnishes a legal presumption, liable to be rebutted, that such road is a public highway.—*Eyman vs. People*, 1 *Gil.*; *Nealy vs. Brown*, *ib.* 10.

Parol evidence is admissible to show where a road is located. Although there should be some uncertainty as to the precise location of the road, yet if the evidence be such as to convince the jury as to its location, it is sufficient for them to act upon.—*Nealy vs. People*, 1 *Gilm.*, 10.

The laying out of a road over the land of a person by the Commissioners of Highways is not taking or appropriating it to the public use.

The land over which a highway is laid out cannot be said to be taken for public use, until it is opened by order of the Commissioners of Highways.

A majority of the Board of Commissioners of Highways may order a road opened, but one Commissioner cannot sign the name of another to such order without his immediate assent and direction.—*The State* ex rel. *Evans vs. James*, 4 *Wis. R.*, 408.

An appeal suspends the powers of the Commissioners of Highways, and until their acts are affirmed by a decision, they cannot open the road. If they do so, they are trespassers—*Clark vs. Phelps*, *Cow.*, 190.

It seems that a road passing through unimproved and unenclosed lands is considered in contemplation of law opened, when established.—*Ferris vs. Ward*, 4 *Gil.*, 499.

If, on an order being made discontinuing a highway, a fence be built across it, an appeal subsequently brought will not have the effect of rendering the fence a public nuisance.—*Drake vs. Rogers*, 3 *Hill*, 604.

it shall and may be lawful for the corporate authorities of such city or village, to cause the Clerk or Recorder of the same, to issue a *venire facias*, directed to the Marshal, or other proper officer of such city or village, directing him to summon and return a jury of (12) twelve freeholders to appear before such Clerk or Recorder, at a time to be therein stated, to inquire into the necessity of taking said lands or premises, and the just compensation therefor to the owners of, or to those interested in said lands and premises, which jury shall be duly sworn by such Clerk or Recorder, faithfully and impartially to inquire into the necessity of taking such lands or premises, and the just compensation to be made therefor.

Duties of Jury.

SEC. 31. The said jury shall then proceed to view the lands and premises proposed to be taken for such public use, and if they shall deem it necessary for such city or village to take such lands or premises for the public use, shall inquire and assess such damage and recompense as they think proper to award to the owner or owners of such lands and premises, according to their respective estates and interests therein, and the said Clerk or Recorder shall, upon the return of such assessment or verdict, report the same to the corporate authorities of such city or village, at their next meeting, and the said corporate authorities may thereupon enter an order confirming the same, or may refuse to confirm the same, and order another jury to be summoned in the manner aforesaid; and such second jury when summoned and sworn as aforesaid, shall proceed to inquire into the necessity of taking such lands and premises for the public use, and assess such damages as aforesaid.

Non-attendance of Jurors.

SEC. 32. If one or more of such jurors shall fail to attend at the time and place mentioned in the *venire facias*, the Justice, Clerk or Recorder before whom such jury were summoned to appear, shall order the Constable, Marshal or person summoning such jury, forthwith to summon a sufficient number of talismen to make up said jury.

Damages, &c., how paid.

SEC. 33. The damage or compensation so assessed by said jury, together with the costs and expenses of such proceedings, shall be assessed, levied and collected upon the property of such city or village in the same manner as other taxes or moneys are levied; such damage and recompense shall be paid or tendered to the claimant or person entitled thereto, before such street, common, lane, alley or highway shall be opened, established or altered; when the damage aforesaid shall have been paid or tendered to the person or persons entitled thereto, it shall be lawful for the corporate authorities of such city or village to cause the said lands and premises to be used and occupied for the purposes aforesaid.

Appointment of Commissioners provided for.

SEC. 34. The Clerk or Recorder aforesaid may, instead of procuring the summoning of a jury as hereinbefore provided, make an application to a court of record for the appointment of (3) three Commissioners, whose duty it shall be to ascertain and determine the necessity of taking the property described in such application, and to appraise the damage thereon, if any is claimed; such application shall be in writing, and describe the premises proposed to be taken for such purpose, and notice thereof shall be given at least (5) five days previous to the time of making such application, to what court such application will be made, and the time of making the same, to the owner or occupant of the lands described in the application, his, her or their agent or attorney, and such notice may be given by the Commissioner of Highways, Clerk or Recorder, as the case may be, in the manner provided in section (4) four of this act.

Their powers and duties.

SEC. 35. The Commissioners so appointed shall, before they proceed to the performance of their duties prescribed in the preceding section, be sworn to ascertain and determine the necessity for taking the property described in the application, and justly and impartially to appraise the damage thereon, if any is claimed; such Commissioners shall then proceed to view the premises proposed to be taken for such public use, and shall within (5) five days thereafter, make return of their doings in writing, signed by them, to the township, city or village Clerk or Recorder, which return shall state if such highway, street, common, lane or alley is laid out or altered, the necessity therefor, the amount of damage appraised and to whom payable, if known, and shall be filed in the office of the township, city or village Clerk or Recorder. The Commissioners so appointed shall be entitled to receive the same compensation as jurors are entitled to under the provisions of this act.

Penalty for neglect to act as Jurors.

SEC. 36. Jurors who have been regularly summoned under the provisions of this act, who shall, without good cause shown therefor, neglect or refuse to appear and act in pursuance to said summons, shall forfeit the sum of (5) five dollars, to be recovered by action, as other forfeitures to townships.

Expenses, &c., provided for.

SEC. 37. The Commissioners of Highways of the several townships may cause a statement to be presented at the annual township meeting, of the improvements necessary to be made in the roads and bridges in such townships for the ensuing year, and an estimate of the probable expense thereof, beyond what the labor to be assessed for that year will accomplish; and such meeting may vote for the raising of a sum not exceeding (½) one-half of (1) one per cent. upon the aggregate valuation of the property in the township, according to the assessment roll of the preceding year, and the sum so voted shall be levied and collected in the same manner as other township expenses.[36]

---

[36]*Statement of Commissioners of Highways, to be presented at Annual Township Meeting.*

The annual statement of Commissioners of Highways concerning improvements in roads and bridges in the Township of *Augusta*, shows as follows:

That the improvements necessary to be made in the roads and bridges in such township for the ensuing year are as follows: *(here set forth what improvements are necessary,)* and it is estimated that the probable expense thereof, beyond what the labor to be assessed for that year will accomplish, will be —— dollars.

Dated this —— day of —— A. D. 18—.

A. B.,
C. D.,
E. F.,
Commissioners of Highways.

Acts repealed.

SEC. 38. Chapter (25) twenty-five of the Revised Statutes of (1846) eighteen hundred and forty-six, also act (88) eighty-eight, entitled an act to amend chapter (25) twenty-five of the Revised Statutes of (1846) eighteen hundred and forty-six, relative to laying out, altering and discontinuing highways, approved March (18) eighteenth, (1848) eighteen hundred and forty-eight; also, act (72) seventy-two, entitled an act to repeal (amend) chapter (25) twenty-five of the Revised Statutes of (1846) eighteen hundred and forty-six, approved March (15) fifteenth, (1848) eighteen hundred and forty-eight, be and the same are hereby repealed, and all acts and parts of acts inconsistent with the provisions of this act, except acts of incorporation of cities and villages, are hereby repealed.

This act is ordered to take immediate effect.

An Act to Provide for Laying Out and Establishing all State and Territorial Roads heretofore Laid Out, or to be hereafter Located within this State. *d*

[*Approved May* 16, 1846. *Took effect June* 15, 1846. *Laws of* 1846, *p.* 240.]

Powers of Board of Supervisors with respect to State roads.

[1081.] SECTION 1. *Be it enacted by the Senate and House of Representatives of the State of Michigan,* That the Board of Supervisors of the several counties within this State are hereby authorized and empowered to cause to be laid out, established, altered, discontinued, or opened, all State and Territorial Roads heretofore, or now laid out, or hereafter to be laid through or within their respective counties, whenever they may deem it for the interest of the public.

When Commissioners of Highways to cause State Roads to be surveyed and located; proceedings of Supervisors thereon.

[1082.] SEC. 2. Whenever the Board of Supervisors of any county are petitioned to by at least twelve freeholders of each of the townships through which any such road or roads may pass, they shall, upon such petition, authorize the Commissioners of Highways of such townships to cause the line of said road or roads within their respective townships to be surveyed and located therein, and such Commissioners shall report such survey and location to the Board of Supervisors of their county, and upon examination of said survey and report, said board may declare such road or roads duly laid out, established, discontinued, opened or altered, as the case may be: *Provided,* That said board shall deem the laying out, establishing, altering, discontinuing, or opening said road or roads for the interest of the public.[37]

(*d*) For general provisions respecting Territorial Roads, see Revision of 1827, p. 402; Laws of 1830, p. 7; Revision of 1833, pp. 173, 174; Laws of 1834, pp. 91, 92.

[37] *Form of Commissioners' Report to Board of Supervisors of Survey of State Road.*

To the Board of Supervisors of the County of *Washtenaw.*

The undersigned Commissioners of Highways of the Township of *Bridgewater,* having been authorized by your Board to cause the line of a State road within said township, to be surveyed and located therein, in connection with the line of said road to be surveyed and located in the Townships of *Saline* and *Bridgewater,* by the Commissioners of Highways thereof, beg leave to report the following survey and location of said road *(here insert the survey and location.)* All of which is respectfully submitted.

Dated this —— day of —— A. D. 18—.

A. B.,
C. D.,
E. F.,
Commissioners of Highways.

[1083.] SEC. 3. Whenever said road or roads shall be surveyed, laid out, altered, or established, under the provisions of this act, it shall be the duty of the Board of Supervisors to whom such petition and report may have been made as aforesaid, to notify and require the Commissioners of Highways of the several townships through which said road or roads may pass, to furnish the several Township Clerks of such townships the minutes of all surveys within their respective townships, and the same shall be recorded by said Clerks in the same manner that township roads are recorded. Township Clerk to be furnished with minutes.

[1084.] SEC. 4. Any person feeling himself aggrieved by the laying out, altering, discontinuing, or opening of any road or roads, may have his damages appraised, and obtain the same in the same manner and under the restrictions made and provided relative to township roads. How appointed and obtained.

[1085.] SEC. 5. In laying out, discontinuing, establishing, altering or opening any road, under the provisions of this act, the counties through which said road or roads may pass, shall be liable for all damages or expenses incurred, in the same manner as is provided for laying out township roads. Counties to be liable for damages and expenses.

Comp. L. 1857, Chap. XXIII., p. 366.

DIVISION XV.—Of the Obstruction of Highways, Encroachments thereon, and Penalties.

Chapter Twenty-Six of Revised Statutes of 1846.

Penalty for obstructing highways, &c.

[1086.] Section 1. Whoever shall willfully obstruct any highway or navigable river, or fill up, or place any obstruction in any ditch, constructed for draining the water from any highway, shall forfeit for every such offence a sum not exceeding twenty-five dollars.

Encroachments on highways.

[1087.] Sec. 2. In every case where a highway shall have been laid out and opened, and the same has been, or shall be encroached upon by fences, the Commissioners of Highways shall make an order under their hands, requiring the occupant of the land through, or by which such highway runs, and of which such fences form a part of the enclosure, to remove such fences beyond the limits of such highway within sixty days, and they shall cause a copy of such order to be served upon such occupant; and every such order shall specify the width of the road, the extent of the encroachment, and the place or places in which the same shall be, with reasonable certainty.[38]

Forfeiture for not removing encroachments.

[1088.] Sec. 3. If such encroachment shall not be removed within sixty days after service of a copy of such order, such occupant shall forfeit the sum of fifty cents for every day after the expiration of that time, during which such fence shall continue unremoved.

Proceedings in case encroachment be denied.

[1089.] Sec. 4. If the occupant upon whom a copy of such order shall be served, shall deny such encroachment, the Commissioners, or some one of them, shall apply to some Justice of the Peace of the

---

[38]*Form of Order of Commissioners for removal of obstruction in case of encroachment.*

Wayne County, }
Township of *Canton*, } ss.

We, the undersigned Commissioners of Highways of the Township of *Canton* in the County of *Wayne*, having ascertained that the public highway in said township leading from *(here describe the highway,)* is encroached upon the —— side thereof, along the lands in the occupation of C. D., by a rail fence erected by the present or some former occupant thereof, which forms a part of the enclosure of said land; and having ascertained the easterly bounds and limits thereof to be upon and according to the following line, to wit, &c., *(here insert the survey,)* and that all that narrow strip or piece of land which lies under said rail fence, *(or* under said rail fence and between the said rail fence and the line above described, *as the fact may be,)* is a part of the public highway aforesaid; it is therefore ordered by the undersigned Commissioners of Highways of said township, that the said rail fence be removed, so that the said highway be open and unobstructed, and of the breadth originally intended, which was —— rods, within sixty days from the date of the service of this order.

Given under our hands at —— this —— day of —— A. D. 18—.

A. B.,
C. D.,
E. F.,
Commissioners of Highways.

county for a precept which shall be issued by such Justice, directed to any Constable of the county, commanding him to summon six disinterested freeholders thereof, to meet at a certain day and place, and not less than four days after the issuing thereof, to inquire into the premises; and the Constable to whom such precept shall be directed shall give at least three days' notice to one of the Commissioners of Highways of the township, and to the occupant of the land, of the time and place at which such freeholders are to meet.[39]

[1090.] SEC. 5. On the day specified in the precept, the jury so summoned shall be sworn by such Justice, well and truly to inquire whether any such encroachment has been made as described in the order of the Commissioners, and by whom; and the witnesses produced by either party shall be sworn by the Justice, and the jury shall hear the proofs and allegations which may be produced and submitted to them; and in case any person so summoned as a juror shall not appear, or shall be incompetent, his place may be supplied by a talesman as in other cases.[40] Ibid.

[1091.] SEC. 6. If the jury find that any such encroachment has been made by the occupant of the land, or any former occupant thereof, they shall make and subscribe a certificate in writing of the particulars of such encroachment, and by whom made, which shall be filed in the office of the Township Clerk; and the occupant of the land, whether such encroachment shall have been made by him, or by any former occupant, shall remove his fences within thirty days after the filing of such certificate, under the penalty of fifty cents for each Ibid.

---

[39] *Form of Precept to summon Freeholders in case of an Encroachment.*

Allegan County,
Township of *Casco.* }

To any Constable of said county, Greeting:

In the name of the People of the State of Michigan, you are hereby commanded to summon six disinterested freeholders of the said county of *Allegan*, to meet at the house of O. P. in said township on the —— day of —— instant, at —— o'clock —M., to inquire whether any encroachment has been made, and by whom, on the highway running by (*or* through) the land now occupied by C. D. in said township, and to give at least three days' notice to one of the Commissioners of Highways of said township and to said C. D. of the time and place at which the said freeholders are to meet, and have you then and there the names of the freeholders summoned by you and this precept.

Given under my hand this —— day of —— A. D. 18—.

A. B.,
Justice of the Peace.

[40] *Form of Oath of Jurors.*

You and each of you do solemnly swear, that you will well and truly inquire whether any encroachment has been made, and by whom, on the highway now in question.

Form of Oath of Witness.

You do solemnly swear, that the evidence you shall give in relation to the encroachment on the highway now in question, shall be the truth, the whole truth, and nothing but the truth.

day after the expiration of that time, during which such fences shall remain unremoved.[41]

Ibid. [1092.] SEC. 7. If the jury find that any such encroachment has been made as aforesaid, the occupant shall pay the costs of such inquiry, and if the same shall not be paid in ten days, the Justice shall issue a warrant for the collection thereof, directed to any Constable of the county, commanding him to levy such costs, and his fees thereon, of the goods and chattels of such delinquent, and make return thereof to such Justice within thirty days from its date; and the Justice, constables, jurors, and witnesses, shall be entitled to the same compensation as for other similar services in proceedings before Justices of the Peace.

If no encroachment found, damages to be paid by complainant. [1093.] SEC. 8. If the jury find that no encroachment has been made, they shall so certify, and shall also ascertain and certify the damages which the then occupant shall have sustained by such proceeding; which damages, together with the costs of the proceedings, shall be paid by the complainant.[42]

When fence may not be removed. [1094.] SEC. 9. No person shall be required to move any fence under the above provisions, except between the first day of November and the first day of April, unless the same shall have been made within three months next before the making of the order for the removal thereof.

Penalty on occupant of land for not removing fallen trees, &c. [1095.] SEC. 10. If any tree shall fall, or be fallen by any person from any occupied land, into any highway, any person may give no-

---

[41] *Form of Certificate of Jury in case of Encroachment.*

Barry County,
Township of *Baltimore*, } ss.

We, the subscribers, freeholders of said county of *Barry*, having been summoned, and assembled, on the day of the date hereof, at the house of R. P. in said township, pursuant to a precept issued by G. H., Esq., a Justice of the Peace of said county, and having been duly sworn by said Justice on the application of the Commissioners of Highways of said township, to inquire whether any such encroachment on the public highway in said township, as is specified in the order of said Commissioners of Highways, dated the —— day of —— last, (*or* instant,) has been made, and by whom, and having heard the proofs and allegations produced and submitted, do certify,* that such encroachment has been made by C. D., the present occupant, (*or* R. F., the former occupant.) And we hereby certify, that the particulars of such encroachment are as follows, to wit: that said encroachment commences on the north side of said road at *(insert a description,)* and that the rail fence along the lands now in the occupation of the said C. D. is upon the public highway, and is an encroachment thereon.

In witness, &c. *(To be signed by all the Jury.)*

[42] *Form of Certificate where no Encroachment is found.*

Branch County,
Township of *Batavia*, } ss.

We, the subscribers, &c., (*as in the previous form to the * and then continue as follows:*) that no such encroachment has been made on the said highway, and we have ascertained and do certify the damages of C. D., the occupant of the land through (*or* by) whose lands the said highway runs, by reason of the said Commissioners of Highways proceedings against him, to be —— dollars.

In witness, &c.

(To be signed by the Jury.)

tice to the occupant of the land from which such tree shall have fallen, to remove the same in two days; and if such tree shall not be removed within that time, but shall continue in such highway, such occupant shall forfeit the sum of fifty cents for every day thereafter, until such tree shall be removed.

Liability for falling trees into highway.

[1096.] SEC. 11. In case any person shall cut down or fall any tree on enclosed land not occupied by him, so that it shall fall into any highway, unless by the order or consent of the occupant, such person shall pay to the occupant of such land the sum of one dollar for every day the same shall remain in such highway, together with all other damages which such occupant may sustain, to be recovered as damages in an action of trespass, or on the case.

Penalty for obstructing rivers, &c.

[1097.] SEC. 12. Whoever shall obstruct the navigation of any river or stream, which now is, or may hereafter be declared a public highway, by falling any tree therein, or by putting into any river or stream so declared a public highway, any refuse lumber, slabs, or other waste materials, on conviction thereof, shall forfeit the sum of five dollars for any such offence.

COMP. L. 1857, Chap. XXIV., p. 369.

DIVISION XVI.—OF THE ERECTION, REPAIRING, AND PRESERVATION OF BRIDGES.

Chapter Twenty-Seven of Revised Statutes of 1846.

When moneys may be raised for building bridges.

[1098.] SECTION 1. Whenever it shall appear to the Board of Supervisors of any county that any one of the townships in such county would be unreasonably burthened, by erecting or repairing any necessary bridge or bridges in such township, such Board of Supervisors may cause such sum of money to be raised and levied upon the county as will be sufficient to defray the expenses of erecting or repairing such bridge or bridges, or such part of such expenses as they may deem proper; and such moneys, when collected, shall be paid to the Township Treasurer of the township in which the same are to be expended, and be applied by the Commissioners of Highways of such township to the purpose for which the same was raised.

Limitation of amount.

[1099.] SEC. 2. No Board of Supervisors shall, under the provisions of the preceding section, cause any sum exceeding one thousand dollars to be raised and levied in any county in any one year.

Commissioners of Highways or Common Council may put up and maintain notice on bridges.

[1100.] SEC. 3. The Commissioners of Highways of any township, or Common Council of any city, or organized company, or the Village Council of any village, may put up and maintain at the expense of their township, city, or company, or village, as the case may be, in conspicuous places, at each end of any bridge in such township, city, or village, maintained at the public or company charge, and the length of whose chord is not less than twenty-five feet, a notice, with the following words in large characters: "One dollar fine for riding or driving over this bridge faster than a walk," and in case any such bridge shall be over one hundred feet in length, or shall have a draw or turn table therein for the purpose of opening the same, then such notice may be, "Five dollars fine for riding or driving on this bridge faster than a walk."[a]

Forfeiture for fast driving over bridge.

[1101.] SEC. 4. Whoever shall ride or drive faster than a walk on any bridge upon which such notice shall have been placed, and shall there be, shall forfeit for every such offence the sum mentioned in such notice, and the same may be collected, in the name of such Highway Commissioners, city, company, or village authorities, as the case may be, or by criminal prosecution.[b]

Penalty for injuring bridge.

[1102.] SEC. 5. Whoever shall injure any bridge maintained at the public charge, shall, for every such offence, forfeit treble damages.

Repairs, &c., of bridges.

[1103.] SEC. 6. If any bridge over a stream intersected by a highway, in any township of this State, has been within the last year, or shall hereafter be injured or destroyed by the occurrence of a freshet,

a b As amended by "An Act to amend sections three and four of Chapter twenty-seven of the Revised Statutes of Eighteen hundred and Forty-Six, entitled, "Of the Erection, Repairing, and Preservation of Bridges," Approved Jan. 29, 1857. Laws of 1857, p. 29.

or from any other cause, it shall be the duty of the Highway Commissioners of such township to proceed with all convenient despatch to repair or reconstruct such bridge, as the case may require, under the personal supervision of one of their number, or by letting a contract therefor under existing provisions of law: *Provided*, That application for such repairs or reconstruction shall first be made to such Commissioners in writing, signed by at least twelve freeholders of the township, and verified by the oath of such applicants, that the public interest requires such repairs or reconstruction: *And Provided*, That the sum to be expended for such repairs or reconstruction shall not in any one year exceed two hundred dollars in any one organized township.[43] [c]

Payment for labor for the same.

[1104.] SEC. 7. In payment for the labor performed, materials furnished, and necessary expenses incurred, for the purpose in the last preceding section specified, the said Highway Commissioners are hereby authorized to draw and issue their orders upon the Township Treasurer, redeemable out of the proceeds of the tax to be levied and collected therefor in the manner provided by the following section.[c]

Moneys, how raised therefor.

[1105.] SEC. 8. For the purposes of levying and collecting such tax, the said Highway Commissioners shall furnish the Township Clerk with the amount of all the orders drawn by them for the objects aforesaid, on or before the first Monday of October thereafter; and the said Township Clerk shall thereupon include such amount in the statement of moneys to be raised for township purposes, to be by him delivered to the Supervisor, under the provisions of existing law.[c]

An Act to oblige the Owners or Occupiers of Mills, or other Water Works, to keep Bridges over their Races, crossing Public Highways.

[*Approved February* 13, 1855. *Laws of* 1855, *p.* 347.]

Owners and occupiers of mills and other water works to maintain bridges over their races.

[1106.] SECTION 1. *The People of the State of Michigan enact*, That it shall be the duty of all owners, occupiers, or possessors of Mills or other Water Works, where any race or races appertaining to

---

[43] *Form of Application by twelve Freeholders to Commissioners to repair Bridge.*

To the Commissioners of Highways of the Township of *Bedford* in the County of *Calhoun*.

The undersigned twelve freeholders of said township do respectfully represent, that the bridge at (*here state the location of the bridge*) over the *Kalamazoo* river has been lately injured by the occurrence of a freshet. We, therefore, request that you will proceed with all convenient despatch and repair said bridge.

Dated at this —— day of —— A. D. 18—.

(*To be signed by twelve freeholders.*)

The persons whose names are subscribed to the foregoing application, appeared before me this day in person, and severally made oath that the public interest requires the repairs of the bridge mentioned in said application.

Dated this —— day of —— A. D. 18—.

L. M.,
Justice of the Peace.

[c] These three Sections were added to this Chapter by Act 137, of 1848, p. 171.

the same may cross a public highway, to keep a good and sufficient bridge or bridges, not less than fourteen feet in width, with a substantial railing on each side thereof, over the same, except where said Mills have been erected and the races dug previous to the formation of said highway.

Duty of Highway Commissioners in case of neglect.

[1107.] SEC. 2. In all cases where the owner or owners, occupiers, or possessors of any such Mill or Mills, or other Water Works, shall refuse or neglect to make such bridge or bridges, or shall refuse or neglect to keep the same in good repair, it shall be the duty of the Commissioners of Highways of the township in which such highway may be, to proceed forthwith to erect or repair such bridge or bridges, at the expense of the person or persons whose duty it was to have erected or repaired such bridges.

Expense a legal charge against owners, &c.

[1108.] SEC. 3. The expenses so made or incurred by said Commissioners of Highways, in erecting or repairing such bridge, or bridges, shall be a legal charge against the owner or owners, occupiers or possessors of such Mill or Mills, or other Water Works, and it shall be the duty of the said Commissioners of Highways to prosecute the person or persons so chargeable, on an action of assumpsit, for the expenses so made or incurred, and to cause the damages recovered in such prosecution to be applied towards the payment of said expenses.

Declaration in suit to recover expenses.

[1109.] SEC. 4. Whenever an action of assumpsit shall be brought, under the provisions of this act, for the recovery of expenses made or incurred in erecting or repairing any such bridge or bridges, it shall be sufficient, without setting forth the special matter, to allege in the declaration that the defendant, being indebted to the plaintiff in the amount of such expenses, according to the provisions of this act, referring to the same by its title and date of approval, undertook and promised to pay the same to the plaintiff; and to every such declaration, the defendant may plead the general issue, and may give in evidence, under such plea, any special matter in bar of the action, or in discharge of the defendant, in the same manner and with like effect, as if a special notice thereof had been given.

Defence.

This act shall take effect immediately.

DIVISION XVII.—MISCELLANEOUS PROVISIONS OF A GENERAL NATURE.

COMP. L. 1857, Chap. XXV., p. 373.

Chapter Twenty-Eight of Revised Statutes of 1846.

[1110.] SECTION 1. All trees standing or lying on any land over which any highway shall be laid out, shall be for the proper use of the owner of such land, or person otherwise entitled thereto, except such of them as may be requisite to make or repair the highways or bridges on the same land, or within one mile of the same; but no trees reserved for shade or ornament shall be used for such purposes. When trees, &c., to be for use of owner of land.

[1111.] SEC. 2. Any person owning or occupying land adjoining any highway not less than three rods wide, may plant or set out trees on each side of said highway contiguous to his land; which trees shall be set in regular rows, at a distance of at least six feet from each other, and within ten feet of the margin of the highway; and if any person shall cut down, destroy or injure any tree that may have been, or shall be so planted or set out, or which shall have been left on the side of such highway for shade, he shall be liable in treble damages to the owner or occupant of such adjoining land, in an action of trespass, or on the case. Trees may be set out along highway, &c.

[1112.] SEC. 3. Whoever shall willfully destroy, remove, injure or deface any milestone, or mile board, erected on any highway; or shall willfully injure or deface any inscription or device upon any guide post or guide board on any highway, or remove, destroy or injure any such guide post or guide board, shall be deemed guilty of a misdemeanor, and on conviction thereof, shall be fined not exceeding fifty dollars, or imprisoned in the county jail not exceeding three months, in the discretion of the Court. Person removing milestone, &c., guilty of misdemeanor.

[1113.] SEC. 4. Whoever shall injure any highway, by obstructing or diverting any creek, water course or sluice, or by drawing logs or timber on the surface of any road or bridge, or by any other act, shall be liable in treble damages, to be recovered in an action of trespass, or on the case, by the Overseer of Highways of the road district within which the injury was done, in his name of office, to be expended by him in the repair of roads in his district.[43a] Liability for injuring highway; Overseer to prosecute.

[1114.] SEC. 5. But if any such injury shall be done, within any road district, by the Overseer of Highways of such district, or with his assent, or if any Overseer of Highways of any road district shall refuse or neglect to prosecute for any such injury done within his district, it shall be the duty of the Commissioners of Highways of the town within which such district is situated to prosecute for such injury When Commissioners to prosecute.

43aA joint action cannot be brought by the Overseers of two adjoining road districts for any injury caused to a bridge which is partly in each district. Nor can the Commissioners of Highways of the township, on the refusal of the respective Overseers to prosecute, sue under the statute and recover in one action for the damages sustained by both districts.—*Highway Commissioners vs. Stockman*, 5 *Mich.*, 528.

in an action of trespass on the case, and cause the damages to be recovered in such prosecution to be expended in the repair of roads in the district within which such injury shall have been done.[a]

Provisions of this title to extend to all parts of State, except, &c.

[1115.] SEC. 6. The provisions of this chapter and of the preceding chapters, relating to highways and bridges, shall be construed to extend to all parts of the State, except where special provisions inconsistent therewith have been, or shall be, made by law in relation to particular townships, counties, cities or villages.

[a] Added by Sec. 21 of Act 206 of 1848. Laws of 1848, p. 315.

DIVISION XVIII.—On the Regulation of Ferries.

Comp. L. 1857, Chap. XXVI., p. 375.

Chapter Twenty-Nine of Revised Statutes of 1846.

License for keeping ferries.

[1116.] Section 1. The Board of Supervisors of each of the counties of this State may grant licenses for keepiug ferries in their respective counties, to as many suitable persons as they may think proper; which licenses shall continue in force for a time to be specified therein by said board, not exceeding ten years.

Laws 1859, p. 465.

Rates of ferriage, how regulated.

[1117.] Sec. 2. The said board, when they shall grant any license to keep a ferry, shall order and direct the rates of ferriage which the person licensed may receive, and may, from time to time thereafter, during the continuance of such license, alter such rates; and they may also direct what and how many hours each day such person shall attend his ferry.

When license not to be granted, except to owner of land.

[1118.] Sec. 3. No such license shall be granted to any person other than the owner of the land through which the highway adjoining the ferry shall run, unless such owner shall consent thereto, or shall neglect to apply for such license, after notice as hereinafter provided.

Ibid.

[1119.] Sec. 4. Whenever application shall be made by any person other than such owner, the board shall not grant a license to such applicant without the consent, in writing, of such owner, unless proof shall be made that such applicant caused notice to be given, in writing, to such owner, at least eight days before such application made, of his intention to make the same.

Bond to be given.

[1120.] Sec. 5. Every person applying for such license shall, before the same be granted, give bond to the People of this State, in such penal sum as the said board shall direct, not less than two hundred dollars, with so many and such sufficient sureties as the said board shall direct and approve, upon condition that he will faithfully keep and attend such ferry, with such and so many safe and convenient boats, and so many men to work the same, together with sufficient implements therefor, during the several hours in each day, and at such several rates as the said board shall, from time to time, order and direct; which bond shall be filed with the County Clerk.

Entry of license by Clerk, &c.

[1121.] Sec. 6. Every such license shall be entered by the County Clerk in a suitable book in his office; and a copy of such license, attested by such clerk, shall be delivered to the person licensed.

When waters divide two counties, license may be obtained in either.

[1122.] Sec. 7. Whenever the waters over which any ferry may be used shall divide two counties, a license obtained in either of the counties shall be sufficient to authorize the person obtaining the same to transport persons, goods, wares, merchandise and effects, to and from either side of said waters.

Persons violating bond guilty of misdemeanor, &c.

[1123.] Sec. 8. Every person who shall violate such bond shall be deemed guilty of a misdemeanor, and on conviction thereof, shall be subject to such fine as the Court may adjudge, not exceeding twenty-five dollars for each offence, and unless such fine, and the costs of prosecution shall be paid within ten days after such fine shall have been imposed, the Prosecuting Attorney for the county shall prosecute such bond for the use of the State.

Persons using ferry without license, guilty of misdemeanor.

[1124.] SEC. 9. If any person shall use any ferry for transporting across any river, stream, or lake, persons, goods, chattels or effects, for profit or hire, unless authorized in the manner directed in this chapter, such person shall be deemed guilty of a misdemeanor, and on conviction thereof, shall be subject to such fine as the Court may adjudge, not exceeding twenty dollars for each offence.

When persons may be prosecuted in either of two counties.

[1125.] SEC. 10. When any offence mentioned in either of the two last preceding sections shall be committed on waters dividing two counties, the person so offending may be prosecuted in either of such counties.

Limitation of provisions of this chapter.

[1126.] SEC. 11. Nothing contained in this chapter shall affect or impair any right or privilege belonging to any individual, or corporation, by virtue of any law of this State.

DIVISION XIX.—OF PRIVATE ROADS.

Comp. L. 1857, Chap. XXVII., p. 377.

An Act to Provide for Laying out Private Roads.[a]

Approved February 7, 1855. Took effect May 16, 1855. Laws of 1855, p. 36.

[1127.] SECTION 1. *The People of the State of Michigan enact,* That whenever application shall be made to the Commissioners of Highways of any township for a private road, they shall give notice to the owner or occupant of the land over which the road is proposed to be laid out, to meet on a day and at a place certain, for the purpose of aiding in the striking of a jury to determine as to the necessity or propriety of such road; at which time and place the jury shall be selected, in the following manner, to wit: Said Commissioners of Highways shall direct some disinterested person to write down the names of eighteen disinterested freeholders, from which list the owner or occupant of said land, and the applicant for said road, shall strike out three names each, and the balance remaining on such list shall form said jury. In case either said owner or occupant, or said applicant, shall refuse to strike, said Commissioners shall strike for the party so neglecting or refusing. Said Commissioners shall issue a citation to said freeholders to appear before them forthwith, to determine as to the necessity or propriety of such road, and the damages resulting therefrom, in case such road shall be deemed necessary by them.[44]

Application for private road.

Jury, how selected and cited.

---

[a]Section Sixteen of the Act of Feb. 17, 1857, (given in Chapter XXII,) would *seem* to be intended as a substitute for the first four sections of this Act; but *quere* if it can have that effect, or be of any validity whatever, where it now stands. See Sec. 20, Art. 4, of Constitution.

[44]*Form of Application of Private Road.*

To the Commissioners of Highways of the Township of *Howard* in the County of *Cass.*

The undersigned respectfully asks, that a private road be laid out in said township as follows: (*here describe the private road and give names of owners or occupants of lands over which the road is desired.*)

Dated this —— day of —— A. D. 18—. A. B.

Form of Notice by Commissioners of Highways of Meeting to select Jury.

To Mr. C. D.

SIR:—Application having been made by A. B. to the undersigned Commissioners of Highways of the Township of *Bengal* in the county of *Clinton,* for a private road as follows: (*here describe the proposed road as contained in the application.*) You are, therefore, hereby notified to meet said Commissioners on the —— day of —— A. D. 18—, at —— o'clock, at ——, for the purpose of aiding in the striking of a jury to determine as to the necessity or propriety of such road.

Dated this —— day of —— A. D. 18—.

A. B.,
C. D.,
E. F.,
Commissioners of Highways.

Jury to be sworn. [1128.] SEC. 2. Such freeholders, when met, shall be sworn well and truly to examine in regard to the necessity and propriety of such road, and in case they shall decide that such road is necessary, to justly and impartially appraise the damages of the owner or owners, or occupant of the land, by reason of laying out such road.[45]

Duty of Jury. [1129.] SEC. 3. If they shall determine that the road so applied for is necessary, they shall make and subscribe a certificate of such determination, and also their appraisal of the damages, and shall deposit the same with the Commissioners of Highways of the township; and the said Commissioners of Highways shall thereupon lay out the road, describing the same particularly by its bounds, courses and distances, and cause a record thereof to be made in the Clerk's office of the proper townships.[46]

How road shall be laid out.

Form of Citation to Freeholders.

Eaton County, }
Township of *Benton*, } ss.

To (*here insert the names of the freeholders.*)

In the name of the People of the State of Michigan, you are hereby required to appear forthwith before the undersigned Commissioners of Highways of said township at ——, to determine as to the necessity or propriety of a private road as follows: (*here describe the road as in the application,*) and to determine also the damages resulting therefrom in case such road shall be deemed necessary by you, and this you are not to omit.

Given under our hands this —— day of —— A. D. 18—.

A. B.,
C. D.,
E. F.,
Commissioners of Highways.

[45]*Form of Oath of Freeholders.*

You and each of you do solemnly swear, that you will well and truly examine in regard to the necessity and propriety of a private road from (*here describe the proposed road as in the application,*) and in case you shall decide that such road is necessary, that you will justly and impartially appraise the damages of the owner or owners, or occupant of the land over which said road is to be laid out, by reason of laying out the same.

[46]*Form of Certificate of Freeholders as to the necessity of Private Road.*

Genesee County, }
Township of *Burton*, } ss.

The undersigned, freeholders of said township, having been selected and duly sworn as a jury to determine as to the necessity and propriety of a private road as follows: (*here describe the road as in the application,*) and having duly and faithfully examined into the premises, do hereby certify, that we have determined said road to be necessary and proper, and that we have assessed the damages resulting from said road to the owners and occupants of lands over which said road is proposed as follows:

To John Doe, owner of (*here describe the land,*) —— dollars.

To (*continue in like manner.*)

In witness whereof we have hereunto subscribed our names this —— day of —— A. D. 18—.

(*To be subscribed by all the freeholders.*)

The record of a private road laid out by the Commissioners, designating the course, distance and quantity of land taken, is sufficiently definite to determine the width of the road, and parol evidence of the result, from the data given, is admissible.—*Herrick vs. Stover*, 2 *Wen.*, 580.

An obstruction of a private road is a mere private injury, in which the public have no concern.—*Fowler vs. Lansing*, 5 *Wen.*, 580.

An obstruction placed in a private road by the owner of the land over which it is laid out, cannot be lawfully removed by one having no right to use the road.—*Drake vs. Rogers*, 3 *Hill*, 604.

[1130] SEC. 4. The damages of the owner or owners, or occupant of the land through which such road shall be laid, when ascertained, as hereinbefore provided, together with expenses of proceedings, shall be paid by the person applying for the road, and when such damages and expenses are paid, the Commissioners of Highways of the township shall proceed to open the road.

Applicant to pay damages and expenses.

When paid, road to be opened.

[1131] SEC. 5. Every such private road, when so laid out, shall be for the use of such applicant, his heirs and assigns, but not to be converted to any other use or purpose than that of a road: *Provided, always,* That the owner or occupant of the land through which such road shall be laid out, shall not be prevented making use thereof as a road, if he shall signify his intention of making use of the same to the jury who ascertain the damages sustained by laying out such road, before the appraisal of the damages by them.

Road to be for use of applicant.

When owner of land may use road

Comp. L. 1857, Chap. XXX., p. 403.

DIVISION XX.—Of Weights and Measures.

Chapter Thirty-One of Revised Statutes of 1846.

Public standards of weights and measures.

[1241.] Section 1. The weights and measures, together with the scales and beams, and those made in conformity therewith, which are now, or may hereafter be deposited in the Treasury of this State, shall be preserved by the Treasurer, and be the public standards.

State Sealer, his duties.

[1242.] Sec. 2. The Treasurer of the State shall be the State Sealer of weights and measures, and he shall have and keep a seal, which shall be so formed as to impress the letter "M." upon the weights and measures, and scales and beams, to be sealed by him, with which he shall seal all such authorized public standards of weights and measures, and all the weights and measures and scales and beams to be provided by the several counties, when examined by said Treasurer, and found to be in conformity with the standard weights and measures, and scales and beams aforesaid.

Supervisors to procure standard from State Sealer, &c.

[1243.] Sec. 3. The Board of Supervisors for each county for which the same have not already been obtained, shall procure for the use and at the expense of their county, a complete set of weights and measures, and scales and beams, in exact conformity with those remaining in the State Treasury; except that the same may be made of such suitable materials as the Supervisors may direct, which shall be tried and proved by the said Treasurer, and by him sealed and certified.

County standard to be deposited with Clerk; his duties.

[1244.] Sec. 4. When so sealed and certified, such weights and measures, scales and beams, shall be deposited with the County Clerk, who shall be the sealer of weights and measures for the county, and the same shall be kept by him as the standard of weights and measures for the county; and the said clerk shall also provide and keep a seal similar to the seal required to be kept by the State Treasurer, with which he shall seal the weights and measures, and scales and beams, to be provided by the several townships.

County standard to be tried once in five years.

[1245.] Sec. 5. Once in every five years from the first day of January, eighteen hundred and forty-five, each County Clerk for the time being shall cause the said standards in his keeping to be tried, proved, and sealed by the State standards, under the direction of the State Treasurer.

When county standard to be procured by Treasurer.

[1246.] Sec. 6. If the Board of Supervisors of any county which has not heretofore provided such standards, shall neglect for six months to provide the same, and cause them to be tried and proved, and sealed as aforesaid, and delivered to the clerk of the county, it shall be the duty of the clerk to notify the County Treasurer of such neglect, and such County Treasurer shall immediately provide such standards, and cause the same to be tried, proved, sealed, and deposited as aforesaid, at the expense of his county.

[1247.] SEC 7. The Township Board of each township shall procure to be made and provided, when it shall not heretofore have been done, for the use and at the expense of the township, a complete set of weights and measures, and scales and beams, in conformity with the standards kept by the clerk of the county, which shall be tried, proved and sealed, and certified by the County Clerk, by the standards remaining in his office, and such weights and measures, scales and beams, so tried, sealed and certified, shall be delivered to, and kept by the clerk of the township, as standards for the township; such township standards to be made of such suitable materials as the Township Board shall direct; and the said board shall also provide a seal similar to the State seal, to be kept by the Township Clerk. Standard for each township, how procured, &c.

[1248.] SEC. 8. The Township Clerk of each township shall be the Sealer of weights and measures therein, and shall have the care and custody of the standard weights and measures of his township, and shall seal weights and measures, scales and beams, used within his township, after having tried and proved them by the township standards. Township Sealer, his duty.

[1249.] SEC. 9. The clerk of each township shall, once in each year, some time in the month of April, put up a written notice in three of the most public places in the township, stating therein the time and place when and where he will attend such of the inhabitants as live within the limits described in the several notices aforesaid, and seal all such of their great and small scales, beams, weights and measures, as are found to be accurate, and as they shall bring for that purpose.[47] Ibid.

[1250.] SEC. 10. The Township Clerk shall be entitled to demand and receive from the person from whom the service is rendered, for trying, proving, and sealing as aforesaid, three cents for each scale, beam, weight or measure found not to be conformable thereto, and two cents for each scale, beam, weight or measure found to be conformable thereto. Compensation of Township Clerks.

[1251.] SEC. 11. The Township Clerk shall go, once in every year, to the houses, stores and shops of such merchants, traders, retailers of spirituous liquors, and of such other of the inhabitants of the township, using scales, beams, weights and measures, for the purpose of buying and selling, as shall neglect to bring or send in their scales, beams, weights and measures, and he shall there try, prove, and seal them. When Clerk to go to stores, &c., and try weights and measures.

---

[47] *Form of Township Clerk's Notice of time and place of Sealing Weights and Measures.*

Public notice is hereby given, that the undersigned Township Clerk of the Township of *Allen* will, on the —— day of —— A. D. 18—, at —— o'clock, at ——, attend such of the inhabitants as live within the limits described as follows: *(here describe the limits,)* and seal all such of their great and small scales, beams, weights and measures as are found to be accurate, and as they shall bring for that purpose.

Dated this —— day of —— A. D. 18—.

A. B.,
Township Clerk.

Double fees, when to be paid. [1252.] SEC. 12. For the services required in the last preceding section, the Township Clerk shall be entitled to demand and receive of such merchants, or other persons, double the fees hereinbefore provided for the like services, together with four cents for every mile he shall necessarily travel for that purpose, going out and returning home.

Fees of County Clerk for sealing, &c. [1253.] SEC. 13. The County Clerk shall be entitled to receive from each Township Clerk a fee of three cents for the first sealing of every weight, measure, scale, or beam, and two cents for every subsequent sealing of the same.

When Township Clerk to procure standard. [1254.] SEC. 14. If the Township Board of any township, after notice to them that the standard of weights and measures for the county have been deposited with the County Clerk, shall neglect, for the space of six months, to provide standard weights and measures for their township, as above directed, it shall be the duty of the Township Clerk forthwith thereafter to procure the same at the expense of the township.

Penalty on Sealer for neglect, &c. [1255.] SEC. 15. If any Sealer of weights and measures shall neglect to perform his duty, as prescribed in this chapter, he shall forfeit, for each neglect, the sum of five dollars.

Vibrating steelyards. [1256.] SEC. 16. The vibrating steelyards, which have heretofore been allowed and used in this State, may continue to be used; but each beam, and the poises thereof, shall be annually tried, proved, and sealed, by a Sealer of weights and measures, like other beams and weights.

Construction of certain contracts. [1257.] SEC. 17. When any commodity shall be sold by the hundred weight, it shall be understood to mean the nett weight of one hundred pounds avoirdupois, and all contracts concerning goods or commodities sold by weight, shall be construed accordingly, unless such construction would be manifestly inconsistent with the special agreement of the parties contracting.

Weight of grains, &c., to the bushel [1258.] SEC. 18. Whenever wheat, rye, Indian corn, oats, barley, clover seed, buckwheat, dried apples, or dried peaches, shall be sold by the bushel, and no special agreement as to the measure or weight thereof shall be made by the parties, the measure thereof shall be ascertained by weight, and shall be computed as follows: Sixty pounds for a bushel of wheat, or clover seed; fifty-six pounds for a bushel of rye, or Indian corn; thirty-two pounds for a bushel of oats; forty-
1839, p. 218, sec. 9. eight pounds for a bushel of barley; and forty-two pounds for a bushel of buckwheat; and twenty-eight pounds for a bushel of dried apples, or dried peaches.

Measure for charcoal, &c. [1259.] SEC. 19. The half bushel, and the parts thereof, shall be the standard measure for charcoal, fruits, and other commodities customarily sold by heaped measure; and in measuring such commodities, the half bushel, or other smaller measure, shall be heaped as high as may be, without especial effort or design.

DIVISION XXI.—Of the Preservation of the Public Health; Quarantine, Nuisances, and Offensive Trades.

Comp. L. 1857, Chap. XXXVII., p. 430.

Chapter Thirty-Five of Revised Statutes of 1846.

[1337.] Section 1. The Supervisor and Justices of the Peace of every township, respecting which no other provision is, or shall be made by law, shall be a Board of Health for their respective townships, and the township Clerk shall be the clerk of such board, and shall keep a record of their proceedings in a book to be provided for that purpose at the expense of the township. Board of Health.

[1338.] Sec. 2. Every Board of Health may appoint a Physician to the board, who shall be the Health Officer of his township, and shall hold his office during their pleasure, and they shall establish his salary, or other compensation, and shall regulate all fees and charges of every person employed by them in the execution of the Health Laws, and of their own regulations. Appointment of Health Officer, his compensation &c.

[1339.] Sec. 3. The Board of Health shall make such regulations respecting nuisances, sources of filth, and causes of sickness within their respective townships, and on board of any vessels in their ports or harbors, as they shall judge necessary for the public health and safety, and if any person shall violate any such regulations, he shall forfeit a sum not exceeding one hundred dollars. Regulations relating to causes of sickness, &c.

[1340.] Sec. 4. The said board shall also make such regulations as they may deem necessary for the public health and safety, respecting any articles which are capable of containing or conveying any infection or contagion, or of creating any sickness, when such articles shall be brought into, or conveyed from their township, or into, or from any vessel; and if any person shall violate any such regulation, he shall forfeit a sum not exceeding one hundred dollars. Respecting articles capable of conveying contagion, &c.

[1341.] Sec. 5. The said board shall also make all regulations which they may deem necessary for the interment of the dead, and respecting burying grounds, for their township; and it shall also be the duty of said board to purchase in each surveyed township so much land for burying grounds as shall be necessary for burying the dead of such township, provided suitable grounds therefor can be found and procured within the township, and if not, they shall then provide such grounds in the nearest adjoining township where such suitable grounds can be procured. Duty of board as to purchase of burying grounds. Laws 1859, p. 396.

[1342.] Sec. 6. The Board of Health of the township for which such burying grounds shall be procured, and their successors in office, shall hold the fee of such land in trust for such township; and they shall keep the same, or so much thereof as shall be necessary, surrounded with a good and substantial fence; the expenses of the purchase of such lands, and of fencing and regulating the same, to be certified to the Town Board by the Board of Health, and by the Board to hold lands in trust. Ibid. Expenses, how paid.

Town Board, provided for as a part of the contingent expenses of the township: *Provided, however,* That the Board of Health may, whenever they think it desirable, sell and convey single or family burial lots in said township burying grounds to such person or persons as may desire to procure the same, and apply the proceeds thereof towards the purchase or improvement of said grounds, certifying the amount of all such sales and expenditures to the Township Board, as above provided.

Proviso.

Notice of regulations, how published.

[1343.] SEC. 7. Notice shall be given by the Board of Health of all regulations made by them, by publishing the same in some newspaper of the township, if there be one published therein, and if not, then by posting them up in five public places in such township; and such notice of said regulations shall be deemed legal notice to all persons.

Board to examine into nuisances, &c., and destroy, remove or prevent the same.

[1344.] SEC. 8. The Board of Health shall examine into all nuisances, sources of filth, and causes of sickness that may, in their opinion, be injurious to the health of the inhabitants within their township, or in any vessel within any harbor or port of such township; and the same shall destroy, remove, or prevent, as the case may require.

Proceedings, if nuisance, &c., found on private property.

[1345.] SEC. 9. Whenever any such nuisance, source of filth, or cause of sickness, shall be found on private property, the Board of Health shall order the owner or occupant thereof, at his own expense, to remove the same within twenty-four hours; and if the owner or occupant shall neglect so to do, he shall forfeit a sum not exceeding one hundred dollars.

When nuisance, &c., to be removed by Board at expense of owner, &c.

[1346.] SEC. 10. If the owner or occupant shall not comply with such order of the Board of Health, such board may cause the said nuisance, source of filth, or cause of sickness, to be removed, and all expenses incurred thereby shall be paid by the said owner or occupant, or by such other person as shall have caused or permitted the same.

Court may order nuisance remov'd in certain cases.

[1347.] SEC. 11. Whenever any person shall be convicted, on an indictment for a common nuisance that may be injurious to the public health, the Court may, in its discretion, order it to be removed or destroyed, at the expense of the defendant, under the direction of the Board of Health of the township where the nuisance is found; and the form of the warrant to the Sheriff, or other officer, may be varied accordingly.

Proceeding, when admittance of Board to building or vessel is refused.

[1348.] SEC. 12. Whenever the Board of Health shall think it necessary, for the preservation of the lives or health of the inhabitants, to enter any building or vessel in their township, for the purpose of examining into and destroying, removing, or preventing any nuisance, source of filth, or cause of sickness, and shall be refused such entry, any member of the board may make complaint, under oath, to any Justice of the Peace of his county, whether such Justice be a member of such board or not, stating the facts of the case, so far as he has knowledge thereof.

Ibid.

[1349.] SEC. 13. Such Justice may thereupon issue a warrant, directed to the Sheriff or any Constable of the county, commanding him to take sufficient aid, and being accompanied by any two or more members of said Board of Health, between the hours of sunrise and sunset, to repair to the place where such nuisance, source of filth, or cause of sickness complained of may be, and the same destroy, remove or prevent, under the direction of such members of the Board of Health.

[1350.] SEC. 14. The Board of Health may grant permits for the removal of any nuisance, infected article, or sick person, within the limits of their township, when they shall think it safe and proper so to do.

Board may permit removal of infected articles, &c.

[1351.] SEC. 15. When any person coming from abroad, or residing in any township within this State, shall be infected, or shall lately before have been infected with the small pox, or other sickness dangerous to the public health, the Board of Health of the township where such person may be, shall make effectual provision in the manner in which they shall judge best for the safety of the inhabitants, by removing such sick or infected person to a separate house, if it can be done without danger to his health, and by providing nurses and other assistance and necessaries, which shall be at the charge of the person himself, his parents, or other person who may be liable for his support, if able; otherwise, at the charge of the county to which he belongs.

Board to make provision to prevent spread of small pox, &c.

3 Mich. Rep., 475.

[1352.] SEC. 16. If any such infected person cannot be removed without danger to his health, the Board of Health shall make provision for him as directed in the preceding section, in the house in which he may be, and in such case they may cause the persons in the neighborhood to be removed, and may take such other measures as they may deem necessary for the safety of the inhabitants.

Provision in case infected persons cannot be removed.

[1353.] SEC. 17. The Board of Health of any township near to, or bordering upon either of the neighboring States, may appoint, by writing under their hands, suitable persons to attend any places by which travelers may pass from infected places in other States; and the persons so appointed may examine such passengers as they may suspect of bringing with them any infection which may be dangerous to the public health, and if need be, may restrain them from traveling until licensed thereto by the Board of Health of the township to which such persons may come; and any person coming from such infected place, who shall, without license as aforesaid, travel within this State, unless it be to travel by the most direct way to the State from whence he came, after he shall be cautioned to depart by the persons appointed as aforesaid, shall forfeit a sum not exceeding one hundred dollars.

Board may restrain travelers coming from infected districts.

[1354.] SEC. 18. Any two Justices of the Peace may, if need be, make out a warrant under their hands, directed to the Sheriff, or any Constable of the county, requiring him, under the direction of the Board of Health, to remove any person infected with contagious sickness, or to take possession of convenient houses and lodgings, and to provide nurses, attendants, and other necessaries, for the accommodation, safety, and relief of the sick.

Removal of persons infected.

Infected baggage, clothing and goods, how secured.

[1355.] SEC. 19. Whenever, on application of the Board of Health, it shall be made to appear to any Justice of the Peace that there is just cause to suspect that any baggage, clothing, or goods of any kind found within the township, are infected with any disease which may be dangerous to the public health, such Justice of the Peace shall, by warrant under his hand, directed to the Sheriff, or any Constable of the county, require him to take with him as many men as the said Justice shall deem necessary to secure such baggage, clothing, or other goods, and to post said men as a guard over the house, or place where such baggage, clothing, or other goods shall be lodged, which guard shall take effectual care to prevent any person removing, or coming near to such baggage, clothing, or other goods, until due inquiry be made into the circumstances thereof.[47a]

Impressing houses, &c., for keeping infected goods.

[1356.] SEC. 20. The said Justice may also, by the same warrant, if it shall appear to him necessary, require the said officer, under the direction of the Board of Health, to impress and take up convenient houses or stores, for the safe keeping of such baggage, clothing, or other goods; and the Board of Health may cause them to be removed to such houses or stores, or to be otherwise detained until they shall, in the opinion of said Board of Health, be freed from infection.

Power of officer execut'g warrant.

[1357.] SEC. 21. Such officer, in the execution of such warrant, shall, if need be, break open any house, shop, or any other place mentioned in said warrant, where such baggage, clothing, or other goods shall be; and he may require such aid as shall be necessary to effect the execution of the warrant; and all persons shall, at the command of any such officer, under a penalty not exceeding ten dollars, assist in the execution of the warrant, if able to do so.

Charges to be paid by owner.

[1358.] SEC. 22. The charges of securing such baggage, clothing, or other goods, and of transporting and purifying the same, shall be paid by the owner or owners thereof, at such rates and prices as shall be determined by the Board of Health.

Compensation for houses, nurses, &c.

[1359.] SEC. 23. Whenever the Sheriff or other officer shall take possession of any houses, stores, lodgings, or other necessaries, or shall employ any nurse or attendants, as provided in this chapter, the several parties interested shall be entitled to a just compensation therefor, to be paid by the county in which such person or property shall have been so employed or taken possession of.

When prisoners attacked with dangerous disease may be removed.

[1360.] SEC. 24. Whenever any person confined in any common jail shall be attacked with any disease, which, in the opinion of the Physician of the Board of Health, or of such other physicians as they may consult, shall be considered dangerous to the safety and health of the other prisoners, or of the inhabitants of the township, Board of Health shall, by their order in writing, direct the removal of

---

47a When the Board of Health of a township necessarily incurs expenses in providing for the safety of its inhabitants by removing, &c., any person infected with the small pox or other sickness dangerous to the public health, such person, his parents, or other persons liable for his support, being unable to pay them, said expenses are a charge against the county, which it is the duty of the Board of Supervisors to allow.—*People ex rel. Bristow vs. Supervisors Macomb Co.*, 3 *Mich.*, 475.

The only effect of Sec. 20, Art. 10 of the Revised Constitution is to abrogate the right of appeal from the decision of a Board of Supervisors, which before existed by law. A mandamus will, notwithstanding that provision, lie to compel them to do what the law unconditionally requires of them.—*Ibid.*

such person to some hospital or other place of safety, there to be provided for and securely kept, so as to prevent his escape, until their further orders; and if such prisoner shall recover from the disease, he shall be returned to such jail.

Prisoners removed to be returned, and not to be considered as having escaped.

[1361.] SEC. 25. If the person so removed shall have been committed by order of any Court or under any judicial process, the order for his removal, or a copy thereof, attested by the presiding member of said Board of Health, shall be returned by him, with the doings thereon, into the office of the Clerk of the Circuit Court for the county; and no prisoner, removed as aforesaid, shall be considered as thereby having committed an escape.

When Superintendents of Poor may remove paupers from poor houses.

[1362.] SEC. 26. Whenever any pestilence or contagious disease shall break out in any County Poor House in this State, or in the vicinity thereof, and the physician to such County Poor House, or such other physician as the Superintendents may consult, shall certify that such pestilence or disease is likely to endanger the health of the persons supported at such Poor House, the Superintendents of such County Poor House shall cause the persons there supported, or any of them, to be removed to some other suitable place in the same county, and there to be maintained and provided for at the expense of the county, with all necessary medical attendance and care, until they can safely be returned to such Poor House, or otherwise discharged.

QUARANTINE.

Township Quarantine.

[1363.] SEC. 27. Any township may establish a Quarantine Ground in any suitable place, either within or without its own limits: *Provided*, That if such place shall be without its limits, the assent of the township within whose limits it may be established shall be first obtained therefor.

Quarantine for two or more townships.

[1364.] SEC. 28. Any two or more townships may, at their joint expense, establish a Quarantine Ground for their joint use, either within or without their own limits: *Provided*, That if such place shall be without their limits, they shall first obtain the assent of the township within whose limits the same may be.

Quarantine in townships bordering on certain lakes, rivers, &c.

[1365.] SEC. 29. The Board of Health in each township in this State bordering upon Lake Michigan, Lake Superior, Lake Huron, Lake St. Clair, or Lake Erie, or upon any of the principal rivers or straits connecting together any of the said lakes, or bordering upon any navigable waters uniting with any of the said lakes, rivers or straits, may from time to time establish the Quarantine to be performed by all vessels arriving within the limits of such townships, and may make such Quarantine regulations as they shall judge necessary for the health and safety of the inhabitants.

Quarantine regulations to extend to persons and goods in vessels.

[1366.] SEC. 30. The Quarantine regulations so established shall extend to all persons, and all goods and effects, arriving in such vessels, and to all persons who may visit or go on board of the same.

Penalty for violating Quarantine regulations.

[1367.] SEC. 31. The said Quarantine regulations, after notice shall have been given in the manner before provided in this chapter, shall be observed and complied with by all persons; and any person who shall violate any such regulations, shall forfeit a sum not less than five dollars, and not more than five hundred dollars.

Vessels in certain cases to be removed to Quarantine ground, &c.

[1368.] SEC. 32. The Board of Health in each township bordering upon any of the lakes, rivers, straits, or other navigable waters hereinbefore mentioned, may at all times cause any vessel arriving within the limits of the township, when such vessel or cargo thereof shall, in their opinion, be foul or infected, so as to endanger the public health, to be removed to the Quarantine Ground, and to be thoroughly purified, at the expense of the owners, consignees, or persons in possession of the same; and they may also cause all persons arriving in, or going on board of such infected vessel, or handling such infected cargo, to be removed to any hospital under the care of the said Board of Health, there to remain under their orders.

Master, &c., to answer on oath in regard to infections.

[1369.] SEC. 33. If any master, seaman, or passenger, belonging to any vessel, on board of which any infection may then be, or may have lately been, or which may have been at, or which may have come from any port or place where any infectious disease prevails, that may endanger the public health, shall refuse to answer on oath, to be administered by any member of such board, such questions as may be asked him relating to such infection or disease, by any member of the Board of Health of the township to which such vessel may come, such master, seaman, or passenger, so refusing, shall forfeit a sum not exceeding two hundred dollars; and in case he shall not pay such sum, he shall suffer six months' imprisonment.

Expenses, by whom to be paid.

[1370.] SEC. 34. All expenses incurred on account of any person, vessel or goods, under any Quarantine regulations, shall be paid by such person, or by the owner of such vessel or goods respectively.

SMALL POX, AND OTHER DANGEROUS DISEASES.

Hospitals for reception of persons having small pox, &c.

[1371.] SEC. 35. The inhabitants of any township may establish within their township, and be constantly provided with, one or more Hospitals for the reception of persons having the small pox, or other disease which may be dangerous to the public health.

By whom hospitals to be regulated, &c.

[1372.] SEC. 36. All such Hospitals shall be subject to the orders and regulations of the Board of Health, or a committee appointed by such board for that purpose; but no such Hospital shall be established within one hundred rods of any inhabited dwelling house situated in an adjoining township, without the consent of such adjoining township.

Penalty for inoculating with small pox, except at hospitals.

[1373.] SEC. 37. If any person shall inoculate any other person, or inoculate himself, or suffer himself to be inoculated with the small pox, unless at some Hospital licensed and authorised by law, he shall, for each offence, forfeit a sum not exceeding two hundred dollars.

Physicians, &c., to be subject to regulations of Board, &c.

[1374.] SEC. 38. When any Hospital shall be so established, the physician attending the same, the persons inoculated or sick therein, the nurses, attendants, and all persons who shall approach or come within the limits of the same, and all such furniture and other articles as shall be used or brought there, shall be subject to such regulations as shall be made by the Board of Health, or of the committee appointed for that purpose.

When Board of Health to provide hospital.

[1375.] SEC. 39. When the small pox, or any other disease dangerous to the public health, shall break out in any township, the Board of Health shall immediately provide such Hospital, or place of reception for the sick and infected, as they shall judge best for their accommodation and the safety of the inhabitants; and such Hospitals and places of reception shall be subject to the regulations of the Board of Health, in the same manner as hereinbefore provided for established Hospitals.

When infected persons to be removed to hospital, &c.

[1376.] SEC. 40. The Board of Health shall cause such sick or infected persons to be removed to such Hospitals or places of reception, unless the condition of the sick person be such as not to admit of removal without danger of life; in which case the house or place where the sick shall remain, shall be considered as a Hospital to every purpose before mentioned, and all persons residing in, or in any way concerned with the same, shall be subject to the regulations of the Board of Health, as before provided.

Board to prevent the spread of dangerous disease.

[1377.] SEC. 41. When the small pox, or any other disease dangerous to the public health, is found to exist in any township, the Board of Health shall use all possible care to prevent the spreading of the infection, and to give public notice of infected places to travelers, by such means as in their judgment shall be most effectual for the common safety.

Penalty for violating regulations of hospitals.

[1378.] SEC. 42. If any physician or other person, in any of the Hospitals or places of reception before mentioned, or who shall attend, approach, or be concerned with the same, shall violate any of the regulations lawfully made in relation thereto, either with respect to himself, or his, or any other person's property, the person so offending shall, for each offence, forfeit a sum not less than ten, nor more than one hundred dollars.

Householders to give notice of disease; penalty for neglect.

[1379.] SEC. 43. Whenever any householder shall know that any person within his family is taken sick with the small pox, or any other disease dangerous to the public health, he shall immediately give notice thereof to the Board of Health, or to the Health Officer of the township in which he resides; and if he shall refuse or neglect to give such notice, he shall forfeit a sum not exceeding one hundred dollars.

Penalty on physician neglecting to give notice.

[1380.] SEC. 44. Whenever any physician shall know that any person whom he is called to visit, is infected with the small pox, or any other disease dangerous to the public health, such physician shall immediately give notice thereof to the Board of Health, or Health Officer of the township in which such diseased person may be; and every physician who shall refuse or neglect to give such notice, shall forfeit, for each offence, a sum not less than fifty, nor more than one hundred dollars.

Inoculation with cow pox.

[1381.] SEC. 45. Every township may, at any meeting, make suitable provision for the inoculation of the inhabitants thereof with the cow pox, under the direction of the Board of Health, or the Health Officer of the township, and they shall raise all necessary sums of money to defray the expenses of such inoculation, in the same manner that other township charges are defrayed.

OFFENSIVE TRADES.

Places may be assigned for carrying on offensive trades.

[1382.] SEC. 46. The Township Board of every township, the President and Trustees, or Council, of every village, and the Mayor and Aldermen of every city, respectively, when they shall judge it necessary, shall, from time to time, assign certain places for the exercising of any trade or employment, offensive to the inhabitants, or dangerous to the public health; and they shall forbid the exercise thereof in places not so assigned; and all such assignments shall be entered in the records of the township, village, or city, and they may be revoked when the said township, village, or city officers may think proper.

When places become a nuisance, assignment may be revoked, &c.

[1383.] SEC. 47. When any place or building so assigned shall become a nuisance by reason of offensive smells or exhalations proceeding therefrom, or shall become otherwise hurtful or dangerous to the neighborhood, or to travelers, and the same shall be made to appear on a trial, or the admission of the person exercising such trade or employment, before the Circuit Court for the county, upon a complaint made by the Board of Health, or by any other person, the said Court may revoke such assignment, and prohibit the further use of such place, or building, for the exercise of either of the aforesaid trades or employments, and may cause such nuisance to be removed or prevented.

Action on the case for damages.

[1384.] SEC. 48. Any person injured, either in his comfort, or the enjoyment of his estate, by any such nuisance, may have an action on the case for the damages sustained thereby, in which action the defendants may plead the general issue, and give any special matter in evidence.

BOARDS OF HEALTH IN CITIES AND VILLAGES.

Who to constitute Board in cities and villages.

[1385.] SEC. 49. The Mayor and Aldermen of each incorporated city, and the President and Council, or Trustees of each incorporated village in this State, shall have and exercise all the powers, and perform all the duties of a Board of Health, as provided in this chapter, within the limits of the cities or villages respectively of which they are such officers.

DIVISION XXII. — OF THE DRAINING OF SWAMPS, MARSHES, AND OTHER LOW LANDS, THAT AFFECT INJURIOUSLY THE PUBLIC HEALTH.

Comp. L. 1857, Chap. XXXVIII. p. 441.

Chapter One Hundred and Thirty-One of the Revised Statutes of 1846.

OF THE DRAINING OF SWAMPS AND OTHER LOW LANDS.

Owner of swamp, &c., may apply to Township Board. 1839, p. 153.

[1386.] SECTION 1. Any person owning or possessing any swamp, marsh, or other low land, who shall desire to drain such land, and who shall deem it necessary, in order thereto, that a ditch or ditches should be opened through lands belonging to other persons, in case the owners of any such lands shall refuse to permit the opening of such ditch, or ditches, through the same, may make application, in writing, to the Township Board of the township where such marsh, swamp, or other low lands shall be situated, to inquire and determine whether such marsh, swamp, or other lands are a source of disease to the inhabitants, and whether the public health will be promoted by draining the same.[48]

Determination, certificate of Board, and application for summons.

[1387.] SEC. 2. Upon such application being made to the Township Board, they, or a majority of them, shall inquire and determine, and certify under their hands, whether the marsh, swamp, or other low lands, are a source of disease, and whether the public health will be promoted by draining the same, and if they shall certify that the same are a source of disease, and that the public health will be promoted by draining the same, the person or persons making such application may file such certificate with any Justice of the Peace of the township in which the lands are situated, through which any such ditch is proposed to be opened, and apply for such summons as is hereinafter specified.[49]

---

[48] *Form of Application to Township Board for draining Swamp, Marsh, or other low lands.*

To the Township Board of the Township of *Amboy* in the County of *Hillsdale.*

The undersigned, owning the following described lands *(here describe the lands)* in said township, which lands *(or a greater part thereof, or as the case may be,)* are swamp lands, and being desirous to drain such lands, and deeming it necessary thereto that a ditch or ditches should be opened through lands belonging to other persons, to wit: L. M., O. P., &c., who refuse to permit the opening of the same through their lands, do hereby make application to you and ask that you will inquire into the matter and take such measures as will be necessary for the opening of such ditch or ditches.

Dated this —— day of —— A. D. 18—. JOHN JACKSON.

[49] *Form of Certificate by Township Board, where swamp or low lands are a source of disease.*

Ingham County,
Township of *Wheatfield,* } ss.

Application in writing having been made by *John Jackson* to us, the undersigned Township Board of said township, for that purpose we did on the —— day of —— A. D. 18— proceed to inquire, as to whether a certain marsh, ex-

Summons to be issued by Justice.

[1388.] SEC. 3. The Justice to whom such application shall be made, shall thereupon issue a summons, directed to the Sheriff or any Constable of the same county, requiring him to summon nine reputable freeholders of such county, who are not interested in the said lands, nor in any of them, nor in any wise of kin to either of the parties, to be and appear on the premises, at a certain time to be specified in such summons, not less than ten, nor more than twenty days from the date thereof.[50]

Summons to direct notice to be given to owner.

[1389.] SEC. 4. Such summons shall also direct the Sheriff or Constable to give at least six days' notice to the owner of such lands, of the time at which such jury is to appear.

Summons, how executed.

[1390.] SEC. 5. The officer to whom such summons shall be delivered, shall execute the same by summoning such jurors, in the same manner, and with the like authority, as upon venires issued in cases pending before Justices of the Peace, and shall in like manner make return thereof, and of the fact of his having given the notice therein required.

Justice to attend Jury and administer oath, &c.

[1391.] SEC. 6. The Justice shall attend at the time and place specified in the summons, and if it appear that due notice has been given, as required in the summons, and if six or more of the nine free-

---

tending over lands owned by said *John Jackson*, described as follows: *(here describe the lands of the applicant,)* is a source of disease, and as to whether the public health will be promoted by draining such marsh, and do hereby certify, that such marsh is a source of disease, and that the public health will be promoted by draining the same, and that a ditch for that purpose will be required through the lands of L. M. and O. P., &c.

In witness whereof, the persons composing the Township Board have hereunto set their hands this —— day of —— A. D. 18—.

A. B.,
C. D.,
E. F.,
G. H.,
Township Board.

[50] *Form of Justice's Summons for a Jury.*

Ionia County, }
Township of *Boston*, } ss.

To the Sheriff or any Constable of said county, Greeting:

Whereas, *John Jackson* has filed with the undersigned Justice of the Peace of said township a certificate of the Township Board of said township, setting forth that a certain marsh, extending over lands owned by said *John Jackson*, described as follows: *(here describe the lands.)* is a source of disease, and that the public health will be promoted by draining the same, and that a ditch for that purpose will be required through the lands of L. M. and O. P., &c.; these are therefore in the name of the people of the State of Michigan, to require you to summon nine reputable freeholders of said county, who are not interested in the lands before described, nor in the said lands of the said L. M. and O. P., &c., nor in any of them, nor in any wise of kin to either of the parties hereinbefore mentioned, to be and appear on said premises on the——day of—— A. D. 18—, at —— o'clock. And you are directed to give at least six days' notice to the said L. M., O. P., &c., of the time at which such jury is to appear as herein specified, and hereof fail not.

Given under the hand and seal of said Justice, this ——— day of ——— A. D. 18—.

JOHN OAKS,
[SEAL.] *Justice of the Peace.*

holders, as above specified, shall then and there appear, he shall administer to each of them an oath or affirmation, well and truly to examine and certify, in regard to the benefits or damages which will result from the opening of such ditch or ditches.

Proceedings by Jury.

[1392.] SEC. 7. The person applying to have such ditch or ditches opened, shall then deliver to the jury a map of the land through which the same are proposed to be opened, on which map the plan, length, width and depth of such ditch or ditches shall be particularly designated; and thereupon the jury shall personally examine the premises, and hear any reasons that may be offered in regard to the question submitted to them; and they may, if they think proper, vary the dimensions of any ditch so proposed to be opened; but in such case they shall designate on the said map the alterations made by them.

Inquisition of Jury to be certified.

[1393.] SEC. 8. If, after taking all the circumstances into consideration, the jury shall be satisfied that the opening of such ditch or ditches is necessary and proper, they shall so certify by inquisition in writing; and if so satisfied, they shall further certify by such inquisition, that the benefits which will accrue to the owner of the lands, from the opening of such ditch or ditches, will or will not be equal to any damages that he will sustain thereby; and if such benefits shall be certified not to be equal to the damages, the jury shall assess the damages which, in their judgment, will be sustained by such owner, and certify the same in like manner.[51]

Inquisition to be delivered to Justice; fees of officers and Jury.

[1394.] SEC. 9. Every such inquisition shall be signed by all the jurors, and delivered to the Justice; and the Justice, jurors, and officer serving the summons, shall be entitled to receive the same fees for their services under the provisions of this chapter, as are allowed by law for similar services in causes tried before Justices of the Peace.

When applicant may enter and open ditch.

[1395.] SEC. 10. Upon payment or tender of the damages assessed by the jury, and the costs of such assessment, or if no damages shall have been found by them, upon payment of the costs of the proceedings, and the delivery of the certificate of the jury to the Justice, it shall be lawful for the person applying for such summons to enter, with his servants, teams, carriages, and necessary implements, upon such lands, and then and there to cut and open such ditch or ditches as were designated on the said map, according to the plan and dimensions therein specified and adopted by the jury, not deviating materially from such dimensions.

---

[51]*Form of Certificate of Jury in relation to Opening Ditches.*

We, the undersigned Jury, being summoned and duly sworn for that purpose, having proceeded and truly examined as to the necessity and propriety of opening a ditch, as shown by the annexed map, *(let the map be annexed,)* and having heard all the reasons that were offered in regard to the question submitted to us concerning the opening of said ditch, do hereby certify that, after taking all circumstances into consideration, we are satisfied that the opening of such ditch is necessary and proper, and do so declare; and we do further certify, that the benefits which will accrue to L. M., O. P., &c., owners of lands through which said ditch is to be opened, from the opening thereof, will be equal to any damages that they will sustain thereby.

Witness our hands, this —— day of —— A. D. 18—.

(To be signed by all the Jury.)

Ditch may be cleared and scoured from time to time.

[1396.] SEC. 11. After such ditch or ditches shall have been opened, it shall be lawful for the said applicant, his heirs or assigns, forever thereafter, from time to time, as it shall be necessary, to enter upon the lands through which such ditch or ditches shall have been opened, for the purpose of clearing out and scouring the same, and then and there to clear and scour such ditch or ditches, in such manner as to preserve the original length, depth, and width thereof.

Double damages for obstructing or injuring ditch, &c.

[1397.] SEC. 12. Any person who shall dam up, obstruct, or in any way injure any ditch or ditches so opened, shall be liable to pay to the person owning or possessing the swamp, marsh or other low land, for the draining of which such ditch or ditches shall have been opened, double the damages that shall be assessed by the jury for such injury, and in case of a second, or other subsequent offence by the same person, treble such damages.

Justice to cause maps to be filed with Township Clerk.

[1398.] SEC. 13. The Justice before whom such proceedings shall be had, under this chapter, shall cause the map delivered by the applicant, and the inquisition of the jury, which he shall certify to have been taken before him, to be filed in the office of the clerk of the township wherein the premises shall be situated, to be kept in his office, as a record of the proceedings between the parties.

An Act to Provide for the Draining of Swamps, Marshes, and other Low Lands.

[*Approved February* 17, 1857. *Laws of* 1857, *p.* 431.]

Board of Supervisors to appoint Commissioners to superintend drainage of lands.

[1399.] SECTION 1. *The People of the State of Michigan enact*, That the Board of Supervisors in any organized county of this State shall have power to appoint three Commissioners, to superintend the drainage of swamps, marshes, and other low lands, in their respective counties, according to the provisions of this act, as do in their judgment affect injuriously the health of the inhabitants.

Oath. Laws 1859, p. 499.

[1400.] SEC. 2. Before entering upon their duties as Commissioners, they shall severally make oath, before some person duly authorized to administer oaths, that they will justly and impartially discharge the duties assigned them by this Act; which oath shall be by them filed in the County Clerk's office; and they shall, thereupon, choose one of their number chairman, and one as clerk, which shall constitute them an organized Board of Commissioners.

Board of Commissioners.

Construction of ditches. Laws 1859, p. 499.

[1401.] SEC. 3. Upon application, in writing, to said Commissioners, by any ten or more resident freeholders of the township or townships, where said ditch is desired to be constructed, for the construction of any ditch or ditches, pursuant to the provisions of this Act, it shall be the duty of said Commissioners to examine personally, the marshes and other low lands designated in such application; to make such observations and surveys as they may deem necessary to determine the route and dimensions of the several ditches required to be cut in, or from the same, together with their length, breadth and depth. And if, in the opinion of said Commissioners, such ditch or ditches should be constructed, the chairman of the board shall thereupon issue a venire, under his hand, directed to any Constable of said

Proceedings.

Provision for jury

county, commanding him to summon twelve freeholders, therein named by said Commissioners, and not directly or indirectly interested therein, of the township or townships where such ditch or ditches are to be constructed, to be and appear before said Commissioners, at such time and place in said county as may be designated in said venire, to determine the necessity for the construction of any such ditch or ditches, and the amount of damages sustained by any person or persons, owning or interested in any of the lands through which the same shall be constructed.

Commissioners to estimate and apportion expense of ditches and cause maps to be made.

[1402.] SEC. 4. Said Commissioners shall also make an estimate of the sum necessary to be raised to pay the expenses of making such ditches or drains, including all incidental expenses. They shall also make an estimate of the sum that ought to be levied on each section, or part of a section of land in such marshes or other low lands, in such proportion as they shall deem just, according to the benefit that will accrue to each by making any such ditches or drains; and they shall cause maps of said lands to be made, designating thereon the length, depth, width, position and direction of every ditch or drain by them laid out or contemplated; said map shall also contain a description of every section, or part of a section upon which estimates have been made, with the amount of such estimate; also the aggregate amount to be collected in each township.

To contract for making ditches.

[1403.] SEC. 5. Said Commissioners shall contract for the performance of the work and materials required to complete such ditches and drains; but contracts shall be upon reasonable public notice, published not less than three weeks in some newspaper printed in the county, or if no paper be printed in the county, in a newspaper printed in some county nearest thereto, and such other notice as to them shall seem proper, and shall be subject to the action and judgment of the Circuit Court, as hereinafter specified.

Report to Circuit Court. Laws 1859, p. 499.

[1404.] SEC. 6. Said Commissioners shall make a full report to the Circuit Court of all their doings in the premises, accompanied by maps, estimates, statements of contracts, and other matters necessary to a full exhibition and understanding of their action. Such report shall be filed in the office of the County Clerk of said county at least three weeks before it be acted upon by said Court; and the Commissioners shall give notice at least three weeks, by publication in a newspaper printed in the county, or if no newspaper be printed therein, by posting notices upon the outer door of the Court House in said county, and in five or more public places in each township or townships in which such ditch or ditches, or drains, are to be made, that they will on some day, to be by them specified, present said report to the Circuit Court for confirmation; and on such day, or some other day thereafter as may be appointed by said Court, any person interested may appear and object to the confirmation of said report, and the Court may, for good cause shown, amend or set aside said report, and direct new examination or surveys, when, in the opinion of the Court, justice or equity requires it; but if no good cause be shown against it, the Court shall confirm the report; but if the aggregate estimate

Notice.

Confirmation of report.

When confirmation not required.

for the construction of any ditch or drain shall not exceed the sum of fifteen hundred dollars, it shall not be necessary for said Commissioners to apply to the Court for confirmation of the report, but they may proceed at once in the construction of such ditch or drain, conforming in all other respects to the provisions of this act.

Confirmed report, when filed. Laws 1859, p. 499.

[1405.] SEC. 7. The Commissioners shall cause a copy of the report, confirmed by the Circuit Court, (where a confirmation is required by the preceding section,) to be filed in the office of the Auditor-General of the State, and in the office of the Treasurer of the county. They shall also cause a copy of the same to be laid before the Board of Supervisors of said county, at their annual session on the second Monday in October following; and the said board shall charge the aggregate sums as they are apportioned, against the proper townships, and shall direct the Supervisor of each township in which any portion of said ditches or drains may be constructed, or tax levied, to levy the same upon the several sections or parts of sections, and other lands, described as being in his township, and direct the Township Treasurer to collect and pay said sums to the County Treasurer, in like manner and at the same time with other county taxes; and where no confirmation of the Circuit Court is required, they shall make a report in like manner to the Auditor-General, County Treasurer, and to the Board of Supervisors of said county, as is required in cases where a confirmation is required.

Duty of Board of Supervisors.

Delinquent for taxes.—Ibid.

[1406.] SEC. 8. All lands upon which a delinquent tax shall be levied by virtue of this act for taxes which may be returned to the office of the Auditor-General delinquent for such tax, shall be advertised and sold for such taxes, at the same time and in the same manner, and subject to like redemption, as lands delinquent for other taxes.

Re-location of drains.—Ibid.

Proviso.

[1407.] SEC. 9. Said Commissioners shall have power to locate or re-locate ditches or drains, or to alter or vary the size thereof: *Provided*, That no such alteration or variation shall be made without the consent of the contractor; but if at any time said Commissioners shall extend, alter, locate, or re-locate any drain, the estimated cost of which shall exceed fifteen hundred dollars, so as to increase the expense of such drain, then and in such case, they shall make report of their doings from time to time, according to the facts, to the Circuit Court of the proper county, who shall in all cases act in accordance with the provisions of this act.

Report to Circuit Court.

Power of Commissioners to deepen, widen and clear out ditches.

[1408.] SEC. 10. The power herein conferred upon said Commissioners for digging and draining, shall also extend to, and include deepening, widening, and clearing out any ditches that have heretofore, or may be hereafter constructed.

Fine for injuring drain.

[1409.] SEC. 11. If any person shall willfully or maliciously obstruct, or injure any drain laid out by, and under the provisions of this act, he shall be subject to a fine not exceeding ten dollars, together with such sum as will be required to repair such damage, and costs of suit, which fine may be recovered in an action of debt at the suit of any one of said Commissioners, before any Justice of the Peace of the proper county, and when any recovery shall be made, and the same collected, it shall be paid to the complainant, and be by him deposited with the Township Treasurer in the township where such damages occurred, for the benefit of highways in such township.

[1410.] SEC. 12. No money shall be paid by any County Treasurer of any county in which a tax is assessed for the purposes of drainage under this act, or any warrant drawn by the said Commissioners, out of any other fund than that derived from such taxes.

Money not to be paid by County Treasurer for drainage out of any other fund. Laws 1859, p. 499.

[1411.] SEC. 13. The Commissioners shall each be entitled to receive one dollar and fifty cents per day for the time actually spent by them in performing their duties under this act; but before they shall receive any pay, their respective accounts shall be sworn to by them, and taxed by the Judge of the Circuit Court of the county, and the bills filed in the office of the Treasurer of said county, who shall pay them out of the moneys collected by virtue of this act, and not otherwise.

Compensation of Commissioners.

[1412.] SEC. 14. Whenever any order drawn by the Commissioners shall be presented to the County Treasurer, and there shall be no funds in his hands applicable to the payment thereof, the County Treasurer shall endorse thereon the date of such presentation, with his signature thereto. Such orders shall draw interest from and after such presentation and endorsement.

When orders may draw interest.

[1413.] SEC. 15. Whenever any drain shall be laid upon any public road, or where drains have been laid, and roads shall hereafter be laid out beside said drain, it shall be the duty of Commissioners of Highways and Overseers of their respective districts to keep said drains opened and free of all obstructions.

Keeping drains open.

[1414.] SEC. 16. All claims arising under the preceding sections of this act, whether on contract, labor performed, or any other services, shall be audited by the Commissioners, (except for their services as Commissioners,) and paid on their order by the County Treasurer of the county out of any funds in his hands created by this act, and not otherwise.

By whom claims audited and by whom paid.

[1415.] SEC. 17. All bids made for any of the lands which may be sold for taxes assessed under the provisions of this act, may be paid in warrants drawn under the provisions of this act, by the Commissioners, on the Treasurer of said county in which the lands sold are situated, if drawn for the construction of the said ditch, or Commissioner's service, for which said lands are to be sold, and such warrants shall, if tendered, be received by the Auditor-General, or Treasurer of the county in which they were drawn, in payment for any such tax that may be returned delinquent.

Bids at sale may be paid in warrants drawn under this act.

[1416.] SEC. 18. For the information of all persons concerned, the said Commissioners shall make a full report in writing to the Board of Supervisors of the proper county, at the next and each annual session thereafter, setting forth as near as practicable:

Annual report of Commissioners.

1. What proportion of the ditches or drains for the construction of which a tax has been levied, are completed, and the amount paid therefor;

2. What proportion is under contract and not completed, and the amount to be paid therefor, and whether such contract or contracts are likely to be performed; also the proportion not yet under contract, and the estimated cost of their construction; and whether there is a sufficient amount of unexpended funds created by such tax to complete the work;

3. What amount of such funds had been expended and for what purpose, exhibiting the items of such expenditure as fully as may be practicable; and also what amount of warrants has been drawn by them against such fund, and shall also report all such other matters in relation to the subject as they may deem necessary, or said Board of Supervisors may require.

Powers of Boards of Supervisors with respect to Commissioners and drains.

[1417.] SEC. 19. The Board of Supervisors of the several counties in which such Commissioners shall be appointed, shall have full power and authority to control the action of such Commissioners, and may make any order in relation to such ditches or drains, or other matters relating thereto, not inconsistent with the public interest or the rights of individuals, which order shall be binding on such Commissioners. The Board of Supervisors shall also have power and authority, for any cause by them deemed sufficient, to remove any or all of such Commissioners, and appoint others in their stead, with like powers and subject to the same liabilities: *Provided*, That nothing contained in this act shall be construed as to affect any contract, vested right or interest existing, made or created at any time previous to the passage of this act. All acts or parts (of acts) contravening the provisions of this act, are hereby repealed.

Jury. Laws 1859, p. 499.

[1418.] SEC. 20. Upon the return of the venire issued pursuant to the provisions of section three of this act, if the jurors shall not all appear within one hour after the time of appearance named in the venire, the chairman of the board shall direct the officer to summon a sufficient number of freeholders, naming them in the vicinity, as talesmen, to complete the panel; and when the jurors have appeared, the chairman shall administer unto each of said jurors an oath well and truly to examine and determine the necessity for constructing such ditch or ditches, and to assess the damages sustained by any person or persons owning the lands through which the same shall pass.

Oath of Jurors.

Jury to estimate and assess damages.—Ibid.

[1419.] SEC. 21. The jury shall thereupon proceed to examine such swamp, marsh, or other low land, to determine the necessity for constructing such drain or drains, and if they shall, on a careful examination of the whole matter, be of the opinion that it is necessary to construct said drain or drains, they shall proceed to assess the damage which any person or persons shall sustain by reason of the construction of the same, and shall certify in writing their doings, and the amount of any damage so assessed, to the chairman of said Board of Commissioners, and said jurors shall be entitled to receive one dollar per day each, and six cents per mile for traveling in going to the place or places where such drain or drains shall be located, to be paid according to the provisions of this act.

Compensation of Jurors.

Damages, how paid.—Ibid.

[1420.] SEC. 22. If damages shall be assessed by any jury, under the provisions of this act, and certified as aforesaid, said Commissioners shall thereupon issue their order upon the County Treasurer of said county, for the amount of such damages, to any person or persons, their agents or attorneys, entitled thereto; such order or orders shall be paid by said Treasurer out of any money in the treasury, in pursuance of the provisions of this act.

Applicant to pay cost, when request is not granted.—Ibid.

[1421.] SEC. 23. Whenever application shall be made, as provided in the third section of this act, to said Commissioners to examine any swamp, marsh, or other low land, and said Commissioners shall proceed to examine the same, and it appears, on such examination, that there was no sufficient cause for making such application, and the Commissioners shall determine that no ditch or ditches asked for by said applicants is needed, said applicants shall be liable to said Commissioners for the amount of all costs and expenses incurred by them in making such examination; and if said applicants shall neglect to pay the same on demand thereof being made, said Commissioners may recover the same in an action of assumpsit, or on the case, before any Justice of such county.

Special Commissioners to assess damages.—Ibid.

[1422.] SEC. 24. Said Commissioners shall have power to apply to any Judge of a Court of Record of such county, for the appointment of three Commissioners to determine the necessity for constructing any ditch or ditches, and to assess the damages to which any person or persons shall be entitled by reason of the construction thereof, in the same manner and under the same restrictions imposed on a jury of freeholders in section twenty-one of this act, and in such case it shall not be necessary to empannel any jury as provided by this act.

Prior contracts, &c., not affected. Ibid.

[1423.] SEC. 25. Anything contained in these amendments or in the act hereby amended, shall not be construed or held to annul or avoid any engagement, contract or undertaking heretofore entered into by the Commissioners of any county under the act hereby amended.

This act is ordered to take immediate effect.

Comp. L. 1857, Chap. XXXIX., p. 451.

DIVISION XXIII.—Of the Support of Poor Persons by their Relatives.

Chapter Thirty-Seven of Revised Statutes of 1846.

Certain persons to support poor relations.

[1418.] Section 1. The father, mother, and children, being of sufficient ability, of any poor person who is blind, old, lame, impotent, or decrepit, so as to be unable to maintain himself, shall, at their own charge, relieve and maintain such poor person, in such manner as shall be approved by the Directors of the Poor of the township where such poor person may be.

In case of failure, Superintendents to apply to Circuit Court.

[1419.] Sec. 2. Upon the failure of any relative to relieve and maintain any such poor person, it shall be the duty of the Superintendents of the Poor of the county where such poor person may be, to apply to the Circuit Court for the county where such relative may dwell, for an order to compel such relief; of which application at least fourteen days' notice in writing shall be given, by serving the same personally, or by leaving the same at the dwelling place of the person to whom it may be directed, in case of his absence therefrom, with some person of sufficient age.

Court to make order.

[1420.] Sec. 3. The Court to which such application may be made, shall proceed in a summary way to hear the proofs and allegations of the parties, and shall order such of the relatives aforesaid of such poor person, as appear to be of sufficient ability, to relieve and maintain such poor person, and shall therein specify the sum which will be sufficient for the support of such poor person, to be paid weekly.

Order in which relations are liable.

[1421.] Sec. 4. The said Court shall also in such orders direct the relative or relatives who shall perform that duty, in the following order: the father shall be first required to maintain such poor person, if of sufficient ability; if there be no father, or he be not of sufficient ability, then the children of such poor person; if there be no such children, or they be not of sufficient ability, then the mother, if she be able to do so.

Contribution, when to be ordered.

[1422.] Sec. 5. If it shall appear that any such relative is unable wholly to maintain such poor person, but is able to contribute towards his support, the Court may, in its discretion, direct two or more relatives of different degrees to maintain such poor person, and shall prescribe the proportion which each shall contribute for that purpose; and if it shall appear that the relatives liable as aforesaid are not of sufficient ability wholly to maintain such poor person, but are able to contribute something therefor, the Court shall direct the sum, in proportion to their ability, which such relations shall severally pay weekly for that purpose.

Order what to specify; may be varied in certain cases.

[1423.] Sec. 6. Such order may specify the time during which the relatives aforesaid shall maintain such poor person, or during which any of the said sums so directed by the Court shall be paid, or it may be indefinite, or until the further order of the Court; and the said Court may from time to time vary such order, whenever circumstances shall require it, on the application either of any relative affected thereby, or of any Superintendent of the Poor, upon fourteen days' notice being given in the manner aforesaid.

[1424.] SEC. 7. The costs and expenses of any application under the provisions of this chapter, shall be ascertained by the Court, and paid by the relatives against whom any order may be made, and the payment thereof, and obedience to the order of maintenance, and to any order of such Court for the payment of money as aforesaid, may be enforced by process of attachment from such Court.

Payment of costs and expenses, &c. how enforced.

[1425.] SEC. 8. If any relative who shall have been required by such order to relieve or maintain any poor person, shall neglect to do so in such manner as shall be approved by the Directors of the Poor of the township where such poor person may be, and shall neglect to pay to the Superintendents of the Poor of the county, weekly, the sum prescribed by the Court for the support of such poor person, the said Superintendents may maintain an action against such relatives, as for moneys paid, laid out and expended, and shall recover therein the sum so prescribed by the said Court for every week the said order shall have been disobeyed, up to the time of such recovery, with costs of suit, for the use of the poor.

Action may be brought by Superintendents in case of neglect, &c.

[1426.] SEC. 9. Whenever the father, or the mother, being a widow, or living separate from her husband, shall abscond from his or her children, or a husband from his wife, leaving any of them chargeable, or likely to become chargeable upon the public for their support, the Superintendents of the Poor of the county where such wife or children may be, may apply to any two Justices of the Peace of any county in which any estate, real or personal, of the said father, mother or husband may be situated, for a warrant to seize the same.

When Superintendents may apply for warrant to seize estate of person abscond'g.

[1427.] SEC. 10. Upon due proof of the facts aforesaid, the said Justices shall issue their warrant, authorizing the said Superintendents to take and seize the goods, chattels, effects, things in action, and the lands and tenements of the person so absconding; and the said Superintendents, by virtue of such warrant, may seize and take the said property, things in action, and effects, wherever the same may be found in the same county, and they shall be vested with all the rights and title to the said property, things in action, and effects, which the person so absconding had at the time of his or her departure.

When warrant to issue, and duty of Superintendents thereon.

[1428.] SEC. 11. All sales and transfers of any personal property left in the county from which such person absconded, made by him or her after the issuing of such warrant, whether in payment of an antecedent debt, or for a new consideration, shall be absolutely void; and the said Superintendents shall immediately make an inventory of the property, things in action, and effects so seized by them, and return the same with their proceedings, to the next Circuit Court for the county in which such Superintendents reside, there to be filed.

Sales by owner after warrant issued to be void.

Inventory and return by Superintendents.

Circuit Court may confirm or discharge warrant, &c.

[1429.] SEC. 12. The said Circuit Court, upon inquiry into the facts and circumstances of the case, may confirm the said warrant and seizure, or may discharge the same; and if the same be confirmed, such Court shall, from time to time direct what part of the personal property shall be sold, and how much of the proceeds of such sale, and of the rents and profits of the real estate, if any, shall be applied towards the maintenance of the wife and children of the person so absconding.

Order for sale.

Sale of property and application of proceeds.

[1430.] SEC. 13. The Superintendents shall sell, at public vendue, the property so ordered to be sold, and receive the rents and profits of the real estate of the person so absconding, and shall apply the same to the maintenance and support of the wife or children of the person so absconded, and for that purpose shall draw on the County Treasurer therefor; and they shall account to the said Circuit Court for all moneys so received by them, and for the application thereof, from time to time, and may be compelled by said Court to render such account at any time.

When two Justices may discharge order.

[1431.] SEC. 14. If the party so absconding return and support the wife or children so abandoned, or give security to the Superintendents of the Poor of such county, to be approved by two Justices of the Peace of such county, that the wife or children so abandoned shall not become, or thereafter be chargeable to the county, then such warrant shall be discharged by an order of such Justices, and the property taken by virtue thereof, and remaining unappropriated, or the proceeds thereof, after deducting the expenses of the proceedings aforesaid, shall be restored to such party.

DIVISION XXIV.—Of the Support of Poor Persons by the Public.

Comp. L. 1857, Chap. XL., p. 455.

Chapter Thirty-Eight of Revised Statutes of 1846.

OF THE SUPPORT OF POOR PERSONS BY COUNTIES.[a]

[1432.] Section 1. Every poor person who is blind, old, lame, sick, or decrepit, or in any other way disabled or enfeebled, so as to be unable to maintain himself, and who shall not be relieved or maintained by his relatives as provided in the preceding chapter, shall be maintained by the county in which he may be, according to the following provisions: *Poor persons, when to be maintained by county.*

[1433.] Sec. 2. It shall be the duty of the Board of Supervisors of each county, at their annual meeting in each year, to appoint three discreet freeholders of such county to be Superintendents of the Poor within the same, who shall hold their offices for one year, and until others shall be appointed in their places and duly qualified, and who shall take the oath of office prescribed in the twelfth article of the Constitution, and file the same with the County Clerk. *Appointment of Superintendents, their oath of office.* *Const., Art. 18.*

[1434.] Sec. 3. A majority of the persons so appointed shall be at all times competent to transact business, and to execute any powers vested in the Board of Superintendents; and they shall be allowed such sum for their actual attendance and services, as the Board of Supervisors of the county shall deem reasonable. *Compensation.*

[1435.] Sec. 4. They shall be a corporation by the name of the Superintendents of the Poor of the county for which they shall be appointed, and shall possess the usual powers of a corporation for public purposes, and they shall meet as often as the Board of Supervisors of the county shall direct, at the County Poor House, if there be one, and if not, then at the place of holding the Circuit Courts in their county, and at such other times and places as they shall deem necessary. *To be a corporation, their powers as such, &c.*

[1436.] Sec. 5. They shall have the general superintendence of all the poor who may be in their respective counties, and shall have power, and it shall be their duty: *Specification of certain powers and duties.*

1. To have charge of the County Poor Houses that have been or shall be erected, and to provide suitable places for the keeping of such poor, when so directed by the Board of Supervisors, when houses for that purpose shall not have been erected by the county, and for that purpose to rent a tenement or tenements, and land not exceeding eighty acres, and to cause the poor of the county to be maintained at such places;

[a] In 1849 an Act was passed authorizing the County Superintendents of the Poor of Berrien County to contract with one or more persons for the support of all, or any, of the County Poor of that County. Laws of 1849, p. 188.

Specification of certain powers and duties.

2. To ordain and establish prudential rules, regulations, and by-laws, for the government and good order of such places so provided, and of the County Poor Houses, and for the employment, relief, management, and government of the persons therein placed; but such rules, regulations, and by-laws shall not be valid until sanctioned by the Judges of the County Court;

3. To employ one or more suitable persons to be keepers of such houses or places, and all necessary officers and servants; and to vest in them such powers for the government of such houses as shall be necessary, reserving to the paupers who may be placed under the care of such keepers, the right to appeal to the Superintendents;

4. To purchase the furniture, implements, and materials that shall be necessary for the maintenance of the poor, and their employment and labor, and to sell and dispose of the proceeds of such labor, as they shall deem expedient;

5. To prescribe the rate of allowance to be made by any persons for bringing paupers to the County Poor House or place provided for the poor, subject to such alterations as the Board of Supervisors may, by general resolution, make;

6. To authorize the keepers of such houses or places to certify the amount due to any person for bringing such paupers; which amount shall be paid by the County Treasurer, on the production of such certificate, countersigned and allowed by any two of the Superintendents;

7. To direct the commencement of suits by any Directors of the Poor, who may be entitled to prosecute upon any recognizances, bonds, or securities, taken for the indemnity of any township, or of the county, and in case of the neglect of any such Directors to commence and conduct such suits, without the authority of such Directors, in their names;

8. To draw, from time to time, on the County Treasurer for all necessary expenses incurred in the discharge of their duties; which drafts shall be paid by him out of the moneys placed in his hands for the support of the poor;

9. To render to the Board of Supervisors of their county, at their annual meeting, an account of all moneys received and expended by them, or under their direction, and of all their proceedings;

10. To pay over all moneys remaining in their hands to the County Treasurer, within fifteen days after the expiration of their office.

Board of Supervisors may determine to erect Poor House, and direct Superintendents to purchase land.

[1437.] SEC. 6. The Board of Supervisors of any county in this State, in which a County Poor House is not already erected, may, at any annual or special meeting thereof, determine to erect such house, for the reception of the poor of their county; and upon filing such determination with the Clerk of the county, they may direct the Superintendents of the Poor of such county to purchase one or more tracts of land, not exceeding three hundred and twenty acres, and to erect thereon one or more suitable buildings, for the purpose aforesaid.

[1438.] Sec. 7. To defray the expenses of such purchase and buildings, the said Board of Supervisors may raise, by tax on the taxable real and personal property within the same county, a sum not exceeding seven thousand dollars, in such installments, and at such times as they may judge expedient; and such tax shall be raised, assessed, and collected in the same manner as the other county charges, and shall be paid by the County Treasurer, upon the order of the Superintendents of the Poor, to be applied for the purposes aforesaid.

Tax to defray expenses of building, &c.

[1439.] Sec. 8. When any person shall apply for relief to any Director of the Poor, or to any Superintendent, he shall inquire into the state and circumstances of the applicant, and if it shall appear that the person so applying is in such indigent circumstances as to require permanent relief and support, and can be safely removed, the Director or Superintendent shall, by a written order, cause such poor person to be removed to the County Poor House, to be relieved and provided for, as his necessities may require.

When poor person to be remov'd to Poor House.

[1440.] Sec. 9. Every such person so removed shall be received by the keeper of the County Poor House, and shall be supported and relieved therein, under the direction of the Superintendents, until it shall appear to them that such person is able to maintain himself, when the said Superintendents may, in their discretion, discharge him.

To be received and relieved.

[1441.] Sec. 10. The expense of such removal shall be paid by the County Treasurer, on the certificate of the keeper, countersigned as aforesaid, at the rate which shall have been prescribed by the Superintendents.

Expense of removal, how paid.

[1442.] Sec. 11. The Directors of the Poor House shall be allowed such sums necessarily paid out, or contracted to be paid by them, for the relief or support of any such pauper previous to such removal, as the Superintendents shall judge were reasonably expended while it is improper to remove such pauper; which sums shall be paid by the County Treasurer, on the order of the Superintendents.

Directors, when to be allowed moneys paid out by them.

[1443.] Sec. 12. If it shall appear that any such poor person so applying for relief as aforesaid, requires only temporary relief, or is so sick, lame, or otherwise disabled that he cannot be safely or conveniently removed to the Poor House, and the application be made to a Director, he shall apply to a Justice of the Peace of the same township, who shall examine into the facts and circumstances, and shall, in writing, order such sum to be expended for the temporary relief of such poor person as he shall deem the circumstances of the case to require.

When Justice to order amount to be expended for temporary relief.

[1444.] Sec. 13. Such order shall entitle the Director to receive any sum which he may have paid out or contracted to pay within the amount therein specified, from the County Treasurer; but no greater sum than twenty dollars shall be so expended or paid for the relief of any one person, or one family, without the sanction, in writing, of one of the Superintendents of the Poor of the county, which shall be presented to the County Treasurer with the order of the Justice.

County Treasurer to pay amount expended, &c.

Provisions for support of idiots and lunatics out of Poor House.

[1445.] SEC. 14. The Superintendents may provide for the support of paupers that may be idiots or lunatics, out of the County Poor House, in such place, and in such manner as shall best promote the interests of the county, and conduce to the comfort and recovery of such paupers.

Punishment for remov'g paupers from one county to another.

[1446.] SEC. 15. Any person who shall send, carry, transport, remove, or bring, or who shall cause or procure to be sent, carried, transported, removed, or brought, any poor or indigent person from any county, into any other county, without legal authority, and there leave such poor person, or who shall entice such poor person so to remove, with intent to make any such county to which the removal shall be made, chargeable with the support of such pauper, shall be deemed guilty of a misdemeanor, and on conviction thereof, shall be imprisoned in the county jail not exceeding one year, or fined not exceeding two hundred dollars, or both, in the discretion of the Court.

Paupers removed &c., where to be maintained; notice may be given

[1447.] SEC. 16. The pauper so brought, removed or enticed, shall be maintained and provided for by the Superintendents of the Poor of the county where he may be, and the said Superintendents may give notice to either of the Superintendents of the Poor of the county from which such pauper removed, or was brought or enticed, informing them of such improper removal, and requiring them forthwith to take charge of such pauper.

Superintendents receiving notice to pay expenses, &c., or deny the allegation of removal within twenty days.

[1448.] SEC. 17. The Superintendents to whom such notice may be directed shall, within thirty days after the service thereof, take and remove such pauper to their county, and pay the expenses incurred in giving such notice, and in maintaining such pauper from the time of his becoming a charge to the county in which he is maintained; or they shall, within the time aforesaid, notify the Superintendents from whom such notice was received, or either of them, that they deny the allegation of such improper removal or enticing.

If Superintendents to whom notice is given, omit to remove pauper, &c., they and their successors liable.

[1449.] SEC. 18. If the Superintendents to whom a notice shall have been given, as provided in the sixteenth section of this chapter, shall omit to take and remove such pauper, and also neglect to notify such denial within the time aforesaid, they shall be liable for said expenses so long as such pauper shall remain a charge; and an action for such expenses may be maintained from time to time by, and in the name of the Superintendents incurring the same, or their successors in office, against the Superintendents so made liable, and their successors in office.

On receiving notice of denial, action to be commenced; consequence of neglect.

[1450] SEC. 19. Upon receiving any such notice of denial as aforesaid, the Superintendents upon whom the same may have been served, shall, within three months thereafter, commence an action against the Superintendents of the Poor of the county to whom the first notice was directed, for the expenses of supporting such pauper, as for moneys paid, laid out and expended, and shall prosecute the same to effect; and if such action be not commenced within the time aforesaid, the same shall be for ever barred, and no action shall thereafter be brought for any expenses incurred in supporting or maintaining such pauper.

[1451.] SEC. 20. No Supervisor of any township, Prosecuting Attorney of any county, County Clerk, or County Treasurer, shall be appointed to, or hold the office of Superintendent of the Poor. Who not to be Superintendent.

[1452.] SEC. 21. The keeper of every Poor House shall be exempt from all service in the militia, and from serving on juries, during the time he shall be such keeper. Keepers exempt from militia service, &c.

[1453.] SEC. 22. The places which shall be provided for the reception of the poor by the County Superintendents, pursuant to the provisions of this chapter, shall in all cases be deemed to be the County Poor House; and all the provisions of this chapter, applicable to County Poor Houses, shall extend and apply to such places. Places provided by Superintendents to be deemed Poor Houses.

[1454.] SEC. 23. Wherever there shall be in any county ten or more paupers, over five and under eighteen years of age, the Superintendents of the Poor of such county shall cause the same to be taught and educated in an apartment of the County Poor House, to be fitted up for that purpose, if it shall be convenient, and if not, then in some building or apartment to be provided by them for that purpose; and there shall be taught in such school the branches usually taught in the primary schools of this State; and the Superintendents are required to provide for the education of such paupers for at least one-half of the time they shall be under their charge, and the expenses thereof shall be paid in the same manner as other contingent expenses are paid for the support of such paupers: *Provided*, That when the number of such persons shall be less than ten, then the said Superintendents shall make such provisions for their education as to them shall seem just and proper. Education of paupers. Laws 1859, p. 200. Expense, how paid. Proviso.

[1455.] SEC. 24. Any person who shall bring or remove, or cause to be brought or removed, any poor or indigent person, from any place without this State, into any county within it, with intent to make such county chargeable with the support of such paupers, shall forfeit and pay fifty dollars, to be recovered before any Justice of the Peace of the county into which such pauper shall be brought, or in which the offender may be; and shall also be obliged to convey such pauper out of the State, or support him at his own expense. Liability of person removing pauper from another State.

[1456.] SEC. 25. It shall be lawful for the Justice or Court before whom such person shall be convicted for a violation of the provisions of the preceding section, to require of such person satisfactory security that he will, within a reasonable time, to be named by the Justice or Court, transport such person out of the State, or indemnify such county for all charges and expenses which may have been, or may be incurred in the support of such pauper; and if such person shall neglect or refuse to give such security when required, it shall be the duty of the Justice or Court to commit him to the county jail for a term not exceeding three months. Magistrate may require security.

SEC. 26.[b]

[1457.] SEC. 27. All moneys which shall be collected by any Superintendents, or by the Directors of the Poor of any township, or re- Moneys received by Directors and Superintendents to be paid to Treasurer, &c.

---

[b]Relative to the disposition of Moneys received for Licenses to Tavern Keepers, Common Victuallers, or Retailers of Spirituous Liquors. No Law for such Licences is now in force.

ceived by any of them on any bond or other security given for the benefit or indemnity of any county, or of any township, and all other moneys which shall be received by such Superintendents or Directors for the benefit of the poor, shall be by them paid over, within thirty days after the receipt of the same, to the County Treasurer; and if not so paid, the same may be recovered in an action as for money had and received, to be brought by, and in the name of the County Treasurer, with interest, at the rate of ten per cent. from the time the same should have been paid over.

Liability of Superintendents for neglect to account, &c.

[1458.] SEC. 28. Every Superintendent who shall neglect or refuse so to render an account or statement, or to pay over any moneys as required in this chapter, shall forfeit the sum of two hundred and fifty dollars, and shall also be liable to an action by, and in the name of the County Treasurer, as for moneys had and received, for all moneys which may be in his hands after the expiration of his term of office, with interest thereon, from the time when the same ought to have been paid over.

Estimate of amount necessary for support of poor, and collection thereof.

[1459.] SEC. 29. The Superintendents of the Poor in each county shall present to the Board of Supervisors at their annual meeting in each year, an estimate of the sum which, in their opinion, will be necessary during the ensuing year for the support of the county poor; and the said Supervisors shall cause such sum as they may deem necessary for that purpose to be assessed, levied and collected, in the same manner as the other contingent expenses of the county; to be paid to the County Treasurer, and by him to be kept as a separate fund, distinct from the other funds of the county.

Accounts of Directors and Justices, how audited and paid.

[1460.] SEC. 30. The accounts of the Directors of the Poor, and of Justices of the Peace, for any personal or official services rendered by them in relation to the poor, shall be audited and settled by the Superintendents, and be paid on their order by the County Treasurer; but no allowance shall be made to any officer for attending any board with accounts, for the purpose of having the same audited or paid.

Annual report of Superintendents.

[1461.] SEC. 31. It shall be the duty of the Superintendents of the Poor of each county, on or before the twentieth day of December in each year, to report to the Secretary of State, in such form as he shall direct, the number of paupers that have been relieved or supported in such county the preceding year, the whole expense of such support, specifying the amount paid for the transportation of paupers, and any other items which do not constitute any part of the actual expense of maintaining such paupers, and the allowance make to Superintendents, Directors, Justices, keepers and officers, the actual value of the labor of the paupers maintained, and the estimated amount saved in the expense of their support in consequence of their labor.

Penalty for neglect to make report, &c.

[1462.] SEC. 32. Any Superintendent who shall neglect or refuse to make such report as aforesaid, or who shall willfully make any false report, shall forfeit one hundred dollars; and the Secretary of State shall give notice to the Prosecuting Attorney of the county of every such neglect or refusal, or misconduct.

[1463.] SEC. 33. The Secretary of State shall *annually* lay before the Legislature, during the first month of its session, an abstract of said report. Duty of Secretary of State.

An Act to Amend Chapter Thirty-Eight of the Revised Statutes of Eighteen Hundred and Forty-Six.[c]

[*Approved March* 1, 1849. *Laws of* 1849, *p.* 44.]

SECTION 1. *Be it enacted by the Senate and House of Representatives of the State of Michigan*, That chapter thirty-eight of the Revised Statutes of eighteen hundred and forty-six be, and the same is hereby amended, by adding thereto a section to be numbered thirty-four, as follows:

[1464.] SEC. 34. Whenever, at the annual meeting of the Board of Supervisors of any county, two-thirds of all the Supervisors elected shall vote to restore the distinction between town and county poor, a record of such vote shall be made by the clerk of such county, and thereafter the system of maintaining the poor by townships, as it existed by law on the twenty-eighth day of February, A. D. one thousand eight hundred and forty-six, shall be deemed as adopted and of force in such county: *Provided*, That by a similar vote of two-thirds, the Supervisors of such county may restore the provisions of chapter thirty-eight of the Revised Statutes. Distinction between town and county poor may be restored in certain cases. See Sec. 345, Clause 11.

SEC. 2.[d]

[1465.] SEC. 3. If any township shall not be charged with the relief or support of any township poor, by the time of the annual meeting of the Board of Supervisors in each year, or if the charges made by the County Treasurer against any township do not amount to the sum or sums paid into the Treasury by such township, then the balance found due each township respectively up to that time shall be deducted from the amount of State and County tax apportioned to each of the respective townships to which the County Treasurer stands indebted. Townships to be charged or credited with certain balance.

SEC. 4. This act shall take effect and be in force from and after its passage.

Chapter Two, Title Nine, Part One, of Revised Statutes of 1838.[e]

[1466.] SECTION 1. Every poor person who is blind, lame, old, sick, impotent, or decrepit, or in any way disabled or enfeebled, so as to be unable by his work to maintain himself, and who shall not be relieved or maintained by his relatives, as provided for in the prece- Poor persons, when to be maintained by county or township.

---

c This Act, as well as the Chapter from the Revised Statutes of 1838, relative to County or Township Poor, is believed not to be in force, except in those counties in which the distinction between County and Township Poor was restored prior to April 8, 1851, and which have not since abolished it. See Chapter X., Sec. 345, Clause 11. And except, perhaps, in the County of Saginaw.

In 1857, a special act was passed authorizing the Supervisors of Saginaw County to restore the distinction between Township and County Poor by a two-thirds vote, at any regular meeting. Laws of 1857, p. 205.

For Special Acts on the same subject, relating to the counties of Wayne, Calhoun, and Van Buren, see Laws of 1847, p. 145; Laws of 1848, p. 241; Laws of 1849, p. 29.

d Related to License Moneys. See note *b*.

e See note *c*. This Chapter was in force February 28, 1847.

The office of County Commissioner was abolished by Act No. 19, of 1842, (Laws of 1842, p. 22,) and the powers of the Board of Commissioners conferred, and its duties imposed upon the Board of Supervisors.

ding chapter, shall be maintained by the county or township in which he may be, according to the following provisions:

Distinction between county and township poor may be abolished.

[1467.] SEC. 2. The Board of County Commissioners of any county in this State, at any annual meeting, or at any special meeting called for that purpose, may determine to abolish all distinction between county poor and township poor in their counties respectively, and to have the expense of maintaining all the poor a county charge; and shall thereupon file such determination, duly certified by the clerk of the board, with the County Clerk.

Superintendents of the Poor, three to be appointed in each county.

[1468.] SEC. 3. It shall be the duty of the Board of County Commissioners in every county to appoint three discreet freeholders of such county, to be Superintendents of the Poor within the same, who shall hold their offices for one year, and until others shall be appointed in their places, and who shall take the oath prescribed in the Constitution of this State. A majority of the persons so appointed shall be at all times competent to transact business, and to execute any powers vested in the Board of Superintendents; they shall be allowed such sum for their actual attendance and services, as the Board of County Commissioners of their county shall deem reasonable.

To be a body corporate; have care of county poor.

[1469.] SEC. 4. They shall be a corporation, by the name of the Superintendents of the Poor of the county for which they shall be appointed, and shall possess the usual powers of a corporation for public purposes; they shall meet as often as the Commissioners of the county shall direct, at the County Poor House, if there be one, or at the place of holding Courts in their county, or at one of the places of holding Courts, if there be more than one, and at such other times

Powers and duties

and places as they shall think expedient; they shall have a general superintendence and care of the county poor who may be in their respective counties; and shall have power, and it shall be their duty:

Have charge of county poor.

First. To have the charge of the County Poor Houses that have been, or shall be erected; or to provide suitable places for the keeping of such poor, when so directed by the Commissioners of any county, where houses for that purpose have not been erected by the county; and for that purpose to erect a tenement or tenements, and land not exceeding fifty acres, and to cause the poor of the county to be maintained in such places.

To establish By-Laws.

Second. To establish and ordain prudential rules, regulations and by-laws, for the government and good order of such places so provided, and of the County Poor Houses, and for the employment, relief, management, and government of the persons therein placed; but such rules and regulations shall not be valid, until sanctioned by the Board of County Commissioners.

Employ keeper of Poor House.

Third. To employ one or more suitable persons to be keepers of such houses or places, and all necessary officers and servants, and to vest such powers in them for the government of such houses as shall be necessary, reserving to the paupers who may be placed under the care of such keepers the right of appeal to the Superintendents.

To purchase materials for manufactures, &c.

Fourth. In counties where a Poor House is erected, or other place provided for the poor, to purchase the furniture, implements and materials that shall be necessary, from time to time, for the maintenance of the poor therein, and their employment in labor or manufactures, and to sell and dispose of the proceeds of such labor as they shall deem expedient.

Fifth. To prescribe the rate of allowance to be made to any persons for bringing paupers to the County Poor House, or place provided for the poor, subject to such alterations as the Board of Commissioners may, by a general resolution, make. To prescribe rate of allowance for bringing paupers to Poor House.

Sixth. To authorize the keepers of such houses or places so provided, to certify the amount due to any person for bringing any such paupers; which amount shall be paid by the County Treasurer, on the production of such certificate, countersigned and allowed by any two Superintendents. To authorize keepers to certify amount.

Seventh. In counties where the distinction between township and county poor is not abolished, to decide any dispute that shall arise concerning the settlement of any poor person, summarily, upon a hearing of the parties; and for that purpose to issue subpœnas to compel the attendance of witnesses, and to administer oaths to them in the same manner, with the like power to enforce such process, as is given to Justices of the Peace in any matter cognizable by them; their decisions shall be filed in the offiee of the County Clerk, within thirty days after they are made, and shall be conclusive and final upon all parties interested. To decide settlement of paupers.

Eighth. To direct the commencement of suits by any Directors of the Poor who shall be entitled to prosecute for any penalties, or upon any recognizances, bonds, or securities taken for the indemnity of any township or of the county; and in case of the neglect of any such Director, to commence and conduct such suits, without the authority of such Directors, in their names. To direct the commencement of suits.

Ninth. To draw from time to time on the County Treasurer for all necessary expenses incurred in the discharge of their duties, which drafts shall be paid by him out of the moneys placed in his hands for the support of the poor. To draw on County Treasurer for amount of expenses incurred.

Tenth. To render to the Board of Commissioners of their county, at their annual meeting, an account of all moneys received and expended by them, or under their direction, and of all their proceedings. To render account

Eleventh. To pay over all moneys remaining in their hands, within fifteen days after the expiration of their office, to the County Treasurer or to their successors. To pay over moneys.

[1470.] SEC. 5. The Board of Commissioners of any county in this State, in which a County Poor House is not already erected, may, at any annual or special meeting thereof, determine to erect such house for the reception of the poor of their county; and upon filing such determination with the clerk of the county, they may direct the Superintendents of the Poor of such county to purchase one or more tracts of land, not exceeding three hundred and twenty acres, and to erect thereon one or more suitable buildings for the purpose aforesaid. To defray the expenses of such purchase and buildings, the said board may raise, by tax on the real and personal estate of the inhabitants of Commissioners may erect Poor Houses.

May raise a sum by tax to defray expenses.

the same county, a sum not exceeding seven thousand dollars, by such installments, and at such times as they may judge expedient. The said tax shall be raised, assessed, and collected in the same manner as the other county charges, and shall be paid by the County Treasurer to the Superintendents of the Poor, to be applied in defraying the expenses aforesaid.

When distinction between township and county poor abolished, duty of Clerk of Board of Commissioners.

[1471.] SEC. 6. In those counties where the Commissioners shall determine to abolish the distinction between township poor and county poor, and to have all the poor a county charge, it shall be the duty of the Clerk of the Board of Commissioners immediately to serve notice of such determination on the Directors of the Poor, and Clerk of every township, and clerk of each village or city within the county. Within three months after the service of such notice, the Directors of the Poor of every township shall pay over all moneys which shall remain in their hands, after discharging all demands against them as such Directors, to the County Treasurer, to be applied by him towards the future taxes of such township; and the Directors of the Poor and Township Boards of the several townships of such county, and the officers of every city or village therein shall pay over to the Treasurer of the county, *all moneys which shall thereafter be received for licenses to tavern keepers, retailers, or common victuallers,*[f] *and* all moneys which are directed to be paid to the Directors of the Poor, or for the use of the Poor of the county, within thirty days after the receipt thereof; and in counties where the distinction of county and township poor is not abolished, such moneys shall be paid over to the Directors of the Poor of the township in which the same shall be collected. In case of neglect to pay over such moneys, the County Treasurer or any Director of the Poor may maintain an action therefor, in which he shall recover interest, at the rate of ten per cent. per annum, on all moneys withheld, from the time they should have been paid.

When and to whom Directors to pay over moneys; how to be applied.

When poor a county charge.

[1472.] SEC. 7. In those counties in which the distinction between township and county poor shall have been abolished, all persons entitled to support from the public, shall be maintained at the expense of such counties respectively; and all costs and charges attending the examinations, conveyance, support and necessary expenses of paupers within said counties, shall be a charge upon the said counties, without reference to the number or expense of paupers which may be sent to the Poor House of said counties, from or by any of the townships therein. The said charges and expenses shall be reported by the Superintendents of the Poor of the said counties to the Boards of Commissioners therein respectively, and shall be assessed, levied and collected of and upon the taxable real and personal estate in the said counties, in the same manner as other county charges.

To defray expense: how paid.

When poor to be supported at expense of township

[1473.] SEC. 8. In those counties in which the distinction between township and county poor shall not be abolished by the Boards of Commissioners, the poor having a settlement in any township in such counties shall be supported at the expense of such township, and

f No Law for such Licenses is now in force.

the poor not having such settlement shall be supported by the county in which they may be. *And in said counties, all excise money collected in any township, when received, shall be paid over to, or collected by, the Directors of the Poor of the several townships in said counties, and applied to the use of the poor of the townships in which such money and penalties shall be collected.*[g] Excise money, to whom paid and how applied.

[1474.] SEC. 9. Every person of full age, who shall have been a resident and inhabitant of any township for one year, and the members of his family who shall not have gained a separate settlement, shall be deemed settled in such township. A minor may be emancipated from his or her father, and may gain a settlement: What deemed a settlement in township.

First. If a female, by being married and living one year with her husband, in which case the husband's settlement shall determine that of the wife.

Second. If a male, by being married and residing separately from the family of his father.

Third. By being bound as an apprentice, and serving one year by virtue of such indentures.

Fourth. By being hired and actually serving for one year for wages to be paid such minor.

[1475.] SEC. 10. A woman of full age, by marrying, shall acquire the settlement of her husband, if he have any. And until a poor person shall have gained a settlement in his own right, his settlement shall be deemed that of his father or mother; but no child born in any place used and occupied as a residence for the poor of the township, city or county, shall gain any settlement merely by reason of the place of such birth; nor shall any child, born while the mother is a county pauper, gain any settlement by reason of the place of its birth; and no residence of any person as a pauper, in the county Poor House, or place provided for the support of the poor, or in any township, while supported at expense of any township or county, shall operate to give such pauper a settlement in the township where such actual residence may be had. Settlement of paupers.

[1476.] SEC. 11. No person shall be removed as a pauper from any city or township to any other city or township of the same, or any other county, nor from any county to any other county; but every poor person shall be supported in the township or county where he may be, as follows: Poor persons, where to be supported, &c.

First. If he has gained a settlement in any township in such county, he shall be maintained by such township.

Second. If he has not gained a settlement in the county in which he shall become poor, sick or infirm, he shall be supported by the Superintendents of the Poor, at the expense of the county.

Third. If such person be in a county where the distinction between township and county poor is abolished, he shall, in like manner, be supported at the expense of the county, and in both the cases aforesaid, proceedings for his relief shall be had as hereinafter directed. County Poor.

[g] See Note *f*.

Township Poor.

Fourth. If such pauper shall be in a county where the respective townships are liable to support their poor, and has gained a settlement in some other township of the same county than that in which he may then be, he shall be supported at the expense of the township where he may be, and the Directors of the Poor shall give notice in writing to the Directors of the Poor of the township to which such pauper shall belong, or to one of them, requiring them to provide for the relief and support of such pauper.

Settlement of pauper may be contested.

[1477.] SEC. 12. If within ten days after the service of such notice, the Directors of the Poor to whom the same was directed, shall not proceed to contest the allegation of the settlement of such pauper, by giving the notice hereinafter directed, they, their successors, and the township which they represent, shall be forever precluded from contesting or denying such settlement. They may, within the time aforesaid, give notice in writing to the Directors of the Poor of the township where such pauper may be, that they will appear before the County Superintendents, at a place and on a day therein to be specified, which day shall be at least ten days, and not more than thirty days, from the time of the service of such notice, to contest the said alleged settlement.

Notice to be given

Who to determine controversy, &c.

[1478.] SEC. 13. The County Superintendents shall convene whenever required by any Directors of the Poor, pursuant to such notice, and shall proceed to hear and determine the controversy, and may award costs, not exceeding ten dollars, to the prevailing party, which may be recovered in any action before a Court of competent jurisdiction. The decision of the Superintendents shall be final and conclusive.

Support of paupers in certain cases.

[1479.] SEC. 14. The Directors of the Poor of the township in which it may be alleged any pauper has gained a settlement, may at any time after receiving such notice requiring them to provide for such pauper, take and receive such pauper to their township, and there support him. If they omit to do so, or shall fail to obtain the decision of the County Superintendents, so as to exonerate them from the maintenance of such pauper, the charge of giving such notice, and the expenses of maintaining such pauper, after being allowed by the County Superintendents, shall be laid before the Board of Commissioners at their annual meetings, from year to year, as long as such expenses shall be incurred; and the Commissioners shall annually add the amount of the said charges to the tax to be laid upon the township to which the pauper belongs, together with such sum in addition thereto as will pay the township incurring such expenses the lawful interest thereon, from the time of expenditure to the time of repayment, which sums shall be assessed, levied and collected, in the same manner as the other contingent expenses of such township. The said moneys, when collected, shall be paid to the County Treasurer, and be by him credited to the account of the township which incurred the said expenses.

Paupers not county charge without sanction of Superintendents.

[1480.] SEC. 15. The support of any pauper shall not be charged to the county without the sanction of the Superintendents. If a pauper be sent to the County Poor House, or place provided for the poor, as a county pauper, the Superintendents in those counties where the respective townships are required to support their own poor, shall immediately inquire into the fact, and if they are of opinion that such pauper has a legal settlement in any township of the said county, they shall, within thirty days after such pauper shall have been received, give notice to the Directors of the Poor of the township to which such pauper belongs, that the expenses of his support will be charged to such township, unless the said Directors, within such time as the said Superintendents shall appoint, not less than twenty days thereafter, show that such township ought not to be so charged. And on the application of the said Directors, the Superintendents shall re-examine the matter, and take testimony in relation thereto, and shall finally decide the question, which decision shall be final.

When Superintendents to inquire into settlement of paupers.

[1481.] SEC. 16. In those counties where no County Poor House or other place is provided, no person shall be supported as a county pauper, without the direction of at least one Superintendent. In such cases the Directors of the Poor of the township where such person may be, shall immediately give notice to one of the Superintendents, who shall inquire into the circumstances; and if he is satisfied that such person has not gained a legal settlement in any township of the said county, he shall give a certificate to that effect, and that such pauper is chargeable to the county. He shall report every such case to the Board of Superintendents, at their next meeting, who may affirm such certificate, or may annul the same, on giving due notice to the Directors of the Poor of the township interested, and after hearing the allegations and proof in the premises.

When pauper is chargeable to county, Superintendent to give certificate to that effect.

[1482.] SEC. 17. If the Superintendent to whom the Directors of the Poor may have given such notice, shall neglect or refuse to give the certificate aforesaid, the Directors may apply to the Board of Superintendents, who shall summarily hear and determine the matter, and whose decision shall be conclusive.

If Superintend'nt neglect, how to proceed.

[1483.] SEC. 18. The decisions of the Board of County Superintendents, in relation to the settlement of any paupers, or to their being a charge upon the county, shall be entered in books to be provided for that purpose, and certified by the signatures of such of the said Superintendents as make such decisions; and a duplicate thereof, certified in the same manner, shall be filed in the County Clerk's office within thirty days after the making of any such decision. Such original duplicate, or a copy thereof, duly certified, shall be conclusive evidence of the fact therein contained.

Decisions in relation to settlement of paupers; how to proceed.

[1484.] SEC. 19. When any person shall apply for relief to any Director of the Poor, in any county where a Poor House is established or other place provided for the poor, such Directors, or any one of them, shall inquire into the state and circumstances of the applicant. If it shall appear that the applicant is in such indigent circumstances as to require permanent relief and support, and can be safely removed, the Directors, or any one of them, shall, by a written order, cause the poor person to be removed to the County Poor House, or to the place provided as aforesaid, to be relieved and provided for as the necessi-

Poor persons, when to be removed to County Poor House.

ties of such applicant may require. If the said county be one of those where the respective townships are required to support their own poor, the Directors shall designate, in such order of removal, whether the pauper be chargeable to the county or not; and if no such designation be made, such pauper shall be deemed to belong to the township whose Directors or Director made such order.

Expense of removal, how paid.

[1485.] SEC. 20. The expense of such removal shall be paid on the certificate of the keeper of the Poor House or other place, countersigned as aforesaid, at the rate that shall have been prescribed by the Superintendents; and the Directors shall be allowed such sums as may have been necessarily paid out or contracted to be paid, for the relief or support of such pauper, previous to the said removal, as the Superintendents shall judge was reasonably expended, while it was improper to remove such pauper, which sum shall be paid by the County Treasurer on the order of the Superintendents, and shall be charged to the county, if such pauper be a county charge, or the township sending him, if he be not a county charge.

Persons so removed to be supported in Poor House.

[1486.] SEC. 21. The person so removed shall be received by the Superintendents or their agents, and be supported and relieved in the County Poor House, or such other place as shall have been provided, under the direction of the said Superintendents, until it shall appear to them that such person is able to work and maintain himself, when the Superintendents may, in their discretion, discharge him.

Justice of the Peace may make order for relief, &c

[1487.] SEC. 22. If it shall appear that the person so applying requires only temporary relief, or is sick, lame or otherwise disabled, so that he or she cannot be conveniently removed to the County Poor House, or to such place as shall have been provided by the County Superintendents, the Directors of the Poor, or any one of them, shall apply to a Justice of the Peace of the same township, who shall examine into the facts and circumstances, and shall, in writing, order such sum to be expended for the temporary relief of such poor person, as the circumstances of the case shall require; which order shall entitle the Director to receive any sum he may have paid out or contracted to pay, within the amount therein specified, from the County Treasurer, to be by him charged to the county, if such person be a county charge; if not, to be charged to the township where such relief was afforded; but no greater sum than ten dollars shall be expended or paid for the relief of any one poor person or one family, without the sanction in writing of one of the Superintendents of the Poor of the county, which shall be presented to the County Treasurer, with the order of the Justice.

If no Poor House in county, order for weekly allowance.

[1488.] SEC. 23. If application for relief be made in any of those counties where no County Poor House, or other place, shall have been provided, as aforesaid, for the reception of the Poor, the Directors of the Poor shall, with the assistance of some Justice of the Peace of the same township, inquire into the facts and circumstances of the case, and shall make an order in writing for such allowance, weekly or otherwise, as the said Justice and one of the said Directors shall think required by the necessities of such poor person.

[1489.] SEC. 24. If such pauper have a legal settlement in the township where such application is made, or in any other township of the same county, the Directors shall apply the moneys so allowed to the relief and support of such pauper; the moneys paid by them, or contracted to be paid, pursuant to such order, shall be drawn by them from the County Treasurer, on producing said order, out of the funds in his hands belonging to such township.

If pauper have a legal settlement, how supported.

[1490.] SEC. 25. If such pauper have no legal settlement in the same county, the Directors shall immediately give the notice hereinbefore directed to one of the County Superintendents; and until the County Superintendents shall take the charge of the support of such pauper, the Directors shall provide for his relief and support as aforesaid, and the expense thereof, from the time of giving such notice to a County Superintendent, shall be paid to the said Directors by the County Treasurer, on the production of such order and of proof by affidavit, of the time of the giving such notice, and shall be by him charged to the county.

If not, how to proceed.

[1491.] SEC. 26. Whenever the County Superintendents take charge of the support of any county pauper, in those counties where no Poor House is provided, they may authorize the Directors of the Poor of the township in which such pauper may be, to continue to support him, on such terms and under such regulations as they shall prescribe; and thereafter no moneys shall be paid to the said Directors for the support of such pauper, without the order of the Superintendents; or the said Superintendents may remove such pauper to any other township, and there provide for his support, in such manner as they shall deem expedient.

Superintendents may in certain cases authorize Directors of Poor to support certain paupers.

[1492.] SEC. 27. In those counties where the respective townships are required to support their poor, the County Treasurers thereof shall respectively open and keep an account with each township, in which the township shall be credited with all the moneys received from the same, or from its officers, and shall be charged with the moneys paid for the support of the poor chargeable to such township. And if there be a County Poor House, or other place provided in such county for the support of the poor, the Superintendents of the Poor of the county shall, in each year, before the annual meeting of the Board of Commissioners of such county, furnish to the County Treasurer a statement of the sums charged by them, as hereinafter directed, to the several townships for the support of their poor, which shall be charged to each township respectively, by the County Treasurer in his accounts.

When and how County Treasurer to keep an account of moneys received and paid out for support of poor.

[1493.] SEC. 28. In those counties in which a Poor House shall be established, or a place provided by the Superintendents for the reception of the poor, and in which the several townships shall be liable for the support of their poor respectively, it shall be the duty of the Superintendents, annually, and during the week preceding the annual meeting of the Board of Commissioners, to make out a statement of all the expenses incurred by them the preceding year, and of the moneys received, and exhibiting the deficiency, if any, in the funds

Duty of Superintendents of the Poor in certain cases.

provided for the defraying of such expenses; and they shall apportion the said deficiency among the said several townships in proportion to the number and expenses of the paupers belonging to the said townships respectively, who shall have been provided for by the said Superintendents, and shall charge the said townships with the said proportions; which statement shall be by them delivered to the County Treasurer as before directed.

County Treasurer when to account to County Commissioners.

[1494.] SEC. 29. At the annual meeting of the Board of Commissioners, the County Treasurer shall lay before them the account so kept by him; and if it shall appear that there is a balance against any township, the said board shall add the same to the amount of taxes to be levied and collected upon such township, with the other contingent expenses thereof, together with such a sum for interest, at the rate of seven per centum per annum, as will reimburse and satisfy any advances that may be made, or that may have been made, from the County Treasurer for such township; which moneys, when collected, shall be paid to the County Treasurer.

Duty of Commissioners.

Estimate of expense by Superintendents to be assessed and collected.

[1495.] SEC. 30. The Superintendents of the Poor in each county shall annually present to the Board of Commissioners, at their annual meeting, an estimate of the sum which in their opinion will be necessary, during the ensuing year, for the support of the county poor; and the said Commissioners shall cause such sum as they may deem necessary for that purpose to be assessed, levied and collected in the same manner as the other contingent expenses of the county, to be paid to the County Treasurer, and to be by him kept as a separate fund, distinct from the other funds of the county.

Directors of Poor to keep an account; how to be kept.

[1496.] SEC. 31. In those counties where there are no County Poor Houses established, the Directors of the Poor of the respective townships shall enter, in books to be provided at the expense of their townships, an account of all matters transacted by them relating to their official duties; of all moneys received by them, specifying from whom, and on what account; of all moneys laid out and disbursed by them, to whom, and by what authority, and specifying in each case whether to county poor or to township poor; the names of all persons applying for relief, and ordered to be relieved as aforesaid; the day and year when they were admitted to have relief; the weekly or other sums of money allowed for that purpose, and the cause of giving such relief.

When Directors to account to Township Board: duty of Board.

[1497.] SEC. 32. On the Tuesday next preceding the annual township meeting of every township, the Directors of the Poor shall lay the said original books before the Township Board, together with a just and true account of all moneys by them received and expended for the use of the poor, and in what manner, together with an account of the earnings of the poor persons by them employed; which account shall be verified by the oaths of the Directors, and shall be filed with the Township Clerk. The Township Board shall compare the said account with the entries in the poor books aforesaid; shall examine the vouchers in support thereof, and shall audit and settle the same, and state the balance due from such Directors, or to them, as the case may be. No credit shall be allowed to any Director for moneys paid, unless it shall appear that such payment was made pursuant to a legal order.

Forfeiture for neglect.

[1498.] SEC. 33. Every person who, having been a Director of the Poor, shall refuse or neglect to present such original books, or to exhibit such accounts to the Township Board, as required in the last section, shall forfeit the sum of two hundred and fifty dollars, to be recovered by, and in the name of the Directors of the Poor of such township.

Township Clerk in certain cases to exhibit at annual meeting accounts of preceding year.

[1499.] SEC. 34. In those counties where the respective townships are made liable for the support of their poor, it shall be the duty of the Township Clerk to examine, at the annual township meetings, the accounts for the support of the poor therein the preceding year, as the same shall have been allowed and passed by the Township Board, which accounts shall be openly and distinctly read by the clerk of the meeting; and the Directors of the Poor shall also present an estimate of the sum which they shall deem necessary to supply any deficiency of the preceding year, and to provide for the support of the poor for the ensuing year.

Inhabitants to vote sum to be assessed; to whom paid.

[1500.] SEC. 35. The inhabitants of such township shall thereupon, by a vote of a majority of the persons qualified to choose Township Officers, determine upon the sums of money which shall be assessed upon the said township the ensuing year for the purpose aforesaid. The sum so voted, when raised and collected in those counties where a county Poor House, or other place shall have been provided for the reception of the poor, shall be paid to the County Treasurer, and by him placed to the credit of the township; in all other counties, the sum so voted by any township shall be paid to the Directors of the Poor thereof.

Certain accounts to be audited by Board of Commissioners, and paid by County Treasurer.

[1501.] SEC. 36. The accounts of Directors of the Poor and of Justices of the Peace, for any personal or official services rendered by them, in relation to the poor, except county paupers, shall be audited and settled by the Board of Commissioners, and the sums thus audited and allowed shall be paid by the County Treasurer; and if such services were rendered in behalf of any township liable to support its own poor, the same shall be charged to such township. No allowance for time or services shall be made to any officer for attending any board with any accounts, for the purpose of having the same audited or paid.

Superintendents to settle accounts

[1502.] SEC. 37. The Superintendents of the Poor in the several counties in this state shall audit and settle all accounts of Directors of the Poor, Justices of the Peace, and all other persons, for services relating to the support, relief or transportation of county paupers; and shall, from time to time, draw on the County Treasurer for the amount of the accounts which they shall audit and settle.

Forfeiture for enticing paupers from one township to another.

[1503.] SEC. 38. Any person who shall send, carry, transport, remove or bring, or who shall cause to be sent, carried, transported, brought or removed, any poor or indigent person, from any city, township or county, to any other city, township or county, without legal authority, and there leave such poor person, with intent to make any such city, township or county to which the removal shall be made, chargeable with the support of such pauper, or who shall entice any such poor person so to remove, with such intent, shall forfeit fifty dollars, to be recovered by, and in the name of the Directors of the Poor of the township to which such pauper shall be brought or removed, or in the name of the Superintendents of the Poor of the county into which the said poor person shall be removed; and shall, moreover, be deemed guilty of a misdemeanor, and on conviction, shall be imprisoned not exceeding six months, or fined not exceeding one hundred dollars, or both, in the discretion of the Court.

How liable in addition to forfeiture.

Superintendents to maintain pauper, give notice to Directors, &c.

[1504.] SEC. 39. The pauper so removed, brought or enticed, shall be maintained by the County Superintendents of the county where he may be. They may give notice to either of the Directors of the Poor of the township from which he was brought or enticed, if such township be liable for his support; and if there be no township in the county from which he was brought or enticed liable for his support, then to either of the County Superintendents of the Poor of such county, informing them of such improper removal, and requiring them forthwith to take charge of such pauper.

Duty of Directors on receiving notice.

[1505.] SEC. 40. The County Superintendents, or the Directors of the Poor to whom such notice may be directed, shall, within thirty days after the service thereof, take and remove the pauper so brought or enticed, to their county or township, and there support him, and pay the expense of such notice and of the support of such pauper; or they shall within the said time, by a written instrument under their hands, notify the County Superintendents from whom such notice was received, or either of them, that they deny the allegation of such improper enticing or removal, or that their township is liable for the support of such pauper.

Consequence of neglect to remove pauper.

[1506.] SEC. 41. If there shall be a neglect to take and remove such pauper, and also to notify such denial, within the time above prescribed, the said County Superintendents and Directors respectively, whose duty it was so to do, their successors, and their respective counties or townships, shall be deemed to have acquiesced in the allegations contained in such first notice, and shall be forever precluded from contesting the same; and their counties and townships respectively, shall be liable for the expense of the support of such pauper, which may be sued for and recovered, from time to time, by the County Superintendents incurring the said expenses, in actions against the Superintendents of the Poor of the county, or the Directors of the Poor of the township, as the case may be, so liable for such expenses.

What time Superintendents to commence suit; consequence of neglect.

[1507.] SEC. 42. Upon the service of any such notice of denial, the County Superintendents upon whom the same may be served, shall, within three months, commence a suit against the Directors of the Poor of the township, or the County Superintendents of the Poor of the county to whom the first notice was directed, or against their successors in office, for the expenses incurred in the support of such pauper, and shall prosecute the same to effect; if they neglect to do so, they, their successors, and their county, shall be forever precluded from all claim against the county or township to whose officers such first notice was directed, or any of their officers, for any expense that may have been, or may be incurred for the support of such pauper.

[1508.] SEC. 43. Every County Superintendent who shall neglect to render any account, or statement, to the Board of Commissioners as herein required, or to pay over any moneys within the time prescribed by law, shall forfeit two hundred and fifty dollars, to be sued for and recovered by, and in the name of the County Treasurer. The Superintendents shall also be liable to an action, either jointly or severally, by the County Treasurer, for all moneys which shall be in their hands after the time the same should have been paid over according to law, with interest thereon, at the rate of ten per cent. per annum, from the time when the same should have been paid over.

Forfeiture for neglect to render account; liable to action.

[1509.] SEC. 44. Any person who shall bring or remove, or cause to be brought or removed, any poor or indigent person, from any place without this State, into any county or township within it, and there leave or attempt to leave such person, with intent to make such county or township chargeable with the support of such paupers, shall forfeit and pay fifty dollars, to be recovered before any Justice of the Peace of the county into which such pauper shall be brought, to be sued for and recovered by, and in the name of the Superintendents of the County Poor of said county, or by the Directors of the Poor of the township into which such pauper shall be brought, and moreover, shall be obliged to convey such pauper out of the State, or support him at his own expense; and it shall be lawful for the Justice before whom such person shall be convicted for a violation of the provisions of this section, to require of such person satisfactory security that he will, within a reasonable time, to be named by the Justice, transport such pauper out of the State, or indemnify the township or county for all charges and expenses which may be incurred in the support of such pauper; and if such person shall refuse to give such security when so required, it shall be the duty of the Justice to commit him to the common jail of the county, for a term not exceeding three months.

Persons bringing paupers into this State to forfeit fifty dollars; liable in addition to forfeiture.

[1510.] SEC. 45. All penalties imposed under the provisions of this or the preceding chapter, when recovered, shall be paid to the County Treasurer; if not paid by the persons collecting the same, when demanded by the County Treasurer, he may maintain an action therefor in his name of office.

Penalties to be paid to County Treasurer.

[1511.] SEC. 46. Whenever it shall be made to appear to the satisfaction of any Director of the Poor, either upon complaint, or otherwise, that a penalty has been incurred by the violation of any provisions of the law of this State, which such Director is required by law to collect, it shall be his duty immediately to commence a suit for such penalty, and to prosecute the same diligently to effect.

Directors in certain cases to collect penalties.

To be allowed costs in certain cases, and pay for attending suits.

[1512.] SEC. 47. In auditing the accounts of the Directors of the Poor, by the Township Boards, allowance shall be made to them for all costs to which they may have been subjected, or which may have been recovered against them, in any suit brought by them pursuant to law; and they shall also be allowed the same daily pay for attending to any such suit, as is allowed them for the performance of their official duties.

Allowances credited in accounts.

[1513.] SEC. 48. Such allowances may be credited to them in their accounts for moneys collected for penalties, and may be deducted from such moneys; and the balance of such penalties shall be paid over to their successors in office, or to the County Treasurer, as directed by law, in respect to such penalties.

When to be township charge.

[1514.] SEC. 49. If there be not sufficient moneys in their hands to satisfy such allowances, the same shall be paid as other township charges.

Poor Houses, &c., exempt from taxation; Keeper from service in militia.

[1515.] SEC. 50. Every Poor House, Alms House, or other place provided by any city, township or county, for the reception and support of the poor, and all real and personal property whatever, belonging to or connected with the same, shall be exempt from all assessment and taxation, levied either by the State, or by any county, township, city or village; and the keeper of every Poor House, Alms House, or other place provided as aforesaid, shall be exempt from all service in the militia, from serving on juries, and from all assessment for labor on the highways.

Support of idiots, &c., out of Poor House.

[1516.] SEC. 51. In those counties where County Poor Houses may be established, the Superintendents may provide for the support of paupers that may be idiots, or lunatics, out of such Poor House, in such manner as shall best promote the interests of the county, and conduce to the comfort and recovery of such paupers.

Certain paupers to be educated; expense of, how paid.

[1517.] SEC. 52. The Superintendents of the Poor of each county, or the Directors of the Poor of each township, liable for the support of its own poor, are hereby required to cause the paupers of such county or township respectively, who may be over five and under sixteen years of age, under their charge, to be taught and educated, in the same manner as other children are taught in the primary schools of this State, at least one-fourth part of the time the said paupers shall so remain under their charge; and the expense therefor shall be paid in the same manner as other contingent expenses are paid for the support of said paupers.

Superintendents to make annual report; what to contain.

[1518.] SEC. 53. It shall be the duty of the Superintendents of the Poor of each county in this State, on or before the twentieth day of December in each year, to report to the Secretary of State, in such form as he shall direct, the number of paupers that have been relieved or supported in such county the preceding year, distinguishing the number of county paupers from the number of township paupers, if any; the whole expense of such support, specifying the amount paid for transportation of paupers, and any other items which do not compose any part of the actual expense of maintaining the paupers, and the allowances made to the Superintendents, Directors, Justices, keepers and officers; the actual value of the labor of the paupers maintained, and the estimated amount saved in the expense of their support in consequence of their labor.

Township Clerk to report to Board of Commissioners; what to contain.

[1519.] SEC. 54. It shall be the duty of the clerk of every township in those counties where all the poor are not a county charge, to report to the Clerk of the Board of County Commissioners, within fifteen days after the accounts of the Directors of the Poor have been settled by the Township Board, in each year, an abstract of all such accounts for the preceding year, which shall exhibit the number of paupers that have been relieved or supported in such township the preceding year, specifying the number of county paupers, and of township paupers, the whole expense of such support, and specifying the allowance made to Directors, Justices, Constables, or other officers, and any other items which shall not comprise any part of the actual expense of maintaining the paupers. The said abstract shall be delivered by the Clerk of the Board of Commissioners to the County Superintendents, to be included by them in their report aforesaid.

Abstract to be delivered to Superintendents.

Forfeiture for neglect; duty of Secretary of State

[1520.] SEC. 55. Any Superintendent or County Clerk, or Clerk of the Board of County Commissioners, who shall neglect or refuse to make such reports, abstracts or copies aforesaid, or who shall willfully make any false report, abstract or copy, shall forfeit one hundred dollars, to be recovered by the Prosecuting Attorney of the county, in the name of the People of this State, and to be paid into the County Treasury. The Secretary of State shall give notice to the Prosecuting Attorney of the county, of every such neglect or misconduct; and it shall be the duty of the Prosecuting Attorney, on receiving such notice, or in any way receiving satisfactory information of such neglect or misconduct, to prosecute for the recovery of such penalties.

Duty of Secretary of State.

[1521.] SEC. 56. The Secretary of State shall annually lay before the Legislature, during the first month of its session, an abstract of the said returns and reports.

Comp. L. 1857, Chap. XLV., p. 504.

DIVISION XXV.—Of the Law of the Road, and the Regulation of Public Carriages.

N. Y. Rev. Stat., Title 13, Chap. 20, Part 1.

Chapter Forty-Four of Revised Statutes of 1846.

Persons meeting with carriages, &c., to turn to the right. 2 Gray, 181.

[1592.] Section 1. Whenever any persons shall meet each other on any bridge or road, traveling with carriages, wagons, carts, sleds, sleighs, or other vehicles, each person shall seasonably drive his carriage or other vehicle to the right of the middle of the traveled part of such bridge or road, so that the respective carriages, or other vehicles aforesaid, may pass each other without interference.

Penalty, &c., for violating preceding section.

[1593.] Sec. 2. Every person offending against the provisions of the preceding section, shall, for each offence, forfeit a sum not exceeding twenty dollars, and shall also be liable to the party injured for all damages sustained by reason of such offence: *Provided*, That proceedings shall be commenced for the recovery of such forfeiture within three months after the offence shall have been committed, and any action for such damages shall be commenced within one year after the cause of action shall have accrued.

Penalty for employing driver addicted to drunkenness.

[1594.] Sec. 3. No person owning, or having the direction or control of any coach, or other carriage or vehicle running or traveling upon any road in this State, for the conveyance of passengers, shall employ, or continue in employment, any person to drive such coach, carriage, or other vehicle, who is addicted to drunkenness, or to the excessive use of intoxicating liquors; and if any such person shall violate the provisions of this section, he shall forfeit at the rate of five dollars per day for all the time during which he shall have kept such driver in such employment.

Owner of coach, &c., to discharge driver, on notice of his being intoxicated.

[1595.] Sec. 4. If any driver, whilst actually employed in driving such coach, carriage, or vehicle, shall be guilty of intoxication, it shall be the duty of the owner or person having the charge or control of such coach, carriage, or other vehicle, on receiving written notice of the fact, signed by any passenger who witnessed the same, and certified by him under oath, forthwith to discharge such driver from such employment; and every person who shall retain, or have in such service, within six months after the receipt of such notice, any driver who shall have been so intoxicated, shall forfeit at the rate of five dollars per day for all the time during which he shall keep any such driver in such employment after receiving such notice.

Driver running horses guilty of misdemeanor, &c.

[1596.] Sec. 5. No person driving any carriage or vehicle for the conveyance of passengers for hire upon any road or highway in this State, with or without passengers therein, shall run his horses, or cause or permit them to run, upon any occasion, or for any purpose whatever; and every person who shall offend against the provisions of this section shall be deemed guilty of a misdemeanor, and on conviction thereof, shall be punished by a fine not exceeding one hundred dollars, or by imprisonment in the county jail not exceeding thirty days, or both, at the discretion of the Court.

[1597.] Sec. 6. It shall not be lawful for the driver of any carriage used for the conveyance of passengers for hire, to leave the horses attached thereto, while any passenger remains in or upon the same, without making such horses fast with a sufficient halter, rope or chain, or without some suitable person to take the charge and guidance of them, so as to prevent their running; and if any such driver shall violate the provisions of this section, he shall forfeit a sum not exceeding twenty dollars; but no prosecution shall be commenced therefor after the expiration of three months from the time of committing the offence.

Penalty on driver for leaving horses unfastened.

[1598.] Sec. 7. The owners of every carriage running or traveling upon any turnpike road or public highway, for the conveyance of passengers for hire, shall be liable, jointly and severally, to the party injured, in all cases, for all injuries and damage done by any person in the employment of such owners as a driver, while driving such carriage, to any person, or to the property of any person, whether the act occasioning such injury or damage be willful, negligent or otherwise, in the same manner as such driver would be liable.

Owners of carriage liable for injuries done by persons in their employ.

Comp. L. 1857, Chap. XLVII., p. 507.

DIVISION XXVI.—Of Lost Goods, and Stray Beasts.

Chapter Forty-Seven of Revised Statutes of 1846.

Notice of finding goods, &c., how given.

[1603.] Section 1. When any person shall find any lost money, or lost goods, if the owner thereof be known, he shall immediately give notice thereof to such owner; if the owner thereof be unknown, and such money or goods be of the value of three dollars or more, the finder shall, within two days, cause notice thereof to be posted in two public places within the township where the same were found; and shall also, within seven days, give notice thereof, in writing, to the Township Clerk of such township, and pay him twenty-five cents for making an entry thereof in a book to be kept for that purpose.[52]

Ibid.

[1604.] Sec. 2. If the money or goods so found be of the value of ten dollars or more, and the owner thereof be unknown, the finder thereof shall also, within one month after such finding, cause notice thereof to be advertised in some newspaper in the same county, if one be published there, and if not, then in some newspaper published in an adjoining county, and continued therein for six successive weeks.

Taking up stray animals.

[1605.] Sec. 3. It shall be lawful for any resident freeholder of any township in this State to take up any stray horses, mules or asses, by him found going at large in such township, beyond the range where such horses, mules or assses usually run at large; and also to take up, between the months of November and March, any stray neat cattle, sheep or swine by him found going at large therein, beyond the range where such animals have usually run at large.

Notice to owner, and entry on township book. 13 Ill. Rep., 64.

[1606.] Sec. 4. Such finder shall immediately give notice thereof to the owner of any such animal, if known to him; but if the owner thereof be unknown, such finder shall, within ten days, cause notice thereof to be entered with the Township Clerk, in such book as aforesaid, containing a description of the color, age, and natural and artificial marks of such animals, as near as may be, and the name of such finder, and shall pay such clerk twenty-five cents for entering the same; and shall also cause such notice to be posted up in two of the most public places in such township.[53]

---

[52] *Form of Notice to the Township Clerk of Finding Lost Goods.*

To the Township Clerk of the Township of *Concord.*

Sir:—You are hereby notified, that I did on the —— day of —— A. D. 18—, in the public highway, near the house of L. M., in the township aforesaid, find the following goods: *(here describe the goods,)* which are now in my possession.

Dated this —— day of —— A. D. 18—. A. B.

[53] *Form of Notice of taking up Stray Animal to be entered with Township Clerk.*

To the Township Clerk of the Township of *Liberty.*

The undersigned hereby gives notice, that he did on the —— day of ——

[1607.] SEC. 5. If the owner of any such animal or animals shall not, within one month, appear and reclaim them, and such animal or animals taken up at the same time shall be of the value of ten dollars or more, the finder shall cause such notice to be published in a newspaper in the same county, if one be published there, and if not, then in a newspaper published in an adjoining county, and continued therein for six successive weeks.

When notice to be published in newspaper.

[1608.] SEC. 6. Every finder of lost goods or stray animals, of the value of ten dollars or more, shall, within three months, and before any use shall be made thereof, procure an appraisal of the same to be made and certified by a Justice of the Peace of his township, which appraisal he shall, within said three months, cause to be filed with the Township Clerk; and he shall pay to such Justice fifty cents for such appraisal and certificate, and six cents for each mile necessarily traveled by him in such service, and to the clerk six cents for filing the certificate.

Appraisal of lost goods and stray beasts.

[1609.] SEC. 7. If the owner or person entitled to the possession of any such money or goods, other than stray animals, shall appear at any time within one year after such entry with the Township Clerk, and make out his rights thereto, he shall have restitution of the same, or of the value thereof, upon his paying all the costs and charges aforesaid, together with a reasonable compensation to the finder for keeping and taking care of the same, and for his necessary travel and expenses in the case; which charges shall, in case of disagreement between the owner and finder, be determined by some Justice of the Peace of the township, who shall certify the same.

When owner, &c. to have restitution.

[1610.] SEC. 8. If no owner or person entitled to the possession of the same shall appear in one year, then such lost money or goods shall remain to the finder, he paying one-half of the value thereof to the Treasurer of the township, according to said appraisement, after deducting from such value all the fees and charges aforesaid, to be determined and certified by a Justice of the Peace as aforesaid; and upon the neglect or refusal to pay the said half of the value, the same shall be recovered by the Township Treasurer, in an action of debt, or on the case.

When goods, &c., shall remain with finder, and township entitled to one half of value.

[1611.] SEC. 9. If the owner or person entitled to the possession of any such stray beast, shall appear within six months after such entry with the Township Clerk, and shall make out his right thereto, he shall have restitution of the same, upon paying all lawful charges as before provided in the case of lost goods.

When owner, &c. to have restitut'n of stray beasts.

[1612.] SEC. 10. If such owner or person entitled to the possession of the same, shall not appear and make out his title to the animals, within the said six months, such animals shall be sold at the request of the finder, by any constable of the township, at public auction,

Sale of stray beasts and disposition of proceeds

A. D. 18— find one certain stray horse, found by him going at large in the township aforesaid, at *(state where the horse was found,)* being beyond the range where horses usually run at large, which horse is still in possession of the undersigned.

Dated this —— day of —— A. D. 18—. A. B.

upon first giving notice thereof in writing, by posting up the same in three of the most public places in such township at least ten days before such sale, and the finder may bid therefor at such sale; and the moneys arising therefrom, after deducting all the lawful charges aforesaid, and the fees of the Constable, which shall be the same as upon a sale on execution, shall be deposited in the Treasury of the township.

When owner, &c. to receive moneys deposited with Township Treasurer.

[1613.] SEC. 11. If the owner or person entitled to the possession of any such animal, shall appear within one year after the entry with the Township Clerk as aforesaid, and establish by his own affidavit, or otherwise, to the satisfaction of the Township Treasurer, his title thereto, he shall be entitled to receive the money so deposited in the Township Treasury, from the proceeds of the sale; and if no owner or person entitled to the possession of the same shall appear within the said year, such money shall belong to the township.

Finder neglecting to advertise, &c., to lose benefit of this chapter.

[1614.] SEC. 12. If the finder of any lost money, goods, or stray beasts shall neglect to cause the same to be entered, advertised, or notice thereof to be posted, as directed in this chapter, he shall be precluded from all the benefits of this chapter, and from all claim for keeping such goods or animals, or on account of any charges in relation thereto.

Liability of person unlawfully taking stray animals.

[1615.] SEC. 13. If any person shall unlawfully take away any animal, taken up as a stray pursuant to the provisions of this chapter, without paying all the lawful charges incurred in relation to the same, he shall be liable to the finder thereof to the value of such animal, which may be recovered in an action of trespass, or on the case.

When horses, &c. may be moderately worked by finder.

[1616.] SEC. 14. If any horses, mules or oxen of sufficient age and strength, and used to work, shall be taken up under the provisions of this chapter as strays, and shall not be reclaimed by the owner within one month after the entry thereof with the Township Clerk, the person taking up the same may moderately and carefully work such horses, mules, or oxen, within the township where they were so taken up; and the value of such labor shall be deducted from the charges aforesaid.

DIVISION XXVII.—OF CERTAIN MUNICIPAL REGULATIONS OF POLICE.

Comp. L. 1857, Chap. L., p. 517.

Chapter Forty-Nine of the Revised Statutes of 1846.

THEATRICAL EXHIBITIONS AND PUBLIC SHOWS.

[1637.] SECTION 1. The Township Board of any township, or the corporate board of any village, may at any meeting held for that purpose, license theatrical exhibitions, public shows, and such other exhibitions as they deem proper, to which admission is obtained on payment of money, upon such terms and conditions as they shall think reasonable, and may regulate the same in such manner as they shall think necessary for the preservation of order and decorum, and to prevent any danger to the public peace; but no such license shall be in force for a longer time than the officers granting the same shall have been elected to office. Township Board may license shows and exhibitions.

[1638.] SEC. 2. Any person who shall set up or promote any such exhibition or show, or shall publish or advertise the same, or otherwise aid or assist therein, without a license first obtained, as provided in the preceding section, or contrary to the terms and conditions of such license, or while the same is suspended, shall be deemed guilty of a misdemeanor, and on conviction thereof, shall be punished by a fine not exceeding two hundred dollars. Punishment for setting up shows without license.

GUNPOWDER.

[1639] SEC. 3. The inhabitants of every township or incorporated village may, at any regular meeting, order that no gunpowder shall be kept in any place within the limits of such township or village, unless the same shall be kept in tight casks or cannisters; and that no gunpowder above the quantity of fifty pounds, shall be kept or deposited in any shop, store or other building, or in any ship or vessel, which shall be within the distance of twenty-five rods from any other building, or from any wharf; that no gunpowder above the quantity of twenty-five pounds, shall be kept or deposited in any shop, store or other building, within ten rods of any other building; and that no gunpowder above the quantity of one pound, shall be kept or deposited in any shop, store, or other building, within ten rods of any other building, unless the same shall be well secured in copper, tin or brass cannisters, holding not exceeding five pounds each, and closely covered with copper, brass or tin covers. Inhabitants of townships, &c., may make regulations in relation to keeping.

[1640.] SEC. 4. Upon complaint made on oath to any Justice of the Peace, by any township or village officer, that he has probable cause to suspect that gunpowder is deposited or kept within the limits When search warrant may be issued.

of the township or village, contrary to any such order, such Justice may issue his warrant, directed to any Constable of such township, or the Marshal of such village, ordering him to enter any shop, store or other building, or vessel specified in said warrant, and there to make diligent search for the gunpowder suspected to have been deposited or kept as aforesaid, and to make return of his doings to such Justice forthwith.

Forfeiture for violating two preceding sections.

[1641.] SEC. 5. If any person shall commit either of the offences mentioned in the two preceding sections, he shall forfeit a sum not exceeding twenty dollars; but the two preceding sections shall not extend to any manufactory of gunpowder, nor in any case prevent the transportation thereof through any township, or from one part of any township to another part thereof.

OF DOGS.

Regulations by township, &c., relating to dogs.

[1642.] SEC. 6. The inhabitants of any township or incorporated village, may make such by-laws concerning the licensing, regulating and restraining of dogs going at large, as they shall deem expedient, and may affix any penalties not exceeding ten dollars, for any breach thereof; but no such by-laws shall extend to any dog not owned or kept in such township, and no person shall be obliged to pay more than two dollars annually for any license granted under the provisions of this chapter.

Moneys received for licenses to be paid to Treasurer.

[1643.] SEC. 7. All money received for the several licenses mentioned in this chapter, shall be paid to the Treasurer, for the use of the township or village, as the case may be.

SEC. 8, 9.[a]

An Act for the Protection of Sheep and other Domestic Animals, and for other purposes.

Approved March 28, 1850. Laws of 1850, p. 155.

When dogs may be killed.

[1644.] SECTION 1. *Be it enacted by the Senate and House of Representatives of the State of Michigan*, That any person may kill any dog that he may see chasing, worrying, wounding, or killing any sheep, lambs, swine, cattle, or other domestic animal, out of the enclosure or immediate care of the owner or keeper, unless the same be done by the directions or permission of such owner or keeper; or any dog that may suddenly assault him while he is peaceably walking or riding anywhere out of the enclosure of the owner or keeper of such dog.

Owner liable for dogs killing domestic animals.

[1645.] SEC. 2. If any dog shall have killed or assisted in killing, wounding or worrying any sheep, lamb, swine, cattle, or other domestic animal, or that shall assault or bite, or otherwise injure any person while traveling the highway, or out of the enclosure of the owner or keeper of such dog, such owner or keeper shall be liable to the owner of such property or person injured in double the amount of damages sustained, to be recovered in an action of trespass, or on the case, and

[a] Repealed. See Sec. 1648.

it shall not be necessary, in order to sustain an action, to prove that the owner or keeper knew that such dog was accustomed to do such damage or mischief; and upon the trial of any cause mentioned in this section, the plaintiff and defendant may be examined under oath, touching the matter at issue, and evidence may be given as in other cases; and if it shall appear to the satisfaction of the Court by the evidence, that the defendant is justly liable for the damages complained of under the provisions of this act, the Court shall render judgment against such defendant for double the amount of damages proved, and costs of suit; but in no case shall the plaintiff recover more than five dollars costs.

Trial; parties may be examined

Judgment.

[1646.] SEC. 3. The owner or keeper of any dog which has been chasing, worrying, wounding or killing any sheep, lamb, swine or cattle (not the property of such owner or keeper,) out of his enclosure, or which has assaulted or bitten any person while peaceably walking or riding out of the enclosure of the owner or keeper, shall, within forty-eight hours after having received notice thereof in writing, cause such dog to be killed. For every neglect so to do, he shall forfeit the sum of three dollars, and the further sum of one dollar and fifty cents for every forty-eight hours thereafter, until such dog shall be killed, unless it shall satisfactorily appear to the Court before which a suit shall be brought for the recovery of said penalty, that it was not in the power of such owner or keeper to kill such dog. But no recovery shall be had, unless it shall satisfactorily appear that such dog has done the mischief of which such owner or keeper has had notice as aforesaid.

Owner shall cause dog to be killed.

Penalty for neglect.

[1647.] SEC. 4. Whenever a citizen of any township where the trespass has been committed, shall make a complaint in writing, verified by his oath or other testimony, to the satisfaction of the Supervisor thereof, that a penalty imposed by the provisions of this act has been incurred, he shall commence a suit for the recovery thereof in his name of office, and prosecute the same with due diligence; and the moneys recovered shall be by him paid into the Township Treasury, to be applied towards the incidental expenses of the township.

Supervisor to sue for penalty.

Moneys to be paid into Township Treasury.

[1648.] SEC. 5. That sections eight and nine of chapter forty-nine of the Revised Statutes of 1846, are hereby repealed: *Provided*, Such repeal shall not affect any action pending.

Sections 8 and 9, Chap. 49, R. S., 1846, repealed.

SEC. 6. This act shall take effect, and be in force from and after its passage.

Comp. L. 1857, Chap. LI., p. 521.

DIVISION XXVIII. — Of the Destruction of Wolves, and other Noxious Animals.

Chapter Fifty-One of Revised Statutes of 1846.

Bounty for killing wolves, &c.

[1649.] Section 1. Every person, being an inhabitant of this State, who shall kill a full grown wolf, or a wolf's whelp, in any organized township in this State, shall be entitled to a bounty of eight dollars for each wolf over three months old, and four dollars for each wolf's whelp under the age of three months, to be allowed and paid in the manner hereinafter provided.

Wolf or wolf's head, &c., to be taken to Justice.

[1650.] Sec. 2. Every person intending to apply for such bounty, shall take such wolf or wolf's whelp killed by him, or the head thereof, with the ears and skin entire thereon, to one of the Justices of the Peace of the township within which such wolf or whelp shall have been taken, who shall thereupon associate with him another Justice, or an Assessor, or Commissioner of Highways of such Township, to act with him in deciding upon such application.

Examination of applicant.

[1651.] Sec. 3. The person claiming such bounty shall then be sworn by such Justice, and state on oath the time and place, when and where every wolf and wolf's whelp, for which a bounty is claimed by him, was taken and killed; and he shall also submit to such further examination on oath, concerning the taking and killing of such wolf or whelp, as the Justice and officer associated with him may require, and the statement made by him shall be reduced to writing in the form of an affidavit, which shall be subscribed by the person making it.

When certificate to be given.

[1652.] Sec. 4. If it shall appear to the Justice and officer associated with him, that the wolf or whelp was taken and killed within such township by the person applying for such bounty, and that the mother of any such whelp was not taken before she brought forth the same, they shall cut off and burn to ashes the ears and scalp of such wolf or whelp, and deliver to the person so applying a certificate of the facts, and whether the same was over or under the age of three months when taken, annexing thereto the original affidavit made and subscribed by such person.

Certificate to be delivered to Supervisor.

[1653.] Sec. 5. Such certificate, with the affidavit annexed, shall, within fifteen days after the date thereof, be delivered to one of the Supervisors of the same county; and if such Supervisor shall doubt the correctness of the certificate or affidavit, he shall give notice to the person claiming the bounty to give further evidence of the correctness thereof, and shall retain the papers in his hands until such further proof shall be made.

Certificate to be laid before Board of Supervisors, &c.

[1654.] Sec. 6. If such Supervisor shall have no doubt as to the correctness of such certificate and affidavit, or if his doubts shall be removed by further proof, he shall lay such certificate and affidavit before the Board of Supervisors at their next meeting, and if the board shall be satisfied that such certificate and affidavit are just and correct, they shall award to the person to whom such certificate shall have been granted the bounty above specified, and shall cause the certificate and affidavit to be filed with their clerk.

Duplicate certificates of bounties to be delivered to Treasurer, and bounties paid.

[1655.] SEC. 7. Duplicate certificates, stating all the bounties that shall have been allowed by the board at any meeting, shall be made under their direction, and after being signed by their chairman and clerks shall be delivered to the County Treasurer, who shall thereupon pay to the several persons named in such certificate, out of any moneys in the Treasury for defraying the contingent expenses of the county, the bounties to them respectively allowed.

One half of bounties to be charged to State Treasurer &c.

[1656.] SEC. 8. The County Treasurer shall charge to the Treasurer of the State the one half of all the bounties allowed by the Board of Supervisors, and shall transmit an account thereof to the Auditor General, accompanied by one of the duplicate certificates received from the Board of Supervisors; and shall also procure and transmit with such account, a certified copy of the original certificates and affidavits filed with the Clerk of the Board of Supervisors, upon which the bounties mentioned in such account shall have been allowed.

Auditor General to examine acc'ts &c.; proceedings thereon.

[1657.] SEC. 9. The Auditor General shall examine every account so transmitted to him, and if he shall discover any defect or irregularity, which shall induce him to believe the same ought not to be allowed, he may suspend, in whole or in part, as he may think proper, the payment of such account, until satisfactory proof be made to him, by affidavit or otherwise, of the justice of such account; and if the further proofs produced to him shall not be satisfactory, he shall reject such portion of the account as shall have been suspended, and his decision thereon shall be final and conclusive.

Sums audited to be paid out of State Treasury.

[1658.] SEC. 10. Every sum audited and allowed by the Auditor General, upon any such account, not exceeding the one half of the bounties allowed by the Board of Supervisors, shall be paid out of the Treasury of the State, to the Treasurer of the county from which such account was transmitted.

Additional bounties.

[1659.] SEC. 11. The Boards of Supervisors of the several counties of this State shall have power, at the expense of their respective counties, to award and allow such other and further bounties for the destruction of wolves, wolf whelps, and such bounties for the destruction of panthers and other noxious animals within their respective counties, as they may think proper; and the same proof shall be required in such case as is hereinbefore prescribed, and such additional and other bounties, when duly allowed and certified, shall be paid out of the County Treasury.[a]

Giving false certificate a misdemeanor.

[1660.] SEC. 12. If any Justice of the Peace, or other officer, who shall be applied to for a certificate under the provisions of this chapter, shall willfully give a false certificate in the premises, such Justice or other officer shall be deemed guilty of a misdemeanor, and on conviction thereof, shall be punished by a fine not exceeding five hundred dollars, or imprisonment in the county jail not exceeding one year.

[a]See Subdivision 13, of Section 345, p. 189.

COMP. L. 1857, Chap. LIV., p. 540.

DIVISION XXIX.—OF COUNTY AND TOWN AGRICULTURAL SOCIETIES.

An Act for the Encouragement of Agriculture, Manufactures, and the Mechanic Arts.

(*Approved March* 16, 1849. *Laws of* 1849, *p.* 97.)

Where County Agricultural Society raise annually $100 or more, Supervisors to levy a tax.

[1687.] SECTION 1. In any county in this State where the inhabitants thereof have organized and established, or may hereafter organize and establish a Society for the encouragement and advancement of Agriculture, Manufactures, and the Mechanic Arts, and shall raise from said Society annually the sum of one hundred dollars or over, for the promotion of the above objects, in said county, which fact shall be certified by the President and Secretary of the Society under oath, and a certificate thereof shall be filed with the Clerk of the Board of Supervisors, the Board of Supervisors of said county, at their annual session in each and every year, are hereby required to levy a tax of not less than one fortieth, nor more than one tenth of one mill on the dollar, on the assessment roll of the county, which tax shall be collected and paid to the Treasurer of the county, in the same manner that other taxes are collected and paid.[a]

County Treasurer to hold same subject to order of Supervisors.

[1688.] SEC. 2. The Treasurer of the county shall keep the sum so raised subject to the order of the Board of Supervisors of said county.

Moneys to be expended for benefit of County Agricultural Society.

[1689.] SEC. 3. The said Board of Supervisors shall draw upon the said Treasurer for the sum so raised, and the same shall be expended, under the direction of said Board, for the benefit of said Society in the purchase of premiums, the diffusion of valuable agricultural, manufacturing, and mechanical knowledge, or in such other way as shall, in the opinion of the Board, be calculated to promote and encourage the important objects above specified.

Certain act repealed. 1844, p. 23.

[1690.] SEC. 4. The Act entitled "An Act for the Encouragement of Agriculture," approved March second, eighteen hundred and forty-four, is hereby repealed.

Any citizen of the county may become member of County Society.

[1691.] SEC. 5. Any citizen of any county in which a Society of the kind above named is or shall be organized, shall have a right to become a member thereof by complying with the rules and regulations of said Society.

SEC. 6. This act shall take effect and be in force from and after its passage.

---

[a] As Amended by "An Act to Amend an Act entitled, 'An Act for the Encouragement of Agriculture, Manufactures, and the Mechanic Arts,' Approved March 16, 1849." Approved February 6, 1855. Laws of 1855, p. 26.

An Act to Authorize the Formation of County and Town Agricultural Societies.

Approved February 12, 1855. *Laws of* 1855, *p.* 150.

[1692.] SECTION 1. *The People of the State of Michigan enact,* That any ten or more persons, inhabitants of this State, who shall desire to form a town or county Agricultural or Horticultural Society, in any county, town, city or village of this State, may make, sign and acknowledge duplicate articles of association, before any officer authorized to take acknowledgements of deeds in this State, and file the same in the office of the Secretary of the State Society, and also in the office of the County Clerk of the county in which the business of the Society is to be conducted; in which articles shall be stated the name by which such Society shall be known in law, the particular business and objects of such Society, the number of Trustees, Directors or Managers, who shall manage the same, and the names of such Directors, Trustees, or Managers thereof, for the first year of its existence. **How County and Town Societies may be organized.**

[1693.] SEC. 2. Upon filing such articles of association as aforesaid, the persons who shall have signed the same, and their associates and successors, shall thereupon, and by virtue of this act, become a body politic and corporate, by the name stated in such articles: *Provided,* No two Societies shall assume the same name; and by that name they and their successors shall and may have succession, and shall be persons in law capable of suing and being sued; and they and their successors may have and use a common seal, and the same may alter and change at pleasure; and they and their successors, by their corporate name, shall in law be capable of taking and receiving, purchasing and holding real estate for the purpose of their incorporation, but for no other purpose, to an amount not exceeding the sum of twenty-five thousand dollars in value, if a county Society, and ten thousand dollars if a town, village, or city Society, and of personal estate for a like purpose, to an amount not exceeding ten thousand dollars, if a county Society, and five thousand dollars if a town, village, or city Society; and may make all necessary by-laws for the management of said Society, not inconsistent with the laws of this State or of the United States. **Incorporation of; what property they may hold.**

[1694.] SEC. 3. Any person who shall pay into the Treasury of said Society, annually, in such time and manner as the by-laws thereof shall direct, a sum of money not less than fifty cents nor more than one dollar, and subscribe to the articles of association, shall be a stockholder therein, and entitled to all the privileges and immunities thereof. **Who to be stockholders.**

[1695.] SEC. 4. The officers of said Society shall consist of a President, a Secretary and Treasurer, and at least five Directors, and they shall be elected annually by the stockholders of said Society; and said officers shall constitute a board for the management of the concerns of said Society, a majority whereof shall be a quorum; and it shall be the duty of said officers to manage the property and concerns **Officers of societies.**

of said Society, as will best promote the interests of Agriculture, Horticulture, and Mechanic Arts; and they may hold fairs and exhibitions, and may distribute premiums for the best and most meritorious animals or articles exhibited in these several departments, as shall be by their by-laws and regulations provided.

Societies may hold fairs and award premiums.

Number of societies limited.

[1696.] SEC. 5. There shall be but one County Society in any one county of this State, nor shall there be more than one Town Society in any one town, village, or city, but two or more towns may join and organize a Town Society for such towns.[b]

When and how societies may be authorized to sell real estate.

[1697.] SEC. 6. The said Society may, in case the uses and convenience thereof so require, upon application to the Circuit Court of the county where such Society is organized and located, obtain and have authority to sell, from time to time, the whole or any part of its real estate, the granting of such authority to be in the discretion of the Court, and such application to be made only when authorized by said Society, at an annual meeting thereof, by a vote of not less than two-thirds of the members of such Society present at such meeting, and notice of the intention to vote for such application having been published in some newspaper published in said county, if there be one published, and if not, then in some newspaper published in an adjoining county, once a week for three months next preceding such annual meeting.

Stockholders individually liable for labor.

[1698.] SEC. 7. The stockholders of all corporations, organized under this act, shall be individually liable for all labor performed for such corporation or association.

Officers to make report to State Society.

[1699.] SEC. 8. The President, Secretary and Treasurer of said Society shall, on or before the twentieth day of December in each year, make out and transmit to the Secretary of the State Agricultural Society, at his office, a statement of the transactions of said Society for the preceding year, and giving a full detail of the receipts and expenditures thereof, with a list of the premiums awarded, and to whom and for what purpose.

Act subject to certain provisions See Chap. 73.

[1700.] SEC. 9. This act shall be subject to the provisions of chapter fifty-five, title ten, of the Revised Statutes of eighteen hundred and forty-six, so far as applicable to associations formed under this act.

SEC. 10. This act shall take effect immediately.

---

[b] As Amended by "An Act to Amend Section Five of an Act entitled, 'An Act to Authorize the Formation of County and Town Agricultural Societies,' Approved February twelfth eighteen hundred and fifty-five." Approved February 16, 1857. Laws of 1857, p. 398.

INDEX.

A.

A*

B.

D.

E.

F.

Forms.

G.

H.

L.

M.

N.

O.

P.

Q.

R.

S.

T.

U.

V.

W.

www.ingramcontent.com/pod-product-compliance
Lightning Source LLC
LaVergne TN
LVHW020229110826
845151LV00003B/862

* 9 7 8 1 4 2 5 5 3 0 8 0 8 *